A Poverty of Objects

A Poverty of Objects

The Prose Poem and the Politics of Genre

Jonathan Monroe

Cornell University Press · *Ithaca and London*

For my mother and father
and for Mary

Contents

Preface

In the United States, where the prose poem had received at best limited attention before the 1960s, the publication in 1976 of Michael Benedikt's *The Prose Poem: An International Anthology* betokened a sudden surge of interest in the genre among American poets and a newly acquired respectability for it. The appearance that same year of Ulrich Fülleborn's *Deutsche Prosagedichte des 20. Jahrhunderts*—a collection that is, like Benedikt's, the first of its kind—signaled a similar interest among German writers. More recently, evidence that the growing interest in the prose poem now extends outside of France not only to those writing *in* the genre but to those who might write *on* it as well has been provided by the publication in 1983 of *The Prose Poem in France*, a collection of critical essays edited by Mary Ann Caws and Hermine Riffaterre which bears the distinction of being the first volume to be concerned with a broad spectrum of French prose poetry since Suzanne Bernard's monumental study of the late 1950s, *Le poème en prose de Baudelaire jusqu'à nos jours*. Although the introduction to the collection coedited by Caws and Riffaterre still speaks of the prose poem as a genre practiced chiefly by French writers, it was published, significantly, not in France but in America.

The recent appearance of three volumes in English and German devoted entirely to the prose poem and the evidence they provide of the number of contemporaries from non-French-speaking countries working in and on the genre indicate clearly enough that the prose

9

poem can no longer justly be thought of, as it has been in the past by proponents and detractors alike, as a more or less exclusively French preoccupation. Since the prose poem has become in our time a truly international phenomenon, it seems appropriate to broaden the focus of critical attention on the genre to include not only France but other countries as well, and to view present and past examples in light of one another. Accordingly, this book offers an investigation of the prose poem's development that is at once historical and comparative. Not surprisingly, since the French prose poem tradition remains of crucial importance for any serious attempt to come to terms with the genre, I have devoted considerable attention to canonically accepted works by Charles Baudelaire, Arthur Rimbaud, Max Jacob, and Francis Ponge. Included as well, however, are readings of German and American texts—by Friedrich Schlegel, Novalis, Gertrude Stein, Ernst Bloch, Robert Bly, and Helga Novak—that I believe merit more attention with regard to the prose poetry problematic than they have previously been given.

A question guiding my drawing together of this constellation of texts has been that of the historical function of this problematic, from the late eighteenth century up to and including the genre's current reception in America and elsewhere after so many years of neglect. In dealing with this question, which is a crucial one for virtually any hermeneutic, I have not sought to define the prose poem as an unchanging essence or to provide an exhaustive functional taxonomy. I have attempted only to identify certain functions that have seemed paradigmatic for the genre over the course of its relatively brief history. One function that I believe is of particular importance is the prose poem's gesture toward the partial restoration of lost voices whose prosaic speech and everyday struggles—the struggle, among other things, for the power of speech—have been considered by generations of writers and critics unworthy of literary attention. Suffering to a great extent, ironically, the same fate as those it has represented—whether we are speaking of Baudelaire's poor, of Stein's female objects and the commonplace things for which Ponge takes up a position (his *parti pris*), or of Novak's factory laborers and landless peasants—the prose poem itself has been until recently outside of France not only a relatively muted voice even within literature but also one that remains to this day virtually unheard in society at large.

The introduction's discussion of Fredric Jameson and Mikhail Bakhtin and the first two chapters on Schlegel and Novalis are intended especially to situate the French prose poem's project as a genre within a larger aesthetic and historical context. In accordance with the objectlike density and compactness of its form, the prose poem has evidenced over the course of its relatively brief history an extraordinary preoccupation with the prosaic world of everyday material objects. In accordance with the tension hinted at in its name, it has tended also to engage itself directly and indirectly not only with ongoing struggles of genre in the more narrow aesthetic sense but also with more manifestly political struggles of gender and class. In Baudelaire's prose poetry one function of the genre's brevity and condensation is to establish a point of resemblance and contact with the verse lyric in order then to point to its deficiencies and weaknesses from both a more narrowly aesthetic and a more broadly sociopolitical perspective; subsequently, writers such as Rimbaud and Jacob would realize that the prose poem's mode of printing sets it up also to mount a critique of the novel as the paradigmatic form for the imaging of historical/narrative progress (a critique that remains at a more implicit level in Baudelaire). Like Rimbaud and Jacob, Stein saw the genre's potential for dismantling dominant narrative as well as lyric modes; like them as well, albeit with reference especially to male sexual dominance as experienced from a woman's point of view, Stein also conceived of the struggle of literary genres as a symbolic enactment of the politics of gender, in its inclusive sense. Bloch and Ponge react strongly in their work against what they perceive to be philosophy's lack of concreteness; in different ways their oeuvres constitute an ongoing polemic against abstract theorizing and poetic/literary activity divorced from everyday experiences with material objects, class struggle, and concrete political praxis. Like Bloch and Ponge, but from a less philosophical and relatively depoliticized point of view, Bly is concerned in his prose poetry with expanding our ability to respond to aspects of everyday experience we might otherwise tend to neglect. Finally, Novak engages herself with the conflicts of gender and class and the aesthetic/generic struggles that the prose poem since Baudelaire has characteristically addressed by exploring the reified day-to-day existence of factory laborers and the relationship of literary discourse to journalistic and overtly political discursive practices.

The prose poem has functioned throughout its history as a self-reflexively inclusive but highly charged, intensely concentrated yet hybrid form for the mingling and confrontation of various literary and extraliterary speech types. In the condensed heteroglot texts of collections of prose poems from Baudelaire to Novak, the genre has consistently served as a reminder, by means of its self-thematizations and its foregrounding of the relationship between form and content, of ongoing antagonistic social relations and of the sociopolitical impasses and exclusionary literary (and more broadly sociolinguistic) practices that remain to be overcome. The recent international resurgence of interest in the prose poem suggests the extent to which the underlying nature of those relations, impasses, and exclusionary practices has persisted, from Baudelaire's day to our own.

Special thanks are due to the Deutscher Akademischer Austauschdienst (German Academic Exchange Service) for an initial one-year grant that enabled me to conduct research on the prose poem and in literary theory at the University of Constance in West Germany, and to Wolfgang Iser, Hans Robert Jauss, and the DAAD for making possible an additional year of support during which I was able to write initial drafts of the greater part of the book. I am especially grateful to Irving Wohlfarth for his contributions to this project and for his invaluable support over the years. I thank others as well who have read part or all of the manuscript at various stages and contributed to its development: in particular, Paul Armstrong, Mary Ann Caws, Walter Cohen, Peter Gontrum, Peter Hohendahl, Wolfgang Holdheim, Linda Kintz, Mary Lash, Satya Mohanty, Roger Nicholls, Steven Rendall, Wolf Sohlich, Janet Somerville, Richard Terdiman, Kingsley Weatherhead, David Welberry, and Alan Wolfe. I am grateful, finally, to Bernhard Kendler of Cornell University Press for his interest and assistance, and to Kay Scheuer at the Press and Emily Wheeler for their skillful editing of the manuscript in its final stages of preparation.
Versions of chapters 2 and 3 appeared in *Studies in Romanticism* 22 (Spring 1983) and *Stanford French Review* 9 (Summer 1985), respectively. Material from the former appears by courtesy of the Trustees of Boston University. Chapter 7 is forthcoming in *New German Critique*. In order to make the text as readable as possible for those without French and German, I have retained the original French and German only in block quotations and in other specific instances where for various reasons it has seemed necessary or useful to do so. Translations are my own unless otherwise indicated; translations not my own have occasionally been emended.

JONATHAN B. MONROE

Ithaca, New York

A Poverty of Objects

Les meubles ont l'air de rêver . . .
(The furniture seems to be dreaming . . .)

—BAUDELAIRE, "La chambre double"

Introduction: The Prose Poem
as a Dialogical Genre

The prose poem today is a genre that does not want to be itself. In a sense, of course, the prose poem has always been the genre that wants *out* of genre and still finds itself, for all that, inscribed *in* genre. In keeping with the prose poem's fundamentally polemical function within the network of genres it seeks to undermine and transform, my own discussions in the chapters that follow are designed expressly to call into question among other things the still prevalent dichotomization of aesthetics and politics, and to present these two categories as a dialectical interpenetration. The descriptions offered here of the genre called the prose poem are thus understood from the outset to be particular *representations* of that genre. Although my procedure involves extensive close readings, I have not intended these readings to be ends in themselves or to serve merely for the elucidation of especially difficult passages. Such passages are numerous in many of the texts I have chosen to discuss, and although I would of course hope my readings might contribute toward their elucidation in ways previously unconsidered, my primary intention has been to examine individual texts as, in Fredric Jameson's words, "'utterances' in an essentially collective or class discourse."[1] Measuring what the genre has been and is against what it has gestured toward becoming at crucial moments in its history,

1. Fredric Jameson, *The Political Unconscious* (Ithaca: Cornell University Press, 1981), p. 80; hereafter cited as *PU*.

this book offers a reading of the prose poem which sees its literary-historical significance as above all that of a critical, self-critical, utopian genre, a genre that tests the limits of genre.[2]

In *The Political Unconscious*, Jameson identifies two types of hermeneutic, a positive hermeneutic that emphasizes affinities and identity, thereby tending to filter out historical differences, and a negative hermeneutic that would seek, by contrast, "to sharpen our sense of historical difference" (*PU*, 130). I have attempted in what follows to balance both projects and to take advantage of the "twin reopenings upon history" made available by both approaches to genre (*PU*, 129). If I have tended at times to place a somewhat greater emphasis on connections and continuities among various writers and texts than on discontinuities and ruptures among them, I have done so in part as a response to those kinds of historiography that place too great an emphasis on a given text in isolation, thereby making a fetish of individual differences. In part too, I have done so to brush against the grain of manifest discontinuities, to see strikingly disparate texts as part of what Jameson has called "a single great collective story" (*PU*, 19). In this case, the story concerns a genre fascinating in part precisely because of what has been called its "polymorphism, indescribability and elusiveness."[3] Given those qualities and the highly varied, complex, often close to impenetrable texts I have sought to account for—those of Rimbaud, Max Jacob, Gertrude Stein, and Francis Ponge, in particular—I have been conscious throughout of the difficulty of preventing the often radically nondiscursive language of literature from seeming at times superfluous through the rationalizing discursiveness of critical commentary.[4] This difficulty, common to some extent to all criticism, is

2. I am indebted for the latter phrase to Dominick LaCapra's *History and Criticism* (Ithaca: Cornell University Press, 1985), in which LaCapra uses a similar formulation with specific reference to Bakhtin's view of the novel (116): "For Bakhtin the novel was a genre that tested the limits of generic classification." As I will argue below, the antigeneric function Bakhtin ascribes to the novel is manifest in the prose poem as well, though on a more microcosmic level.

3. Michel Beaujour, "Short Epiphanies: Two Contextual Approaches to the Prose Poem," in *The Prose Poem in France*, ed. Mary Ann Caws and Hermine Riffaterre (New York: Columbia University Press, 1983), p. 49.

4. Seeking to avoid this obstacle in his essay on Rimbaud's *Illuminations* in *Les genres du discours* (Paris: Seuil, 1978), p. 210, Tzvetan Todorov has written that the meaning of Rimbaud's prose poems is precisely that there isn't any meaning (*il n'y en a pas*). Such a reading seems as reductive in its way, however, as the "totalizing" interpretations to which he seeks to offer an alternative, and very much opposed to the "complication de texte" he calls for (207) to replace the standard "explication de texte." Although I agree on the importance of taking seriously what Todorov calls "la difficulté de lecture" (207)

nowhere more evident than for large-scale generic-historical investigations such as the present one, especially for those concerning poetry,
which has always been, in part for this very reason, "a step-child of
literary sociology."[5]

My project in any case has been to map out what in Jameson's terms
might be referred to as the "ideology of form" of the prose poem, to
isolate and examine the "essentially antagonistic collective discourses"
("ideologemes") of gender and class which have played such a crucial
role, indeed a defining role, in the genre's history. A paradigmatic
example of what Jameson has called the "symbolic enactment of the
social within the formal and the aesthetic" (*PU*, 76–77), the prose poem
dramatizes real antagonisms of gender and class as a conflict between
and among various modes of literary discourse as directly and explicitly
as any other genre *qua genre*. Apparently a contradiction in terms, the
prose poem is, first and foremost, a mode of discourse that speaks
against itself in the very act of defining itself. It marks a determined
effort to display socio-aesthetic oppositions, conflicts, and apparent
contradictions and play out the question of their possible or impossible
resolutions. As a paradigmatic genre of *concentrated dialogical struggle*,
resembling what Mikhail Bakhtin calls the "novelistic" in its discursive
heterogeneity but differing from the novel more narrowly defined by
virtue of its brevity and concentration, the prose poem offers a self-

---

in texts such as the *Illuminations*, I have also attempted to put forward interpretations that
would be in keeping with Baudelaire's dictum that criticism should be "partiale, politique, et passionée." As Theodor Adorno points out, "Actually, art works, notably those
of the highest calibre, are waiting to be interpreted": *Aesthetische Theorie* (Frankfurt:
Suhrkamp, 1970), p. 193; *Aesthetic Theory*, trans. C. Lenhardt (London: Routledge and
Kegan Paul, 1984), p. 186. All subsequent references will be indicated by *AT* followed by
page numbers for both the original and the Lenhardt translation. Translations have
occasionally been modified.

5. Hans Robert Jauss, *"La douceur du foyer*—Lyrik des Jahres 1857 als Muster der
Vermittlung sozialer Normen," in *Rezeptionsästhetik*, ed. Rainer Warning (Munich:
Wilhelm Fink, 1975), p. 401. The English version of Jauss's essay, "La douceur du foyer:
The Lyric of 1857 as a Pattern for the Communication of Social Norms," originally
appeared in *Romance Philology* 65 (1975), pp. 201–20; the essay is now available in Jauss's
Aesthetic Experience and Literary Hermeneutics, trans. Michael Shaw (Minneapolis: University of Minnesota Press, 1982), pp. 263–93. In contrast to the novel, which has been
widely considered a paradigm for the literary communication of sociopolitical realities,
the lyric is characterized, says Jauss, by a high degree of self-reflexiveness and linguistic
overdetermination that make it the most resistant of genres to "the illusion of referentiality" and to referential/discursive modes. Despite this fact, as Jauss goes on to argue,
even the lyric does often play a definite and identifiable role in the communication,
formation, and legitimation of social norms (pp. 401–34). Rarely, if ever, is poetry *only*
ondiscursive,   nonreferential.

conscious attempt to offer imaginary/aesthetic resolutions to real contradictions and conflicts. It thus lends itself particularly well to a crit-
ical/interpretive rewriting of the discourses of class and gender it so
often takes as its objects of investigation and exhibits in intense relationships of dialectical interpenetration and struggle.

Presupposing, with Jameson and Bakhtin, that the normal form of
the dialogical is essentially antagonistic, I have examined the individual
texts considered here as utterances of a system of class discourse in
which class, gender, and generic struggle manifest themselves through
the interaction of opposing discourses wrestling with one another for
positions of dominance and/or for self-preservation. The prose poem
is that place within literature where social antagonisms of gender and
class achieve *generic* expression, where aesthetic conflicts between and
among literary genres manifest themselves concisely and concretely as
a displacement, projection, and symbolic reenactment of more broadly
based social struggles. These struggles are themselves constituted by
and in the struggles of various discursive practices, including those of
gender and class which will be the focal points of the analyses to follow.
Accordingly, since the prose poem is itself the genre of a kind of class
struggle within literature (a struggle also of gender and/as genre), the
prose poem will be considered here as a particularly amenable site for
an examination of antagonisms of class and gender generally and the
kinds of exclusions that are the preconditions of such antagonisms.

The proper use of genre theory is, as Jameson has remarked, to
"project a model of the coexistence or tension between several generic
modes or strands," to define the specificity of a given text or code
"*against* the other genre, now grasped in dialectical opposition to it"
(*PU*, 141–42). I have therefore attempted in all my readings to focus
on the prose poem less in isolation from other genres than as a nexus of
generic interactions. In particular, I have tried to show to what extent
the prose poem's power has been due to its historically bound subversive relation to competing, better established genres such as the verse
lyric and the novel. Formally as well as thematically, the prose poem is a
genre, as Tzvetan Todorov has said, "based on the union of opposites."
As the "appropriate form . . . for a thematics of duality, contrast, and
opposition," it functions as a nexus for the confrontation not only of
"prose and poetry, freedom and rigor, destructive anarchy and con-
structive art,"[6] but also of the individual and the collective, the aesthetic

---

6. Tzvetan Todorov, "Poetry without Verse," trans. Barbara Johnson, in *The Prose
Poem in France.*

and the political. In part because it does so within such a confined space, the prose poem seems exceptionally well-suited for detecting the traces of what Jameson has called the "uninterrupted narrative" of class struggle (*PU*, 20). Exemplifying the symbolic, "counter-discursive" resistance to dominant culture which Richard Terdiman has recently examined in nineteenth-century France,[7] the prose poem is the literary genre in which the repressed and buried reality of this struggle manifests itself most explicitly in terms of the ongoing struggles *among* genres. Such struggles are not merely analogous to the ongoing generic struggles (struggles of class and gender) in society at large. They are rather, as both Bakhtin and Jameson have indicated, the very locus of class struggle within literature.[8] If the uninterrupted narrative of class struggle is accessible, paradoxically, only in fragments, then the prose poem offers itself, by virtue of its rigorously constricted form, as a model for the apprehension of fundamental social as well as more narrowly "aesthetic" conflicts. The prose poem's deliberate formal fragmentation, together with the inclusion of prosaic content it shares with the novel, suggests an awareness that any gesture toward *unmediated* apprehension of the social totality is itself highly problematic and potentially misleading.

In its self-definitions and self-thematizations, the prose poem rejects literature's (especially poetry's) dream of itself as a pure *other* set apart in sublime isolation, like the idealist/lyrical self, from the more

7. Richard Terdiman, *Discourse/Counter-Discourse: The Theory and Practice of Symbolic Resistance in Nineteenth-Century France* (Ithaca: Cornell University Press, 1985), p. 343; hereafter cited as *DCD*. Terdiman's conceptualization of the "counter-discourse" stems most directly, as his introduction indicates (42–43), from the Gramscian notions of "hegemony" and "counter-hegemony," notions that have figured in my own approach to the prose poem as genre as well. As the focal point of Terdiman's final two chapters, the model of what he calls *absolute* counterdiscourse, the prose poem occupies a privileged position in his argument. In contrast to the investigation of the prose poem that the present work offers, which was close to completion when *Discourse/Counter-Discourse* appeared, Terdiman's analysis of the genre is devoted primarily to Mallarmé (with a fair amount of attention as well to Baudelaire and considerably less to Rimbaud and Lautréamont). Despite this major difference—as the underlying importance to both our projects of the key notions of hegemony, ideology, and discursive resistance in part suggests—Terdiman's general theoretical arguments converge in a number of significant respects with the view of the prose poem I develop in this introduction and in subsequent chapters (see especially note 18 below and additional references in the Introduction, the chapters in Part II on Baudelaire and Rimbaud, and the Conclusion). Calling attention to the extent to which, in the prose poem as in other counterdiscursive texts, "the marginal reveals itself as central" (342), Terdiman also draws on the theoretical insights of Jameson and Bakhtin.

8. See also Michel Foucault, *L'ordre du discours* (Paris: Gallimard, 1971), p. 12 (cited in Terdiman, *DCD* 55), and Terdiman, *DCD*, p. 80.

prosaic struggles of everyday life which all too often "go without say-ing." Because it demonstrates with such force the utopian desire of both literature and society to open itself up to previously excluded forms of discourse and the social groups associated with them, the prose poem offers a unique opportunity for the study of efforts to absorb, in both the ideological and utopian senses of the word, the previously marginalized. Like the severely constricted *Jetztzeit* that Wal-ter Benjamin projects as the only possible medium for a socialist revo-lution, the highly compact space of the prose poem and the com-pressed, even explosive tension it permits are all the genre allows itself for the realization of its aspirations. Both prose and poetry, but neither prose nor poetry exclusively, the prose poem is, as Barbara Johnson has pointed out, the place of confrontation between inside and outside where the distinction between these threatens to collapse. It is also the place where this distinction doggedly maintains itself despite itself. Whether we are speaking of the two words "prose" and "poem," or even of the collapsing of these two words into Ponge's "proême," the prose poem depends for its very existence not only on the continued difference of its two defining terms but even on their continued op-positional status.

It is in this sense especially that the prose poem is, as I have already claimed, a genre that does not want to be itself. Although on the one hand the name "prose poem" suggests a synthetic utopian third term, it also implies the continued irresolution of the two opposing terms that constitute it. To study the prose poem is thus to attend to the desire for a resolution of existing contradictions and antagonistic relations, in-cluding what Jameson calls "the reaffirmation of the existence of mar-ginalized or oppositional cultures" (*PU*, 86). It entails an examination as well, however, of the process of the reappropriation, neutralization, and cooptation of a form that originally gestured toward achieving within literature, in the space called poetry—traditionally literature's most exclusive realm—the representation of subordinate or dominated groups. The prose poem marks a crucial moment in literature where the coexistence of various modes of literary production (read genres) becomes, in Jameson's words, "visibly antagonistic" (*PU*, 95).

To approach the prose poem in this way, to examine what we may call after Jameson and Louis Hjelmslev the content of the prose poem's form and of the prose poem as form, is to effect a dialectical reversal whereby the form of the prose poem may be said to carry its own ideological messages. "The strategic value of generic concepts," Jameson has said, "clearly lies in the mediatory function of the notion of a genre, which allows the coordination of immanent formal analysis of the individual text with the twin diachronic perspective of the history of forms and the evolution of social life" (*PU*, 105). If, as I believe, Jameson is right in maintaining that the simplest and most accessible demonstration of the kind of reversal mentioned above may be found in the investigation of the notion of genre in general and of one literary genre in particular, then the prose poem offers an especially auspicious place for such a demonstration. Given that the relationship of form and content is finally, as Jameson has indicated, one of interpenetration and mutual dependence, the two may be provisionally regarded as distinct from each another for the sake of analysis. Thus, although I would not disagree with Jameson's assertion that a form's ideological messages may ultimately be identifiable in themselves (*PU*, 99), I have based my own selection and analysis of individual texts and passages on the premise that the persuasive abstraction of such messages depends in large part on the possibility of identifying the manifest or repressed content that accompanies and shapes these messages from within, the content, in short, that informs the form.

Such an emphasis on content as an integral, defining feature of form itself seems especially important for the prose poem, which is, as Todorov and others have noted, a genre remarkable in part for its relative paucity of formal requirements. Accordingly, the prose poem also seems an especially well-suited place to practice a reversal of the formalist emphasis on technical and formal analysis as an end in itself. Although my own readings are grounded in such analysis, with attention as well to what Jameson has called "the active presence within the text of a number of discontinuous and heterogeneous formal processes," my principal interest in the prose poem and my interpretive priorities in approaching it remain inextricably bound up with the special potential I believe the genre affords for an analysis of the interpenetration of the aesthetic and the sociopolitical. This potential may be located especially, as I have suggested, in the prose poem's frequent self-thematizing figurations of the struggle of literary genres and by means of a contentual/thematic focus on concrete manifestations of gender and class struggle. Thus, for Baudelaire, prose (the prosaic) comes to represent something like the intractable medium of what Jameson calls history (*PU*, 102), that "experience of necessity" which imposes inexorable limits on individual as well as collective praxis. By contrast, poetry represents the desire to transcend such limits and achieve a more authentic integration of the individual and the collective. The prose poem's projected synthesis of the two modes designated by its name—the one the privileged medium of the collective, the other, that of the individual—symbolically enacts the desire to realize such an integration in the more broadly sociopolitical as well as the more narrowly aesthetic sense. By means of its overtly dialogical self-designation and the coexistence its collections establish among discrete individual texts that in themselves enact particular struggles of genre, gender, and class, the prose poem directs our attention to the varying degrees to which dialogue remains latent, manifest, or actualizable, antagonistic, discontinuous, or sequential, the various ways in which dialogue does and does not take place. In this context, it is instructive that, for example, in *Tender Buttons* Stein rewrites the struggle between men and women as a struggle between prose and poetry. These struggles of gender and genre are themselves figured in Stein's text by objects of household labor that are the signs not only of the sexual subordination of women but of their economic subjugation as well, the signs, in other words, of a struggle pertaining directly to class as well as to gender and genre.

Because it gestures toward opening up literature to prosaic speech, themes, and subject matter previously considered unworthy of aesthetic attention, the prose poem serves to legitimate and, at the same time, to undermine literary culture. It legitimates literature most directly by exemplifying literature's willingness to include, if only to a certain extent and on its own terms, what had previously been excluded, its willingness to adapt itself to an increasingly prosaic world—bourgeois, antiaristocratic—in which economic modes of production develop so rapidly that modes of literary production can scarcely hope to keep pace with them. By absorbing what had been considered *other* than literary or "poetic," the prose poem in Baudelaire's time had the affirmative function (in the Marcusean sense) of displaying literature's openness to the newly hegemonic bourgeoisie, which by the mid-1850s had showed clearly its preference for prose as a literary medium. Writing on the prose poem's entanglement in what he calls the "paradoxes of distinction," Terdiman points out that one important dimension of the genre's "dialectic of exclusion and approbation" manifests itself in its marked ambivalence toward the widespread, fully functional association of prose with "intellectual egalitarianism" and "literary democratization."[9] As a critical site of counterdiscursive/class struggle, prose

9. Terdiman, *DCD,* pp. 60, 266–67, and 261–305. On the material basis of this association, see Foucault, *Language, Counter-Memory, Practice* (Ithaca: Cornell University

offers a forum where social distinctions play themselves out and where the newly ascendent bourgeoisie may *impress* itself with the false image of its own universality. The distinction between poetry and prose in the mid-nineteenth century was thus, as Terdiman indicates, historicized, socialized, and even politicized—as it remains even today—in such a way as to designate "a structure of social power organized around the competition for class hegemony."[10] Although in this respect the prose poem had a manifestly ideological function at its point of emergence, its function was not merely ideological. Of equal if not greater importance was the utopian potential the genre suggested for an authentic restoration of history's lost voices (I am thinking especially of Baudelaire's poor) and for the dismantling of the rigid barriers of class, gender, and genre all the more firmly in place following the failed revolution of 1848. By problematizing the supposed validity of such barriers, the prose poem also gestured toward the undermining of privilege, including the privilege of the spiritual aristocracy of literature and the man (n.b.) of letters.

Genres are, as Jameson points out, "essentially literary *institutions,* or social contracts between a writer and a specific public, whose function is to specify the proper use of a particular cultural artifact" (*PU,* 106). Seen in this light, the prose poem may be regarded as offering quite an unusual contract as literary contracts go, a contract that seeks to dismantle the very principles of exclusion and property on which contractual agreements—and other literary genres—are based. Although not all writers have approached literature with equal attention to the fact that forms of *literary* praxis are themselves specific forms of *social* praxis, it is nonetheless true that to choose to write in or on a particular genre is also to choose a particular mode of social, not just narrowly aesthetic intervention. Such a choice inevitably involves a struggle with the resolution of social as well as aesthetic problems that

---

Press, 1977), p. 200 (cited in *DCD,* 56) and the extremely useful and informative chapter in *Discourse/Counter-Discourse* (117–46) on the rise and proliferation of newspaper culture (see also my references to the latter in chapter 3 below).

10. Terdiman, *DCD,* p. 267; see also pp. 274 and 311: "The opposition between 'poetry' and 'prose' might have remained abstract, purely descriptive, and theoretically reversible in some imaginary conjuncture. But in the nineteenth century it carried a highly charged and irreducibly normative signification"; "Oppositions like these are never created ex nihilo. this one had already been broadly institutionalized (and had thus been constituted as an unavoidable social meaning) as early as *Illusions perdues.*" On the difficulties inherent in attempts to define poetry and prose in purely formalistic terms and the fundamentally normative character of the notion of "literature," see chapter 1 of Mary Louise Pratt's *Toward a Speech Act Theory of Literary Discourse* (Bloomington: Indiana University Press, 1977); cited in Terdiman, *DCD,* pp. 60, 296.

are finally not separate problems at all, even if we often tend to see them as such because of the reified specializing consciousness capitalism has so contributed to developing.

In its very beginnings the prose poem anticipated the kinds of reversals of hierarchically dominant oppositional terms which the work of Jacques Derrida and his followers exemplifies. Such reversals may have, as Jameson has indicated, both an ideological and a utopian function. To the extent that prose had already become in the mid-nineteenth century the clearly preferred genre of the bourgeoisie, Baudelaire's turn to prose poetry merely acknowledges the power of the tastes of the newly ascended class. By turning to the prose poem, Baudelaire participates in the bourgeoisie's triumph and extends the field of its dominance to encompass the previously sacrosanct terrain of the lyric. Prose now occupies the terrain of poetry, and its conquest may itself be seen as an aesthetic projection of the bourgeoisie's triumph over the aristocracy. The prose poem thus served ideologically, in Baudelaire's day, as evidence both of the prosaic triumph of the class of prose par excellence and of the bourgeoisie's poetic self-image and aristocratic pretensions. On the other hand, from a utopian perspective the prose poem's incorporation of marginalized prosaic discourse may be seen as gesturing toward a salutary reinsertion of the "sovereign" lyrical subject into a sociopolitical context, a willingness to see this subject, in contrast to more conventional lyric poetry, as irrevocably inscribed in aesthetic and sociohistorical spheres of struggle. Printed in the same block format and of approximately the same length as a short newspaper article—the mode of printing against which Mallarmé would later direct his *Un coup de dés*—the prose poem offers, from the look of it, a more accessible medium than, say, the alexandrine-based verse lyric. The prose poem's apparent democratization, however, like that of the bourgeois society in which it is born, shows itself almost immediately for the *formal* contract it is, a *paper* contract both real and imaginary. If the prose poem's block print and brevity make it look accessible, like a newspaper article, to those with only minimal literacy and verbal sophistication, the genre's polemical tendencies risked from the very beginning making potential bourgeois readers decidedly uncomfortable, if not openly hostile. Already apparent in the suppression during his own lifetime of poems such as Baudelaire's "Assommons les pauvres!", this risk becomes even clearer in the genre in the work of such later writers as Rimbaud, Mallarmé, Stein, and Jacob.

Proffering and withdrawing its democratizing formal gesture in one and the same motion, the prose poem is utopian because and in spite of being ideological, ideological because and in spite of being utopian. As the conspicuous other of aristocratic/poetic discourse, the "prosaic" functions in a similar way within the prose poem. In its role as the bourgeoisie's very image of a one-dimensional, linear, uncomplicated use of language, prose is allowed by the prose poem to enter into literary language—of which poetry may be regarded as the "purest" mode—and participate in it more or less fully, to enjoy, as it were, its privileges. In its role as the language, on the other hand, of the mass of oppressed people left behind by the bourgeoisie's ascendency to power, prose remains the marginal or else coopted speech of the house of literature where only those may enter who, as the poor of "Les Yeux des pauvres" put it, are *other* than they. For all this, Baudelaire's prose poetry does gesture toward including the speech of the marginal and the oppressed previously excluded from poetry. This gesture has a manifestly utopian as well as an ideological function, and the one is not less real or less significant in its effect than the other at the historical moment of its emergence. Even if the ideological does win out for the moment of the prose poem's appearance with Baudelaire and afterwards, it is still possible to retain glimpses of the genre's status as what Bloch might call a repository of (albeit largely unrealized) utopian possibilities.

The novel, for Bakhtin, is not just one genre among others. It is the genre where genre's autocritique takes place through the parodying of other genres *as genres* and through the exposition of the conventionality of their forms and their languages.[11] In those eras when the novel becomes the dominant genre, Bakhtin writes, all literature gets caught up "in the process of 'becoming,' and in a special kind of 'generic criticism'" (*DI*, 5). In this sense, the prose poem at its emergence in the hands of Baudelaire under the sign of the ascendency of the mid-nineteenth century realist novel and the daily newspaper may well be considered a paradigmatic "novelization" or "prosification" of the verse lyric. Although the prose poem's polemic later shifts to some extent, in the prose poems especially of Rimbaud and Jacob, toward a

---

11. Mikhail Bakhtin, *The Dialogic Imagination*, trans. Caryl Emerson and Michael Holquist, ed. Michael Holquist (Austin: University of Texas Press, 1981); hereafter cited as *DI*. My thanks to Satya Mohanty for insights gained in discussions of Bakhtin's work pertaining to the arguments contained herein.

critique of reified popular forms of the novel itself, the verse lyric is the prose poem's initial object of parodic critique.[12]

Like the novel, in the inclusive sense Bakhtin uses the term to designate many texts—including *Eugene Onegin,* Pushkin's "novel in verse"—not traditionally called novels, the prose poem is an antigeneric genre, a hybrid "artistically organized system for bringing different languages in contact with one another, a system having as its goal the illumination of one language by means of another" (*DI,* 361). It is also a genre whose very existence is bound up with a critique of the principles of exclusion on which conventional generic identities and definitions are based. Like Bakhtin's "novel," but by means of condensation and "elegant concentration" rather than "exhaustive presentation,"[13] the prose poem incorporates on a microcosmic scale both what Bakhtin calls "extraliterary heteroglossia"—the heterogeneous weave of the discourses of everyday life which we may call, after Baudelaire, prosaic speech—and the " 'novelistic' layers of literary language" itself conceived in terms of the representation of various generic tendencies. Finally, as the double designation of its name suggests, the prose poem is fundamentally "novelistic" in being *dialogical*—"permeated with laughter, irony, humor, elements of self-parody, . . . indeterminacy, a certain semantic openendedness, a living contact with unfinished, still-evolving contemporary reality (the openended present)"—dependent for its very existence and continued vitality on "changes in reality itself" (*DI,* 7).

Genre is best understood, as Bakhtin has indicated, not merely in a formalistic sense but "as a zone and a field of valorized perception, as a mode for representing the world" (*DI,* 28), and as the level of struggle of literary discourse and of the struggle of literary discourse with its nonliterary others. From this perspective, the prose poem is self-consciously a form of concentrated generic struggle like no other. With Baudelaire, the prose poem emerges as a form whose field of action is indicated by its titular designation. Like its counterpart the verse lyric, it is, in other words, by definition relatively "petit," characterized by a

12. Explicitly thematizing the generation of dialectical perspective, the prose poem is, as Terdiman observes, "a counter-discourse to *each* of its generic antecedents, and its intervention signals a general reorientation of the entire question of literary genre" (*DCD,* 214 and 296). Although reorientation of the question of genre is already signaled in Baudelaire's prose poetry in relation to both poetry *and* prose, in chapters 3 and 4 below I shall argue that it is only with Rimbaud that the prose poem's critique of prose becomes as forceful as that directed against poetry in Baudelaire's *Le spleen de Paris.*

13. The distinction is borrowed from Ian Watt as quoted in the introduction to Bakhtin, *The Dialogic Imagination,* p. xvi.

certain brevity and condensation. Occupying as it does roughly the same compact space formerly reserved for the verse lyric, the prose poem represents a more or less direct challenge to the verse lyric's self-image. If the lyric is the genre where the self comes, however briefly and tenuously, into its own, it is also the genre where the self emerges in its most concentrated instance as a problematic. In the prose poem's frequent imaging of conflicts of gender and class as a conflict of genres—understood as a conflict of the speech types of diverse extra- and intraliterary groups—it symbolically enacts both aesthetic and more broadly social conflicts. In the relationships it establishes of discrete individual texts to one another and to the generically designated ensemble of such texts which is itself a fragmented totality (see especially Baudelaire's preface to the *Petits poèmes en prose*), the prose poem also allows us to see that the problem of the individual's integration into a genuinely collective society is none other than a *generic* problem, a problem fundamentally of gender and class struggle.

Polemically illustrating the extent to which the lyrical self is always already inscribed in a sociopolitical context, the prose poem is thus the place where the verse lyric is driven back to its own prosaic subtext, to the place where the lyrical self loses itself in the verse line's extension to the margin of the page and the disarticulated, disindividuated uniformity of the block-print of prose. The prose poem is the place, in other words, of the lyric's critique of itself as the genre where the self comes into its own voice and "sublime" isolation becomes a privileged mode of being within literature alongside the other two primary modes, drama and novel, with which it competes for literary hegemony. Turning the lyric's valorized self back to the world, the prose poem exposes how comic and fragmented that self really is in the context of the social reality that negates its own sublime pretensions. (For a classic illustration of this strategy see Baudelaire's "Perte d'auréole.") Readjusting our vision to focus on everyday realities we might tend to ignore or repress for the sake of other loftier concerns, the prose poem undermines, among other things, the privileging of the intellectual and theoretical over against the crude shocks of experience that make up the "world of prose." Dragging the lyric into what Bakhtin calls "a zone of contact with reality" (*DI*, 39)—what for our purposes we may call the prosaic—the prose poem turns this privileged "poetic" form of the eternal present—and its correlate, self-presence—into a cliché to be smashed, *form*-ulating it so as to indicate what forms we have become and need to break out of.

In so doing, and in the very process of continuing to try to be itself, the prose poem inevitably risks its own ossification. As Bakhtin points out: "In general any strict adherence to a genre [including, one might add, even an antigeneric, "novelistic" genre such as the prose poem] begins to feel like a stylization, a stylization taken to the point of parody, despite the artistic intent of the author" (DI, 6). Thus, although the prose poem at its beginnings with Baudelaire and Rimbaud showed clear signs of aspiring to be a radical, even revolutionary genre, its impact has been reduced largely to that of a corrective. The verse lyric itself has by now absorbed virtually all of the prose poem's most prosaic motifs, and the prose poem seems unlikely to replace it. Given these developments, it may well be that the prose poem's limited but still significant function will be as a minor (i.e., marginalized) genre that reappears at those moments—such as the close of the age of the new criticism in America in the early 1960s—when the lyric and the lyrical self seem most sublimely autonomous, detached, set apart from reality, only to disappear or decline in importance when the verse lyric begins again to address the more prosaic aspects of daily life it has often tended to ignore.

The importance of length, the textual space a text occupies, is as underestimated in conceptualizations of genre as it is obvious. The novel, Bakhtin says, is "plasticity itself" (DI, 39). And yet, like the prose poem, though at the opposite extreme, the novel has spatial limitations. As a prose poem cannot be too long and still be a prose poem (understood in the now canonical sense given currency by Baudelaire), so too a novel cannot be too short and remain a novel. Suggesting by virtue of its expansiveness that our lives are capable of becoming immeasurably and gradually richer than they are, but also that the poverty of our lives may continue indefinitely, the novel's form offers us an image of ourselves and our world that is at once ideological (affirmative, reassuring) and utopian (critical and self-critical). No less ideological and utopian by virtue of its dramatically more constricting space limitations, the prose poem's form presents us, by contrast, with the tension between severe confinement and relative autonomy generally entailed in encounters with "reality." It presents us as well with a strong sense of both the repressive uniformity of everyday existence and the explosive potential for a new openness and a communally shared freedom which such repression develops. In the critical/liberating relation to other genres it shares with the novel, the prose poem participates in the novelistic process Bakhtin calls a "reorientation toward a real future."

By critically engaging such functional oppositions as that between the notion of a transcendental poetic autonomy and the prosaic, historical situatedness of the individual subject in concrete relations of gender and class, the prose poem also contributes toward reinterpreting reality "on the level of the contemporary present now meant not only to degrade, but to raise reality into a new and heroic sphere" (*DI*, 40).

The critique of literary/poetic language the prose poem provides does not occur at the level of abstractions but, rather, at the level of world views and of living beings who, in Bakhtin's words, necessarily "think, talk, and act in a setting that is social and historically concrete" (*DI*, 49). Polemically responding to what it clearly perceives as the poverty of individual genres—the self-centered lyric, the plot-bound serial novel—the prose poem displays what Bakhtin calls an "interanimation" or "interillumination" of languages. In the process, it also depicts the novelistic, heteroglossic struggles among these languages or genres as social and ideological struggles among ways of seeing and evaluating the world which then become specific *objects of representation* ("images") in their own right (*DI*, 51). Occupying a precarious and polemically interactive position within literature between two of its dominant modes, the novel (the hegemonic form of prose) and the verse lyric (the equivalent form in poetry), the prose poem also mediates in critical utopian fashion between prosaic language, understood in the broader sense as extraliterary language, and poetic/intraliterary language. From this mediated and mediating perspective, language does not serve merely to "reflect" ideological and material struggles in society; it is itself the very locus of such struggles.

Taking the thematization of unresolved generic/discursive conflicts as one of its constitutive projects, the prose poem has the distinction of being the only genre whose very name designates it as a space in which such conflicts are the center of attention. The desire for a synthesis of prose and poetry which appears in Baudelaire's preface is expressed in Baudelaire's three poems on the poor ("Le joujou du pauvre," "Les yeux des pauvres," and "Assommons les pauvres!") as the still unrealized desire for a resolution of conflicts of gender and class. In incorporating and giving voice to the language of the poor, Baudelaire is himself participating in, not merely commenting on or describing, their struggle with the dominant social groups that oppose them. He is himself struggling, in other words, against the complacent "lyrical" (narcissistic) language of lovers aspiring toward a "union of souls" as well as the self-glorifying, self-affirmingly poetic language of the dominant class symbolized by the historical/mythological mural painted on the inside of the café of "Les yeux des pauvres" where the poor cannot enter. Similarly, by directly confronting the beggar's purely *physical* language of self-preservation in "Assommons les pauvres!", Baudelaire himself participates in the struggle to translate the abstract philoso-phizing discourse of social theorists into an authentic sociopolitical praxis. Baudelaire's own attitude toward such struggles is ambivalent, to be sure, and he often seems more interested in keeping oppositions in play than in resolving them. Although his texts often suggest the desirability of a utopian reconciliation and unity, they also continually thematize the lack of such reconciliation and even mock the very ges-ture toward reconciliation as ridiculous. With Baudelaire, the prose poem gestures simultaneously in two directions: on the one hand, to-ward exposing unresolved struggles and oppositions as persistently and insistently prosaic (i.e., inherently unresolvable), and on the other, toward an actual resolution of such struggles and oppositions. In its dialectical formal conception, which implies the possibility that generic oppositions may be canceled, preserved, and raised in the brief space and time the genre allows itself to unfold, the prose poem is manifestly utopian. In the frequent emphasis of its content, however, on the seem-ingly irresolvable nature of existing struggles of gender, class, and genre, the prose poem remains soberly oppositional. It occupies the discomforting position between the possibility and desirability of actu-ally resolving real oppositions and struggles and the impossibility and undesirability of doing without the generative, productive, transfor-mative power of oppositional tensions that continue doggedly to exist despite our will to resolve them.

In marked opposition to what might be regarded as the com-paratively weak generative/transformative power of the idea of mere "difference"—insofar as this idea tends to neglect the question of power and what Bakhtin refers to as the "ideologically freighted" nature of all uses of language—the prose poem is typically concerned with the potential destructive and productive power of coalesced *opposi-tional* forces. If Bakhtin "recoups the class struggle for epistemology" (*DI*, 431)—in part through his recognition that every speaker is an ideologue and every speech-act an ideologeme (*DI*, 333)—the prose poem does much the same for literary genres. Although the idea and experience of difference may be less dangerous, less explosive and controversial, more accommodating and pluralistic than the idea and experiential fact of oppositional (class and generic) resistance, a writer such as Baudelaire might well maintain that they are also probably less productive. Brief, condensed, interruptive, the prose poem asks to be defined both by its formal opposition to the novel (which is lengthy, expansive, continuous) and by its functional resemblance to it as a heteroglossic, hybrid, antigeneric genre. In contrast, for those features just mentioned and excepting the crucial difference in the mode of printing, the prose poem's relationship to the verse lyric is one of formal resemblance and functional opposition (heteroglossic versus monoglossic).

In Baudelaire's hands—and, I would argue, in the hands of his most important successors—the prose poem is both a utopian genre and a genre of an ongoing utopian self-critique. The latter, especially, remains essential to the integrity of the prose poem's utopian aspirations. Rimbaud extends and expands Baudelaire's critique of the lyric to include a critique of uncomplicatedly linear notions of narrative continuity. It is his combined critique of the verse lyric *and* prose narrative, of the self as sovereign subject and of history-as-progress which makes Rimbaud so crucially important to the history not only of the prose poem but of prose, poetry, and literature generally. Friedrich Schlegel and Novalis, whom I have included as precursors of those writers who would later take up the prose poem, directed their critiques especially against hierarchical taxonomic/generic classifications and the disharmonious, finite materiality of everyday existence. Subsequently, the prose poem's objects of critique include: (1) the reified, "non-novelistic" novel (Jacob); (2) the patriarchal sexual/generic stereotypes and exclusions implied by various narrative, lyrical, and even grammatical uses of language (Stein); (3) apolitical notions of reading, writing, and interpretation, whether philosophical, poetic, or pragmatic (Bloch); (4) abstract, philosophical, homocentric language (Ponge, Bly); and (5) the patronizing, exploitative, euphemistic discourse of employers, the alienated speech of factory labor, and the apolitical pretensions and ideological functions of attempts to preserve notions of unilinear narrative, lyrical enthusiasm, and "objective" journalism (Novak).

By virtue of its emphasis on the fact that all verbal discourse, "literary" and "nonliterary" alike, is inherently a *social* phenomenon, Bakhtin's approach to language greatly contributes toward overcoming the conventional dichotomization of form and content and what he refers to as "the divorce between an abstract 'formal' approach and an equally abstract 'ideological' approach" (*DI*, 259). It is thus potentially of great usefulness for the current state of literary studies in general and for the study of a "novelistic" genre such as the prose poem in particular. In its focus on unresolved contradictions and problems of everyday life, the world of prose in which we live and breathe, the prose poem offers a gauge for measuring lyrical, poetic, literary, and one might also say theoretical, philosophical, and speculative language against the prosaic realities and languages that they exclude. According then to the view I am offering here, one crucial aspect of the prose poem's continued and revitalized importance would be its contribution not only to the interanimation of various forms of literary genres with one another and with critical and theoretical/philosophical discourse but also, and perhaps more important, to a greater inclusiveness of marginalized extraliterary and extratheoretical speech generally. The word "dialogicity" suggests pairs, and the prose-poetry pair figures prominently in Bakhtin's analysis of the novel as it does in my own analysis of the prose poem. It is worth recalling at this point, however, that the notion of dialogicity also has reference (as its twin term "heteroglossia" perhaps more clearly indicates) to a much broader and more diversified kind of interaction than the poetry-prose pair at first seems to imply, an interaction that involves the simultaneous interplay of a virtually "boundless" variety of discourses from both high and low culture.[14]

14. In "La structure de l'énoncé" (reprinted in Tzvetan Todorov, *Mikhail Bakhtine/le principe dialogique* [Paris: Seuil, 1981], p. 289), offering what is perhaps his single most succinctly comprehensive list of different "extra-literary" speech types or modes of discourse, Bakhtin mentions (1) the speech of workers, such as one finds in factories and shops, (2) the speech of various professions, such as that of public administrators and bureaucrats, (3) the speech of everyday encounters and conversations in the street and in pubs, and (4) ideological discourse *stricto sensu*, including the discourses of politics, education, science, and philosophy. To these, one might add the following from the texts reprinted in *The Dialogic Imagination* (262–63, 269, 272–73, 289, 293, 296, 299, 301, 305, 311, 369, 381, 386, 401, 417, 418): "generic languages, languages of generations and age groups, tendentious languages, languages of the authorities, of various circles and of passing fashions, languages that serve the specific sociopolitical purposes of the day," "rhetorical genres (journalistic, moral, philosophical and others)," "languages of social groups," "street songs, folksayings, anecdotes . . . the 'languages' of poets, scholars, monks," "the language of the lawyer, the doctor, . . . the politician, the public education teacher," "the language and world of prayer . . . of song . . . of labor and everyday life . . . of local authorities" and the language of the city, the languages of the court, of parliamentary protocol, of newspaper articles, dry business language, the language of speculators, of maxims, aphorisms, and letters, "the conversational language of a literarily educated circle," the languages of "a priest, a knight, a merchant, a peasant, a jurist." It is easy to see from such a list that it could be extended indefinitely. Though I have made frequent use of the Bakhtinian notion of the "speech genre" or "mode of discourse" here, it has not been my intention to "apply" his (itself inexhaustive) tax-

Significantly, the first text of Baudelaire's *Petits poèmes en prose*, "L'étranger," is in the form of a dialogue between two unnamed speakers whose theme is individual isolation, the solitary "lyrical" self that feels more of a kinship with nature ("the marvelous clouds") than with people. This first text nicely figures the situation of lyric poetry in the wake of Romanticism and sets up the destructive project toward the Romantic conception of poetry and literature—regarded as the prototypical poetic/literary conception of Baudelaire's day—which it would be the task of the collection's subsequent texts to carry out. Throughout the collection, dialogue plays a crucial role in both the narrower, more conventional sense, as well as the broader Bakhtinian sense. In contrast to what Bakhtin calls "single-styled genres" or "poetic genres in the narrow sense of the word" (*DI*, 266), the prose poem presents a variety of voices representing various speech types in conflict with one another. This tension manifests itself not only between individual texts and the collection but within individual texts as well. Examples of the prose poem's heteroglossia I have attended to in the following include: (1) Baudelaire's dialogues between men and women and rich and poor; (2) the intersection of religious, economic, scientific, pagan, political, historical, and other modes of discourse in Rimbaud's *Une saison en enfer* and the *Illuminations* and the former's display of rhymed, metrical verse as an outmoded cliché; (3) Jacob's condensed cubist parodies of the popular novel, the prose poems he describes as written "in a style not my own"; (4) Stein's fracturing and intermingling of the languages of method, conversation, domestic life, dinner parties, sex, violence, and detective stories; (5) Bloch's peculiar combination of fiction, parable, critique, philosophical essay, and fairy tale; (6) Ponge's "rhetoric of objects"; (7) Bly's attention to the "speech" of animals and the languages of dreams, businessmen, prophets, and domestic life; and (8) Novak's focus on the languages of factory workers, travelers, journalists, writers, revolutionairies, and peasants.

All language is, in Bakhtin's phrase, "ideologically saturated" (*DI*, 271). In direct opposition to the tendency of lyric poetry (and of later reified forms of the novel as well) to "unite and centralize verbal-

---

onomy systematically throughout. Such an approach would go against Bakhtin's own emphasis on discourse (*parole* as opposed to *langue*) as fluid and inexhaustible. See Katerina Clark and Michael Holquist, *Mikhail Bakhtin* (Cambridge: Harvard University Press, 1984), p. 218: "For Bakhtin, a rigorous poetics of speech genres would have roughly the same invidious status that a normative catalogue of dream symbols would have for Freud."

ideological thought" into "the firm, stable linguistic nucleus of an offi-
cially recognized literary language," the prose poem recognizes and
thematizes poetic/literary language as the expression of a privileged
understanding and a privileged mode of being and relating to the
world. It reveals such language as the formal/symbolic enactment of a
highly refined and exaggeratedly autonomous and self-enclosed relationship to the rest of the world and its various discourses. Arising
contemporaneously with that extreme form of aesthetic privileging
which was art-for-art's-sake "poésie pure," the prose poem responds to
such privileging by refusing to gloss over the struggle for dominance
among various generic/discursive practices. It focuses, instead, directly
upon that struggle. The preoccupation with physical objects which so
strongly characterizes the prose poetry of both Ponge and, earlier,
Stein, leads both writers to call attention to "the encrustation of meanings bonded to any word or object" (*DI*, 432). Exhibiting the resistance
to the word posed not only by the object the word is directed toward
but also by other words around the same object, this same attention
leads as well to the recognition that since each living utterance takes
meaning and shape, in Bakhtin's words, "at a particular historical moment in a socially specific environment," no utterance can fail to participate actively in social dialogue (*DI*, 276). Like the lyric self who
neglects or represses her own sociohistorical situation and thinks of
herself as a detached, truth-bearing agent, the poetic word, according
to Bakhtin, "forgets that its object has its own history of contradictory
acts of verbal recognition, as well as that heteroglossia that is always
present in such acts of recognition" (*DI*, 278). The texts of Ponge
represent a culmination of sorts of the prose poem's antipoetic, heteroglossic tradition in this sense by acknowledging and giving voice to the
"languages" of countless organic and inorganic objects long considered
(before Ponge) unworthy of literary attention. Although Ponge's novelistically humorous, self-parodic texts certainly display to some extent a
self-consciously poetic nostalgia for what Bakhtin calls "the virginal
fullness and inexhaustibility of the object itself"—in other words, ironically, a return to monoglossia—they are also demonstrably "prosaic"
in confronting the "multitude of routes, roads and paths that have
been laid down in the object by social consciousness" (*DI*, 278).

Attending to what Bakhtin later refers to as the "heteroglot socio-
verbal consciousness ensnaring the object" (*DI*, 283), the dialogue of
voices which arises out of the social dialogue of various languages or

speech types, the prose poem stands in direct opposition to the notion of a pure, self-contained "poetic" speech that would betray no sense of historicity or of the social determinations of its own language, no critical or self-critical edge, no irony. It displays, in other words, a radical skepticism toward the notion of a lyrical/poetic discourse in and through which the self might present itself as unmediated, unaffected by social relations. In stark contrast to what Bakhtin has called the "monological" tendency of lyric poetry, the prose poem dialogizes the word. Reinscribing it in the heteroglossia of the surrounding aesthetic and social world, it reveals, finally, the dialogical nature of *all* language.[15] Its project is both to immerse itself in the "poetic" word and at the same time to maintain a critical relationship to it. In this sense, the prose poem aspires to be poetic/literary language's own coming to self-

15. In response to Bakhtin's definition of poetry, Renate Lachmann has recently emphasized that dialogicity is a constitutive feature of poetry *as well as* prose (see "Dialogizität und poetische Sprache," *Dialogizität* [Munich: Fink, 1982], pp. 51–62). In light of this critique, it is important to note that Bakhtin himself acknowledged the ultimate dialogicity of *all* language on a number of occasions (see, for example, Todorov, *Mikhail Bakhtin/le principe dialogique*, p. 212, and Bakhtin's discussion of inner speech as a form of "inner dialogue" in *Marxism and the Philosophy of Language*, trans. Ladislav Matejka and I. R. Titunik [New York: Seminar Press, 1973], 38). Bakhtin's point is not so much that poetry *succeeds* in being monological but, rather, that it tends to conceal its necessary dialogicity as much as possible—especially through adherence to a relatively limited lexicon of "poetic diction"—in what Clark and Holquist, *Mikhail Bakhtin*, have succinctly described as its pursuit of "the ideal of oneness" (291). Like my own, Bakhtin's heuristic strategy is thus designed above all to get at certain dominant tendencies relating to the historicized opposition between poetry and prose (for a similar perspective on the usefulness of the poetry-prose pair in Bakhtin's work, see Wolfgang Preisendanz's response to Lachmann's essay, "Zum Beitrag von R. Lachmann 'Dialogizität und poetische Sprache,'" also in *Dialogizität*, pp. 25–28). Acknowledging the inescapable dialogicity of poetry does not alter the fact that such tendencies do exist. I shall attempt to show that one major aspect of the prose poem's literary historical importance is precisely that in shifting poetry's locus of struggle from verse to prose, the genre dramatizes and thematizes the lyric's *repression* of its own dialogicity and opens poetry onto a more intense dialogical interaction with other modes of discourse. On the role irony plays in this regard as the rhetorical figure of the dialogic in the specific sociocultural context of nineteenth-century discourses, see Terdiman, *DCD*, p. 76 (see also 34–43, and 77): "The nineteenth-century work of counter-discourse constitutes a mapping of the internal incoherence of the seemingly univocal and monumental institution of dominant discourse." Because proponents and antagonists alike hypostatize the dominant itself as dominant, the discourses that counterdiscursive forms such as the prose poem project as their adversaries tend to be, as Terdiman points out (64–68), *rigidified* forms. As a consequence, counterdiscursive struggles often take on a formalized, "apparently contentless quality" that retains nonetheless an "emblematic class character." Hence, for example, the specific importance of the *popular* novel and the more *conventional* manifestations of rhymed, metrical verse to the prose poem's critical project.

consciousness, the place where poet and reader alike become critically aware of the writer's language as "a professional jargon on a par with professional jargons" (*DI*, 289; see especially Baudelaire's "A une heure du matin") and of the poetic/lyric word as an index of generic, sociohistorical tensions and contradictions.

As the allusion to Marx's *The Poverty of Philosophy* contained in the title of this book suggests, my investigation of the prose poem devotes substantial attention to the genre's increasingly characteristic but largely transhistorical focus on ordinary everyday objects of the physical world. My intention in so doing is not so much to redirect attention toward such objects "in themselves," although the evidence of the prose poem emphatically asserts that at least in some provisional sense such attention is important and even necessary. It is rather to draw attention back to ourselves, to our discursive appropriation of these objects and, more particularly, to the prose poem's resistance to the poverty of specific discourses by which we apprehend the world. I have further intended to call attention to the prose poem's resistance to the manifest poverty and reified nature of existing social relations and the inadequacy of our various ways of using language to help us toward an effective, alternative, as-yet-untheorized form of social praxis. The title of the present work thus has reference above all to (1) the poverty of the dominant discourses against which the prose poem has leveled its attacks, including especially high literary language, the poetic/auratic word/object revealed in Baudelaire's "Perte d'auréole" as having become merely the brand-name product of poet X or Z; (2) the de facto impoverishment of the world of phenomenal "objects" (human and nonhuman) which follows from the mediation of our experience by these discourses; and (3) the impoverished social relations that inform and are in turn shaped by these same discursive practices. Beginning with the historically situated formal and functional opposition between prose and poetry, the prose poem projects a utopian aspiration for the resolution of the conflicts figured by this opposition. From the prose poem's heroic age in the wake of the failed revolutions of 1848 and 1870–71, to the violent America of the 1960s when the prose poem began to flourish in this country for the first time, to the revolutionary Portugal of the mid-1970s that informs the work of Helga Novak, the prose poem has tended to flourish at moments in history characterized by revolutionary tension and a failure to harmonize socio-ideological voices, such as those of gender and class, that have coalesced into combative oppositional forces.[16]

One of the early lessons of any effort to write a broadly historical and comparative study of the prose poem at this point in its history must be that the field has expanded in such a way as to render anachronistic the kind of exhaustive approach that Suzanne Bernard utilized only twenty-five years ago. Bernard had set out to encompass the entire corpus of French prose poetry one writer at a time, stretching her manuscript to eight hundred pages in the process; today such a project would be inconceivable, particularly in light of the genre's worldwide dissemination over the last twenty years. The first task of a historical/comparative study of the prose poem such as this one is therefore to select a constellation of writers and texts which seem to represent paradigmatic moments in the prose poem's history. Such moments do not, of course, exist in themselves. They are neither absolutely prior to nor independent of the process of selection. The very construction of such a constellation is itself a writing of history, the choice already a limitation determined to some extent by affinities, preferences, scholarly and linguistic competence, and the impositions of historical circumstances and received traditions.

As the tension in the prose poem between compressed form and inclusive content ironically suggests, the process of selection, concentration and objectification itself necessarily involves at some point the very principle of exclusion—whether we are talking about a prose poem, a novel, or a critical study—against which the prose poem itself represents a reaction. Among those authors I have excluded, two at the very least deserve special mention. In a number of important discussions of the French prose poem, from Bernard's pioneering study to the more recent work of Julia Kristeva and Barbara Johnson, Mallarmé

16. On the displacement of failed social revolutionary force into "the naively hopeful metaphoricity of those *poetic* revolutions of which the nineteenth century made so much," see Terdiman, *DCD*, pp. 67 and 80: "The blockage of energy directed to structural change of the social formation is an important condition of possibility for the *textual* revolution in which the intelligentsia reinvested some of the dynamism of that sociohistorical revolution which never occurred. In this sense, literary 'revolution' is not simply an analogical formation, still less a trendy metaphor. It is the prolongation of social process which was blocked off in more material arenas of productive activity and human struggle. Literary revolution is not revolution by homology, but by *intended function*. However distant from any project of immediate realization, from any material mutation of the social structures which sustain the here-and-now, it is part of the culture of resistance which plays a role in any oppositional movement."

and Lautréamont have figured prominently. The two most innovative works of both these authors—*Un coup de dés, Les chants de Maldoror*—certainly draw upon and extend the prose poem's crucial historical function of dismantling rigid generic boundaries within literature. Both occupy formal spaces that differ in significant ways, however, not only from each other but also, more important for our purposes, from the formal space typically occupied by the prose poem. For this reason I have chosen not to include them here.[17]

Roughly fifty years before Baudelaire's *Petits poèmes en prose*, Schlegel's *Athenäums-Fragmente* and Novalis's *Hymnen an die Nacht*, the focal points of Part I, offer important theoretical and formal anticipations of the prose poem as genre. Conceptually, Schlegel's notion of an *Universalpoesie* still represents one of the most global articulations available of the prose poem's project of a fusion of genres. At the same time, it figures the fragmentary realization of such a project. Novalis's *Hymnen an die Nacht*, on the other hand, enacts the formal struggle between prose and verse and the thematic struggle between the prosaic—the real, the everyday, the material world, diffusion, discord—and the poetic—transcendent, spiritual, ideal harmony—which were to become crucial to Baudelaire's collection.

Following the attention given in Part I to Schlegel and Novalis as precursors of those writers who would later take up the prose poem, Part II focuses on the prose poem's emergence in France in the nineteenth century with Baudelaire and Rimbaud, the two most influential writers within the genre from what I have called its heroic age. Despite important differences between them, their work in the prose poem shares what Mary Ann Caws has identified as the (by now) "traditional qualities recognized in the prose poem—brevity, intensity, and self-containment or integrity."[18] Their work also shares, however, as I shall argue, a subversive, "norm-breaking" function with regard to both

17. For an account of the prose texts of Mallarmé in particular in a spirit of analysis close to my own, see again Terdiman, *DCD*, pp. 261–343. Beginning with the Mallarméan notion of a "poème critique," Terdiman goes on to describe the prose poem from a perspective at once "esthetic *and* social" as a hybrid genre mapping "explicitly social contradictions," a genre of "social poetry" both "subversive and utopian" that provides traces of a historical potentiality for a "transformed future" (262–63, 265, 279, 313, 342–43). In its "impulse . . . to pass beyond fixity, beyond closure," Terdiman writes, "the counter-discursive imagines the liberation of the whole realm of social discourse . . . the plenitude and the cultural richness of a freer discursive economy in which something more like authentic democracy might prevail" (343).

18. Caws, Preface, *The Prose Poem in France*, p. viii.

aesthetic and social formations.[19] With Baudelaire, two principal norms under attack are the habitual, purely formal association of poetry and verse, and the tendency to exclude from texts accepted under the rubric of poetry such prosaic motifs as urban life, crowds, poverty, and class conflict. Although the fragmentariness of the brief prose texts of *Le spleen de Paris* as collection suggests a latent critique of what Jameson has called the "apparently unified form" of the nineteenth-century novel and its efforts to conceal or mask discontinuities (*PU*, 144), Baudelaire's texts are not particularly revolutionary in their approach to narrative. Baudelaire's prose poetry thus appears historically to be directed primarily against the inherited formal and thematic conventions of the verse lyric. In the wake of Baudelaire's collection, Rimbaud's *Une saison en enfer* and the texts of the *Illuminations* stage an even more explicit critique and rejection of poetry-as-verse ("Alchimie du verbe"), as well as a critique of prose undreamed of by Baudelaire. For both Baudelaire and Rimbaud, the prose poem is the locus not only of a projected utopian fusion of genres but also of irreconcilable contradictions and suspended resolutions. In both writers, the genre emerges in response not only to such specifically aesthetic problems as the conventional opposition between poetry and prose but also to sociopolitical antagonisms left unresolved by the failed revolutions of 1848 and 1870–71.

Part III, "The Prose Poem in the Age of Cubism," examines the radically fissured narratives of Jacob and Stein. Like Rimbaud, Jacob uses the prose poem to undermine the generic conventions of both prose ("roman populaire") and poetry ("poème déclamatoire"). Situated aesthetically between Baudelaire's anecdotal style and Rimbaud's aesthetic of discontinuity, Jacob's texts are utopian in their radical refusal of all claims to generic purity. Jacob's theoretical utterances, on the other hand, tend to isolate the prose poem in their attempts to define it, thereby contributing to the assimilation and canonization of the genre in the early twentieth century. Stein's *Tender Buttons*, which doubtless poses greater problems of intelligibility than any other group of texts considered here, presents a grammar of social relations which involves sexual conflict much more than class conflict. My intention in including it has been twofold: (1) to show the extent to which, both

---

19. The terms "norm-breaking," "norm-building," and "norm-sustaining" occur in Jauss's definition of the relationship between literary texts and existing aesthetic and sociohistorical norms in "Racines und Goethes Iphigenie," *Rezeptionsästhetik*, p. 394.

despite and because of these difficulties, it is not only possible but also important and even crucial to Stein's own purposes and the reception of *Tender Buttons* to (re)construct its syntactical/semantic constellations as expressions of generic conflicts in both the aesthetic (prose/poetry) and sexual (male/female) senses of the word, and (2) to suggest in the process something of the importance of Stein's work to a history of the prose poem and its central concerns, particularly in light of the general omission of her texts from previous discussions of the genre.

Focusing on the utopian project of a fusion of genres with particular attention to the interpenetration of narrative and critique and of philosophy and poetry, Part IV, "The Other Side of Things," discusses texts by Bloch and Ponge that bear important resemblances both to Stein's *Tender Buttons* and to one another. Crucial differences in these writers' approaches to language notwithstanding, the texts of all three writers have in common a prose-poetic concentration of form, a manifest preoccupation with the world of material objects, and an intensely political orientation. Avowedly Marxist in their approaches to "literary" and "nonliterary" problems alike, Bloch and Ponge also share an interest in exploring the question of generic interpenetration by investigating the relationship between literature and philosophy, on the one hand, and between literary and philosophical discourse and political praxis, on the other. In contrast to Stein's texts, Bloch's "thought images" (*Denkbilder*) approach objects for what they might reveal about class, more than sexual, conflict. Bloch's approach to objects also differs from that of Stein in its emphasis on the construction of positive utopian narratives that contrast starkly with the fragmentariness and manifest refusal of narrative characteristic of *Tender Buttons*. Ponge's *Le parti pris des choses* is noteworthy in its approach to the prose poem, particularly for its tendency to virtually equate the form with tangible objects of the material world. The utopian dimension of Ponge's work in the genre manifests itself in his acknowledged attempt to show material objects as they might appear in a world of "after the revolution" and thus contribute to a *Grand Oeuvre* that would bring about the union of both a genreless genre and a classless society. Ponge's later texts represent a calculated attempt to bring the prose poem tradition Ponge identifies himself with to its culmination by exploding the genre's brevity and self-enclosed completeness into extended, fragmentary sequences.

The book's final section, "Beyond French Borders: Two Contemporaries," examines the work of Bly and Novak. By concluding with two writers working outside the French language, one American and one German, one male, the other female, one quite well known to readers of poetry and prose poetry in America, the other by and large unfamiliar here though well known inside her own country, I mean above all to underscore the fact that the prose poem has become a genre of transcultural and transgeneric interest, no longer practiced exclusively or even primarily by male writers from France. The prose poem's recent success in America doubtless has something to do with its somewhat exotic appeal as a relatively unfamiliar foreign import of primarily French origin, and it is worth noting that three of the poets most responsible for its introduction to America—Bly, James Wright, and W. S. Merwin—have also been respected translators. The selection of Bly for consideration here was dictated in large part by his role as one of the most influential recent practitioners and proponents of the prose poem in America. His work provides occasion for coming to terms with the genre's function in the context of contemporary aesthetic and political conditions inside the United States. The inclusion of Novak is intended above all as a gesture in keeping with the prose poem's resistance to the reifying tendency of national and generic literary canons toward certain safe and all-too-predictable critical exclusions and marginalizations, for example, the works of women, foreigners, politically minded writers, and even one's own contemporaries.

There are, of course, numerous other writers in many non-French-speaking countries besides the United States and Germany who have produced work in the genre which is at least equally as accomplished. Bly and Novak serve our purposes especially well here, however, because they exemplify, with quite different results, the tendency in the late 1960s and the 1970s among writers of verse poetry to turn to the prose poem—as had Baudelaire and Rimbaud before them—for the opportunity it provides to dramatize those intractably prosaic aspects of everyday experience often considered banal or unworthy of literary attention. Like Stein, Bloch, and Ponge—and to a lesser degree, Novalis, Baudelaire, Rimbaud, and Jacob—and despite their different nationalities and approaches, both writers display that unremitting preoccupation with the world of physical objects which has become one of the prose poem's most characteristic features. Bly's turn to the form coincides, somewhat surprisingly given the prose poem's past norm-breaking function, its history as a genre of revolt, with an increasing depoliticization of Bly's own work. Although Bly's prose poems evidence a certain domestication of the genre for American consumption—or what might be seen from another perspective as an attempt to keep faith with the relative democratization of form and content which characterizes the genre's Baudelairean phase—they also participate in the genre's profound expression of utopian longing.

In Novak's *Geselliges Beisammensein* the emphasis on opposition that has been such a dominant feature of the prose poem since Baudelaire reemerges as ongoing everyday conflicts between workers and owners ("Arbeitnehmer-Arbeitgeber"). Through her focus on the physical objects of factory labor, Novak relentlessly images the reification, alienation, and class conflict that have continued into our own century from the age of Baudelaire and Rimbaud. Evoking a poverty of objects that is really a poverty of human relations, *Geselliges Beisammensein* allows the utopian to come into view only by extreme negation. Finally, in contrast to this earlier collection, Novak's more recent *Die Landnahme von Torre Bela* suggests a positively utopian dimension, a form of collective experience which might offer a more than imaginary resolution to the sorts of real conflicts hinted at in the oxymoron of the prose poem's name, conflicts of gender, class, and genre, of the individual and the collective, conflicts at once aesthetic and political which have found in the genre a highly condensed and suggestive form.

In bringing the socio-ideological struggle of a wide variety of "languages" into a highly compact space where these languages may both fuse with and clash against one another, the prose poem at its best presents an explosive tension. The anecdote that constitutes "Assommons les pauvres!", the penultimate text of Baudelaire's collection which may serve as a paradigm for the presentation of such tension, is itself nothing less than a dramatic performance in which the languages of philosophy, poetry, philanthropy, and the poor quite literally fight it out with one another. Like the speaker in "Assommons les pauvres!", the prose poem as genre displays a marked ambivalence. On the one hand, the prose poem seems to reject the privilege, the exclusiveness from which other genres derive their identity. On the other hand, although it offers resistance to the fate of becoming merely one genre among many, it asks to be recognized as legitimate and distinctive in its own right. The prose poem's own paradoxical, utopian death-wish resides in the aspiration it has figured from the very beginning toward a final resolution of precisely those conflicts of gender, class, and genre which generate it and on which its very existence, if it is to be more than merely an empty form, continues to depend.

PART I

Two Precursors

CHAPTER 1

Universalpoesie as Fragment:
Friedrich Schlegel and
the Prose Poem

A definition of poetry can only determine what poetry should be, not what it really was and is; otherwise the shortest definition would be that poetry is whatever has at any time and at any place been called poetry.

—*Athenäums-Fragment,* 114

In recent years there has been increasing interest in two related literary forms, the fragment and the prose poem, which have yet to be brought closely to bear upon each other. While the fragment—in particular Friedrich Schlegel's *Athenäums-* and *Lyceums-Fragmente,* together with those of his *Literary Notebooks*[1]—has become the focus of increasing attention among literary critics and theorists, the prose poem over the last thirty years has begun to establish itself internationally as a chal-

1. Friedrich Schlegel, *Athenäums-Fragmente,* in *Charakteristiken und Kritiken I (1796–1801),* ed. Hans Eichner, vol. 2, *Kritische Friedrich-Schlegel-Ausgabe,* ed. Ernst Behler (Paderborn: Ferdinand Schöningh, 1967), p. 182; *Friedrich Schlegel's 'Lucinde' and the Fragments,* trans. Peter Firchow (Minneapolis: University of Minnesota Press, 1971), p. 174. Further references to the *Athenäums-Fragmente* will be indicated in the text by *AF* followed by the fragment number and page numbers corresponding to the *Kritische Ausgabe* and Firchow's translations. References to the *Lyceums-Fragmente* will be indicated by *LF,* fragment number, and page numbers corresponding to vol. 2 of the *Kritische Ausgabe* and *Friedrich Schlegel: Dialogue on Poetry and Literary Aphorisms,* trans. Ernst Behler and Roman Struc (University Park: The Pennsylvania State University Press, 1968). References to *Gespräch über die Poesie* (Dialogue on Poetry) will be indicated for the German original (also in vol. 2 of the *Kritische Ausgabe*) by *GP* and for the English translation of Behler and Struc by *DP.* Translations of passages from the *Literarische Notizen 1791–1801 [Literary Notebooks],* ed. Hans Eichner (Frankfurt: Ullstein, 1980) are my own and are indicated by *LN* followed by fragment and page number. Translations not my own have occasionally been modified.

lenge to the free verse forms that dominated poetry during the first half of the twentieth century.[2] Formulated over a half-century before the appearance of Baudelaire's *Petits poèmes en prose*, the theory of a progressive *Universalpoesie* which Schlegel's *Athenäums-Fragmente* articulate anticipates as comprehensively as any before or since the Baudelairean fusion of genres embodied in the prose poem:

> Die romantische Poesie ist eine progressive Universalpoesie. Ihre Bestimmung ist nicht bloß, alle getrennte Gattungen der Poesie wieder zu vereinigen, und die Poesie mit der Philosophie und Rhetorik in Berührung zu setzen. Sie will, und soll auch Poesie und Prosa, Genialität und Kritik, Kunstpoesie und Naturpoesie bald mischen, bald verschmelzen, die Poesie lebendig und gesellig, und das Leben und die Gesellschaft poetisch machen, den Witz poetisieren, und die Formen der Kunst mit gediegenem Bildungsstoff jeder Art anfüllen und sättigen, und durch die Schwingungen des Humors beseelen.
>
> [Romantic poetry is a progressive, universal poetry. Its aim isn't merely to reunite all the separate genres of poetry and to put poetry in touch with philosophy and rhetoric. It tries to and should mix and fuse poetry and prose, inspiration and criticism, the poetry of art and the poetry of nature; and make poetry lively and sociable, and life and society poetic; poeticize wit and fill and saturate the forms of art with every kind of good, solid matter for instruction, and animate them with the pulsations of humour.] (*AF*, 116, 182/175)

2. Evidence of the extent to which interest in the prose poem has recently begun to grow outside of France (where it has maintained a strong tradition since its origins in the form as we tend to think of it today with Aloysius Bertrand's *Gaspard de la nuit* and Baudelaire's *Petits poèmes en prose*), Michael Benedikt's *The Prose Poem: An International Anthology* (New York: Dell, 1976) includes the work of some seventy poets in eleven languages from countries in Western and Eastern Europe, Scandinavia, the Soviet Union, North and South America, and Japan; well over half of those represented are contemporaries or near-contemporaries, and a large number are already among the more influential poets of their respective national literatures. Many of these, Günter Eich of West Germany, the North Americans Robert Bly and James Wright, the Swede Thomas Tranströmer, turned to the prose poem in the late 1960s and early 1970s having already established themselves as verse poets; others, such as the West German Helga Novak, Russel Edson of the United States, and the French poet Francis Ponge, have acquired literary reputations largely if not exclusively on the basis of their prose poetry.

For a sampling of recent critical attention to the fragment see Philippe Lacoue-Labarthe and Jean-Luc Nancy, *L'absolu littéraire* (Paris: Seuil, 1978), and Lawrence D. Kritzman, ed., *Fragments: Incompletion and Discontinuity* (New York: New York Literary Forum, 1981). Among recent critical appraisals of the prose poem in addition to those already mentioned, see especially Barbara Johnson's *Défigurations du langage poétique: La seconde révolution baudelairienne* (Paris: Flammarion, 1977) and Michael Riffaterre's "The Semiotics of Poetry: The Prose Poem" in his *Semiotics of Poetry* (Bloomington: Indiana University Press, 1978), pp. 115–24.

As this celebrated passage makes clear, the problem of the relationship between poetry and prose is conceived of within the framework of Schlegel's project not in isolation but as of a piece with the related problems of the relationships between and among poetry and philosophy, the aesthetic and the political, literature and society.

By virtue of its emphasis on the fusion not only of poetry and prose but of other modes of discourse as well, Schlegel's theory recommends itself as a point of departure for exploring the larger horizon within which the poetry/prose problematic is inscribed and hence the possibilities and limitations of the prose poem as a literary form. Thus, after beginning with an examination of Schlegel's attempted dismantling of the conventional dichotomization of poetry and prose, this first chapter will offer a brief description of the subsequent Hegelian version of the problem, including a synopsis of the related question of the relationship between poetic discourse and speculative discourse as it has been developed in the last decade by Jacques Derrida and Paul Ricoeur; a section on the polemically destabilizing function of the fusion of genres conceived of by Schlegel and Baudelaire vis-à-vis the lyric and the novel; an outline of the problem of the relationship between the individual and the collective raised by both fragments and prose poems once these are gathered together into collections; and a concluding section touching on the shared discursive and sociopolitical horizon bounding the synthetic projects of both forms.

Poetry and Prose

Appearing in the first issue of *Athenäum* in 1798, Schlegel's *Fragments* fall squarely within that five-year period Michel Foucault has described as a turning point from the neoclassical to the modern episteme. The years between 1795 and 1800 are characterized, says Foucault, by two phases, the essentially conservative old order based on empirical analysis, and the other, which breaks radically from this analytical/empirical view, endorsing a synthetic/speculative view that deemphasizes taxonomic identification in favor of a new principle of organization. This principle looks beyond visible structures to the hidden internal workings of these structures.[3] The change is from inductive to deductive reasoning, a posteriori to a priori reasoning, from classification based on external features alone to a systematic unveiling of internal rela-

3. Michel Foucault, *The Order of Things: An Archaeology of the Human Sciences* (New York: Random House, 1970), p. 233 and passim; hereafter referred to as *OT*.

tions. Replacing the dominant question of the seventeenth and eighteenth centuries as to how differences appear against a background of continuity, the modern episteme asks: How can diversity, discontinuity, be brought into synthesis? What continuity is possible against a background of discontinuity?

Schlegel's work between 1795 and 1800 stands at a crossroads of these two orientations. Analytic, taxonomic, one aspect of the *Athenäums-Fragmente* (even more apparent in the *Literary Notebooks*, 1797–1801) looks back to the neoclassical, Enlightenment episteme as Foucault has described it. Yet what is most striking in the *Athenäums-Fragmente* is not Schlegel's efforts at literary classification but the project of a *Universalpoesie* that would entail a breakdown of the taxonomic approach and a fusion or synthesis of genres:

> Soll denn die Poesie schlechthin eingeteilt sein? oder soll sie die eine und unteilbare bleiben? oder wechseln zwischen Trennung und Verbindung? . . . Die gewöhnlichen Einteilungen der Poesie sind nur totes Fachwerk für einen beschränkten Horizont. . . . Im Universum der Poesie aber ruht nichts, alles wird und verwandelt sich und bewegt sich harmonisch. . . . das wahre Weltsystem der Poesie [ist] noch nicht entdeckt.
>
> [Should poetry simply be divided up? Or should it remain one and indivisible? Or fluctuate between division and union? . . . The usual classifications of poetry are mere dead pedantry designed for people with limited vision. . . . But in the universe of poetry nothing stands still, everything is developing and changing and moving harmoniously. . . . the true world system of poetry has not yet been discovered.] (*AF*, 434, 252/237)

The only bad genre, says Schlegel, echoing Voltaire, is the *boring* genre, and the surest way to arrive at it is not to know to which genre one's work belongs. Yet as that "dead pendantry" (*totes Fachwerk*), the usual division of poetry, indicates, it is not so easy to delimit genre as it may at first appear. If Schlegel concerns himself with literary classification, the generic taxonomies of his predecessors, he does so in order to collapse them into each other and so get beyond them. The chemist knows, says Schlegel's friend Novalis, "that through true mixing a third thing arises that is two things at once and at the same time more than each thing separately."[4] As a good chemist wants to have mastered the

4. Novalis, *Teplitzer-Fragmente*, in *Schriften* 2, ed. Richard Samuel (Stuttgart: W. Kohlhammer, 1960), p. 432.

properties of various chemicals before experimenting with them, so Schlegel intends to identify generic properties of literary texts in order to bring about what he sometimes refers to as a "mixing" (*Mischung, Vermischung*) sometimes as a "fusion" (*Verschmelzung*) of literary genres into a kind of genre to end all genres: "Whether there is to be a variety of modes of writing or not, there must still be one mode of writing that unites all others" (*LN*, 120, 34). Such is the project of *Universalpoesie*, the achievement of which is linked up, as it is articulated in the *Athenäums-Fragmente*, with the possibility of system. Yet, Schlegel says, "It is equally fatal for the mind to have a system and to have none. It will simply have to decide to avoid both" (*AF*, 53, 173/167). To have and at the same time to avoid system is a problem to which the *Athenäums-Fragmente* themselves, and after them Baudelaire's *Petits poèmes en prose*, the prose poem and collections of prose poems generally, attempt to provide an answer. If their answers are in no way conclusive, this fact must be attributed at least partially to the character of the modern age, which leads not into an age of organic wholeness and totality but, instead, to increasing fragmentation. As Schlegel himself puts it: "The history of progressive poetry could only then be completely and *a priori* constructed if it were itself complete; as for now we can only point to confirmations of the progressive idea in the history of modern poetry and pursue our speculations [*Vermuthungen*] from there" (*LN*, 96, 32).

In the "history of progressive poetry," and with it of generic classifications, Schlegel's *Fragments* stand Janus-faced between what Peter Szondi refers to as the normative and the speculative theories of genre—"normative" implying an emphasis on visible similarities and differences, "speculative" the attempt to articulate a fundamental unity beneath these.[5] In this sense, Schlegel's *Fragments* marked an important contribution to the newly emerging modern episteme in which classification gave way to the relation of the visible to the invisible, manifest signs to secret architecture. The change from a normative to a speculative genre/poetics was only possible, according to Szondi, once the lyric had firmly established itself as a genre, clearing the way for the tripartite division still dominant today of lyric, drama, and epic (or its modern counterpart, the novel). The rise of the lyric as a generic category and its assimilation in this triadic schema was accomplished, however, only in the last half of the eighteenth century following the

---

5. Peter Szondi, *Von der normativen zur spekulativen Gattungspoetik* in *Poetik und Geschichtsphilosophie*, 2 (Frankfurt: Suhrkamp, 1974), passim; hereafter referred to as *PG*.

appearance of Batteux' *Les beaux arts réduits à un même principe* (The Fine Arts Reduced to a Single Principle) (1746). The idea of such a division appears at least several times in Friedrich's *Literary Notebooks* (most notably, in fragments 322, 1750, and 2065) but does not occur as such in the *Athenäums-Fragmente,* where the pair poetry/prose has a significant role. Granted that in a sense, as Szondi says, the work Schlegel *wanted* to write was written by Hegel, it must be said that although the tripartite schema epic-lyric-drama does enter into the *Athenäums-Fragmente,* it does not play the decisive role it does at the conclusion of Hegel's *Ästhetik.* Indeed, without denying the usefulness and importance of the epic-lyric-drama generic distinction, it is worth remembering that just as the prose/poetry distinction receives the greatest attention in the *Athenäums-Fragmente,* so in Hegel's *Ästhetik* its elaboration precedes and in a sense incorporates the tripartite division.

The latter has its roots, as Szondi reminds us, in the Platonic definitions of literary genre according to modes of oral performance. Drama, the *genus activum* or *imitativum,* is performed by actors in their respective roles; dithyramb, the *genus enarrativum* or *enuntiativum* (subsequently associated with the lyric), is performed by a narrator speaking in the third person; and epic, the *genus commune* or *mixtum,* is a combination of acting and third-person narration (*PG,* 25). What such a tripartite division fails adequately to take into consideration is the extent to which literature, as we know it today and as it has been conceived since the early years of the nineteenth century, has undergone a transition from a principally oral to a principally written phenomenon. From the end of the eighteenth century on, as Foucault observes, literature is no longer made for the voice: "Henceforth it is the primal nature of language to be written" (*OT,* 38). In effect, this change had been preparing itself at least since Gutenberg, the beginning of the age of the mechanical reproduction of writing which led to the loss of aura of the original manuscript. With the advent of mechanical printing, the literary text is detached not only from its origin in the voice but also from the voice's surrogate, the signature, the handwritten text. As such, it becomes for the first time what the modern age experiences as "literature." To the extent that poetry had been thought more or less inextricably bound up with verse until Schlegel's *Universalpoesie* and the emergence of the prose poem with Aloysius Bertrand and Baudelaire, the division of literature into prose and poetry carries an implicit reference to modes of printing rather than to oral performance. It is toward the resolution of the antinomy between poetry and prose that

Schlegel's dialectical schema prose—poetry—*Universalpoesie*, is directed (as would be also Baudelaire's *Le spleen de Paris*, albeit deprived of the third term and seemingly removed further than ever from the possibility of resolution). In this sense, the prose/poetry distinction is at least as fundamental to the conception of literature in Schlegel's time as is the drama-lyric-epic division.

Schlegel's attitude toward a possible fusion of prose and poetry is not without some ambivalence. In 1707–8 he wrote: "Poetry is laughable in prose, prose despicable in poetry" (*LN*, 509, 69). Yet this comment is best understood in conjunction with Schlegel's insistence that only the "boring" genre results from an attempted fusion of genres which is not preceded by a thorough mastery of their elemental properties. Such properties, however, are not easily determined. Once it is admitted that genres do not have the crystalline purity of physical elements, the chemical metaphor itself breaks down. Contrary to his intention, it must be admitted that in a sense, as Philippe Lacoue-Labarthe and Jean-Luc Nancy have remarked, what Schlegel and Romanticism show is that there is no mixing of genres "as such."[6] "What prose might in reality be," Schlegel concedes, "no one has yet said" (*LN*, 584, 76). Nor does he himself develop a systematic distinction between poetry and prose which would liberate him entirely from his own potentially misleading chemical analogy: "There is a prose of nature [*Naturprosa*] and a prose of art [*Kunstprosa*], as in poetry. There is poetry without meter (Meister) and metrical prose (Nathan). The basis of prose is dialectical, that is, logical and political—then grammatical" (*LN*, 584, 76). If nobody before Schlegel had satisfactorily defined what prose might be, his own attempt here does not carry us much further. Even the dialectical, the logical, political, and grammatical are not exclusive properties of prose alone. "Is there in fact a poetic prose or does such a thing annihilate itself? Since there is prosaic poetry (the novel) there must also be a poetic prose" (*LN*, 596, 77). As romantic poetry is split between the metrical and the prosaic, so romantic prose between the metrical and the poetic (*LN*, 557, 73).

Given that classification is "a definition that contains a system of definitions" (*AF*, 113, 181/174), Schlegel's classification is singularly unsystematic. Prose and poetry are clearly distinguished from each other neither as modes of printing—*en bloc* or *en vers*—nor as modes of oral performance. Yet despite this failure clearly to distinguish poetry

6. Lacoue-Labarthe and Nancy, *L'absolu littéraire*, p. 141. Hereafter referred to as *AL*.

from prose, in the *Literary Notebooks* Schlegel maintains the importance of the project most fully developed in *Athenäums-Fragment* 116: "All poetry should be prose, and all prose poetry. All prose ought to be novelistic/romantic [*romantisch*]" (*LN*, 602, 78). Sometimes it appears as if the "fusion" has already taken place: "All prose is poetic. If one distinguishes poetry from prose, then only the logical is prose" (*LN*, 40, 27). Yet for the most part the future of poetry and prose is not, for Schlegel, a given. As was the case with *Charakteristik*, which Schlegel describes as a genre in itself for Plato and antiquity, it remains for the moderns to successfully fuse poetry and prose once again: "Avoid everything poetic in the form; only the spirit and the substance [or material, *Stoff*] should be poetic; the expression as prosaic as possible.— There is then after all true poetic prose. But the poetic falls over so easily into the rhetorical, which is the death of the philosophical, the historical and the philological.—" (*LN*, 14, 24). The fusion of poetry and prose still implies, for Schlegel, the successful melting together of other subgenres or co-genres "within" as well as "outside" literature. In this, the novelistic/Romantic project Schlegel puts forward in his collections of fragments is fundamentally "novelistic" in the Bakhtinian sense and anticipates not only Baudelaire's *Le spleen de Paris*—where the prose poem appears as a nexus of interaction for the novel, the lyric, the short story, the epigram, the aphorism, and other literary and extraliterary speech types—but also Hegel's *Ästhetik*, where poetry and prose are again brought into relation with each other, this time systematically and by means of a third term, philosophy.

The Poetic and the Speculative

The notion of oral performance does not play a significant role in either Schlegel's fragments or Hegel's *Ästhetik*. Although at one point Hegel affirms that works of poetry must be "spoken, sung, read aloud, presented by living subjects . . . like works of music," in another passage he declares it "makes no difference for the truly poetic whether a work of literature is read or heard."[7] Deemphasizing for the sake of system that fragmentation which Schlegel considered decisive for the modern world, Hegel considers the poem "a world closed in on itself," "an organic whole" (*VA*, 231). Poetry and prose are not to be reduced to their forms of expression. Rather than defining poetry and prose in

---

7. G. W. F. Hegel, *Vorlesungen über die Ästhetik* 3 (Frankfurt: Suhrkamp, 1970), pp. 320 and 229; hereafter referred to as *VA*.

terms of oral performance or modes of printing, Hegel follows Aristotle in distinguishing between mimetic and nonmimetic uses of language. Poetry is distinct from prose, on the one hand, philosophy on the other, in that it permits an "internal idea" [*inneres Vorstellen*], a quasi-visual "inner image" [*innerliche Anschauung*] maintaining the golden mean [*schöne Mitte*] between inner and outer worlds (*VA*, 229–57). Prose, poetry, philosophy: each of these is at the same time, for Hegel, language and more than language, a way of perceiving the world.

Although poetry in the modern world draws its material from the world of prose, it is not, like prose, merely a means to an end, but an end in itself. Whereas prose characterizes our habitual perception of things, poetry permits the possibility of new ways of seeing. Finally, where prose represents the world as a place of chance, a mere given in its "external contingency, dependence and hopeless arbitrariness" (*VA*, 260), poetry melts down and recasts the recalcitrant world of prose into works of inner unity and organic wholeness (*VA*, 244). Speculative philosophy shares with poetry, in contrast to prose, the perception of a fundamental unity of self and world but is limited by its abstract character. In contrast to the reasoning process that characterizes speculative philosophy, which hurries to arrive at generalities, or the pragmatic, teleological character of the world of prose, poetry lingers on details. Whereas prose is the perception of finitude, the extremes of either total independence or total dependence of the individual in society, the part and the whole, poetry and philosophy show totality and unity. Poetry, as the visualization of speculative thought, is also a kind of mediation between prose and philosophy. As such, it is always in danger of collapsing into one or the other. Though conceding that the boundaries of prose, poetry and philosophy are sometimes difficult to establish, as in Schiller's philosophical poems, Hegel does not encourage, as Schlegel did, a fusion of genres, the *Verschmelzung* of the aesthetic and the political, of prose, poetry, and philosophy, which lay at the heart of the project of a *Universalpoesie*.

The relation between poetic and speculative discourse, at issue in Hegel's *Ästhetik* as well as in Schlegel's fragments, has resurfaced in the last decade in important critical writings by Derrida and Ricoeur on the subject of metaphor. Like Hegel, Ricoeur sees the principal resemblance between the two kinds of discourse in the perception of similarity each articulates. For Ricoeur, as for Hegel and Aristotle, poetic discourse differs most visibly from philosophical, speculative discourse by its mimetic aspect, the quasi-visualization of a "setting before the eyes."[8] But for Ricoeur the difference does not stop here. Although both poetic and speculative discourse are one in the perception of similarities, poetry is ruled by metaphorical language, philosophy by conceptual language. Metaphor depends on the tension between identity and difference; philosophy presents the resolution of the conflict of identity and difference in the same. Philosophy is conceived (in highly metaphorical terms!) as "watchman overseeing the ordered extensions of meaning," poetry as the discourse of the "unfettered extensions of meaning" (RM, 261). The metaphorical language of poetry may serve in the search for what Ricoeur calls a "non-generic unity" by breaking down old categories of thought and establishing new logical frontiers. But the attainment of this nongeneric unity, which recalls the project of Schlegel's *Universalpoesie,* depends on the passage from poetry (metaphor) to philosophy (analogy) to the "nonmetaphorical and properly transcendental resemblance" of speculative thought. The realm of the speculative is also, for Ricoeur, the realm of religion, the project of onto-theology which encompasses "the horizontal relation of the categories of substance and the vertical relation of created things to the Creator" (RM, 273).

Although Ricoeur maintains that speculative discourse reverses the order of poetic discourse by giving priority to concept (signifying) over metaphor (representing), he argues nonetheless that the "rule of metaphor" characteristic of poetry is also a necessary condition of speculative discourse. According to Derrida, by contrast, the very resemblance-revealing function of metaphor which makes it a necessary condition of speculative discourse also poses the possibility of the *death* of the speculative (whether "philosophical" or "religious"). In its desire for univocality, its dream of being one with itself in a oneness of meaning, speculative discourse represses the metaphorical polyvalence and structural unconscious of words which poetic discourse exploits and reveals. Although metaphor opens up the possibility of what Ricoeur calls the "indifference" of identity and difference in the Same, the meta-oneness of Western metaphysics, it also poses a threat to the speculative, according to Derrida, because of the copresence in metaphor of identity with difference. Whereas poetry depends on the *play* of difference and similarity, speculative discourse depends on the possibility of the *Aufhebung* of these in the Same. Hegel's concept of the

---

8. Paul Ricoeur, *The Rule of Metaphor,* trans. Robert Czerny (Toronto: University of Toronto Press, 1977), p. 34; hereafter referred to as *RM.*

Aufhebung, the cancellation and raising of two opposed terms into a third term that would represent the absolute in-difference of identity and difference, implies for Derrida continuity. As Ricoeur says, summarizing Derrida's position: "Whether we speak of the metaphorical character of metaphysics or of the metaphysical character of metaphor, what must be grasped is the single movement that carries words and things beyond, *meta*" (*RM*, 288). Where Derrida conceives of the *Aufhebung* of metaphor and metaphysics (common to the onto-theological project of both religion *and* philosophy) as a "single movement," Ricoeur perceives two discrete moments, the poetic and the speculative, radically separate from each other. Where Derrida articulates the passage from the metaphorical to the metaphysical as one of *usure*—implying both a wearing away and a speculation, loss as well as gain in the exchange-value of a term—Ricoeur sees the relation between them as one of discontinuity.[9]

Because Ricoeur wishes to maintain a radical distinction between the poetic and the speculative, Derrida's philosophy—along with that of Heidegger and by extension, presumably, that of Schlegel as well—comes to represent for him "a temptation we must shun when the difference between speculative and poetic threatens once again to disappear" (*RM*, 309). Yet Ricoeur himself admits that the boundaries between poetic and speculative thought are not always easily drawn: "Certainly the difference is infinitesimal when the philosopher approves a thinking poetry—that of poets who themselves write poetically on language, like Hölderlin" (*RM*, 310). Note that Hölderlin has the same function in this regard for Ricoeur which Schiller had earlier for Hegel. As Ricoeur's equivocation between "philosopher" and "poets" suggests, both Hölderlin and Schiller write in a margin that makes them and their work difficult to label. Given the existence of such writers and such works, we may well want to ask, as did Schlegel: "Is there not also a philopoetic genre of prose?" (*LN*, 18, 25). The trajectory of Ricoeur's discourse toward the speculative moment of onto-theology is the counterpart of the trajectory of Derrida's discourse toward difference. Paradoxically, Ricoeur would achieve his onto-theological telos of the absolute indifference of identity and difference in the Same by maintaining a radical separation between poetic and speculative discourse. In a more Schlegelian spirit, on the other

9. A further distinction between Derrida's position and that of Ricoeur—and in this case of Schlegel as well—is marked by Derrida's questioning of the possibility of the *Aufhebung* itself as constituting a pure resolution rather than a mere repression, of existing antinomies.

hand, Derrida's *White Mythology* tends to affirm the play of differences by demonstrating the interpenetration of the "poetic" and the "philosophical," as the philosopher's stone is exchanged, at the end of his essay, for that of the poet, the heliotrope that is not only a plant but a "precious stone, greenish and streaked with red veins, a kind of oriental jasper."[10]

Novel, Lyric, Prose Poem

Preceding Baudelaire's prose poetry by more than fifty years, Schlegel's call for a fusion of genres has its "proper" reference, as Szondi has reminded us, in the novel:

> Quite probably the best known and most worked-over text of the young Schlegel, *Athenäums-Fragment* 116, is at the same time the most misunderstood, precisely because the romantic poetry which it puts forward as its project and defines as a progressive universal poetry is not meant to designate the poetry of the romantics, but the writing of novels, the genre of the novel—and only by means of that genre's dominant, tone-setting position the poetry of the romantics and of the modern itself. (*PG*, 144)

Granting this intimate connection between *Universalpoesie* and the novel, between *romantisch* (romantic) and *romanhaft* (novel-like), the question nevertheless remains: How does Schlegel conceive of the novel? The answer to this question will serve, I believe, partially to undermine the very connection Szondi has sought to reestablish and, as I hope to show, displace the relation *Universalpoesie*→novel in a direction similar to *Universalpoesie*→*Petits poèmes en prose*.[11]

   The principal difficulty in maintaining an identity among the terms *Universalpoesie—romantische Poesie—Roman* (universal poetry—Romantic poetry—novel) lies in Schlegel's use of the designation "romantic" for genres other than the novel in the more conventional senses the word has come to be understood since the early nineteenth century. In the *Literary Notebooks*, for example, Schlegel refers to Petrarch's lyric poems as "classical fragments of a novel" (*LN*, 353, 54; see also *LN*, 522,

---

10. Jacques Derrida, *White Mythology*, in *Margins of Philosophy*, trans. Alan Bass (Chicago: University of Chicago Press, 1982), p. 271. For a recent discussion by Derrida on the mixing of genres see his "The Law of Genre," trans. Avital Ronell, in *Critical Inquiry* 7, no. 1 (1980), pp. 55–83. The same article also appears in *Glyph* 7 (Baltimore: Johns Hopkins University Press, 1980).

11. Charles Baudelaire, Preface to *Petits poèmes en prose* (*Le spleen de Paris*), *Oeuvres complètes*, ed. Claude Pichois (Paris: Gallimard, editions Pléiade, 1975), p. 275; hereafter cited as *OC*.

70), identifies the sonnet—that highly condensed and tightly structured example of lyrical expression par excellence—as the Romantic fragment's "most complete form" (*LN*, 435, 62–63), and speaks of a "dichotomy of novelistic/romantic poetry into the metrical and the prosaic" (*LN*, 557, 73). Thus, the modern reader's first expectation of the novel, that it be written in *prose*, is frustrated in Schlegel's theory by his use of the term *romantisch* to refer to modes of writing not typically thought of as "novelistic." "In a sense," he writes, "all poems are really novels, just as all poems have the historical (classical or progressive) merit of belonging to the progression of poetry" (*LN*, 573, 75). Conceptually, Schlegel has in effect already subverted the dichotomization of novel and lyric by conceiving of poetry, traditionally associated with verse, in broad terms that include both verse and prose: "Evidently we often read a lyric poet as a novel; whenever one relates lyric poems primarily to the individuality of the poet, one reads them in a romantic/novelistic manner [*betrachtet man sie romantisch*] (*LN*, 1395, 149).[12]

Schlegel's "read . . . as" in the above sentence anticipates a problem that will subsequently be foregrounded by the prose poem *as collection;* that is, the role of the reader in constructing or seeing a given text as totality or as fragment. One of the most striking aspects of Schlegel's *Universalpoesie* is that, although the theory itself points in the direction of totality, the fragment is its formal unit of articulation. The resulting tension is evident in Schlegel's definition of the novel as "an artfully constructed chaos" (*LN*, 1356, 146), on the one hand, an "absolute system, a book in the highest sense" (*LN*, 1683, 172) on the other. It is obvious, Schlegel writes, that "all the novels of an author not infrequently belong together and are to a certain degree only one novel" (*LF*, 89, 158, 129–30). We may, if we choose, break down the "unity" of a novel into so many links of a chain, or on the other hand we may

12. The point of arguing such a displacement is not to call into question the specific connection between the "Romantic" and the "novelistic" which Szondi rightly emphasizes with reference to Schlegel's own work but, rather, to suggest important differences between the novel as it was conceived by Schlegel and the novel as it might otherwise be conceived today. As will become clear in what follows, my use of the term is designed especially to underscore the disparity between Schlegel's conceptualization of the genre and the popular, serialized forms of the novel which subsequently held sway during the period contemporaneous with the emergence of Baudelaire's prose poetry. Although the novels of such eighteenth-century French writers as Laclos, Marivaux, and Diderot and of such German contemporaries of Schlegel as Novalis, Goethe, and Tieck more closely approximate the Schlegelian notion of what a novel is and should be than do these later forms, they are beyond the scope of my immediate concern here, which is to consider Schlegel's notion of the novel and the "novelistic" in light of the fate of the genre *after* Schlegel and what might be called its institutionalization, conventionalization, or reification in the age of Baudelaire and beyond.

construct out of a collection of lyrics a "novelistic" unity. As for lyric
poetry as a genre in itself, it no longer has a place in the modern era,
Schlegel says, but is "constantly to be woven into novels" (*LN*, 1569,
163). To the extent that the "lyrical" implies situating unity in an individual subjectivity rather than in "objective" reality, Schlegel's notion of
the novelistic seems closer to what is usually conceived of as a lyrical
perspective than to the distanced third-person perspective more conventionally expected of the novel.[13] Despite Schlegel's marked tendency to view the novel in lyrical, subject-centered terms, however, he
envisions the novel finally as a hybrid genre in which the subjective and
the objective are to be synthesized.[14] Thus, "In all novels the subjective
has to become objective; it is an error to think that the novel is a
subjective mode of writing" (*LN*, 828, 99).

A paradigmatic example of the kind of hybrid text Schlegel conceived of under the term "novel" is evidenced by Schlegel's own *Lucinde*. Though generically subtitled *Ein Roman* (A Novel), Schlegel's text
has little in common with the popular notions of what a novel should be
that developed and rigidified as the genre ascended to the hegemony
over other literary forms it has maintained to the present day. The
reassuring images of developing wholeness, logical coherence, closure,
and a unified world view which the bourgeois public of the nineteenth
century came increasingly to expect and demand from the novel find
themselves already undermined by Schlegel's fragments, by *Lucinde*,
and by the prose poetry of Baudelaire. With its heterogeneous and
discontinuous pattern, including a "dithyrambic fantasy," an allegory,
an idyll, epistolary, meditative and reflective strategies alongside and
even dominating narrative structure, *Lucinde* in fact bears a much
closer family resemblance to collections of prose poems such as
Baudelaire's *Petits poèmes en prose* than to subsequent novels charac-

---

13. Citing Schlegel specifically in the first footnote of the essay entitled "From the
Prehistory of Novelistic Discourse," Bakhtin writes: "The Romantics maintained that the
novel was a mixed genre (a mixture of verse and prose), incorporating into its composition various genres (in particular the lyrical)—but the Romantics did not draw any
stylistic conclusions from this" (*The Dialogic Imagination*, p. 42). Compared to Schlegel's
use of the word *romantisch* and Bakhtin's notion of the "novelistic," the term novel
[*Roman*] as it is habitually used tends to designate a much narrower range of phenomena,
novels in the more conventional sense of what Bakhtin calls a "single-styled genre." For
Bakhtin, of course, as we have seen, the novelistic designates a hybrid, antigeneric form
that resists classification.

14. Accordingly, Lacoue-Labarthe and Nancy have written that the unity of
Schlegel's fragments is located somehow outside the work, "in the subject who lets himself be seen or in the faculty of judgement which gives its maxims there" (*AL*, 58).

terized by an emphasis on linear narrative, plot development, and smooth transitional coherence from chapter to chapter.[15]

Although the popular triple-decker serial novels of the mid-nineteenth century develop primarily the aspect of Schlegel's notion of a *Universalpoesie* that points toward totality, Baudelaire's prose poetry tends to carry forward its project of a fusion of genres by thematizing fragmentation and by exposing both the illusory sense of completeness proferred by the detached, "objective" third-person perspective of the popular novel and the illusory sense of independence which tends to characterize the lyrical "I" and thus the lyric as a primarily subjective genre. The complete novel, Schlegel says, would mean a "totality of all individuals" (*LN*, 574, 75). In light of this definition, the prose poem suggests a fragmentation of reified forms of the novel which offer a *false* sense of totality, polemically negates the popular novel's omnisciently "objective" third-person point of view as well as the lyric's privileging of the individual subject, and consequently thematizes the struggles among speech types and the distance separating the individual from the collective which would be truly "novelistic" in the Bakhtinian sense. On display in the *Petits poèmes en prose* is neither the subjective isolation and independence of the lyrical "I" alone, nor a positivistically "objective" nineteenth-century realism. The "absolute impossibility of uniting subject and object" which Schlegel says will be itself "object and subject of poetry in the romantic/novelistic lyric" (*LN*, 726, 90) is but one dimension of the *Petits poèmes en prose*. The collection's other dimension, that which typifies its critical relation not only to the novel but to conventional received forms of the verse lyric as well, is its (re)insertion of the individual into the social context, the dialectical interpenetration of subject and object which discovers their identity and difference.

The Fragment as Form, the Prose Poem as Fragment

Like the fragment, the prose poem distinguishes itself by a relative lack of formally distinctive features. Compared even to free verse the prose poem seems an artless genre, if art be defined by identifiable formal structures. Like the fragment, the prose poem is characterized by concision and brevity, the attempt to condense the maximum verbal power

15. Conceived of by Schlegel as the new synthetic genre par excellence, the novel comes to occupy a position in this regard formerly held in the tripartite schema, as Szondi has indicated, by tragic drama (*PG*, 202–3).

into the fewest possible words. Although Schlegel's fragments are dominated by conceptual language, however, Baudelaire's prose poems exhibit that concern for evoking the visual characteristic of metaphorically concentrated discourse. Both the fragment and the prose
poem have about them the quality of sudden insight, Schlegel's typically more general and abstract (though not devoid of examples, one
would hesitate to speak of illustrations), Baudelaire's more grounded
in the particular case, the anecdotal and the fictional. Schlegel's fragments are generally less developed and rounded off, more "fragmentary" than the poems of *Le spleen de Paris,* an effect partially produced
by the fact that whereas each piece of the latter collection is titled,
Schlegel's individual fragments are not.

The question of form as it relates to the fragment and the prose
poem must be considered with reference, however, not only to the
individual work but to the collection as well. In both cases, arrangements tend to be predominantly paratactic. Although it might well be
argued that the coherence of the *Athenäums-Fragmente* would suffer if,
for example, Fragment 116 were omitted, it would clearly make little
difference to the *Athenäum* or *Lyceum* collections were certain parts to
be displaced to points earlier or later. Similarly, the effect of Baudelaire's collection would not be radically altered by such displacement.
Like Schlegel's texts as well, Baudelaire's texts radically question the
very principle of organic unity and coherence. Although Schlegel's
Literary Notebooks are chronologically arranged, the *Athenäums-* and
Lyceums-Fragmente clearly share with *Le spleen de Paris* a concern for
beginnings as well as for closure which provide a frame setting them
off from the surrounding chaos. Within and among individual prose
poems and individual fragments, both Baudelaire and Schlegel exploit
logical and dialectical principles of generation, though neither does so
systematically. A loosely structured principle of thematic repetition and
variation dominates both cases, so that whatever internal or "hidden"
coherence might emerge in the collections themselves depends more
on the reader's adeptness at building consistency than on a tightly
woven and ineluctable pattern constructed by the author. Like the
poems of *Le spleen de Paris,* the *Athenäums-Fragmente* challenge the reader to construct an organic whole that construction then meets, in each
instance, with at least partial frustration. Through this kind of presentation, each work *as collection* offers to the reader a fragmented world.

Thematizing the problem of boundaries, of self-sufficiency and interdependence, the fragment is that form which is identifiable as part

of a larger whole. Complete in itself, yet open to all sides—"like a miniature work of art . . . isolated from the surrounding world . . . complete in itself like a porcupine" (*AF*, 206, 197/189)—a fragment must be self-enclosed, like a prose poem, yet it must also resist closure. The problem of the individual work of art—the artwork as fragment— is, as both Schlegel and Baudelaire conceived it, the aesthetic counter- part of the problem of the individual per se. Within literature and within society, Schlegel's fragments pose the same question that Baude- laire raises in his preface to *Le spleen de Paris*: "Chop it into numerous fragments [*en nombreux fragments*] and you will see that each one can exist separately." How, in Baudelaire's terms, does "*one* modern life" (une *vie moderne*) relate to "modern life *generally*" (la *vie moderne*, my emphasis)?[16] For, as Schlegel observed, "Isolation is certainly charac- teristically modern" (*LN*, 317, 51). How does each individual fragment or prose poem relate to the collection of fragments, the collection of prose poems? How would the individual and the collective be balanced in society, as the part and the whole in the literary work? How would the respective social, political, and aesthetic fabrics be woven into a unity and to what extent is such a unity capable of emerging with finality? For Schlegel, the answer to all these questions lies in the real- ization of *Universalpoesie*, a never-ending process, a goal whose value is heuristic, not absolute.

For both Schlegel and Baudelaire, the fragmentation of modern life poses two related problems, the problem of understanding it and the problem of conceiving an alternative to it. Unlike the Greeks, Schlegel says, for whom unified works existed, the moderns seem capable of producing only literary fragments that correspond to a fragmented society: "All poetic fragments," he writes, "must be parts of some whole"—and yet—"There is so much poetry, and yet nothing is more rare than a poetic work!" (*LF*, 4, 147/121). What are perceived as unified works among the moderns are in reality only so many tenden-

16. In Batteux' treatise on the fine arts, which was familiar to Friedrich Schlegel through the German translation provided by his father, Johann Adolf, in 1751, the dithyramb is explicitly equated with lyric poetry (see *PG*, 36). The inclusion of a "di- thyrambic fantasy" in *Lucinde* thus provides further evidence of the lyrical underpinning of Schlegel's conception of the novel and of the affinities between his notion of the novelistic and the project of a "poetic prose" put forward in Baudelaire's *Le spleen de Paris* (see especially the preface and the prose poem entitled "Le thyrse").

For Schlegel's perspective on the political implications of the lyric as genre, see his *Geschichte der Poesie der Griechen und Römer*; see also Szondi's discussion of the impact, most notably in the philosophy of Schelling, of Schlegel's notion that the lyric is a specifi- cally *democratic* ("republican") form (*PG*, 269–70).

cies, sketches, studies, fragments, ruins (*LN*, 409, 60). Since isolation and fragmentation are themselves characteristically modern, the project of a fusion of genres shared by Schlegel and Baudelaire seems, for the moments of their texts, incapable of being perceived or articulated as *other* than fragmentary. "Wherever art on its way to concreteness tries to eliminate [*polemisch eliminieren*] . . . a genre . . .," Adorno has remarked, "this negation preserves what it ostensibly eliminates. This state of affairs is constitutive of modern art."[17] Nor has our own situation changed in this regard since Schlegel's fragments and Baudelaire's prose poems were first published, if the problem is still that of perceiving totality and of the possibility of things being otherwise.[18]

The question of form, as of identity and genre, is thus one in Schlegel with the question of the new age to come: "How is it possible," he writes, "to understand and punctuate the contemporary period of the world correctly, if one can't even foresee the general outlines of the subsequent one?" (*AF*, 426, 248/234). Schlegel often speaks of the difference between his own age and the age to come as that between the chemical and the organic. The chemical age, dominated by the French, whom Schlegel describes as "a chemical nation" (*AF*, 426, 248/234), is the age of revolution. Until the age of revolution ends and the new organic age replaces the chemical age at hand, according to Schlegel, no unity, no final sense of the completeness of a form is possible; nor will it be possible to recognize or produce a unified or complete work or society. Only with the arrival of this new age will the relation of individual to collective, of individual works to collections of works become clear. In the meantime, "Even the greatest system is after all only a fragment" (*LN*, 921, 107). The coming of this organic age seems endlessly postponed, however, within the bounds of the notion of a *Universalpoesie*, continually receding toward the horizon even as we progress toward it. Like the Romantic/novelistic mode of writing [*romantische Dichtart*] that will represent this progress, its "real essence" is to be "forever . . . becoming and never completed" (*AF*, 116, 183/175).

The Intersection of the Aesthetic and the Political

Compression, brevity, the appearance on the page *en bloc* as prose, a foregrounding of the relation of the individual piece to the collection—these are the principal features the prose poems of Baudelaire's *Le*

---

17. Adorno, *Ästhetische Theorie*, p. 522; *Aesthetic Theory*, p. 481.
18. In this sense, as Lacoue-Labarthe and Nancy have indicated, *Athenäum* may well

spleen de Paris share with Schlegel's *Athenäums-* and *Lyceums-Fragmente*. But generic identification may not be satisfactorily established on the basis of formal and thematic features alone. Of at least commensurate importance are a genre's aesthetic and more broadly sociohistorical functions. Such considerations are, of course, ultimately inextricable from one another, for form and theme are not separate from or prior to function but coincident with it. By virtue of their shared formal and thematic concerns, both Schlegel's fragments and Baudelaire's prose poems have the historical function of questioning the boundaries between genres. With its concern for order, form, unity on the one hand, openness, possibility, a breakdown of generic and other barriers on the other, the quest for a "non-generic unity," the project of a *Universalpoesie* articulated in Schlegel's *Athenäums-Fragmente*, exhibits tendencies that persist, as the exchange we have examined briefly between Ricoeur and Derrida demonstrates, in the contemporary debate concerning poetry and speculative thought. The distinction between the poetic and the speculative, however, like that between poetry and prose, presents only one dimension of Schlegel's theory. Once again it is the intersection not only of poetry and prose, the poetic and the speculative, but also of the aesthetic and the political which is decisive. In the words of the final *Athenäums-Fragment*:

> Universalität ist Wechselsättigung aller Formen und aller Stoffe. Zur Harmonie gelangt sie nur durch Verbindung der Poesie und der Philosophie: auch den universellsten vollendetsten Werken der isolierten Poesie und Philosophie scheint die letzte Synthese zu fehlen; dicht am Ziel der Harmonie bleiben sie unvollendet stehen. Das Leben des universellen Geistes ist eine ununterbrochene Kette innrer Revolutionen: alle Individuen; die ursprünglichen, ewigen nämlich leben in ihm. Er ist echter Polytheist und trägt den ganzen Olymp in sich.

> [Universality is the interpenetration of all forms and substances. Universality can attain harmony only through the conjunction of poetry and philosophy: and even the greatest, most universal works of isolated poetry and philosophy seem to lack this final synthesis. They come to a stop, still imperfect but close to the goal of harmony. The life of the Universal Spirit is an unbroken chain of inner revolutions: all individuals—that is, all original and eternal ones—live in him. He is a genuine polytheist and bears within himself all Olympus.] (*AF*, 451, 255/240)

---

be said to represent "our place of birth," the fragment its single most striking production, "the sign of its radical modernity . . . the romantic genre par excellence" (*AL*, 17 and 57).

Like Schlegel's fragments, Baudelaire's prose poems project a novelistic interpenetration of modes of discourse often considered to be mutually exclusive. Abandoning the verse lyric for the sake of a collection of brief prose texts that remained unfinished at his death, Baudelaire risked losing his own "halo" as a poet and abandoning the aura of poetry completely. In so doing, he offered the prose poem as a challenge to the world of prose which, as he saw, had in any case already swallowed up much of what was left of poetry.[19] It may well be true that, as Lacoue-Labarthe and Nancy have remarked in connection with Schlegel's work, "what we have perhaps begun to learn is that the future *is* fragmentary—and that there is no place to make a project of it as a finished work" (*AL*, 423). The political question, however, remains open, the relationship between aesthetics and history still undecided. In a formulation of the problem which seems particularly relevant to the current situation of the prose poem, Walter Benjamin has written that in every era "the attempt must be made anew to wrest tradition away from a conformism that is about to overpower it."[20] Seen against the horizon of Schlegel's project of a *Universalpoesie*, does the recent revival of interest in the genre signal a domestication of the prose poem's antigeneric impulses or, rather, a seizing again of that aesthetic and political opportunity evidenced in Baudelaire's *Petits poèmes en prose*? Does it represent a revitalized use or an abuse of the prose poem's initial norm-breaking function?

19. Thus, looking forward to a futureless future from the perspective of a dismal, prosaic present in the section of his *Journaux intimes* called "Fusées," Baudelaire writes: "And you yourself, oh Bourgeois,—even less a poet today than you have ever been,—you won't find anything there to be retold. . . . These times are perhaps very near; who knows if they have not even arrived already . . .!" (*OC*, 1:667).

20. Walter Benjamin, "Theses on the Philosophy of History," in *Illuminations*, ed. Hannah Arendt, trans. Harry Zohn (New York: Schocken Books, 1969), p. 255. Hans Eichner notes that in later years Schlegel considered the synthesis of poetry and history even more important than the synthesis of poetry and philosophy. In *Athenäums-Fragment* 325 Schlegel defines history as "philosophy in a state of becoming" (221) and philosophy as "completed history" (210). History is also "applied poetry.—The highest poetry is itself history" (*LN*, 1647, 169, and note, 289).

For a recent discussion of the aesthetic and the political in the works of Schlegel and Benjamin see Irving Wohlfarth's "The Politics of Prose and the Art of Awakening: Walter Benjamin's Version of a German Romantic Motif," in *Glyph* 7 (1980), pp. 131–48. Prose is for both Schlegel and Benjamin, as Wohlfarth observes, "the medium in which the Messianic scheme is enacted" (131). Evidence that the idea of revolution belongs for Schlegel, in contrast to Benjamin, more to the past than the present or future may be found in *LN*, 2071, 209, where Schlegel writes of his novel, *Lucinde*, as being a "transition from the revolutionary to the romantic/novelistic" (*Uebergang aus der Revoluzionären in die Romantische*).

What is at stake, finally, in the genre called the prose poem, as also in Schlegel's fragments, is not merely a set of established relations between and among various modes of discourse "within" literature (poetry and prose, the lyric and the novel), or even that set of relations existing between literature and elevated "extraliterary" modes of discourse such as the "philosophical" and the "religious," but an entire network of discursive and nondiscursive classifications and generic *distinctions* within society at large. Like Derrida's deconstruction of the distinction between the poetic and the speculative, the project of a fusion of genres, common to Schlegel's fragments and Baudelaire's prose poetry, has a decidedly political dimension. As Schlegel himself explicitly reminds us, the principle of "mixing" exemplified in such a project—which remains "the essence of novelistic/romantic poetry"— is itself a *political* principal [*Selbst das Wesen der R[omantischen] P[oesie], die Mischung ist ein pol[itisches] Prinzip*] (*LN,* 776, 95). If poetry is to become truly social [*gesellig*] and society poetic, Schlegel's description of his own era applies all the more to our own: "A community is not yet at hand" (*LN,* 123, 34).

Poetry, Prose, and the Literary Absolute

Noting the anonymous authorship of many of the *Athenäums-Fragmente,* Lacoue-Labarthe and Nancy have emphasized that the Romanticism that took shape at Jena was a small-scale *collective* enterprise involving roughly ten persons, men and women, working in close collaboration with one another (*AL,* 15–18). This short-lived collective project did not involve simply a crisis within literature but a more general crisis and critique, at once social, moral, religious, and political, which opened onto the historical and conceptual overdeterminations of a critique of literature, the relations literature has maintained with society and politics from their era to our own, and the crisis of modern history itself. Allying themselves with the revolutionary in political as well as aesthetic matters, the Jena group aspired toward a new kind of society that would offer an alternative to the ascending order of the bourgeoisie.

Published in the last two issues of *Athenäum* in what was also to be the last year of the Jena experiment (1800), Schlegel's *Gespräch über die Poesie* (Dialogue on Poetry) provides through its four extended talks and its discussions involving seven different characters or voices what is certainly the most explicit dramatization of the group's collective activities as well as a telling investigation of the privilege the group accorded to the writer in their vision of the creation of a new society. Placed in between a historical survey of the development of literature from the Greeks to the moderns and an essay on the different styles in Goethe's early and late works, Schlegel's "Talk on Mythology" and the "Letter about the Novel" constitute not only the chronological but also the conceptual double center of the work (cf. *AL*, 274–75). Regretting above all else the absence of a collective mythology that would serve as a basis for the creation of modern poetry, the first of these essays indicates that modern writers must create poetry in the absence of "a matrix (*mütterlichen Boden*), a sky, a living atmosphere." They must create, in other words, what Ernst Bloch has since called "poetry in empty space" (*Poesie im Hohlraum*). In contrast to the poets of ancient Greece, poets of the modern period must create "separately." Each work must develop "from its very beginning, like a new creation out of nothing." Modern poetry is thus above all a poetry of the monad, a poetry of isolated subjectivities in search of but not a part of a community. Its primary function is to create a new mythology that can serve as a basis for a new society. It is time, the talk says, "we earnestly work together to create one" (*GP*, 312; *DP*, 81).

In the absence of true community, the new mythology can only arise from the "deepest depths of the spirit," a thoroughgoing investigation of the subject brought forth by idealism which is now understood to be the representative subject of all mankind: "All disciplines and all arts will be seized by the great revolution. . . . idealism—from a practical view nothing other than the spirit of that revolution—. . . is yet only a part, a branch of expression of the phenomenon of all phenomena: that mankind struggles with all its power to find its own center" (*GP*, 312, 314; *DP*, 82–83). As this passage suggests, the "inner revolution" Schlegel has in mind in *Athenäums-Fragment* 451 involves not merely a revolution within a single individual subject in isolation from all others but one involving the masses of such monadic subjects reintegrating themselves into a newly reconstructed social whole. Although the individual subject of idealism is said to provide a basis for both a personal and a more broadly social revolution, idealism in and of itself is not considered sufficient to bring it about; from the matrix of idealism there must and will arise "a new and equally infinite realism." This realism cannot be found in philosophy, the talk goes on to say, but only in poetry, "which indeed is to be based on the harmony of the ideal and real" (*GP*, 315; *DP*, 84). Although the individual subject is taken to be an analogon of humanity as a whole, the individual subject par excellence is, of course, the poet, "an ideal man and a universal artist" (*GP*, 324; *DP*, 90).

Although the *Dialogue* places poetry at the very center of mankind's efforts to achieve genuine community, it is important again to remember that for Schlegel the true poetry of the modern period does not occur in the verse lyric, as it did with ancient Greek poets like Sappho, but rather in the novel. As the remarks in the following chapter, "Letter about the Novel" suggest, although Schlegel rejects, as the prose poem will later also reject, the conventional formal association between poetry and verse, the equally well-established association between poetry and a focus on the individual subject remains the basis for Schlegel's definition of the novel as a kind of poetry: ". . . what is best in the best of novels is nothing but a more or less veiled confession of the author" (*GP*, 337; *DP*, 102–3). In asserting that the realist turn necessary for idealism to become revolutionary must take place in the novel, Schlegel anticipates the more concrete sociohistorical reinscription of the lyric which Baudelaire will later accommodate, shifting poetry's terrain of struggle from verse to prose, from the intrasubjectively "poetic" to the intersubjectively "prosaic," or in Bakhtin's terms, from the monological to the dialogical. The central problem of Romantic poetry thus poses itself in Schlegel as the problem of overcoming monadic individualism per se. Significantly, the final remarks in the *Dialogue* attributed to Ludovico, the speaker of the "Talk on Mythology," place the entire project in doubt: "Do you perhaps consider it impossible to construct future poems *a priori*?" (*GP*, 350; *DP*, 116).

Like Hegel, Schlegel places the specular, self-reflexive subject at the center of the modern era. Unlike Hegel, however, who will represent his own era as the place where the representative subject demonstrates its capacity for absolute self-enclosure by way of a self-recuperating synthesis (*AL*, 21–25), Schlegel characterizes the modern era as that place where the subject simultaneously centers and decenters, realizes and undoes itself, and where literature's autocritique begins to break down the distinction between poetry and philosophy. Schlegel articulates at one and the same time a revolt against reason and the Cartesian subject and an infinitization of the same. As Lacoue-Labarthe and Nancy have pointed out, the "era of the Subject"—what we might also call the era of monadic individualism—attested to by this double articulation has remained our own from *Athenäum* to the present (*AL*, 26–27). The Romantic idea of a perpetual self-critique implied by Schlegel's reference to a "chain of inner revolutions" anticipates the prose poem's subsequent decentering of the subject from its privileged site and the site of its privilege in poetry-as-verse—the prototype of the "literary" par excellence—to the site of its critique and social reinscription in prose, the privileged medium of philosophy, history, and politics. The era ushered in by the German Romantics is thus both the era of a certain privileging of the subject and the era of the subject's autocritique, the era in which philosophy aspires to becoming a "great speculative poem" and literature undertakes its own self-critique by shifting its locus of struggle from poetry-as-verse to poetry-as-prose (AL, 40). Again in contrast to Hegel, who attempts to realize philosophy's dream of absolute self-reflection, Schlegel and the Jena Romantics envision philosophy's realization—as would Nietzsche as well at the close of the next century—in the *aesthetic,* and in particular in the kind of text Mallarmé would later call a "poème critique" where the subject's self-realization and its utter abolition emerge as inseparable.

In the aftermath of the Kantian critique of the subject's self-sufficiency and the consequent displacement of the question of the subject from the philosophical onto the aesthetic which opens up the possibility of Schlegel's Romanticism (AL, 42–43 and 49), the prose poem emerges with Baudelaire and his successors as the genre that offers a critique of the lyric's monological, intrasubjective orientation by displacing the site of poetry's self-critique from verse to prose and by exposing the idealist subject as disintegrated, scattered among the objects and discourses that surround it. In the process of this displacement, as I indicated in the Introduction, the prose poem calls attention to the lyric's own repressed dialogicity and to the fact that subjectivity is itself dialogically and intersubjectively constituted by the discourses of others which it posits as its own. The prose poem's critique suggests, in other words, that however radical the lyric's own self-interrogations might be, they are not as radical as they might be if situated more self-consciously and deliberately within the social and the dialogical. To the extent that philosophy has focused on what Lacoue-Labarthe and Nancy have called "the idea of the subject and the subject in its ideality" as, in Schlegel's words, "the first of all ideas," poetry may be seen as offering the speculative organon par excellence (AL, 50), the place where philosophy may attempt to realize itself and the new mythology it creates give rise to a new subject and a new society. In the modern era, however, as the interchangeability of the terms *poetry* and *novel* in Schlegel's terminology indicates, the subject's self-realization is no longer to be in verse but in prose, which is now understood to be the medium above all of a *critique* of the subject, the site of a self-realization that comes about only through a simultaneous self-abolition.

If the question of poetry in Schlegel—as in the prose poem—is none other than the question of literature itself (*AL,* 265), then what Schlegel's fragments self-consciously demonstrate is the ultimate futility of all attempts to distinguish once and for all between poetry and prose, or between the literary and the nonliterary, other than as the mutually defining ideological manifestations of particular historical periods and the provisional sites of struggle for a synthetic project that would ultimately seek to abolish whatever putative differences have been maintained between them. The prose poem will subsequently demonstrate the same as well in its polemic against lyric poetry's tendency to cordon itself off as a particular discourse monologically unaffected by the discourses that surround and traverse it. Like the prose poem, but on a considerably more abstract level, the fragment offers through the medium of prose a highly compact space where literature and the idealist subject mount a critique of their own insufficiency and dependence on the nonliterary and on the subject's manifold others. As one of the philosophical fragments published after Schlegel's death indicates (see *AL,* 371), in contrast to the tautology of a *transcendental* idealism, what Schlegel intended was rather a *critical* idealism that would take itself and the idealist subject to task. Like Baudelaire in his *Petits poèmes en prose,* Schlegel attributes an important role in this regard to dialogue, which is itself considered to be a kind of nongenre, a genre of *Witz* and irony and a dramatized self-critique, a genre at once prosaic, poetic, and philosophical which is capable of receiving all genres and thus a privileged site for the critique of the very notion of genre. Like dialogue and like the prose poem, the fragment points to the dialogical *situation* of all subjects and all modes of discourse (*AL,* 276–77) and hence to the impossibility of defining fixed boundaries between and among genres. In contrast to verse poetry's monological tendency to treat the problem of identity as one of self-identity, the fragment and the prose poem tend to treat the same problem dialogically, dramatizing what Lacoue-Labarthe and Nancy have called the mediation of identity by nonidentity (*AL,* 66).

Like the fragment, the prose poem presents an analogon of a complete work gesturing toward the utopian nonplace of a collective labor that would constitute a reconstruction of the individual subject and of the subject of humanity as a whole (*AL,* 373). It is both the promise of what Francis Ponge will call the *Grand Oeuvre* and the sign of its continued absence. In shifting the site from verse to prose of the critique of the idealist subject of poetry and the dominant class which is necessary to give *form* to such an *oeuvre*, Schlegel's fragments and Baudelaire's prose poetry provide not so much a "poetry of poetry" (*AL*, 377)—the subject's critique of itself "from within"—as a concretization of the *inter*subjective nature of the *intra*subjective. They thus offer not so much an illumination of the self *by itself* (alone and self-sufficient) as an illumination of the self by the discourses that surround, traverse, and overdetermine it and from which it cannot finally retreat—as Baudelaire's "A une heure du matin" trenchantly suggests—into sublime isolation.

If what constitutes the subject per se is nothing other than the self-engendering power of its own discourse (*AL*, 392), both the fragment and the prose poem call attention to the fact that the discourse of any given subject or genre is never really self-engendering or absolutely autonomous but is instead inextricably bound up with the discourses of others. Both the fragment and the prose poem offer a critique of the world of prose with a view to making poetry possible again through a rejection of the uncritical reproduction of either poetry or prose in isolation. Their critique constitutes nothing less, in other words, than an attempted reconstruction of a unity that is missing in the chaotic fragmentation of the modern world, a reparation of the world, in Ponge's words, as it comes to us, "by fragments." Like Ponge, Schlegel conceives antiquity as the figure of a unified subject and a unified humanity that have been lost. The fragment is both the form this absolute loss takes and the anticipatory articulation of its absolute recuperation (*AL*, 72). (In contrast to Schlegel, but in a no less dialogical fashion, Ponge articulates his own attempted recuperation of the lost unity of the subject and of humanity as a whole, as we shall see, by way of the endless detour of a focus on the "discourses" of the objects of the material world.)

As paradigmatic examples of literature's self-representation, the fragment and the prose poem represent as well a decomposition of literature's claim to being a self-enclosed, self-sufficient discourse, a monumental verbal icon conceivable apart from its relations to other modes of discourse. Although the dialogical nature of all discourse suggests that there is no such thing as a "fusion" of genres as such, the project of such a fusion pushes the notion of literature, as Lacoue-Labarthe and Nancy have pointed out, to its absolute limits and the limits of its "ab-solution" (*AL*, 421). As a consequence of their shared emphasis on this project, both Schlegel's fragments and the prose poetry of Baudelaire and his successors constitute privileged sites at the margins of literature where the necessarily dialogical, conflictual, and inescapably social nature of literary discourse comes into view. In marked contrast to the majority of texts considered in subsequent chapters, the kind of dialogicity or heteroglossia manifest in Schlegel's work is, as we have seen, primarily intraliterary and intraphilosophical. The Jena group's collectivist gestures notwithstanding, the discursive struggles that take place in Schlegel's work occur on a comparatively aristocratic and idealist/high cultural level that has relatively little to do with the more mundane speech genres that literary and philosophical discourse have tended to exclude. In the prose poem, as we shall see, discursive struggle will be dramatized much more self-consciously as a conflict between high and low culture—a conflict also necessarily of class and gender—and in this sense especially as a conflict between the "poetic" and the "prosaic."

CHAPTER 2

Novalis's *Hymnen an die Nacht* and the Prose Poem *avant la lettre*

> We're always looking for the absolute, and everywhere finding only things.
>
> —Novalis, *Blüthenstaub*

The Death of the Sun and the Reign of Prose

To speak of a work as *avant la lettre* does not necessarily imply a fixed origin; it does imply a history of usage. Thus, for example, André Breton credits Apollinaire with inventing the term *surréalisme*, though he himself would doubtless take credit, as well he should, for making the word current.[1] To make a list, then, as Breton goes on to do, of "*surréalistes avant la lettre*" is to provide a retrospective patterning of literary history with reference to a term that earlier was, even if known, not familiar, even if "invented," not in common usage. In the case of the prose poem, a genre that should be of much interest to theorists of contemporary genre not only because of its current wide dissemination but also because it is a genre with a relatively short history, the term *avant la lettre* must have reference to Baudelaire, for it is his collection of *Petits poèmes en prose*, his naming of them as such, which establishes the currency of the prose poem within literature. If Aloysius Bertrand also has a strong claim to being the true inventor of the modern prose poem, as Max Jacob claimed early in the twentieth century, still it must be acknowledged that without Baudelaire, Bertrand's most important reader, the historical value attributed to his *Gaspard de la nuit* would at the very least be severely diminished.

---

1. André Breton, *Manifestes du surréalisme* (Paris: Gallimard, 1973), pp. 36 and 38–39.

It is not my aim in this chapter, however, to consider the emergence of the modern prose poem in France, where it acquires currency as a literary genre for the first time. Nor do I intend to argue that Novalis's *Hymnen an die Nacht* (Hymns to the Night) constitutes the real or true "origin" of the prose poem. Rather, I hope to show that, just as Schlegel's projected *Universalpoesie* provides a broad conceptual horizon within which to situate the prose poem's own project as a genre, so the *Hymnen an die Nacht* provides an early framework within which to consider the conflict between prose and poetry, the prosaic and the poetic which is a constitutive concern of the prose poem from Bertrand and Baudelaire to the present.

In her otherwise peerlessly exhaustive study of the French prose poem, Suzanne Bernard does not make mention of *Hymnen an die Nacht* as a precursor of the prose poem, though she does emphasize the importance of literary translation, especially from verse into prose. In particular, she credits the prose translations of folk ballads, also of Edward Young's *Night Thoughts* and fragments of Macpherson's *Ossian* with a significant role in the prose poem's emergence.[2] Young and Macpherson were translated not only into French but into German as well. A journal entry confirms Novalis's familiarity with Young's *Night Thoughts* at around the time he began working on the *Hymnen an die Nacht,* and he would have had contact with *Ossian* through Goethe's translations at the end of *Werther.* Yet Novalis's *Hymns,* with their alternation of prose and verse, figure in the history of the prose poem in a way that is qualitatively different than either of these other works.

Hymnen an die Nacht is one of the first works in which the relation between prose and poetry is not only conceived but *presented* in antinomial fashion. The relationship between prose, the way the world is, and poetry, the way it might, could, or should be, is set up as the conflict between two modes of printing—the one *en bloc,* the other *en vers.* In this sense, one would have every right to consider *Hymnen an die Nacht* as a prose poem *avant la lettre,* except that the modern prose poem as it emerges with Baudelaire has so to speak "internalized" the conflict between prose and poetry, prose and verse, into prose alone.

---

2. Suzanne Bernard, *Le poème en prose de Baudelaire jusqu'à nos jours* (Paris: Nizet, 1958), pp. 24–47. Although Bernard is silent on *Hymnen an die Nacht,* Ulrich Fülleborn does make occasional mention of it in his synoptic, ground-breaking study, *Das deutsche Prosagedicht* (Munich: Wilhelm Fink Verlag, 1970). Fülleborn points out (6) that as early as 1895 Henri Albert, a critic with ties to the symbolists, referred to Novalis's text as containing "'the most perfect prose poems in German literature.'"

What *Hymnen an die Nacht* does is not so much typify the future form of the prose poem, for the most part all prose, as provide a kind of early battleground for its opposing terms on which some of the earliest fragments of prose poems make their appearance only to be "conquered" by fragments of rhymed metrical verse. As the first issue of *Athenäum* introduces the problematic of a fusion of genres, of prose and poetry and of the poetic and the speculative within the framework of *Universalpoesie* as fragment, so the last issue of *Athenäum*, with the publication of *Hymnen an die Nacht*, develops this problematic in explicitly formal terms that anticipate equally strongly the prose poem's characteristic concerns.

The strategy of dividing up and distributing segments of "ordinary" prose (as, for example, from a newspaper) into lines resembling free verse in order to demonstrate that an act of attention that one may call "literary" does or does not result was described by Barbara Herrnstein Smith as early as 1968 as "only too familiar."[3] Much less discussed is the effect of reworking free verse into prose, as Novalis did between 1797 and 1800 in the two versions of *Hymnen an die Nacht* which have been left us. Composed roughly fifty years before Whitman's *Leaves of Grass* and seventy years before the free verse poems in Rimbaud's *Illuminations,* the handwritten draft of *Hymnen an die Nacht* attests to Novalis's experimentation with free verse, just as the final draft printed in *Athenäum* reveals his even bolder experimentation with a form resembling the modern prose poem. Both innovations serve, in their respective versions, as the ground on which is figured the rhymed metrical verse of *Hymnen an die Nacht.* With slight alterations and some omissions, each section printed in free verse in the handwritten draft is replaced in that of *Athenäum* by prose, while the rhymed metrical verse remains, again with slight variations, constant from one draft to the next. The effect of the change from free verse to prose is to intensify the figure/ground relationship considerably. This intensification is not only highly appropriate to the poem's thematic concerns generally but also lends a visible formal dimension to the poem's conflict between the world of prose and the world of poetry, the real world and the ideal world, which would be lacking had the prose passages been left in free verse.

3. Barbara Herrnstein Smith, *Poetic Closure* (Chicago: University of Chicago Press, 1968), p. 22. Two other well-known examples, one preceding and one following Smith's book, may be found in E. D. Hirsch, Jr., *Validity in Interpretation* (New Haven: Yale University Press, 1967), pp. 94–98, and Jonathan Culler's *Structuralist Poetics* (London: Routledge and Kegan Paul, 1975), pp. 161–64.

Free verse may be seen as a kind of intermediary form between poetry, understood conventionally as rhymed and/or metrical verse, and prose.[4] It is a form with which Rimbaud also experimented, but its role in his poetic innovation is clearly subordinate to that of the prose poem. The latter implies a revolutionary break with conventional verse, as opposed to the compromising gesture of free verse. If free verse is an attempt to "reason" with the world of prose as well as the world of conventional verse, to mediate as it were diplomatically between them, the prose poem is a genre of provocation; it sets the two worlds into direct contact with each other. Whether this proximity results in harmonic reconciliation or in explosive confrontation may vary considerably from writer to writer and from poem to poem. That *Hymnen an die Nacht* begins in prose and ends in verse, after what may be described as a protracted, if "foreordained," struggle between the two, indicates more than a formal preference on Novalis's part. The distribution of prose and verse among the various sections exemplifies the thematic development of the poem as a whole and is rigorously integrated into it.[5]

In a short tribute to his friend Novalis, Friedrich Schlegel writes, "You are not one of those who hovers at the threshold; in your spirit, poetry and philosophy have deeply penetrated one another" (*RI*, 493). As for Schlegel, for Novalis the fusion of poetry and philosophy was a major concern. "Schlegel's writings," says Novalis, "are lyrical philosophemes. . . . The lyrical prosaist will write logical epigrams" (*B*, 462/105). Yet just as Schlegel's fragments seem more appropriately considered to be speculative, philosophical discourse, so Novalis's *Hymnen an die Nacht* would seem strangely situated were one to consider it to be other than poetic discourse, first and foremost. Indeed for

4. Thus, Bernard writes: "free verse is born of a desire to render classical verse more supple and bring it closer to the rhythms of prose" (*Poème en prose*, 92).

5. Previous studies of the *Hymns* have tended either to overlook the formal strategy of the poem's division into prose and verse entirely or to treat it as arbitrary, merely incidental to theme and imagery, rather than seeing the integrity of these formal combinations of the thematic and imagistic dimensions with which they are so tightly interwoven. In citing the work of Novalis I have used the three-volume *Schriften*, ed. Paul Kluckhohn and Richard Samuel (Stuttgart: W. Kohlhammer, 1960). The following abbreviations (followed by page and, where applicable, by fragment number) are used in the text: from *Schriften*, vol. 2, *Das philosophische Werk I—Blüthenstaub* = B, *Logologische Fragmente* = LF, *Anekdoten* = A, and *Teplitzer Fragmente* = TF; from *Schriften*, vol. 3, *Das philosophische Werk II—Randbemerkungen zu Friedrich Schlegels 'Ideen'* (*1799*) = R, and *Fragmente und Studien 1799–1800* = FS. References to *Hymnen an die Nacht* are drawn from *Schriften*, vol. 1, *Das dichterische Werk*, and are indicated in the text by S followed by page number.

Novalis, poetry is the key to philosophy, its goal and significance: "If the philosopher only orders everything and sets everything upright, the poet is the one who would break all bonds" (*LF*, 533/32); further, "Poetry is the true absolute real. This is the core of my philosophy. The more poetic, the more true" (*TF*, 647/473).

The "all-joyful light" (*S*, 131), the sun, which opens *Hymnen an die Nacht*, is as Derrida has observed one of the most frequent of metaphors, common both to poetic and speculative, philosophical discourse. It is even possible to claim, as does Derrida, that "the turning of the sun always will have been the trajectory of metaphor":

> Does not such a metaphorology, transported into the philosophical field, always, by destination, rediscover the same? The same *physis*, the same meaning (meaning of Being as presence or, *amounting to the same*, as presence/absence), the same circle, the same fire of the same light revealing/concealing itself, the same turn of the sun? What *other* than this return of the same is to be found when one seeks metaphor? that is, resemblance? and when one seeks to determine *the dominant* metaphor of a group, which is interesting by virtue of its power to assemble? What other is to be found if not the metaphor of *domination*, heightened by its power of dissimulation which permits it to escape mastery: God or the Sun?[6]

What else, in *Hymnen an die Nacht*, but the sun as a double metaphor—in the first instance for that dominant framework against which Novalis's poetic discourse situates itself, that Hymn of Hymns to the sun as the metaphor of human reason, Enlightenment philosophy; in the second instance the sun as metaphor for the Son, Christ, whose religion the sun of the Enlightenment threatened to extinguish.[7] "Whoever had no taste for religion," Novalis says, "would have to have something in its place which would be for him what religion is for others" (*FS*, 563/53). *Hymnen an die Nacht* presents a kind of hymn to onto-theology, yet its concern is less explicitly with the mixing or fusion of poetry and philosophy, than of poetry and religion. The latter is described by Novalis, in his notes to Schlegel's *Ideen*, as "a surrounding sea" (*RI*, 489). What Philippe Lacoue-Labarthe and Jean-Luc Nancy have said of the early Romantic view of the artist in general is especially true for Novalis: "The artist is only able to assure his function of mediator to the precise extent that, in him, poetry and philosophy

---

6. Derrida, *White Mythology*, pp. 251, 266. Further references will be indicated by *WM* followed by page number.

7. A motif Novalis treats in *Christenheit oder Europa*.

manage to be reconciled or to 'fuse' with one another. Inasmuch, that is, as he is a religious man."[8] Whereas Schlegel typically values most the interpenetration of poet and philosopher, Novalis holds the reunification of poet and priest above all: "In the beginning, poet and priest were one, and only in later times have they become separated. The true poet, however, is always a priest, just as the true priest has always remained a poet. And shouldn't the future give rise again to the old state of things?" (B, 441/71). Thus, against the advice of Friedrich Schleiermacher to entitle the work only *An die Nacht,* Novalis insisted on *Hymnen an die Nacht,* the latter title suggesting from the outset the specifically religious, Christian dimension to be developed in the poem without which it would be entirely different.

Novalis is far from rejecting the Enlightenment metaphor of the sun as it stands for human reason. Man, he says, "is a son—his senses are his planets" (FS, 573/130), and light is the "vehicle of community— of the universe—is the true presence of mind [*Besonnenheit*] in the intellectual/spiritual sphere [*in der geistigen Sfäre*] not likewise" (TF, 619/435). Yet Novalis will not stop here, content with the resemblance of man to the sun. "Like us," he says, "the stars are suspended in alternating illumination and eclipse" (TF, 619/436). *Hymnen an die Nacht* emerges not so much as a rejection of the visible, of what can be understood in the light of reason, as an attempted balancing of reason and unreason, the visible and the invisible, of life and death, presence and absence. The term *illumination,* or *enlightenment,* is one that resists the neat separation of kinds of discourse such as poetry, philosophy, and religion. In contrast to merely additive knowledge in a fixed ground of knowing, illuminating knowledge helps us see connections among previously disparate domains of knowledge.[9] For the speculative thought of onto-theology and of Christianity, enlightenment implies the ongoing process of perceiving an underlying unity among similarities and differences. Thus, Novalis begins by acknowledging the principal source of illumination in the physical world, the sun. Following the title, this beginning comes as a shock. The presence of the sun, which alone opens up the marvelousness of the kingdom of earth even as it reigns over it, is also in this opening paragraph the presence of man. Not mentioned explicitly at this point in the poem is

8. Lacoue-Labarthe and Nancy, *L'absolu littéraire,* p. 193; hereafter referred to as *AL.*

9. My thanks to Austin Quigley for this concise differentiation.

the Son of man, Christ, who is, however, implicitly present. As the poem progresses, it will name Christ in increasingly specific terms, from mention of the "King of earthly nature" (*König der irdischen Natur*) and the "heavenly image" (*himmlisches Bild*) of the first section, through the "barren hill" (*dürren Hügel*) of section 3, the "holy grave" (*heiligen Grabe*) and "cross" (*Kreuz*) of section 4 and the "Son of the first Virgin and Mother" (*Sohn der ersten Jungfrau und Mutter*) of section 5, to "Jesus, the beloved" (*Jesus, dem Geliebten*) among the poem's final verses. As during the night the sun is buried in memory only to be followed by its simultaneous presence and absence at dawn when it appears as itself in the morning sky, so the present sun of man is to be replaced by the past and future Son of man, the reign of Christ over men. This progress corresponds to the movement of the poem from its beginnings in prose (sections 1–3) through the middle sections' alternations of prose and verse (sections 4 and 5) to its verse conclusion (section 6).

Just as the speaker's high praise of the sun creates a shock following the title *Hymnen an die Nacht,* so he surprises the reader a second time by turning "Down . . . to the holy, unspeakable, mysterious night" (*S,* 131). The strategy is a highly effective one, creating what may aptly be called a "conceptual need."[10] In this case the conceptual need created is for a reunification of day, the absence of which is felt all the more intensely because of the praise lavished upon it, with night, which is praised even more highly. The separation of day from night could be described in the speculative thought of onto-theology as a split between the philosopher's sun and the theologian's Son. The latter is presented here in the beginning not in the absolute presence of his true self but as night, the absence of philosophy. Mediating between them in order to bring about the desired reconciliation is the poet, the "singer" who emerges only in section 5, coincident with Christ's birth. Before this reunification can take place, however, the speaker—and with him the reader—must move through a poetic sequence that presents what Derrida calls, with reference to philosophical metaphor, "a detour within (or in sight of) reappropriation, parousia, the self-presence of the idea in its own light" (*WM,* 253).

The sun separates because it delineates; its blessing, like that of metaphor, is ambiguous. If it permits us to see similarities, it also allows for the play of difference which in its negative aspect will be perceived

---

10. The phrase occurs in Ricoeur's discussion of "semantic shock" in *The Rule of Metaphor,* p. 296.

as separation. For the thinker or poet of an onto-theological perspective, such as Novalis, this separation is, although painful, only a surface phenomenon. This is why the onset of night makes the day appear in retrospect as "poor and childish" (*S*, 133); beneath the world of non-human objects ("the sparkling, ever resting stone, the sensible, sucking plant, and the wild, burning animal of many forms") and beneath the human world as well ("the magnificent alien with the meaningful eyes") (*S*, 131), both of which are revealed by the light of day, the night seems to provide evidence of a fundamental unity. In the night difference is less perceivable; hence the feeling of the infinite that contrasts so sharply with the day's sense of limits, definitions. In the absence of the sun things draw towards a state of nondifferentiation, that absence of difference that would promise its obverse—the absolute presence of self to self, self to others and self to world. In the night is the welcome chaos of origin and of the return to origin, "your return—in the days of your distance" (*deine Wiederkehr—in den Zeiten deiner Entfernung*), as well as the end of sexual separation in union with the "gentle loved one—lovely sun of night" (*S*, 133). This return to origin in the reunion with the loved one is, however, at the end of the first section a thing hoped for, a promise rather than an accomplished fact.

Thus, section 2 begins, "Must morning always come again?" "Morning" here suggests the world of work, that "accursed industry" (*Unselige Geschäftigkeit*) in which everything is separated and measured: "The light has its allotted time; but night rules over time and space" (*S*, 133). The world of work is the world of prose, of separation and difference, the way things are rather than the way things might be, of unity and identity; it is the present and the threat that the future will continue as the same. Given this state of affairs, the function of the third section is to explain how things got the way they are. Thus, the past tense dominates for the first time: "Once, when I shed bitter tears" (*S*, 135). The personal pain of the speaker at the loss of his loved one is linked, still implicitly, to Christ's death on Calvary, the "barren hill." Yet this same hill becomes the place of a reversal comparable to the turning away from day to night in the first section. In contrast to the hard definitions of objects in daylight, the hill suddenly appears as a transparent cloud of dust, through which the loved one appears. The promise implied by this vision is still not actualized, however, in the real world: "It was the first, the only dream" (*S*, 135).

Section 4, with its beginning, "Now I know when the last morning will be" (*S*, 135), provides an answer to the question posed in the

second section. Having indicated how the speaker arrived at the painful sense of separation in which he finds himself, as well as the promise
of an end to that separation, the poem returns to the present and the
possibilities of the future. The pilgrimage to the grave of the loved one,
"to the holy grave, hugging the cross," has served as a reminder of the
promise of Christ's death. The present of the speaker, however, remains "the bustle of the world [*das Treiben der Welt*] . . . where the light
lives in eternal unrest" (*S*, 137). Allowed a glimpse into "the new land,"
which will soon be heralded by the first appearance of verse in the
poem, the speaker nevertheless cannot for the time being leave the
obligations of the everyday world: "Once again, bright light, you wake
the weary to work." He performs his job as overseer faithfully:

> Gern will ich die fleißigen Hände rühren, überall umschaun, wo du
> mich brauchst—rühmen deines Glanzes volle Pracht—unverdrossen
> verfolgen deines künstlichen Werks schönen Zusammenhang—gern
> betrachten deiner gewaltigen, leuchtenden Uhr sinnvollen Gang—
> ergründen der Kräfte Ebenmaß und die Regeln des Wunderspiels un-
> zähliger Räume und ihrer Zeiten. (*S*, 137)

> [I'll gladly stir hard-working hands, look round everywhere, where you
> need me—praise the full magnificence of your bright gaze—tirelessly
> pursue the beautiful coherence of your artful/artificial works—gladly
> observe the ingenious running of your enormous shining clock—inves-
> tigate the symmetry of forces and the rules of the miracle play of
> innumerable spaces and of their times.]

Yet although he goes about his task "gladly" (*gern*) with lip service paid
to the meaningfulness of the day's progress and his own everyday work
activities (their *sinnvollen Gang*), his heart is not in it. He remains true to
the dream of the end of the separation of labor and love: "Inside I feel
an end to your industry [*In mir fühl ich deiner Geschäftigkeit Ende*]—
heavenly freedom, blessed return" (*S*, 139). As the speaker's recollection of Christ suggests, the way things are is not the way things have
been or must be: "Truly I was, before you were." The promise of
Christ is also the promise of the end of the workaday world of prose.
Hence, for the first time in the poem, verse appears. Yet because it
ends section 4, the status of such a "blessed return" (*selige Rückkehr*) to
the world of poetry, of rhymed metrical verse, is still uncertain:

> Ich lebe bei Tage,
> Voll Glauben und Mut
> Und sterbe die Nächte
> In heiliger Glut.

(S, 139)

[I live by day
Full of courage and faith
And die at night
In holy fire.]

Like the worker who returns home at the end of a grueling day to
drown his sorrows, the speaker dreams of a better day to come, which,
however, turns out to be all too much like the day he has just spent. He
is still in the world of prose, and this first appearance of verse provides
only the drunkard's delusion of escape from it.

Naturprosa and *Kunstprosa*

As section 4 provides an answer to section 2, section 5 returns, like
section 3, to the past. At issue here, however, is less the personal situation of the speaker of that earlier section than the collective fate of
mankind. It is in this, the longest section of the *Hymns*, that the struggle
between the world of prose and the world of poetry-as-verse is carried
out most directly. The conflict is not as simple as it may first appear, for
the text actually presents two worlds of prose. One of these, to which
the reader has been exposed throughout the first four sections, is the
workaday world of the present, of what might be called, to use a term
familiar to Novalis which we have previously encountered in Schlegel,
Kunstprosa (artificial/artful prose); the other, standing at the very origin
of the world like an Eden from which we have been expelled, is that of
Naturprosa (natural prose). In the world of *Naturprosa*, there is no freedom or language as such: "Long ago an iron destiny ruled over the
widely scattered tribes of man with silent power" (S, 141). Yet this
world is at least not one of tragic separation as is the *Kunstprosa* that
characterizes the modern period. Life in the age of *Naturprosa* is "an
eternally bright and colorful celebration [*ein ewig buntes Fest*]" (S, 143).
In contrast to the poverty of objects and of the physical world in the
modern age, enchantent and animation reign over everything: "Rivers,
trees, flowers and animals had human sense [*menschlichen Sinn*]" (S,
141).

The principal difficulty is that this world never really existed: "It
was only an idea, a terrible vision" (*Ein Gedanke nur war es, Ein entsetzliches Traumbild*) (S, 143). Placed as they are as the very hinge of the
transition in section 5 between prose and verse, the words "*Ein Gedanke
nur war es, Ein entsetzliches Traumbild*" may be read both backwards and
forwards; they have as their double referent both the vanished harmo-

ny and unity of *Naturprosa,* which because it never existed in the first place is indeed a "mere thought" and is death, the "mere thought" of which disperses the myth of *Naturprosa* and calls forth the possibility of an alternative harmony and unity to be restored with Christ's second coming. The figure of death exposes the mythically harmonious age as itself incomplete; it is the sign that the golden age too was only an idea, the mark of the imperfection that even the gods could not erase and that Christ has come to cancel and raise in the manner of an *Aufhebung.* That deceptive image of a golden age of the past which Schlegel describes in *Athenäum* 243 as presenting one of the greatest obstacles to the golden age to come is here reproduced only as a distant echo of the latter which would function to guarantee its possibility. Since it proves to be only a thought, however, a thought at one with the thought of death, its position in the text is less reassuring than it might want to be. That the tale of death's appearance is written in verse may be seen as paradoxical at first, for death, one would think, belongs to the world as it is, the world of prose. Yet this interpretation does not do justice to the dual function of verse as Novalis uses it here. First, verse, the division of thought into lines of unequal length, functions here to disrupt the original vision of the age of *Naturprosa,* suggesting difference as well as similarity. Its artifice marks an end to that mythical state that was only an idea (*Ein Gedanke*). Second, although death, like the sun, separates, delineating the difference between the animate and the inanimate and thus ushering us into the world of *Kunstprosa* which is our own, it anticipates the Son, Christ, whose death will mark an end to death.

Following the three-verse stanzas that have introduced the reader to death but also to the as yet "undeciphered . . . Night,/The earnest sign of a distant power," which will be realized in the triumph of the new sun/Son, Christ, over death, of poetry over prose, the poem brings us back to the world of *Kunstprosa.* As Christ's birth contains within it the seed of his death and his triumph over death, no sooner is the world of *Kunstprosa* born than it begins coming to an end: "The old world drew to a close" (*S,* 145). The old world here is not to be confused with the world of *Naturprosa* which was never more than a dream. Rather, it is the world of *Kunstprosa,* the end of which was proclaimed by the hour of Christ's birth but which has been waiting ever since to be realized by the second coming. Once again the reader is back in the world of separation, loneliness, the banishment of Christ, and, which is the same for Novalis, poetry.

In the first section, even though the world of objects and of plants and animals is presented as separate from that of men, the breathing of the "sparkling, ever resting stone" functions as a sign of former animation and nondifferentiation from the living. In section 4, by contrast, the last signs of the impoverished life of objects are extinguished. Although in the world of *Naturprosa* there was an eternally bright and colorful celebration but no language as such, in the modern world there is language, but it is inadequate to connect the inner and the outer worlds. In the world of *Naturprosa*, it is as if words were characterized by a transparency that allowed unmediated access to the world of objects. In the real world of the modern era which is that of *Kunstprosa*, however, if a never-before-known freedom of language from the world of objects is acquired, it is only at the cost of the loss of language's transparency: "Nature stood alone and lifeless . . . the measureless flower of life fell apart in dark words as in dust and breezes. Imagination . . . had fled" (*S*, 145).

As Novalis writes elsewhere: "The days are gone when the mind of God was knowable. The meaning of the world has been lost. We have remained stuck at the letter" (*A*, 594/316). In order to restore the transparency of absolute presence of self, of the world and of God, some mediation is necessary: "Nothing is less dispensable for true religiosity than a middle term that connects us with the godhead. Without mediation, man simply cannot measure up to it. In the choice of this middle term, man must be completely free" (*B*, 441–42/74). The selection of a means of mediation must remain free, yet clearly, for Novalis, poetry is the privileged mode of discourse, the linguistic mediation par excellence. Poetry is "presentation of the spirit—of the inner world in its entirety. Words, its medium, already suggest this, for they are the outer manifestation of that inner realm of power. . ." (*FS*, 650/553). Words are the outer manifestation of the inner person, yet in the age of *Kunstprosa* they cannot be other than inadequate. Thus, a sense for poetry "has much in common with the feeling for mysticism. . . . It presents the unpresentable. It sees the invisible, feels the unfeelable" (*FS*, 685/671). "Language," Novalis says, "is not the right medium of presentation for philosophy" (*FS*, 573/124). In the world of prose, language in its various modes is ambivalent: "Self-expression is the source of all degradation, as well as, on the contrary, the ground of all true elevation. The first step is to look inward, isolated contemplation of self. Whoever stops here, arrives only half-way. The second step must be to look effectively outward, spontaneous, prolonged observation of the outer world" (*B*, 423/24). Only with the birth of the Christ-child, according to the narrative logic of Novalis's *Hymns,* will the gap between the outer and the inner worlds, difference and similarity, the visible and the invisible, between absolute signification in absolute unfreedom (*Naturprosa*) and meaningless freedom (*Kunstprosa*) be breached.

The Banishment of Prose and the Son's Return

Christ emerges in the *Hymns* as the poet-mediator who brings "inexhaustible words," the "Singer" who offers "a comforting sign in the darkness" (*S*, 147). Like the tune whistled by the little boy in the dark, the Singer's eight lines of verse are preceded and followed by two longish blocks of prose. The return to prose is necessary because Christ must die in order to be born again. Thus, the speaker says: "The hour of birth of the new world neared in terrible fear. . . . The weight of the old world [*der Druck der alten Welt*] lay heavily on him." It is tempting to understand the German word *Druck* not only as in "the *weight* of the old world" but also as in "the *print* of the old world," for as we have seen, the birth of the new world has been figured all along in verse. Thus the hour of birth of the new world, which is really, for Novalis, the world of Christ, of poetry-as-verse, will be marked by the banishment of prose and the final triumph of rhymed, metrical verse at the end of section 5 and in the final section, "Sehnsucht nach dem Tode" (Longing for Death).

The banishment of prose is heralded in the text by the removal of the stone from Christ's (prefiguring the loved one's) "dark grave" (*S*, 149). Stone, as symbol of the world of objects at its most opaque and inanimate, must be *Gehoben,* raised by the death and rebirth, the re-animation of Christ necessary for poetry to reappear. Also a symbol of separation, the stone must be penetrated to get through to the invisible unity of things which Christ embodies in the poem. Christ's resurrection announces the renewal of poetry, when words and things will once again be adequate to each other, "inexhaustible" (*Unerschöpflich*).[11]

---

11. In an eight-line free-verse stanza from the handwritten draft which is omitted in the version published in *Athenäum*, the absence of Christ is figured as the absence not only of poetry but of speech altogether:

> Von ihm will ich reden
> Und liebend verkünden
> So lang ich
> Unter Menschen noch bin.
> Denn ohne ihn
> Was wär unser Geschlecht,

Once again, however, the time of such a renewal is postponed and the poem returns abruptly, still in the world of prose, to the present:

> Noch weinen deine Lieben Tränen der Freude, Tränen der Rührung und des unendlichen Danks an deinem Grabe . . . Worte sagen, wie vom Baum des lebens gebrochen; sehen dich eilen mit voller Sehnsucht in des Vaters Arm, bringend die junge Menschheit, und der goldnen Zukunft unversieglichen Becher. (*S,* 149)

> [Still your loves cry tears of joy, tears of emotion and of infinite thanks at your grave . . . say words, as if broken from the tree of life; see you hurry full of longing in the Father's arm, bringing the young human race and the golden future's inexhaustible cup.]

The golden future that echoes the golden age of the past remains like it a mere thought (*Ein Gedanke nur*) unrealized in the present. The closest we can get to it in the world of the present is suggested among the closing lines of the final prose passage, where the most regular nonverse rhythms of the poem are located: "*und Tausende zogen aus Schmerzen und Qualen, voll Glauben und Sehnsucht und Treue dir nach*" (and thousands drew near you in sorrow and pain, full of longing, loyalty and faith) (*S,* 149). These one and a half lines of prose, set off as they are only by dashes from the surrounding text, are easily read as two lines of verse, the first a full, the second an approximate alexandrine. As such they anticipate the new age of poetry-as-verse to come which is yet, for the present so full of sorrow and pain, more a matter of faith, longing, and loyalty, still more dream than reality.

The seven stanzas of rhymed metrical verse which conclude the

---

> Wenn sie nicht sprächen von ihm
> Ihrem Stifter, Ihrem Geiste. (*S,* 140)

> [I want to speak of him
> And lovingly proclaim his word
> So long as I'm
> Still here among men.
> For without him
> What would become of our kind,
> If we didn't speak of him
> Of our Author, our Spirit.]

These lines may well have been omitted in part because they speak of the salvation of poetry through the resurrection of Christ in such an unrhymed and prosy fashion, in contrast to the rhymed metrical verses that normally have this function in the poem. For Novalis, of course, Christianity is the sum of all religions: "There is no religion that would not be Christianity" (*Es giebt keine Religion die nicht Xstenthum wäre*) (*FS,* 566/82). Without religion, poetry is drowned in the workaday world of prose.

fifth section, figuring the triumph of poetry over prose and of eternal life over death, also attempt to unify the personal with the collective, similarity with difference. Christ's resurrection, the renewal of language as poetry, is also the resurrection of humanity, which is to be realized as for the first time: "*Gehoben ist der Stein—/Die Menschheit ist erstanden*" (The stone is removed—/humanity is risen) (*S*, 149). Not only are human beings imaged for the first time in the poem as at one with themselves and at one with their language in the absolute presence of their own voices which Christ, as poet/mediator, has restored to them, but the separation of sexuality is also overcome. Replacing the "shadow life" (*Schattenleben*) (*S*, 150) of sexual difference is a new androgyny, a nongeneric unity in which man and woman are one. Schlegel's comment, "If Christ were to come again, he would be one with Mary,"[12] is echoed in Novalis's *Hymns* by the poem's conclusion. Yet despite the *formal* triumph of verse over prose and the positing of a nongeneric unity that would end all separation, thematically the poem affirms that the world of prose is still with us.

> So manche, die sich glühend
> In bittrer Qual verzehrt
> Und dieser Welt entfliehend
> Nach dir sich hingekehrt . . .
>
> (*S*, 151)
>
> [So some, consumed
> In bitter, burning pain
> Have fled this world
> And turned to you . . .]

Maria, the "you" (*dir*) of the last verse here is, like rhymed metrical verse itself, like Christ, like religion, a turning away from the present, from the modern world of prose and its separations of labor and love to a world that does not exist: "*Getrost das Leben schreitet/Zum ewgen Leben hin* (Confident life strides forth/To gain eternal life) (*S*, 153). Although the verse conclusion of section 5 speaks of a life where there is "no more separation . . . the full life" (*keine Trennung mehr . . . das volle Leben*), poetry remains unrealized in life. The affirmation of a new world of poetry in verse carries its own reminder that verse is itself a form of separation, of line breaks in contrast to the even distribution and unified appearance on the page of prose.

12. Schlegel, *Literarische Notizen (1797–1801)*, p. 221, fragment 2188. Hereafter referred to as *LN*, followed by fragment and page number.

"Sehnsucht nach dem Tode," the final and only titled section of *Hymnen an die Nacht*, is also the only section in the poem entirely in verse. As such, it confirms the triumph of the world of poetry over the world of prose which is one in the poem with the triumph of Christ over death. Having begun in prose with praise of life and of the day, the poem ends in verse with a return to the night of death which the title had initially affirmed. Whether the text as a whole achieves a truly dialectical resolution of contraries, first and foremost in its antinomial alternation of prose and verse, remains doubtful, however. Although the poem concludes with praise of the night as the carrier of the seed of the new day, its final note, as the title of the final section indicates, is one of longing (*Sehnsucht*) rather than of the actualization of poetry in everyday life: "*Was sollen wir auf dieser Welt/Mit unsrer Lieb und Treue*" (What's here for us to do on earth/With all our love and faith) (*S*, 155). Sounding somewhat wooden against the background of the more supple and interesting (because less predictable) prose, the harmonies of the final section's rhymed metrical verse find no echo in the real world. To the prose complaint of the section preceding—"Nature stood alone and lifeless"—the verse of section 6 can only offer confirmation: "*O! einsam steht und tiefbetrübt/Wer heiß und fromm die Vorzeit liebt*" (Oh! he who passionately, piously loves/Past ages stands alone and deeply sad) (*S*, 155). Its measured rhythms provide no final consolation for the way things are: "*In dieser Zeitlichkeit wird nie/Der heiße Durst gestillet*" (The hot thirst never will be stilled/In this life here on earth). The fullness of absolute presence which Christ's coming had promised turns out still to be its opposite: *Das Herz ist satt—die Welt ist leer*" (The heart is full—the world is empty) (*S*, 157). As the world of *Naturprosa* presented at the beginning of section 5 never existed, so too the promise of the second coming has yet to be fulfilled in reality: "*Ein Traum bricht unsre Banden los/Und senkt uns in des Vaters Schoß*" (A dream breaks open all our bonds/And sinks us in the Father's womb). The hopeful androgyny implied by "*süßen Braut/Zu Jesus, dem Geliebten*" (to the sweet bride/to Jesus, the beloved) as also in "*des Vaters Schoß*" (the Father's lap or womb), is undercut by the final image of sinking in the last line as the dream is swallowed up by reality.

"What is called prose has arisen," says Novalis, "out of the restriction of the absolute extremes—it is only there *ad interim* and plays a subordinate, temporal role. A time is coming when it will no longer be. For restriction has turned into interpenetration [*Durchdringung*]. A true life has arisen, and through this life prose and poetry are most intimately united and set in alternation [*in Wechsel gesetzt*]" (*LF*, 536/61). As in Schlegel's *Universalpoesie*, not only prose and poetry, the poetic and the speculative, but the three ages of Greek poetry as well—epic, lyric, and dramatic—are to be melted together or fused, so also for Novalis, in what he refers to as "*Universalgeschichte*" (universal history, *LF*, 537/54). Yet Schlegel's understanding of history and of poetry, and of how the fusion of genres is to come about, differs from that of Novalis in at least one decisive feature. This feature may be most clearly indicated by two opposing terms that occur frequently in their respective works—for Schlegel, *Universalpoesie* is first and foremost *progressive*; for Novalis, on the other hand, *Universalgeschichte* will be conceived of as a *return*. In the last section of the poem, shortly after three stanzas each beginning with the words "past ages" (*Die Vorzeit*), the speaker sums up this attitude with the line, "What holds up our return" (*S*, 157). That Novalis decides the conflict between the present world of prose and the past world of poetry in favor of poetry-as-verse indicates an aesthetic of return which by and large turns its back to the present as well as to the future. The significance of having not just metrical verse but rhymed verse in *Hymnen an die Nacht* lies in this aesthetic of the harmonious return which rhyme, more than any other stylistic device, tends to enforce.

The discursive struggles enacted in the *Hymns* are neither as abstract as those typical of Schlegel's work nor as sociohistorically concrete as those we shall discuss in the next chapter on Baudelaire's *Spleen de Paris*. The specific dialogicity of Novalis's text inheres above all, as we have seen, in the confrontation between two modes of printing (the one *en bloc*, the other *en vers*) and the "prosaic" and "poetic" worlds they figure. Prose and poetry prove to be emblematic for Novalis of competing, putatively reconcilable philosophical and religious (Enlightenment and Christian) ideologies and, to a lesser extent, of a similar confrontation between the more abstract discourses of poetry, philosophy, and religion (all three of which might be grouped together as "speculative" discourses) and the more concrete "extraliterary," "extraphilosophical" discourses of physical labor and everyday life.

In contrast to Schlegel's *Universalpoesie*, the whole movement of the *Hymns* tends to be retrograde, from light to dark, differentiation to nondifferentiation, prose to poetry, from the increasingly secularized world of the present to the religious past. A correspondence between a past and a future golden age is more or less explicit in both writers, but

Novalis tends to posit the future resolution of contraries as a pure return to the past, with the present losing its significance as the place of struggle on which any resolution must be based. For Schlegel, by contrast, the present plays the more decisive role—it is the novel, not the epic, prose, not poetry (as verse) that provides the base for *Universalpoesie*. Thus, in *Hymnen an die Nacht*, the old conventional form, verse, emerges victorious over the more contemporary form of prose. The formal struggle that Bertrand, Baudelaire, and Rimbaud each in his turn would decide in favor of prose, the printed medium of the modern age, is anticipated by Novalis briefly, brilliantly. Just as quickly, however, like the speaker turning "Down . . . to the holy, unspeakable, mysterious night," where the world lies "far down and away [*Fernab*]," Novalis turns away from this struggle to the security of a vanished age, that of the reign of Christianity, and to verse as its representative form. It is because both Christianity and verse come to seem increasingly anachronistic in the post-Enlightenment, postrevolutionary bourgeois world of the nineteenth century that *Hymnen an die Nacht* looks in retrospect like a rearguard attempt to resist the overwhelming "progress" of the modern world. It is in response to this challenge of the modern world and against the background of the hegemony of the novel among literary forms that the prose poem will be born. If, for Novalis, the world of prose is only here *ad interim*, as an ephemeral surface phenomenon, Bertrand, Baudelaire and the prose poets who come after them perceive it as a world that is here to stay. From the nineteenth century on, as Schlegel says, "If prose and poetry are to be mixed, the whole must be 'manifestly' prosaic" (*LN*, 1024, 114).

As Lacoue-Labarthe and Nancy have pointed out, German Romanticism may be said to offer two fundamentally opposed critical gestures—the first that of Schelling and subsequently of Hegel involving the subject's *Aufhebung* through its own critical self-representation, the other the Schlegelian critique of the very possibility of such a self-recuperation (*AL*, 378–83). Seen in relation to these two dominant orientations, Novalis's work clearly tends toward the former. Where Schlegel's *Athenäum* fragments articulate a prose critique of the notion that any individual subject, discourse, or genre may be undialogically cordoned off from its overdetermining others, the formal figuration of the return of Christ the singer-poet in the rhymed, metrical verse that concludes the *Hymns* gestures toward a wished-for restoration of the monological through the mediation of a single representative, re-

demptive, unifying, "poetic" voice.[13] While the former exemplifies the
"first romanticism's" turn to prose as the site of a necessary critique of
the idealist subject and of poetry's subject-centeredness, the final decision of the *Hymns* to privilege poetry-as-verse over poetry-as-prose
tends rather to confirm the more widespread popular image of Romanticism as the site not of a rigorous self-critique but of mere self-
expression and self-affirmation. Since in fact, as Lacoue-Labarthe and
Nancy have also pointed out (*AL*, 372), Schlegel produced relatively
little poetry compared to Novalis and to his own production of critical
and theoretical texts, it is not altogether surprising that the latter view
of Romanticism and of poetry should have gained wider currency. In
any case, however regrettable this popular image might be of Romantic
poetry—and indeed of poetry in general—as "pure lyricism," and
however much writers and critics have fought against it, it has been a
formative one not only for the popular imagination but also for those
who have made a more serious commitment to reading and writing
poetry from the nineteenth century through the surrealists and beyond
(*AL*, 287). It is largely with reference to this functional, historically
situated "mythology" or informing ideology of the "poetic" that the
prose poem has carried on its own dialogical struggle with the verse
lyric, from Baudelaire and Rimbaud to the present.

13. The favorable treatment of the character named "Fabel" and the unfavorable
treatment and ultimate expulsion of the antagonist called "Schreiber" in the "Klingsohrs
Märchen" section of *Heinrich von Ofterdingen* offers further evidence of Novalis's nostalgia for a kind of monological wholeness and his rejection of the modern, secular world of
prose in favor of the antiquated, religious world of poetry-as-verse. Significantly, although prose, not verse, is the dominant mode of printing in the novel, the prose is itself
highly poeticized. In the movement of the narrative toward poetry and myth (which are
associated with the mother, the past, harmony, and unity) and away from prose (which is
associated, by contrast, with the father, the present, discord, and disintegration), the
novel enacts precisely those sets of associations with the "poetic" and the "prosaic" which
Hegel would later codify in his *Ästhetik*. For an illuminating extended analysis of the
Fabel-Schreiber opposition as a structuring principle in *Heinrich von Ofterdingen*, see
Friedrich A. Kittler's "Die Irrwege des Eros und die 'absolute Familie'. Psychoanaly-
tischer und diskursanalytischer Kommentar zu Klingsohrs Märchen in Novalis *Heinrich
von Ofterdingen*," in *Psychoanalytische und Psychopathologische Literaturinterpretation*
(Darmstadt: Wissenschaftliche Buchgesellschaft, 1981). "Dialogues 1 et 2" (*AL*, 428–33),
with which Lacoue-Labarthe and Nancy conclude *L'absolu littéraire*, demonstrates an
atypical, more forward-looking and Schlegelian Novalis in its suggestion that the reconstruction of a genuine totality from the false totality of the "world of reality" as it
currently exists depends on a willingness to work *through* the world of prose made
manifest in the dialogically "fragmented world of books."

PART II

The Prose Poem in Its Heroic Age

CHAPTER 3

Baudelaire's Poor: The *Petits poèmes en prose* and the Social Reinscription of the Lyric

> All that is solid melts into air, all that is holy is profaned, and
> man is at last compelled to face with sober senses, his real
> conditions of life, and his relations with his kind.
> —Marx, *Manifesto of the Communist Party*

The Writer in the Marketplace

The principal force behind the modern prose poem was a writer already accomplished, before coming to the genre, not only in the verse lyric but in critical prose as well. Clearly, this combination is significant both for the genre's emergence and for its subsequent development. As his own commitment to critical activities indicates, Baudelaire was acutely aware of the importance of the question of the relationship between author and reader and of the de facto impotence of a work of art without an audience.[1] Yet however much Baudelaire was, as Walter Benjamin has said, his own impresario, he remained badly placed on the literary market during his lifetime. Although it was possible for such novelists as Eugène Sue and Alexandre Dumas to earn fortunes through their writing, by the mid-1850s conditions for the reception of lyric poetry were already considerably less favorable.[2]

---

1. Few have been more conscious than Baudelaire that, as Michael Riffaterre has remarked in a different context ("The Stylistic Approach to Literary History," *New Literary History* 2, no. 1 [1970], p. 46), "no work is a work of art if it does not command the response of a public."

2. Walter Benjamin, *Zentralpark*, in *Gesammelte Schriften*, ed. Rolf Tiedemann and Hermann Schweppenhauser (Frankfurt: Suhrkamp, 1980), I, 2, 535 and 665. See also "Central Park," trans. Lloyd Spencer, *New German Critique*, no. 34 (Winter 1985), pp. 38

Although poets have long since grown all too accustomed to an extremely limited audience, the rapidly growing size of the reading public in the mid-nineteenth century, evidenced by the success of the serial novel (or *roman feuilleton*), must have held out prospects to the poet which seemed continually to be snatched from his hand by the writer of prose. Seeing the success of a writer such as Victor Hugo, for whom he had great respect, Baudelaire was far from averse to taking advantage of the possibilities. In the "Salon of 1848" he writes, already with some irony: " . . . the bourgeois . . . is quite respectable; you've got to please those at whose expense you want to live."[3] Baudelaire's attitude toward the bourgeois public—his brother, the "hypocrite reader"—was one of growing disdain over the years, a consequence perhaps in part of his having tried and failed to gain the broad audience he desired. Although the achievement of a collection such as Baudelaire's *Petits poèmes en prose* (*Le spleen de Paris*) is not, of course, reducible in any way to a mere function of his economic situation as a writer/producer in "the age of high capitalism," Baudelaire's correspondence indicates clearly the extent to which his efforts in the genre are bound up with financial concerns and market strategy. The contract Baudelaire signed on January 13, 1863, giving Pierre-Jules Hetzel the rights to reprint the *Fleurs du mal* and to publish the *Petits poèmes en prose* for the first time in their entirety brought Baudelaire 600 francs in advance for each of the two works, a total of only 1,200 francs. In a letter to Hetzel two months later (March 20, 1863) referring to the "great importance" he attributed to the unfinished prose collection,

---

and 54: hereafter cited as *CP*. Translations are my own unless otherwise indicated. References to *Charles Baudelaire: Ein Lyriker im Zeitalter des Hochkapitalismus*, in *Gesammelte Schriften* I, 2 (Frankfurt: Suhrkamp, 1980) will be drawn from Harry Zohn's translation, *Charles Baudelaire: A Lyric Poet in the Era of High Capitalism* (London: New Left Books, 1973), and indicated in the text by *CB* followed by page number. *Les fleurs du mal* (The Flowers of Evil) was itself a book, Benjamin wrote, "which from the beginning had little prospect of becoming an immediate popular success." And as Benjamin adds: "there has been no success on a mass scale in lyric poetry since Baudelaire" (*CB*, 607).

3. Charles Baudelaire, *Oeuvres complètes*, 2, ed. Claude Pichois (Paris: Gallimard, éditions Pléiade, 1975), p. 352. References to Baudelaire's writings will be indicated in the text by *OC* followed by volume and page numbers; quotations appear by permission of Editions Gallimard. Specific references to the *Petits poèmes en prose* (*Le spleen de Paris*) and Louise Varèse's translation, *Paris Spleen* (1947; reprint, New York: New Directions, 1970; copyright © 1970 by New Directions Publishing Corporation; portions reprinted by permission of New Directions), will be indicated by *OC*, 1, and *PS* respectively. *Cor* (followed by volume and page numbers) will refer to the two-volume Pléiade edition of Baudelaire's *Correspondance* (1973), ed. Claude Pichois.

Baudelaire writes: "I believe that, thanks to my nerves, I won't be ready before the 10th or 15th of April. But I can guarantee you a *singular book that will be easy to sell*" (*un* livre singulier et facile à vendre) (*Cor*, 2: 205).

In a previous letter to Madame Aupick dated March 29, 1862, Baudelaire's impatience at not having finished the collection is again expressed in financial terms: "The *Poèmes en prose* will also go to *La Presse*. A thousand francs! but, alas! it's not FINISHED" (*Cor*, 2: 237). Since in the twentieth century most "serious" poets have become accustomed to publishing the bulk of their work prior to book publication in so-called little magazines with only minimal circulation, it is worth recalling the important role in the history of printed media played by the journal that was destined to be the first to publish texts later collected in the *Petits poèmes en prose*. *La presse*, which published the first twenty of Baudelaire's prose poems over the course of three issues (August 26, August 27, and September 24, 1862), was not merely or even primarily a literary journal but, rather, a daily newspaper founded in 1836 by Emile de Girardin and Moïse Millaud. As Richard Terdiman has pointed out in his illuminating discussion of the rise of newspaper culture in nineteenth-century France, *La presse* was at the vanguard of the discursive/publishing innovations that led to the deliberate depoliticization and commercialization of the daily newspaper and its establishment as "an authentic *mass* medium."[4] Seen in the context of Baudelaire's literary production, the circulation figures Terdiman has assembled reveal to what extent the period that immediately concerns us here, that of Baudelaire's work in the prose poem, was a period as well of an unprecedented massification of the written word. By July 1863, roughly a year after *La presse* published Baudelaire's first prose poems—including the celebrated preface to Arsène Houssaye, the daily's literary editor—the circulation of another Millaud daily, *Le petit journal*, had attained a circulation of 38,000. By 1869, the year of the first publication of the *Petits poèmes en prose* in its entirety (following Baudelaire's death two years earlier), the circulation of *Le petit journal* had jumped to more than 300,000, a figure over five times that of all Paris papers in 1830 (see *DCD*, 133).

Although Baudelaire initially entertained hopes that the prose poetry of *Le spleen de Paris* would find a broader public than did the verse poetry of *fleurs du mal*, it soon became clear that prose poetry could not compete with the novel either. In the same letter to Madame Aupick,

---

4. Terdiman, *Discourse/Counter-Discourse*, pp. 129–30; hereafter referred to as *DCD*.

Baudelaire goes on to speak admiringly of Flaubert's "next novel" and the coming publication of Hugo's *Misérables* in ten volumes as "one more reason" for his *Petits poèmes en prose* not to be rushed onto the marketplace (*Cor,* 2: 238). A letter to Auguste Poulet-Malassis of December 13, 1862, confirms Baudelaire's suspicion that the competition would be too great: "As for *Salammbô,* great, great success. One two thousand volume edition bought up in two days" (*Cor,* 2: 271). If the *Petits poèmes en prose* had been completed, with all of the one hundred prose poems Baudelaire had planned for it, it would itself have approximated a medium-length novel more closely than the fifty-poem collection that has been left to us. In the end, although the collection remained unfinished, Baudelaire continued to hope against hope even as late as 1865 that the singular, easily saleable book he had promised Hetzel three years earlier would bring him the financial success that had eluded him: "Now, supposing that of these last fifty there were twenty which were unintelligible or repulsive to the newspaper's public, there will still be plenty of material to be able to ask a good price" (letter to Julien Lemer, October 13, 1865, in *Cor,* 2: 534).

In the dedicatory preface to Houssaye, Baudelaire shows himself as, among other things, a salesman of his own literary wares. As our first and principal access to the work, the preface provides a vantage point from which to consider the relations of the author/producer not only to his publisher/middleman but also to the reader/consumer. The importance of the latter is suggested in the preface by its designation of the work not as an organic unity but as "neither head nor tail, both head and tail, alternately and reciprocally" (*ni queue ni tête . . . à la fois tête et queue, alternativement et réciproquement*) (*OC,* 1: 275; *PS,* ix). Considering the emphasis in literary studies on the role of the reader over the last decade, it is surprising that a passage such as the following, and prose poem collections generally, should have attracted so little attention:

> Considérez, je vous prie, quelles admirables commodités cette combinaison nous offre à tous, à vous, à moi et au lecteur. Nous pouvons couper où nous voulons, moi ma rêverie, vous le manuscrit, le lecteur sa lecture, car je ne suspends pas la volonté rétive de celui-ci au fil interminable d'une intrigue superflue.

> [I beg you to consider how admirably convenient this combination is for all of us, for you, for me, and for the reader. We can cut wherever we please, I my dreaming, you your manuscript, the reader his reading; for I do not keep the reader's restive mind hanging in suspense on the threads of an interminable and superfluous plot.] (*OC,* 1: 275; *PS,* ix)

The fragmented, antiorganic composition of Baudelaire's collection attested to here exemplifies that phenomenon of "ordered disorganization" which is a characteristic feature, as Terdiman remarks, of both the newspaper and the department store. Similarly, individual prose poems—which Baudelaire hoped, as we recall, would be "easily saleable"—bear a strong and, as seems likely, more than incidental resemblance in their form to newspaper "articles" and "faits divers" (*DCD,* 122–27). It is in the newspaper after all that, in Terdiman's words, "page space was measurable in money . . . the column *itself* became readable as a machine to make money" (*DCD,* 186). Accordingly, in Baudelaire's preface, the potential reader is clearly envisaged, though certainly not without irony, as a consumer, the texts themselves as products—convenient commodities—to be consumed with as little annoyance as possible.

The author thus emerges not only as a producer of literary wares but also as his own agent, the work of art not as a pure end in itself but as a means for acquiring both an audience and an income. There may never have been a letter or, for that matter, any piece of writing that contained, between the opening "Mon cher ami" and the closing "Votre bien affectionné" more "deep duplicity" (*CB,* 527) and calculation than Baudelaire's preface to a new genre. Examples of such duplicity abound: the "whole serpent" Baudelaire dares to dedicate to Houssaye in the hope that some of what he refers to as its "fragments" (*tronçons*) will be sufficiently alive to "please," "amuse," and also no doubt to disturb the reader—both Houssaye and the broader public accessible to him through *La presse;* the statement raising up Aloysius Bertrand's ghost only to banish it into the shadow of his own accomplishment; the concealment of false modesty under the aegis of integrity in Baudelaire's reference to his own work as a mere "accident which anyone else would glory in" (*accident dont tout autre que moi s'en-orgueillirait sans doute*) (*OC,* 1: 276; *PS,* x). Finally, this duplicity manifests itself in Baudelaire's not terribly subtle attempt to flatter Houssaye by intimating that, no less than Bertrand, Houssaye was—in his efforts to "translate in a song the *Glazier's* strident cry . . . and to express in a lyric prose all the dismal suggestions this cry sends up through the fog of the street to the highest garrets"—Baudelaire's true "mysterious and brilliant model," that same Houssaye who authored the prose poem, "La chanson du vitrier," so acidly parodied by Baudelaire's own "Le mauvais vitrier." Following this letter of introduction, it is less a wonder that a number of the later *Petits poèmes en prose* were not published before Baudelaire's death than that most of them were—and by Houssaye!

Around 1850, Roland Barthes has said, "Literature begins to be confronted with the problem of its own justification: writing starts looking for alibis."[5] In what has become one of its most celebrated passages, Baudelaire's preface (1861–62) refers to "a poetic prose, musical, without rhythm and without rhyme, supple enough and rugged enough [*assez heurtée*] to adapt itself to the lyrical impulses [*mouvements lyriques*] of the soul, the undulations of reverie, the jibes [*soubresauts*] of conscience?" (*OC*, 1: 275–76; *PS*, x). Musicality, the impulses of the soul, dreams, even meditative consciousness—these are the traditional stock-in-trade of Romantic poetry, and especially of the subjective verse lyric. In the *Petits poèmes en prose,* certainly, these have an important role, yet more in a position of negation than affirmation, a negation beneath the weight of the "huge cities" (*villes énormes*) and the "medley of their innumerable interrelations" (*croisement de leurs innombrables rapports*). Speaking of the "lyrical impulses of the soul" is Baudelaire's alibi for presenting the individual not as self-sufficient or transcendent but, rather, as radically situated in the social matrix.

Nowhere is there a clearer presentation of the situatedness of the authorial "I" than in the prose poem, "A une heure du matin" (One O'Clock in the Morning). The demands Baudelaire makes of his prose poetry, that it be supple and tough enough to adapt itself to the undulations of dream and the jolts of consciousness, are those required not by the lyrical soul in splendid isolation but by the individual in society. For the writer, this society includes, most immediately, other writers and potential publishers. Thus, strategically placed after the parodic demolition of Houssaye's "La chanson du vitrier" (The Song of the Glazier) in Baudelaire's own "Le mauvais vitrier" (The Bad Glazier), "A une heure du matin" begins with the double exclamation: "At last! Alone!" (*Enfin! seul!*) (*OC, 1: 187; PS,* 15). That five more exclamations follow before the text begins to recapitulate the day's events in the third paragraph suggests how long it takes the speaker to recover from the encounters about to be listed. How absorbed the speaker is by the social life of his big-city environment is indicated by the text's initial pronoun, which is not the conventional lyric's first-person singular, *je,* but the impersonal third person, *On* (serving in this case in its everyday sense as an alternative for the first person plural). *On* is then followed in the

5. Roland Barthes, *Le degré zéro de l'écriture* (Paris: Seuil, 1972), p. 46.

second sentence by the other collective first person plural form, *nous;* only after "the tyranny of the human face has disappeared" does the first *je* of the poem appear, followed by the more intimate first-person privacy of *moi-même* (myself). The first paragraph thus presents a shift from the impersonal and the collective to the private and personal, a shift expressed, significantly, in terms of private ownership, the desire to "possess silence, if not rest" (*nous* posséderons *le silence, sinon le repos;* my emphasis).

Having arrived home at his solitary room, immediately the speaker double-locks the door: "It seems to me that this turn of the key increases my solitude and strengthens the barricades that currently separate me from the world" (*Il me semble que ce tour de clef augmentera ma solitude et fortifiera les barricades qui me séparent actuellement du monde*). Ironically resonant with the revolution of 1848 in "barricades," this willed separation is undermined by the memories of the day which succeed each other relentlessly in the third paragraph. Following the exclamations, "Horrible life! Horrible city!" the text returns to the impersonal, this time in the form of a sequence of past infinitives: "avoir vu . . . avoir disputé . . . avoir salué . . . avoir distribué . . . être monté . . . avoir fait ma cour . . . m'être vanté . . . avoir nié . . . avoir refusé . . . et donné" (to have seen . . . to have disagreed . . . to have greeted . . . to have distributed . . . to have gone up to . . . to have made my rounds . . . to have boasted . . . to have denied . . . to have refused . . . and given) (*OC,* 1: 287–88). The effect of this sequence is of a confessional, a kind of litany or mea culpa in which the speaker recounts his *business,* his daily bread. The figures he encounters belong for the most part to his professional milieu, "several men of letters . . . the editor of a review . . . a theatrical director" (*OC,* 1: 288; *PS,* 15), but include also "twenty or more persons, of whom fifteen were unknown to me . . . a dancer [*une sauteuse*] who asked me to design her a costume for *Venustre* . . . a friend . . . and . . . a perfect rogue" (*OC,* 1: 288; *PS,* 15–16). In fact, this second list of acquaintances, encounters, friends, and enemies *also* belongs to the speaker/writer's professional circle, for as the paragraph and its conclusion suggest, the circle continues round indefinitely: "Ugh! is there no end to it?" (*ouf! est-ce bien fini?*).

For the writer, as for every member of a competitive society concerned with getting ahead (or even staying in the same place), no stone can be left unturned. That the speaker turns in the last paragraph—unhappy, in his words, with everyone, including himself—to the consolations of religion ("*Seigneur mon Dieu!*") would but be in keeping with the ideology of his class were it not for his implicit demystification of that same religious idelogy: " . . . *je voudrais bien me racheter . . .* " (I long to redeem myself). The verb *racheter*, with its specifically Christian connotation, "to redeem," should be understood here also in its economic sense, "to buy back," which echoes the verb "to possess" (*nous posséderons*) in the first paragraph. The speaker would like to buy *himself* back, to be in possession of himself, not to be subjected to the laws of the marketplace.[6] Yet no matter how much he pleads to the "souls" of "those [he] has loved and celebrated in song" (*ceux que j'ai aimé . . . ceux que j'ai chantés*) he will not be able to shut himself off from that market and continue to live. Even his double-lock will not keep the "contaminating fumes" (*vapeurs corruptrices*) of the social world from seeping into his most private room or from fixing even his most lyrical self in its matrix.

Knowing this, the speaker prays to God for a strange kind of grace. *Dieu* emerges here as a substitute for the poetic muse, the inspiration that is to allow the speaker to "produce" something ("some beautiful verses") which will set him above his kind, not for the liberation of forgiveness, of self and others, but to prove to himself that he is not "the lowest of men" (*le dernier des hommes*), "inferior to those [he] scorns" (*inférieur à ceux que je méprise*). Although the desire these lines express not to be *inferior* does not necessarily imply a need to feel *superior* to others, the speaker's admitted scorn for those with whom he compares himself strongly suggests such an interpretation. If we are inclined to interpret the speaker's prayer as a desire to be no more than equal to others, then his invocation to God may strike us as sincere and even self-effacing. The fact, however, that the speaker desires not only to redeem himself but also to "boost [his] own pride at the expense of others" (*m'enorgueillir un peu*), may well lead us to interpret his appeal to God, though not his desire to produce beautiful poetry, as at least partially ironic. Christian grace is not given because one has or has not earned it. It is, rather, a gift that may be accorded to even the most unworthy. Thus, an ironic reading seems called for especially by the speaker's desire to *prove* his own worth, and above all to himself ("*qui me prouvent à moi-même*"), rather than to a Christian God who would require no such proof, whether through the creation of beautiful poetry or through any other means. In any case, poetry is here inseparable

6. See Irving Wohlfarth, " 'Perte d'auréole': The Emergence of the Dandy," *Modern Language Notes* 85 (1970), p. 541.

from what Hegel calls "the world of daily life and of prose." With its sober, forceful indication of the extent to which poets are themselves, like anyone else, trapped in this world of prose and hence no longer able to maintain "that appearance of autonomous and complete vitality and freedom which is the very foundation of beauty," "A une heure du matin" offers itself as a paradigmatic text for the *Petits poèmes en prose* as a whole. Although the individual in such a world may desire to see himself as, in Hegel's words, "a sealed unity," he finds himself comprehensible, like the speaker in "A une heure du matin," only through his relationships to other people, on whom he is wholly dependent.[7]

Baudelaire's Poor

Academic critics have traditionally slighted Baudelaire's prose poetry in favor of the verse poetry of the *Fleurs du mal*.[8] Even so profound and radical a critic as Benjamin managed to all but ignore the *Petits poèmes en prose* in his important studies of Baudelaire's work. It is almost as if Baudelaire criticism has been suffering from a kind of aestheticist repression of that very "world of prose" which Baudelaire thematized in his later work, not just as a pendant or ornament to the *Fleurs du mal*, but to "brush against the grain" of the earlier poems. Barbara Johnson has noted that, although critics have largely neglected Baudelaire's prose poetry, poets have consistently considered it among his most interesting work.[9] Only relatively recently has the surprising lack of attention given to the *Petits poèmes en prose* in Baudelaire criticism begun to see some redress.[10] In the 1970s in particular, there seems finally to

7. Quotations from Hegel are drawn from the translation on pp. 150–52 of the *Ästhetik* appearing in Fredric Jameson's *Marxism and Form* (Princeton: Princeton University Press, 1971), pp. 352–53.

8. Fritz Nies, *Poesie in prosaischer Welt* (Heidelberg: Carl Winter, 1964), notes in his study of Bertrand and Baudelaire that among 5,200 titles of W. T. Bandy's comprehensive bibliography, *Répertoire*, only around 1 percent deal with *Le spleen de Paris* or the prose poem generally.

9. Johnson, *Défigurations du langage poétique*, p. 14.

10. In addition to those already cited, the rapidly growing list of recent discussions of Baudelaire's prose poetry includes the following: Donald Aynesworth, "Humanity and Monstrosity in *Le spleen de Paris*: A Reading of 'Mademoiselle Bistouri,'" *Romanic Review* (March 1982), pp. 209–21; Cynthia Chase, "Paragon, Parergon: Baudelaire Translates Rousseau," in *Difference in Translation*, ed. Joseph F. Graham (Ithaca: Cornell University Press, 1985), pp. 63–80; Fernande De George, "The Structure of Baudelaire's *Petits poèmes en prose*," *L'Esprit créateur* 13, no. 2 (1973), pp. 13: 144–53; Maurice Delcroix, "Un poème en prose de Charles Baudelaire: 'Les Yeux des pauvres,'" *Cahiers d'Analyse Textuelle* 19 (1977), pp. 46–75; Jeffrey Mehlman, "Baudelaire with Freud: Theory and Pain," *Diacritics* (Spring 1974), pp. 7–13; Charles Mauron, *Le dernier Baudelaire* (Paris:

have emerged a broader consensus that the more revolutionary Baudelaire is not necessarily to be found in his verse poetry. Now more than ever before it is possible to speak credibly of what Johnson has called the "second Baudelairean revolution" as equally enduring.

Exemplifying on a small scale the dialogical, heteroglossic, mixed mode of discourse Mikhail Bakhtin associates with the novel and prose forms generally, the prose poem in Baudelaire's hands demonstrates the kind of "self critique of the literary language of the era" Bakhtin has said is carried out not at the level of abstraction but through images of language which are "inseparable from images of various world views and from the living beings who are their agents—people who think, talk, and act in a setting that is social and historically concrete."[11] Far more extensively and concretely than the dialogical struggles enacted in Novalis's and especially in Schlegel's texts, those in Baudelaire's prose poems incorporate discourses other than the predominantly literary and philosophical. This broadening of the dialogical from a virtually exclusive focus on struggles *within* high culture to include a concern with struggles *between* high and low culture is crucial to the social reinscription of the lyric that the prose poem advances as it emerges with Baudelaire. In the remainder of this chapter, I will bring together three prose poems that have not previously been examined in detail in close relation to one another despite several worthwhile studies of them in isolation. The three poems I will consider are those that deal most explicitly with the poor: "Le joujou du pauvre" (The Poor Child's Toy), "Les yeux des pauvres" (The Eyes of the Poor), and "Assommons les pauvres!" (Let's Beat Down the Poor!). Though Baudelaire's treatment of the poor in the *Petits poèmes en prose* is not at all limited to these three texts, they offer an especially useful interpretive constellation. Much of their pathos, like that of Baudelaire's prose poetry and the prose poem generally, stems from their symbolic enactment of the impossibility of

---

José Corti, 1966); Dolf Oehler, "'Assommons les pauvres!' Dialektik der Befreiung bei Baudelaire," *Germanisch-romanische Monatsschrift* (1975), pp. 25: 454–62; Oskar Sahlberg, *Baudelaire und seine Muse auf dem Wege zur Revolution* (Frankfurt: Suhrkamp, 1979); and Virginia E. Swain, "The Legitimation Crisis: Event and Meaning in Baudelaire's 'Le vieux saltimbanque' and 'Une mort héroique,'" *Romantic Review* (November 1982), pp. 452–62.

11. Mikhail Bakhtin, *Die Ästhetik des Wortes*, ed. Rainer Grübel (Frankfurt: Suhrkamp, 1979), pp. 168–219, and *The Dialogic Imagination*, p. 49 and passim. Oppositions between individuals in Baudelaire's prose poems typically manifest themselves as what in Bakhtinian terms may be called "surface upheavals of the untamed elements in social heteroglossia" (*Dialogic Imagination*, 326).

resolving existing antagonisms in the absence of the kind of *collective praxis* necessary for such a resolution to come about. Seen in relation to one another, the three prose poems on the poor suggest an "internal" dynamic, three moments of a single dialectical relation. In the aspiration they figure, both individually and collectively, toward a dialectical resolution of oppositional forces; in their staging of the urgency and extreme difficulty of the same, they offer paradigmatic examples of the prose poem's own gesture as genre.[12]

"In every aspect of daily life in which the individual worker imagines himself to be the subject of his own life," Georg Lukács has remarked, "he finds this to be an illusion that is destroyed by the immediacy of his experience."[13] As a prose poem such as "A une heure du matin" suggests, the writer is scarcely more the "subject of his own life" (a lyrical perspective) than any other worker or wage laborer. In its presentation of the lyrical subject's unwilling dependence on others, its imaging of the individual's ineradicable situatedness within determinately social contexts, "A une heure du matin" exemplifies the turn taken by the *Petits poèmes en prose* toward more concretely and explicitly social motifs than the verse poetry of the day seems to have allowed.[14]

12. Cf. Terdiman, *DCD*, p. 269: "Because it refuses to conceive the oppositions which it represents as immutable, because it inscribes history as determinant not only in its own constitution but in all elements of social reality, the prose poem functions as a dialectical structure." See also p. 338: "A certain displaced image of another way of living and of thinking about the world, a project of the resolution of these intolerable deformations, is therefore implicit in the very existence of the prose poem and in its attempt to take on its antagonist in the realm of his ideological strength." The following discussion of Baudelaire's prose poems on the poor was written in the spring of 1983 and appeared in much the same form as that offered here in the summer 1985 issue of *Stanford French Review*. In the interim, *Discourse/Counter-Discourse* (315–18) made available its own brief but useful discussion of the three prose poems. Though the book considers each of the texts individually as examples of Baudelaire's thematization of the "historical dialectic around midcentury" (315) and consequent "representation of class relations" (318), it does not examine them in detail, nor does it trace the dialectical relation among the texts which is my specific concern here.

13. Georg Lukács, *History and Class Consciousness*, trans. Rodney Livingston (Cambridge, Mass.: MIT Press, 1971), p. 165.

14. Baudelaire's inclusion of explicitly social motifs is not, of course, exclusively limited to his prose poetry. There are certainly precedents for a related orientation in earlier verse poems. For a discussion of Baudelaire's turn from a Romantic "subjective" to a more modern "objective" aesthetic, see Hans Robert Jauss, "Baudelaires Rückgriff auf die Allegorie," in *Formen und Funktionen der Allegorie*, ed. Water Haug (Stuttgart: Metzler, 1979), pp. 688ff. The "Spleen" poems of the *Fleurs du mal*, in particular, on which Jauss focuses attention, look forward in this sense to the *Petits poèmes en prose*, where Baudelaire's social reinscription of the lyric in the prose poem achieves its most revolutionary form. For a similar assessment, see Terdiman, *DCD*, p. 294: "Baudelaire's

In "A une heure du matin" and elsewhere, Baudelaire's prose poetry shows him as having developed, by means of his literary praxis, an intense awareness of himself *as object*, of his sensibility and his texts as exchangeable goods within the commodity structure of society. There is, accordingly, an intimate connection between Baudelaire's awareness of his own precarious situation as a literary producer and the presentation of the poor in the *Petits poèmes en prose*.[15] It is questionable whether this awareness enables Baudelaire to get entirely beyond that contemplative subject-object dualism Lukács describes as characteristic of bourgeois thought. Still, as we shall see, the penultimate poem of the *Petits poèmes en prose*, "Assommons les pauvres!", shows signs if not of a breakthrough, then at least of a movement in that direction.

Through its frequent focus on the first-person singular of subjective, "lyrical" consciousness, the prose poem offers, on the one hand, an implicit critique of the putative "objectivity" of prose.[16] On the other hand, by virtue of its dislocation and reinsertion of the self into the social context of third-person narrative (with particular emphasis on the anecdote), the prose poem also suggests a critique of the "subjective" lyric. In the case of Baudelaire, it seems most useful to emphasize the genre's critique of lyric poetry, both because the inventor of the modern prose poem has been primarily known as a writer of the verse lyric and because the prose poem's implied critique of prose becomes

---

closest approaches to the reality of these social processes occur in the prose poems (which Benjamin does not extensively discuss). It is these texts which represent his most explicit penetration into the world of modern capitalism, into its discourses and its dissonances, which he re-situates in the counter-discourse of *Le spleen de Paris*."

15. A man's relation becomes "*objective* and *actual* for him," Marx wrote, "through his relation to the other man." (*Economic and Philosophic Manuscripts of 1844*, in *Collected Works* [New York: International Publishers, 1975], 3: 278). In terms of class relations, Baudelaire's position is that of the petty bourgeois, described by Marx as "fluctuating between proletariat and bourgeoisie" where the individual members of this class "are being constantly hurled down into the proletariat by the action of competition" (*Manifesto of the Communist Party, Collected Works*, 6: 509). Thus, Benjamin has written: "It is exceptionally important . . . that Baudelaire stumbled on relations of competition in poetic production. . . . [, on] the transposition of such rivalry into the sphere of competition on the open market. . . . It was a real discovery of Baudelaire's that he was ranged against *individuals*. . . . With Baudelaire the public as such moves for the first time into the field of vision" (*CB*, 688; *CP*, 54).

16. As Terdiman points out, the successful commercialization and massification of the daily newspaper in the nineteenth century both depended on and encouraged the widespread acceptance of this view of prose as an objective discursive mode. Notwithstanding the counterdiscursive gestures of the prose poem and of such novelists as Balzac and Flaubert, as Terdiman indicates, the novel in the nineteenth century remained largely caught up in this view of prose (see *DCD*, 132–34 and chaps. 1 and 5).

foregrounded only somewhat later, in the work, for example, of Rimbaud, Lautréamont, and Max Jacob. In the "ordinary" novel, Barthes has said, "the 'I' is the witness; it is the 'he' who is actor."[17] Thus, the "I" in Baudelaire's prose poems, according to Fritz Nies, speaks mostly from the standpoint of the observer, "occasionally retreating so far into the background that in many texts it doesn't even make an appearance."[18] This denial of the primacy of the "I" is indeed a prominent aspect of the *Petits poèmes en prose* and an important part of its critique of the verse lyric, but it is only one dimension of this critique and by no means final. John Lyons has written that the collection comprises mostly narratives, "anecdotes . . . hallucinatory adventures, with the structural core . . . generally a story of someone doing something . . . the protagonist *acts*."[19] That these acts are recounted in the first person as well as in the third person suggests an alternation between lyrical and novelistic, poetic and prosaic perspectives, between "the poet observing himself . . . and the poet observing others."[20]

In an otherwise admiring letter to Sainte-Beuve (dated January 15, 1866), whom Benjamin considered the poet most responsible before Baudelaire for incorporating social motifs into the lyric, Baudelaire indicates his reservations about the aestheticizing tendencies of his friend's work: "In certain places of Joseph Delorme, I find a little too much of *luths*, of *lyres*, of *harps* and *Jehovahs*. It taints the Parisian poems. Besides, you had come to destroy that" (*Cor*, 2: 585). Earlier in the letter, Baudelaire speaks of *Le spleen de Paris* as itself "a new Joseph Delorme attaching its rhapsodic thought to each incident of his idleness and drawing from each object a disagreeable moral" (*Cor*, 2: 583). The difference between Baudelaire's treatment of the poor and Sainte-Beuve's is suggested in part by the *disagreeable* moral Baudelaire, in contrast to Saint-Beuve, wishes to draw from the prosaic world.[21] Although Benjamin's analysis of social motifs in Baudelaire's poetry focuses on the *Fleurs du mal*, the *Petits poèmes en prose* displays an even greater emphasis on such motifs, as well as, perhaps, the greater insights; while the verse collection tends to turn mud into gold, poeticiz-

17. Barthes, *Le degré zéro*, p. 29.
18. Nies, *Poesie*, pp. 29 and 270.
19. John D. Lyons, "A Prose Poem in the Nominal Style: 'Un Hémisphère dans une chevelure,'" *L'Esprit créateur* 13, no. 2 (Summer 1973), p. 137.
20. De George, "The Structure of Baudelaire's *Petits poèmes en prose*," p. 146.
21. For an example and illustration of Sainte-Beuve's aestheticization of poverty in a Parisian setting drawn from *Les consolations* (also mentioned in Baudelaire's January 15, 1866, letter), see Benjamin, *CB*, p. 21.

ing (versifying) social relations even as it ironizes them. In the prose poems of *Le spleen de Paris,* by comparison, as Suzanne Bernard has said, "mud stays mud."[22]

"Le joujou du pauvre"

Thus, "Le joujou du pauvre" (*OC,* 1: 304–5), first published in 1862, does not greatly change or poeticize the prosaic objects it excerpts from the essay, "Morale du joujou" (*OC,* 1: 581–87), which first appeared nine years earlier. Except for some slight additions, including the list of three exemplary toys in the second paragraph and the breaking up of the second paragraph of the original into the prose poem's eight paragraphs, the two texts remain substantially the same. The most striking difference besides these, and the one that makes the prose poem, is the establishment of a symmetrical frame in the form of a two-line opening and two-line closing paragraph. The latter two lines are completely new, the former partially drawn from the earlier text. Inside this frame, with its "*Je*" on one end and "*les deux enfants*" (two children) on the other, the narrator situates himself as a pure observer. The almost immediate shift away from the first person in "Le joujou du pauvre" contrasts with the extended first-person anecdote that begins "Morale du joujou," where Baudelaire recounts a personal event from his own childhood as background to his fascination with toys as an adult. The isolation from this original context of the paragraphs that make up the prose poem effectively cancels much of the subjective, "poetic" first-person intimacy of the earlier essay in favor of a more distanced, objective and "prosaic" account. Although the second paragraph suggests contact between the first and third persons, the subject and object of contemplation, it does so only in the uncertain temporal space between future and imperative, and by means of an ambiguous second person: "When you go out in the morning . . . fill your pockets" (*Quand vous sortirez le matin . . . remplissez vos poches*). Of the poor children who are to receive toys and who would run away like cats to savor them, the speaker says: "You will see their eyes open unbelievably wide" (*Vous verrez leurs yeux s'agrandir démesurément*). There is no guarantee, however, that these children will "actually" receive anything (from us? the speaker? Baudelaire?), as the children well know, "having learned to be wary of man" (*ayant appris à se défier de l'homme*). Contact is postponed indefinitely, leaving speaker and reader suspended in the space/time between two verb tenses.

22. Bernard, *Le poème en prose de Baudelaire jusqu'à nos jours,* p. 108.

In the third paragraph, the verb tense changes, and the speaker, who remains unidentified except as an "I" who contemplates the (im)possibility of an "innocent diversion," begins to recount the principal anecdote of the poem, a static portrait. On one side of a fence a wealthy child stands passively on the grass beside a splendid toy; across from him, like an outcast from Eden, "on the highway" (*sur la route*), there is another child described as "pitifully black and grimy" (*sale, chétif, fuligineux*). The two children and their objects are presented in a frozen, dualistic world. What is referred to in "Morale du joujou" as "that immense *mundus* of childhood" (*OC*, 1: 584) is in fact two worlds, the insecure world of poverty and the road separated by "symbolic bars" from the cozy, domestic world of the rich. If the toy is, as Baudelaire writes in the earlier essay, "the first initiation of the child to art" (*OC*, 1: 583), then the literary art to which the poor child receives initiation would certainly be unadorned prose, that of the rich child the aristocratic art of classical French poetry with its intricate rhyme schemes and other aesthetic devices and adornments. The phrase Baudelaire uses to describe the rich child's toy—"*verni, doré, vêtu d'une robe pourpre, et couvert de plumets et de verroteries*" (gilded and shining, dressed in purple, and covered with plumes and glittering beads)—suggests the latter in the preciosity of its diction and subject matter, in the conspicuous assonance and alliteration of "*verni . . . vêtu . . . verroteries*" and "*pourpre . . . plumets*," and in its concealed approximation of a double alexandrine ("*verni . . . pourpre*"/"*et . . .verroteries*").[23]

Corresponding to this symbolic reading on the literary/aesthetic level, the two worlds of the poor and the rich child suggest on the social level the class relations of proletariat and bourgeoisie. In an earlier verse poem from his "Révolte" cycle, "Abel et Caïn," Baudelaire lays out a similar set of relations, where the race of Cain may be identified with the proletariat and the race of Abel with the bourgeoisie.[24] Recall-

---

23. Exemplary of such aristocratic art is the work of Théophile Gautier, about which Baudelaire wrote: "His poetry, at once majestic and precious, moves magnificently, like aristocrats in full attire" (*Sa poésie, à la fois majestueuse et précieuse, marche magnifiquement, comme les personnes de cour en grande toilette*). Baudelaire goes on to praise Gautier for having introduced (in *Emaux et Camées*) "the majesty of the alexandrine into octosyllabic verse" and for "the regular and symmetrical purple of a rhyme that is more than exact." Some of Gautier's poems, Baudelaire says, are sculptures, some flowers, others jewels, but all are "dressed up in a finer or more brilliant color than the colors of China or India, . . . and of a purer cut than objects of marble or crystal" (*Cor*, 2: 126).

24. Such an interpretation is offered by Wolfgang Fietkau in his book, *Schwanengesang auf 1848* (Rowohlt: Reinbek bei Hamburg, 1978), p. 394.

ing not only the poor child "on the road" in "Le joujou du pauvre" but also the beggar family in "Les yeux des pauvres," in "Abel et Cain" Baudelaire writes: *"Race de Caïn, sur les routes/Traîne ta famille aux abois"* (Race of Cain, on the roads/drag along your family with your backs to the wall) (*OC*, 1: 123). Like Abel in the biblical version of the story, the rich child in "Le joujou du pauvre" stands inside the garden from which the poor child is excluded. In contrast to "Abel et Caïn," however, with its open call to rebellion, the tone of "Le joujou du pauvre" is more detached; the speaker is one who keeps his distance and self-possession, "the eye of a connoisseur." The dominant verbs in the latter poem have to do with observation, the calm *durée* of the imperfect tense: *"regardait," "nettoyait"* used to refer to the act of divining "an authentic master under . . . the disgusting patina of misery" (*une peinture idéale sous . . . la répugnante patine de la misère*). The closest the children come to action is, momentarily, in the poor child's "showing" (*montrait*), the rich child's "examining" (*examinait avidement*) the live rat that is the shared focus of their gaze, "drawn from life itself" (*tiré de la vie elle-même*).

The only real center of activity in the poem, the rat the poor child agitates violently, is quite literally caged up. Clothed in a proliferation of adjectives, the children face each other across what seems for the moment of the text a secure partition, but the activity of the poor child exciting the rat inside its cage on one side of the "symbolic bars" is suggestive of the energy that might be released by the proletariat in class struggle. Up to the very end, the speaker of Baudelaire's poem keeps his distance, though the "fraternal" smiles, "of an *equal* whiteness" (*d'une* égale *blancheur*), serve as an ironic reminder that the promises of the French revolution for liberty, fraternity, and equality have been realized only by those on the right side of a class barrier that has yet to be broken down by successful revolutionary praxis. As with the man looking at his own reflection in the prose poem, "Le miroir" ("according to the immortal principles of '89, all men are equal before the law" [*d'après les immortels principes de '89, tous les hommes sont egaux en droits*]), an empty formal likeness is here reflected alongside unresolved, potentially explosive difference. The mirror, Pierre Macherey has said: "does not reflect things (in which case the relationship between the reflection and the object would be one of mechanical correspondence). The image in the mirror is deceptive: the mirror enables us to grasp only *relationships* of contradiction. By means of contradictory images the mirror represents and evokes the historical contradictions of the period."[25] The prose poem in Baudelaire's hands is not only the site of a potential and actual confrontation between literary modes, between poetry and prose, it is also the location, as "Le joujou du pauvre" makes abundantly clear, of a strong emphasis on societal oppositions, potential and actual antagonisms stemming from class relations.[26] In "Les yeux des pauvres," the second of Baudelaire's poems on the poor we will consider, conflict involves not only class relations and literary antagonisms of the form prose/poetry but also another kind of "generic" conflict, the gender-based sexual antagonisms between men and women.

"Les yeux des pauvres"

In "Le joujou du pauvre," as we have seen, the speaker keeps his distance, and with it, his anonymity, considering the poor from the point of view of a "connoisseur." The overall effect of the poem is to situate poverty as an object of contemplation, as spectacle. In "Les yeux des pauvres" (*OC*, 1: 317–19; *PS*, 52–53), subject—poetry, the speaker, the lyrical "I"—and object—prose, the poor, the narrative "he"—continue to be held apart in a relation of mutual exclusion, but at a closer distance than in "Le joujou du pauvre." The latter text, as we have seen, takes the form of a monological anecdote, with the speaker present only as an observer and narrator. "Les yeux des pauvres," by contrast, suggests a dialogical relationship that includes the speaker as a more active participant, though even here his position is best de-

25. Pierre Macherey, *A Theory of Literary Production*, trans. Geoffrey Will (London: Routledge and Kegan Paul, 1978), p. 126.

26. If a work of art may be said to "reflect" the social contradictions of a given period, what it reflects, as Jameson has said, "is not so much the class in itself as some autonomous cultural configuration, or rather the situation of that class, or, in short, class conflict" (*Marxism and Form*, 381–83). Despite Jameson's attempt, not unlike that of Macherey in his chapter on Lenin in *A Theory of Literary Production*, to revitalize the reflection metaphor by acknowledging "a fairly wide range of possibilities in the mode of reflection itself," we may agree with Terry Eagleton (*Criticism and Ideology* [London: Verso Editions, 1976], p. 65) that "one does not escape from reflectionist models by imagining a somewhat more complicated mirror." Though Jameson's revised formulations in *The Political Unconscious* (where he no longer speaks of reflection, but of displacement, projection, symbolic enactment, etc.), and Eagleton's alternative notion of the relation between literary text and society, text and author, and text and reader in terms of production have clear advantages over reflection metaphors, I have chosen to stay with the latter metaphor here because of its specific relevance to Baudelaire's work. As I hope to demonstrate, it is precisely the contemplative, distanced, reflectionist approach to reality evident in both "Le joujou du pauvre" and "Les yeux des pauvres" that the Baudelaire of "Assommons les pauvres!" attempts to break through, smashing the mirror, as it were.

scribed as one of oscillation: "inside" the frame of the lover's relationship, he remains "outside" the frame of the poor. Suggestive of a
dialectical reversal of the subject/object relation in "Le joujou du
pauvre," however, the eyes of the poor in the prose poem that bears
their name take in the speaker at least as much as he takes in the poor.

"Les yeux des pauvres" begins, like other crucial prose poems such
as "A une heure du matin," "Perte d'auréole" and "Assommons les
pauvres!", with an exclamation, one of those linguistic shocks suggesting intensified awareness: "Ah! So you want to know why I hate you
today?" At this stage, "you" (*vous*) remains powerfully ambiguous. As
opposed to the "you" of "Le joujou du pauvre," which functions primarily to parry attention away from a detached "I," "you" in this case
serves to immediately implicate the reader in a way reminiscent of the
verse poem "Au lecteur" (To the Reader). The reader is of course also
implicated by the problematic of innocence and guilt which begins "Le
joujou du pauvre," but the emphasis in that poem falls first on the
speaker rather than, as here, on the reader. Though we may continue
to read "you" in reference to ourselves as readers, and we are indeed
implicated, the pronoun begins to take on its other and primary connotation with the attribute, "the most perfect example of feminine
impermeability." Beyond this, the first sentence of the second paragraph, "We had spent a long day together which to me had seemed
short," places the speaker in a past that separates him from the reader.
Thus, as the focus shifts from the second person plural *vous* to the first
person plural *nous*, the speaker's place in the narrative gives way to a
third "other," his female companion.

The couple, the narrator tells us, has promised to share all their
thoughts with each other. These thoughts, however, and the gener-
ic/sexual problematic the poem thematizes, are not to be separated
from a problem of class relations which stands implacably, in the speaker's words, "directly in front of us." Obtruding on the speaker's romantic desire for a utopian oneness with his female companion—"We had
duly promised each other . . . that our two souls would henceforth be
but one—a dream which . . . has been realized by none"—is the prosaic
reality of class, as well as sexual, difference, and the crisis of conscience
which results from the disparity between rich and poor. The contrast
between the ornate, lavish surroundings of the new café where the
speaker and his lover are seated and the poor man "of about forty, with
tired face and graying beard" holding two small boys, one "too weak to

walk," could not be more pointedly drawn. All three "in rags," the members of the poor family contemplate the conspicuous display of wealth in front of them with serious eyes and an admiration "equal in degree but differing in kind according to their ages" (*une admiration égale, mais nuancée . . . par l'âge*). Ironically "equal" in their admiration of cultural achievements that do not belong to them but only to a privileged few, the poor, we might say, cannot present themselves, they must be represented.[27] And so here the poor are attributed words we take to be their own in a world that excludes them even as it takes them in: "a house where only people who are not like us can go" (*une maison où peuvent seuls entrer les gens qui ne sont pas comme nous*).

Theirs is the world of prose; the speaker's world, that of the poetic "café neuf" of history and mythology: "All the gold of the poor world had come to adorn those walls" (*on dirait que tout l'or du pauvre monde est venu se porter sur ces murs*). This autocritique of French Romantic poetry's aestheticization of poverty, the poeticization of a prosaic world,[28] is further developed in the beginning of the penultimate paragraph:

> Les chansonniers disent que le plaisir rend l'âme bonne et amollit le coeur. La chanson avait raison ce soir-là, relativement à moi. Non seulement j'étais attendri par cette famille d'yeux, mais je me sentais un peu honteux de nos verres [read also "verses"—*vers*][29] et de nos carafes, plus grandes que notre soif.

> [Song writers say that pleasure ennobles the soul and softens the heart. The song was right that evening as far as I was concerned. Not only was I touched by this family of eyes, but I was even a little ashamed of our glasses/verses and decanters, bigger than our thirst.] (*OC*, 1: 319; *PS*, 53)

27. See Marx, *The Eighteenth Brumaire of Louis Bonaparte*, in *Collected Works* (New York: International Publishers, 1979), 11: 187.

28. In addition to Sainte-Beuve and Gautier, the exemplary poet of the era for Baudelaire is, of course, Hugo: "Our neighbors say: Shakespeare and Goethe! We can answer them: Victor Hugo and Théophile Gautier!" (*OC*, 2: 125). Author of the influential aestheticist collection *Les orientales*, Hugo is for Baudelaire the poet of the "sadnesses of the poor," the "painter of history" (*OC*, 2: 136). Of Hugo's combination of myth and history in *La légende des siècles* Baudelaire writes: "With what majesty he has made the centuries unfurl before us, like ghosts who would come out of a wall . . . each one endowed with its favorite costume. Such art could not move at ease except in the legendary milieu: It is this . . . choice of terrain that facilitated the spectacle's evolutions" (*OC*, 2: 140–41). While Gautier offers "the love of painting," Hugo counsels "a taste for archeology" (*OC*, 2: 124).

29. In *Défigurations du langage poétique*, Johnson (154) has offered a similar reading in connection with "Le mauvais vitrier."

Like "Le joujou du pauvre," "Les yeux des pauvres" presents poverty as an object of contemplation, even delectation, though here, significantly, the eyes of the poor *look back;* the distance between the "I" and the other(s) has diminished. Yet though the poor have come closer and their eyes have engaged the speaker, his response is not to confront what stands right before his eyes but to turn away. What he turns toward is a typical substitute for pressing social concerns—romantic love. The eyes of the poor give way to the eyes of the lover, yet the text ends with the static relation of incommunicability. When the speaker's visual intoxication is dispelled, when the lover speaks, the effect is to increase rather than diminish the sense of irreconcilable generic, sexual, and class differences, to accentuate the distance between men and women as well as between social classes: " 'Those people are insufferable with their eyes wide open like carriage doors! Can't you tell the proprietor to send them away?' " (*'Ces gens-là me sont insupportables avec leurs yeux ouverts comme des portes cochères! Ne pourriez-vous pas prier le maître du café de les éloigner d'ici?'*).

"Assommons les pauvres!"

As at the conclusion of "Le joujou du pauvre," in "Les yeux des pauvres" a static set of relations remains firmly in place, unchallenged by any notion of an intervening praxis that might resolve existing tensions. Although the subject/object relation of the former remains completely one-sided, however, with the narrator/subject contemplating the frozen, dichotomized world of rich and poor alike, "Les yeux des pauvres" displays a contrasting reciprocity in which the speaker, seated complicitously with his lover in a bourgeois café, contemplates the beggarly characters of his anecdote only to have these objects of his contemplation look back at and even "speak" to him (albeit in his own words). These acts of speech distinguish "Les yeux des pauvres" from the voiceless landscape of "Le joujou du pauvre,"[30] yet both poems exhibit a fundamentally contemplative orientation to the problem of class relations—significantly, in "Les yeux des pauvres," it is the *eyes* that do the talking. In "Assommons les pauvres!", by contrast to these two earlier poems, contemplation gives way to action, an exchange of words to an exchange of blows, reciprocal glances between the speaker and the poor to physical interaction and confrontation. Although the

---

30. What Delcroix calls the "surging up of speech in that universe of the glance" ("Un poème en prose," 64).

probable consequences of such a confrontation are ambiguously drawn in Baudelaire's poem, the change of emphasis in question recalls Marx's fundamental claim that the resolution of theoretical antitheses ("subjectivity and objectivity, spirituality and materiality, activity and suffering") "is *only* possible in a *practical* way, by virtue of the practical energy of man. Their resolution is therefore by no means merely a problem of understanding but a *real* problem of life, which *philosophy* could not solve precisely because it conceived this problem as *merely* a theoretical one."[31]

Le spleen de Paris combines, as we have noted, a markedly social thematic with lyrical brevity and compression. Although often maintaining the lyric "I," individual prose poems as well as the collection as a whole tend to displace the lyrical subject from the center of attention. In the poems we have looked at so far, we have seen this subject (re)situated within decidedly social contexts. In "Assommons les pauvres!" (*OC*, 1: 357–59; *PS*, 101–2), the "I" is much more an explicit focus of attention than in either of the other two poems on the poor:

> Pendant quinze jours je m'étais confiné dans ma chambre, et je m'étais entouré des livres à la mode dans ce temps-là (il y a seize ou dix-sept ans); je veux parler des livres où il est traité de l'art de rendre les peuples heureux, sages et riches, en vingt-quatre heures.
>
> [For fifteen days I had shut myself up in my room and had surrounded myself with the most popular books of the day (that was sixteen or seventeen years ago); I am speaking of those books that treat of the art of making the people happy, wise and rich in twenty-four hours.] (*OC*, 1: 357; *PS*, 101)

Since "Assommons les pauvres!" was written in 1865, the anecdotal narrative of some sixteen or seventeen years earlier which it recounts takes place around 1848, the year of the failed social revolution that here emerges as the immediate horizon within which to situate Baudelaire's radical formal experimentation in the *Petits poèmes en prose*. The subject presented to us has a certain distance from his past which allows him to perceive himself as the speaker of the two previous poems we have considered perceived the poor, that is, as an *object* within the historical process. As a consequence of this temporal distancing, the "I" in "Assommons les pauvres!" approaches an awareness of himself as both subject and object.

31. Marx, *Collected Works*, 3: 302.

Following the speaker's self-imposed immersion in social theory, the intensive fifteen-day period of reading alluded to above, he does something that is, if not unheard of, at least fairly unusual among the generally contemplative speakers of Baudelaire's prose poems—he *acts:* "And I left my room with a terrible thirst" (*Et je sortis avec une grande soif*). At first, this activity takes the most familiar, relatively passive form of Baudelairian activity, that of the *flâneur.* We are on the verge of following him, however, into a release of energy that is unsurpassed by any other speaker in Baudelaire's work with the possible exception of "Le mauvais vitrier," that poem to which "Assommons les pauvres!" bears perhaps the closest resemblance. The former begins, in a manner suggesting spontaneous individual, much more than collective, praxis: "There are certain natures, purely contemplative and totally unfit for action, which nevertheless, moved by some mysterious and unaccountable impulse, act at times with a rapidity of which they would never have dreamed themselves capable" (*OC,* 1: 285; *PS,* 12). The amount of time the speaker in "Assommons les pauvres!" spends confined in his room reading suggests his contemplative affinity with the earlier speaker. Although his immersion in theoretical problems also suggests the search for a well-grounded praxis that might differ qualitatively from the perverse spontaneity of the speaker in "Le mauvais vitrier," the course of action he chooses is scarcely less perverse, the action's outcome no less ironic. Like his predecessor in "Le mauvais vitrier," the speaker here has his demon or, rather, his good angel, yet in contrast to that of the speaker in the earlier poem, the demon/angel of "Assommons les pauvres!" is explicitly linked to philosophy—"Since Socrates had his good Demon, why shouldn't I have my good Angel"—as well as to two *aliénistes* of the era, Lélut and Baillarger, who had maintained that Socrates was insane. The principal difference, the speaker says, between his own demon and that of Socrates, is that his is "a demon of *action*" (*un Démon d'action, un Démon de combat*). His counsel: " 'A man is the equal of another only if he can prove it, and to be worthy of liberty a man must fight for it' " (*Celui-là est l'égal d'un autre, qui le prouve, et celui-là seul est digne de la liberté, qui sait la conquérir*).

Such a position is quite different from the prevailing attitudes of the speakers in "Le joujou du pauvre" and "Les yeux des pauvres." What follows in the text is a parodic example or test case of a noncontemplative, violent approach to solving a "theoretical" problem in which the speaker physically attacks a beggar only to get back twofold everything he delivers to him:[32]

> Tout à coup, ô miracle! ô jouissance du philosophe qui vérifie l'excellence de sa théorie!—je vis cette antique carcasse se retourner, se redresser . . . le malandrin . . . me pocha les deux yeux, me cassa quatre dents. . . . Par mon énergique médication, je lui avais donc rendu l'orgueil et la vie.

> [Suddenly,—O miracle! oh joy of the philosopher when he sees the truth of his theory verified!—I saw that antique carcass turn over, jump up . . . the decrepit vagabond . . . proceeded to give me two black eyes, to knock out four of my teeth. . . .—Thus it was that my energetic medication had restored his pride and given him new life.] (*OC*, 1: 358; *PS*, 102)

After this "discussion," which ends by mutual agreement, the defeated speaker ironically acknowledges the beggar ("Sir, *you are my equal*"), shares his purse with him, and advises him ("if you are really philanthropic") to apply the same theory to his "colleagues" (*confrères*), supposedly in order to benefit them as well. There is more to this anecdote, to be sure, than a perverse version of the adage, "The Lord helps those who help themselves." In contrast to the speaker of "Le joujou du pauvre," who maintains his contemplative distance from what he observes, the speaker in "Assommons les pauvres!" turns dramatically from theory to praxis. What kind of praxis is, of course, another question. Equality, the decisive problematic at the end of "Le joujou du pauvre," is imaged as something to be taken by force—or, if need be, by violent action. But to be taken by whom? The speaker's use of the term *colleagues* sends us back to the title's first-person plural, but the question still arises: Who is the implied "we" of this poem?

As so often in Baudelaire, and as we have already seen in the beginnings of "Le joujou du pauvre" and "Les yeux des pauvres," the text sets up an inescapable complicity between author and reader, both producers of the contradictions and antagonisms of the social context

---

32. For the prototypically novelistic character of the speaker's testing of a theoretical/ideological position and discourse in "Assommons les pauvres!", see Bakhtin, *The Dialogic Imagination*, p. 334: "the person in a novel may *act*—but such action is always highlighted by ideology, is always harnessed to the character's discourse . . . is associated with an ideological motif and . . . ideological position. The action and individual act of a character in a novel are essential in order to expose—as well as to test—his ideological position, his discourse."

and text itself. In this case, however, complicity is no longer that of an aesthetic contemplation that makes of the poor one more commodity for pleasurable though guilty consumption. It is, rather, a complicity of praxis, to "beat down" the poor. Although the directive to commit acts of physical violence against the poor is in all likelihood best understood ironically, the particular kind of irony in question is less certain. However we take it, the question of class affiliation arises, and it is difficult to pin down the speaker's own standpoint toward such an imperative: one of "us," or one of "them." The speaker, who is himself not a beggar, gives us no other immediate clues as to his own class alliance, though if we read the poem in the context of the preceding prose poems, Baudelaire's other writings, and his situation as a literary producer in the age of high capitalism, ample evidence is available: "the literary life, the only element where certain classless beings can breathe" (*la vie littéraire, le seul élément où puissent respirer certains êtres déclassés*) (*OC*, 2: 302). The "we" of "Assommons les pauvres!" should stand as a warning to all those intent on "rescuing" Baudelaire's motivations and intentions by assuming a Marxist or historical materialist perspective.[33] One of the problems with such a reading is its tendency to minimize or repress the antisocialist aspects of the poem along with that deep duplicity Benjamin rightly maintained as characteristic of Baudelaire. The ambivalence and contradictoriness Oskar Sahlberg says must be emphasized with regard to Benjamin's work obtain even more in that of Baudelaire.[34]

Jean-Paul Sartre's claim that the writers of 1848 missed the chance to ally themselves with the proletariat, "the subject par excellence of a literature of *praxis*,"[35] applies particularly well to Baudelaire. Insofar as the literary market of the nineteenth century was first of all, as Sahlberg has remarked, "a great opportunity, and a greater battlefield than it had ever been before,"[36] Baudelaire's turn to the prose poem as

33. Oskar Sahlberg verges on such a totalization when he says in *Baudelaire und seine Muse auf dem Wege zur Revolution*, p. 185: "The poet is now active and *in solidarity*" (my emphasis). Although I would agree with Sahlberg that "Assommons les pauvres!" is the "goal of a long road" insofar as it demonstrates movement from a predominantly contemplative to a predominantly active approach to social reality, the speaker's (and Baudelaire's) solidarity with the poor remains about as difficult to pin down as the most effective mode of praxis at a given historical moment.

34. Oskar Sahlberg, "Die Widersprüche Walter Benjamins: Ein Vergleich der beiden Baudelaire-Arbeiten," *Neue Rundschau* 85 (1974), p. 487.

35. Jean-Paul Sartre, *Qu'est-ce que la littérature?* (Paris: Gallimard, 1948), pp. 148–54.

36. Sahlberg, "Die Widersprüche Walter Benjamins," p. 483.

genre suggests among other things a final attempt to gain for himself a greater share of the rapidly growing bourgeois reading public. Perhaps more important, however, the aesthetic experimentation and social reinscription of the lyric evidenced in the *Petits poèmes en prose* also suggest an effort on Baudelaire's part to create a new and expanded audience by *breaking* with the accepted norms and expectations of bourgeois readers as to what a poem should be. As Claude Pichois has remarked: "In the modern era, isn't respecting rules—even those that presided over the elaboration of the *Fleurs du mal*—a sign of submission [asservissement]? To respect the hierarchy of genres in the nineteenth century is perhaps to accept the hierarchy of social classes" (*OC*, 1: 1295). The wealth of devices and artifice characteristic of rhymed, metrical verse, in particular the classical alexandrine, had become by the mid-nineteenth century its peculiar poverty. Responding to this situation, Baudelaire's prose poetry offers itself as a dialogization, pros-ification, and relative democratization of the verse lyric and a renuncia-tion of the aestheticist tendencies Baudelaire had earlier praised in the work, for example, of Théophile Gautier.[37] Arising as it does in the wake of the failed social revolution of 1848, the critique of such ten-dencies manifest in the *Petits poémes en prose* arrives too late, however; their aesthetic revolution goes underground, to be revived by Rimbaud at that "moment of danger" in the early 1870s when the social force of the proletariat begins to show itself again.[38] Full of contradictions, *Le*

37. In 1858, a year after the publication of the *Fleurs du mal*, Baudelaire had praised Gautier by saying: "It is after all the character of true poetry to have a regular flow . . . and to avoid haste and jerkiness (*la saccadé*). . . . All that is abrupt and broken displeases him" (*OC*, 2: 126). Written only a few years later, the letter to Arsène Houssaye, which would become the preface to the *Petits poèmes en prose*, proposes by contrast, as we have seen, a "poetic prose . . . without rhythm and without rhyme, supple enough and rugged enough to adapt itself . . . to the jibes of conscience." On the "democratic suppleness of the prose apparatus" and the association of prose discourse in the nineteenth century with "literary democratization," "middle-class democracy and ideological egalitarian-ism," see Terdiman, *DCD*, pp. 266–67 and 275.

38. (The phrase "moment of danger" refers to W. Benjamin's "Theses on the Philos-ophy of History," *Illuminations*, p. 255.) One aspect of the prose poem's aesthetic revolu-tion is, as I have indicated, the *turn* Baudelaire's prose poetry represents toward a social reinscription of the lyrical subject. Another is its decisive turn away from and break with the conventional association of poetry and rhymed, metrical verse. As a relatively un-adorned, potentially more accessible medium than verse, the literary code of an aesthetic élite, Baudelaire's prose poetry offers a case study within literature of what Jameson in *Marxism and Form* has called a "reversal of limits," in which "the drawbacks of a given historical situation [e.g., the exhaustion of rhymed, metrical verse forms, the hegemony of the novel] turn out in reality to be its [in this case, poetry's] secret advantages, in which what looked like built-in superiorities [the novel's plot emphasis, the easy accessibility of a

spleen de Paris gestures to both bourgeoisie and proletariat, and this double gesturing is responsible for much of the work's tension. Such tension manifests itself nowhere more dramatically than in "Assommons les pauvres!", where the ambiguous deictic "we" suggests Baudelaire's unwilling economic solidarity with prostitutes, beggars, and unemployed wage laborers, the true "confrères" of the poet within the commodity structure.

It is well known that Baudelaire once planned to end "Assommons les pauvres!" with the apostrophe, *"Qu'en dis-tu, Citoyen Proudhon?"* (What do you say to that, Citizen Proudhon?) (*OC*, 1: 1350). With or without the deletion, the text suggests a critical appraisal of Proudhon's social theory. Although Baudelaire had warned as early as 1851 against what he called "socialist sophistry" (*OC*, 2: 41), his sympathies at that time, as earlier in 1848, were on the whole closely allied with those of Proudhon, a writer, he said "whom Europe will always envy us" (*OC*, 2: 40). By 1865, however, the year both of Proudhon's death and of the completion of "Assommons les pauvres!", Baudelaire's own relation to the philosopher had grown more complex. In a letter to Narcisse Ancelle on February 8, 1865, Baudelaire concedes the weakness of Proudhon's aesthetic ideas, while defending him in economic matters as "singularly respectable" (*Cor*, 2: 453). A year later, in his January 2, 1866, letter to Sainte-Beuve, Baudelaire writes that he will never pardon Proudhon for not having been a dandy; he also defends him, however, as, with pen in hand, "un bon bougre" (*OC*, 2: 563). Despite the fact that this letter to Sainte-Beuve was written on the occasion of Sainte-Beuve's own recent appraisal of Proudhon, its special relevance for "Assommons les pauvres!" has been left unaccounted for by previous assessments of the poem. With the statement, "I have read him a lot, and known him a little," the letter does indeed document, as Wolfgang Fietkau has pointed out,[39] Baudelaire's intimate acquantaince with Proudhon's work. Beyond this, however, it also suggests, both by what it says and by what it does not say, that "Assommons les pauvres!"

---

narrative continuum] suddenly prove to set the most ironclad limits on its future development" (309). In contrast to the verse lyric's emphasis on subjectivity, but also to the realist novel's positivistic objectivity, Baudelaire approaches in his poems on the poor and in the *Petits poèmes en prose* generally a thinking that sees the interpenetration of subject and object, reckons "the position of the observer into the experiment itself," and is conscious both of "the thinker's position in society and in history itself" and of "the limits imposed on this awareness by his class position" (340).

39. Fietkau, *Schwanengesang*, p. 38.

may be read as a symbolic enactment on Baudelaire's part of his own attempts to come to terms with, on the one hand, the contemplative aesthetic of the "midwife of souls" represented for him by Sainte-Beuve, and, on the other hand, the revolutionary social praxis represented for him by Proudhon. Of Sainte-Beuve's own recently completed work on Proudhon, Baudelaire writes: "I'll say nothing to you . . . You have more than ever the air of a midwife of souls. The same was said, I believe, of Socrates, but the gentlemen Baillarger and Lélut declared, on their conscience, that he was insane" (OC, 2: 563). Echoing unmistakably the passage in "Assommons les pauvres!" quoted earlier which refers to Socrates, these lines suggest that the speaker's "good angel" may be a composite of both figures: Sainte-Beuve, the poet and aesthetician whom Baudelaire elsewhere called "profound in his skepticism" (Cor, 2: 193), and Proudhon, the most influential French social theorist of his day.[40]

40. In the sardonic "Les bons chiens," which follows "Assommons les pauvres!" as the concluding text of Le spleen de Paris, Baudelaire refers to Sainte-Beuve explicitly: "Where do dogs go? Nestor Roqueplan once asked in an immortal article which he has doubtless forgotten, and which I alone, and perhaps Sainte-Beuve, still remember today./Where do dogs go, you ask, oh unobservant man? They go about their business" (OC, 1: 361; PS, 105). Baudelaire also invokes Sainte-Beuve in the essay quoted earlier comparing Pierre Dupont to Proudhon: "as Saint-Beuve said, if Dupont wanted to be completely free and independent, he remained for all that no less cognizant of the past" (OC, 2: 30). Baudelaire's portrayal of Dupont (via Sainte-Beuve) as a sort of dandy with a social conscience closely resembles a portrait one might draw of Baudelaire himself; the text of "Assommons les pauvres!" turns precisely on Baudelaire's cognizance of the past of sixteen or seventeen years earlier, the past of the 1848 revolution.

On March 1, 1865, Baudelaire wrote a letter to Auguste Poulet-Malassis (OC, 2: 469–70) which supports the idea that the speaker's struggle with the beggar in "Assommons les pauvres!" is in part a displacement and "prose-poetic" reworking of an actual encounter over dinner between Baudelaire and Proudhon in 1848. Proudhon's initial, formally polite dinner invitation to Baudelaire, "'Citoyen . . . voulez-vous que nous dînions ensemble?'" ('Citizen . . . would you like to have dinner together?'), is echoed by the mischievously familiar second-personal singular of "Qu'en dis-tu citoyen Proudhon?" (my emphases), with which Baudelaire once planned to conclude "Assommons les pauvres!" Similarly, the speaker's concluding statement to the beggar—"'Sir, you are my equal! I beg you to do me the honor of sharing my purse'"—echoes the conclusion of the anecdote Baudelaire recounts to Poulet-Malassis: "I ought to add—since you attach an often legitimate importance to the smallest details—that, when the meal was finished and I called the waiter to pay our shared expense, Proudhon so vigorously opposed my intention that I let him take out his own purse, but then he astonished me a little by paying strictly for his own dinner.—You will perhaps infer from this a decided taste for equality and an exaggerated love of justice" (Cor, 2: 470; my emphasis). A comparison of the above anecdote with its reworking in "Assommons les pauvres!" suggests that in espousing the cause of equal rights for all, Proudhon assumed perhaps too readily that equality could be agreed upon without violent struggle. The critique of philanthropy so strongly implied in "Assommons les pauvres!" may have as its unwished-for result an "every-man-for-himself" attitude—each pays for his own din-

In his well-known letter to P. V. Annenkov of December 28, 1846, responding to what he considered a grave misunderstanding and misrepresentation of the dialectic in Proudhon's recently published, *Système des contradictions économiques ou philosophie de la misère*, Marx refers to Proudhon as "the declared enemy of every political movement." "The solution of present problems," Marx says, "does not lie for him in public action but in the dialectical rotations of his own head."[41] It is little wonder that Proudhon should have represented for Marx an impediment to social praxis. In a letter written to him as early as May 17, 1846, Proudhon rejected violent revolutionary praxis as a means of social reform because "this supposed means would be quite simply an appeal to force, to the arbitrary."[42] Nevertheless, although Proudhon hoped instead for what he called "slow, measured, rational, philosophical progress" (letter to M. F***, March 2, 1840, in *Cor*, 1: 363), Baudelaire thought of him as one of the leading forces behind the February 1848 revolution, a role Proudhon himself privately wished to deny. In the first of three articles on his long-time friend, the socialist chansonnier Pierre Dupont, Baudelaire hails Proudhon as the very embodiment of the "genius of action" (*OC*, 2: 34).[43] Accordingly, whereas the "prohibitive Demon" of "Assommons les pauvres!" calls to mind the "poor Socrates" whom Baudelaire associates with Sainte-Beuve in his letter of January 2, the "Demon of action" which the prose poem's

---

ner—that could be used to rationalize even the most uncharitable behavior. Certainly, "Assommons les pauvres!" exhibits to some extent what Fietkau (*Schwanengesang*, 395) has called a "critical turning away" from the Proudhon Baudelaire hailed in 1848 as the harbinger of "absolute emancipation and immediate happiness" (*OC*, 2: 1012). In 1848, praising the February revolution as the occasion of "a fraternal and mystical union,—a union we thought definitive," Baudelaire writes: "We take pride in having shared this sublime illusion" (*OC*, 2: 1060). In 1865, by contrast, Baudelaire declares that he is "not a dupe!": "I have never been a dupe. I say *Long live the Revolution!* as I would say: *Long live Destruction! Long live Explosions! Long live Punishment! Long live Death!*" And he continues: "Not only would I gladly be victim, I would not mind also being executioner,—to feel the Revolution in both ways" (*OC*, 2: 961). Similarly, in "Assommons les pauvres!" the speaker is first cast in the role of bully, then in the role of victim, experiencing both sides of the conflict.

41. Marx, *The Marx-Engels Reader*, ed. Robert C. Tucker (New York: W. W. Norton, 1978), p. 141.

42. Letter to M. F***, March 2, 1840, in *Correspondance*, 1 (Paris: Librarie Internationale, 1875), p. 363. Further references to Proudhon will be indicated in the text as follows: *Solution du problème sociale*, in *Oeuvres complètes*, 6 (Paris: Librarie Internationale, 1868), hereafter cited as *SP*; *De la capacité politique des classes ouvrières*, in *Oeuvres complètes*, 4 (Paris: Marcel Rivière, 1924), hereafter cited as *CP*.

43. Fietkau, *Schwanengesang*, p. 398. Speaking of the philosopher's "secret affinity" with Dupont, Baudelaire refers to the "sublime mouvement de Proudhon" as one in spirit with Dupont's lines: " '*Allons, du courage/Braves ouvriers/Du coeur à l'ouvrage!/Soyons*

speaker claims for himself recalls Baudelaire's vision, if not Marx's, of Proudhon as a philosopher of praxis.

Given the movement enacted in "Assommons les pauvres!" from a contemplative theoretical approach to social reality toward one based on praxis, the question remains as to what specific kind of praxis, if any, might be most effective. In the *Petits poèmes en prose* generally, as in "Assommons les pauvres!" in particular, possible answers to this question are articulated less through affirmative proposals or suggestions than by negation. The "correct" praxis is inscribed in Baudelaire's poem as a conspicuous absence—collective, perhaps, rather than individualistic. Nowhere a given, it is everywhere to be *fought* for. Yet the possibility that such violence will result in benevolent change coexists at the end of "Assommons les pauvres!" with the possibility that it will, instead, make matters worse.[44] In 1865, describing his proposed "universal application of the principle of reciprocity" (*SP*, 260) or "mutualism," Proudhon spoke in favor of "the ancient law of the *talion, an eye for an eye, a tooth for a tooth* . . . so to speak reversed and transferred from criminal law and the infamous practices of the vendetta to economic law, to the workers' tasks and the good offices of free fraternity" (*CP*, 125).[45] That same year, alluding to the failed revolution of seventeen years earlier, "Assommons les pauvres!" subjects such a principle

---

les premiers' " ('Let's go, have faith/Good workers/On to work with good cheer!/Let's be the first'). In the same essay, Baudelaire praises Dupont for furthering the cause of "popular poetry": "Poetry's destiny is a great one! Joyous or elegiac, it always carries within itself the divine utopian character" (*OC*, 2: 35). That Proudhon was for Baudelaire the great social theorist of the day (*le grand bouc*, as he calls him) is indicated by two letters Baudelaire wrote in 1848 warning Proudhon directly of a possible assassination attempt. Baudelaire excerpted a passage out of that same *Philosophie de la misère* to which Marx's *The Poverty of Philosophy* was a critical response, and he was in all probability familiar as well with three important pamphlets Proudhon distributed between March and June 1848: *Solution du problème social*, *Organisation du crédit*, and *Résumé de la question sociale, banque d'échange* (*Cor*, 2: 394 and 563).

44. If what Oehler ("Dialektik der Befreiung bei Baudelaire," 458) refers to as the "dialectic of liberation" in "Assommons les pauvres!" suggests the possibility of a reversal "where the elimination of pauperism turns into the elimination of capitalism," it offers no guarantees. As Fietkau has pointed out (*Schwanengesang*, 213): "Marx's idea that even a series of defeats represents an advance, insofar as it produces with the concluded counterrevolution its revolutionary opposite, is at the very least not applicable for fascism."

45. "The theory of mutuality or of the *mutuum*," Proudhon had written in *Philosophie de la misère*, "that is to say of natural exchange . . . is, from the point of view of the collective being, the synthesis of the two ideas of property and community; a synthesis . . . which . . . is none other than the return of society to its primitive practices." (*Système des contradictions économiques ou philosophie de la misère, Oeuvres complètes*, 1–2 [Paris: Marcel Rivière, 1923], 410–11).

to a parodic spectacle: where the speaker pokes out only one of the beggar's eyes, the beggar pokes out both of his; where the speaker knocks out two of the beggar's teeth, the beggar knocks out four. Already in 1848, with reference to the June insurrections, Baudelaire had written: "And see how violence, turmoil, impatience and crime retard the questions rather than advance them" (*OC,* 2: 1012). Pointing to an indefinite suspension of the synthesis aimed at by revolutionary praxis rather than its permanent realization, the desperate comedy which "Assommons les pauvres!" enacts suggests that one of the manifestations of Proudhon's notion of primitive "exchange in kind" may be physical violence that ends, as the most recent revolution itself had in fact ended, neither in a true dialectical synthesis nor even in a provisional resolution of opposing forces which would be as beneficial to all parties as Proudhon hoped.[46] Although the beggar in "Assommons les pauvres!" gets a share of the speaker's purse, both he and the speaker come away badly injured, and the future is no more secure for either of them than it was before their bloody encounter. Resolution, no resolution, a "wrong" solution (beating down the poor),—all these are coterminous at the text's conclusion.

The reader of *Le spleen de Paris* is not bound, in Baudelaire's words, "on the thread of an interminable and superfluous plot." As a collection, it allows for multiple entrances and exits, combinations and recombinations of texts such as the dialectical relation I have (re)constructed among "Le joujou du pauvre," "Les yeux des pauvres," and "Assommons les pauvres!" *Le spleen de Paris* represents an important gesture toward what Benjamin has referred to in "The Author as Producer" as a "melting-down process of literary forms."[47] In Baudelaire's

46. Ironically, in light of the challenge that was to be thrown down by Baudelaire's deleted last line, Proudhon had himself come to a similar conclusion in his 1858 book, *De la justice dans la révolution et dans l'église*, a conclusion reiterated in 1863–64 in *Théorie de la propriété*. In these later works, Proudhon reverses the earlier position of *Philosophie de la misère* by repudiating Hegel's belief that thesis and antithesis were to be resolved in a third, superior term of synthesis. Not only do the two terms of the antinomy never become resolved—their fusion, Proudhon says, would be death—they are "the generating cause of movement, life, progress." To believe in a synthesis, Proudhon now says, was "an error of logic as much as of experience. . . . THE ANTINOMY DOESN'T RESOLVE ITSELF: this is the fundamental vice of the entire Hegelian philosophy. The two terms of which it is composed BALANCE themselves. . . . But a balance is not a synthesis as Hegel understood it, and as I had supposed along with him" (*Théorie de la propriété*, in *Oeuvres posthumes*, 1 [Paris: Librarie Internationale, 1866], 52–53).

47. Walter Benjamin, *Reflections*, trans. Edmund Jephcott (New York: Harcourt Brace Jovanovich, 1978), p. 231.

prose poems, this process is not without its conservative side. Pieces of the thread of the "interminable and superfluous plot" the *Petits poèmes en prose* refuses *as collection* show up unmistakably in the predominantly anecdotal structures of many of its individual texts. It is not until Rimbaud's *Une saison en enfer* that the prose poem challenges narrative, as it were, from within. What is conservative at one historical juncture, however, may be revolutionary at another. For as much as "Assommons les pauvres!" represents a critical turning away on Baudelaire's part from the revolutionary Baudelaire/Proudhon of February 1848 and "universal panaceas . . . against poverty and misery" (*OC*, 2: 1062), the text also suggests, as does the prose poem itself as form, at least a partial rejection of the "gilded words" (*OC*, 2: 1062) and contemplative aspect of French Romanticism.[48] Proudhon, Sainte-Beuve once remarked to Baudelaire, "should have been the man to whom you were least sympathetic. All these philosophers and socialists want literature to be nothing but a tool of instruction, a moralizing instrument for the people. This is a point of view radically opposed to our own" (*Cor*, 2: 568). If the ghost of Proudhon emerges, in "Assommons les pauvres!" as now the good demon of action, now the author of dubious social theories, this contradiction is suggestive of a growing ambivalence on Baudelaire's part toward Proudhon in particular and socialist theories in general in the aftermath of the failed February revolution. Despite such ambivalences, the poem's very treatment of Proudhon indicates the extent to which, contrary to what Sainte-Beuve might have expected, Proudhon continued to be for Baudelaire, as he had been in 1848, a figure to be reckoned with, as compelling in his way as the merely "prohibitive demon" of a Sainte-Beuve, the "poor Socrates" of Baudelaire's January 2, 1866, letter.

In the *Petits poèmes en prose*, the anecdotal, teleological narrative aspect of individual texts has the progressive function—at once aesthetic and political—of allowing a more radical (re)insertion of the individual subject into concrete social contexts than the verse poetry of Baudelaire's immediate predecessors and contemporaries, including Sainte-Beuve, had seemed to allow. As resolutely cohesive in its individual texts as it is fragmented as a collection, *Le spleen de Paris* marks

48. In his notes for *Le hibou philosophique*, Baudelaire mentions Gautier and Sainte-Beuve together as two writers on whom he wants to write separate articles (*OC*, 2: 50). In the first essay on Gautier, Baudelaire places Sainte-Beuve, along with Hugo and Vigny, in the first wave of French Romanticism. Together with Balzac and Auguste Barbier, Gautier represents the second wave (*OC*, 2: 110).

the persistence of organicist notions of form even as it begins to effect the break with such notions later manifest in the more radically *anti-organic* texts of a Rimbaud or a Mallarmé.[49] Commenting on Baudelaire's prose poetry, Bernard has not hesitated to speak of the "destructive effect that a philosophical, moral, didactic digression can have on the fragile alchemy of poetry."[50] Yet the very interplay of various modes of discourse manifest in Baudelaire's collection is surely one of its greatest strengths. By staging the interpenetration of such "high" and "low" discourses as those we have seen in this chapter—including the languages of poetry, prose, salesmanship, private ownership, the artist's milieu, religion, social unrest, history, philosophy, myth, philanthropy, social theory, and political confrontation; the languages as well of adults and children, men and women, rich and poor— Baudelaire's prose poetry demonstrates an acute awareness of how greatly the "fragile alchemy" of mid-nineteenth-century French Romantic poetry was, if anything, in some need of destructive effects. Of the author as producer, Benjamin asks: "Does he have suggestions for the reorientation of the novel, the play, the poem?"[51] Baudelaire's *Petits poèmes en prose* provides just such a suggestion.

49. Cf. Terdiman, *DCD,* p. 269. Describing organicism as "a product of bourgeois thought in its still-revolutionary phase," Terdiman points out its "decisively progressive role" in allowing a "theorization of the social world as constituted by contradictions."

50. Bernard, *Le poème en prose de Baudelaire,* p. 125.

51. Benjamin, "The Author as Producer," in *Reflections,* p. 238. My translation differs slightly here from that of *Reflections.* Jephcott chooses to leave the word *Umfunktionierung,* which I have translated as "reorientation," untranslated in his English version. The word means literally a transformation of function.

CHAPTER 4

Narrative, History, Verse Undone: The Prose Poetry of Rimbaud

"Mauvais sang"

The second and longest section of Rimbaud's *Une saison en enfer,* "Mauvais sang," evokes a vision of history and narrative which the sequence as a whole struggles to overcome. As an affair of "Bad Blood," Rimbaud presents history as something beyond his, and ultimately perhaps beyond man's, control. Beginning with an illusion to the Gallic ancestors from whom the speaker has inherited "blue-white eyes, a narrow skull, and clumsiness in wrestling,"[1] the narrative immediately takes on an autobiographical dimension that is at the same time inextricable from the history of a people. As numerous critics have noted, "Mauvais sang" and *Une saison en enfer* in its entirety figure not merely a personal history but also a collective one.[2] The relation of

1. Rimbaud, *Une saison en enfer,* in *Oeuvres de Rimbaud,* ed. Suzanne Bernard (Paris: Garnier, 1966), p. 213; *Rimbaud: Complete Works, Selected Letters,* trans. Wallace Fowlie (Chicago: University of Chicago Press, 1966; copyright © 1966 by the University of Chicago), p. 175. Further passages from *Une saison en enfer* and the *Illuminations* will be indicated in the text by *O* (referring to Bernard's edition) and *CW* (referring to Fowlie's translation) followed by their respective page numbers. Translations have been emended where necessary.

2. Cf. Atle Kittang, *Discours et jeu* (Grenoble: Presses Universitaires de Grenoble, 1975). Kittang (138) speaks of *Une saison en enfer* both as a text in which the problematic of the cogito and the drama of the self are emphatically situated at the center and as a *"historical* document of the first order." See also Margaret Davies, *"Une saison en enfer"* *d'Arthur Rimbaud* (Paris: Archives des Lettres Modernes, 1975), C. A. Hackett, *Rimbaud, A*

these two histories is rendered complex, ambivalent, and problematic, however, by the narrative's oscillation between an intertwining and a dissociation of the speaker's personal genealogy and private condition with that of man generally. Already in the first paragraph, the speaker makes gestures in both directions, aligning himself with his ancestors ("My clothes are as barbaric as theirs") but also differentiating himself from them ("But I don't butter my hair") (*O*, 213; *CW*, 175).[3]

Rimbaud's intermingling of individual and collective history is accomplished in part, as C. A. Hackett has pointed out, through the frequent juxtaposition and alternation of impersonal, epigrammatic statements with predominantly personal utterances.[4] Thus, in the fourth paragraph of "Mauvais sang," the first three sentences move from the individualizing first-personal singular to the collectivizing third-person plural to the third-person singular definite article characteristic of epigrammatic discourse: "I loathe all trades [*J'ai horreur de tous les métiers*]. All of them, foremen and workmen, are base peasants [*paysans, ignobles*]. The writer's hand is no better than the ploughman's." These lines suggest simultaneously a rapprochement and equation of the speaker's personal life as a writer with the life of the society he scorns ("*La main à plume vaut la main à charrue*"), and a distancing and differentiation between them. Horrified at the idea of devoting his life to manual labor, and as a consequence holding himself apart from the mass of men, he nevertheless cannot claim to be more in possession of his own life than they ("I will never possess my hand"). Although the speaker has apparently managed to live from his writing, he feels himself to be largely controlled by, rather than in control of, language: "But who made my tongue so perfidious that it has guided and preserved my sloth up until now?" (*Mais! qui a fait ma langue perfide tellement, qu'elle ait guidé et sauvegardé jusqu'ici ma paresse?*). Rimbaud's famous comment in his letter to Georges Izambard during the period of the Commune (May 13, 1871)—"It's wrong to say: I think. One should say: I am thought" (*C'est faux de dire: Je pense. On devrait dire: On*

Critical Introduction (Cambridge: Cambridge University Press, 1981), and Edward Ahearn's recent comparative study, *Rimbaud: Visions and Habitations* (Berkeley: University of California Press, 1983).

3. For discussions of this typically Rimbaldian practice of affirmation and negation, assertion followed by immediate qualification, see Davis, "*Une saison en enfer*" *d'Arthur Rimbaud*, and Renée Hubert's "The Use of Reversals in Rimbaud's *Illuminations*," *L'esprit créateur* 9, no. 1 (Spring 1969), pp. 9–18.

4. Hackett, *A Critical Introduction*, p. 91.

me pense) (*O.* 343; *CW,* 303)—resonates in these lines from "Mauvais sang" in the speaker's suggestion that history makes us more than we make it and that it is less correct to say "I write" than "I am written."

Although section 1 of "Mauvais sang" begins with apparent allusions to the hunting tribes of man's prehistory ("barbaric. . . . The Gauls were flayers of animals and the most inept scorchers of grass in their time"), and ends by mentioning the French Revolution's Declaration of the Rights of Man, its formal and thematic structure is too complicated to suggest a simple historical/narrative progress from a barbaric past into a civilized present. In fact, by claiming to have inherited "all the vices" of his inglorious ancestors, the speaker suggests that, at least insofar as he is the present embodiment of ancestral tendencies, the barbaric past continues to manifest itself in the not so civilized present. Having hyperbolically stated his affinities to all members of the human "family" at the conclusion of section 1 ("I know every family in Europe. . . . families like my own"), the speaker in section 2 immediately jumps to the other extreme, denying completely any continuity between his own personal genealogy and that of the French people: "If only I had ancestors at some point in the history of France!/No! no antecedent." What before had appeared to be an identity between the speaker and his ancestors, his past and his present, is now imaged as difference, with the speaker's identity dislocated among various places and times: "As a serf I would have made the journey to the Holy Land. In my mind I have roads. . . . I, a leper, am seated. . . . Later, as a mercenary, I would have bivouacked under German nights" (*O,* 214; *CW,* 175).

Discontinuity is figured above all in section 2 through the projection of a split between a Christian past and a secularized present. Recalling the history of France as that of the "eldest daughter of the Church" (*O,* 213; *CW,* 175), the speaker expresses his sense of alienation from Christianity even as he acknowledges his inability to see himself apart from it. And where the speaker in section 1 had claimed familial ties all over Europe, in section 2 he completely denies any such ties: "I don't remember farther back than this land and Christianity. I shall never have enough of seeing myself in that past. But always alone. Without a family. Yes, what was the language I spoke?" (*O,* 214; *CW,* 177). As these lines demonstrate, the question of language—raised in section 1 in conjunction with pagan/secular concerns such as luxury, the speaker's horror at all kinds of physical and mental labor, laziness, and the "manual century" (*siècle à mains*)—is raised again in section 2 in conjunction with France's Christian past. Oscillating between two social languages or modes of discourse, one Christian, belonging primarily to the past, the other a secular, scientific, and political hodgepodge of the present ("the people, as they say; reason, the nation, and science"), the speaker's relationship to past and present is paradoxical if not simply contradictory. Having declared his inability to see himself other than in a properly Christian past, the speaker turns this completely around in the next paragraph by identifying himself exclusively with the present: "What was I in the last century? I recognize myself only today."

In effect, the text makes it impossible to separate modes of discourse, past and present, neatly from one another, for the past of Christianity continues into the present of science and progress. The latter may represent "the *new* nobility" (my emphasis), but as such it may also be considered the modern secularized extension of an essentially Christian vision: "It is the vision of numbers. We are moving toward the *Spirit*." If the dominant discourse of the present is that of science and progress, and if this mode of discourse is easily assimilable to the dominance of Christian discourse in the past, the third most prominent mode of discourse in "Mauvais sang," which may be called primitive or pagan, proves more resistant, leading at the end of section 2 to a momentary refusal of any discourse whatever: " . . . not knowing how to explain this without using pagan words, I prefer to be silent." If in section 2 what seemed at first to be a stark opposition—Christianity/science—reveals itself eventually as a relation of hidden continuity or interpenetration (a oneness of spirit), the first paragraph of section 3 reveals a similar relation. In these opening lines, the previous section's apparent opposition between Christian/scientific modes of discourse, on the one hand, and "pagan words" on the other, is itself complicated by a juxtaposition of pagan with spirit: "The pagan blood comes back. The Spirit is near" (*O*, 215; *CW*, 177). At first, this juxtaposition seems to suggest that a return of the more distant pagan past will bring with it a return of the Christian past as well. As subsequent lines indicate, however, such a coincidence of the pagan and the Christian fails to take place: "Why doesn't Christ help me by giving my soul nobility and freedom? Alas! the Gospel has gone by!" (*O*, 214; *CW*, 177). Although the newly paganized speaker awaits God gluttonously (*avec gourmandise*), his salvation is indefinitely postponed: "I am of an inferior race from all eternity."

The following paragraph accentuates the sense of a dissolution and dislocation of the self and of history and narrative previously figured in section 2:

Me voici sur la plage armoricaine. Que les villes s'allument dans le soir. Ma journée est faite; je quitte l'Europe. . . . les climats perdus me tanneront. . . . boire des liqueurs fortes . . . —comme faisaient ces chers ancêtres autour des feux.

Je reviendrai . . . on me jugera d'une race forte.

[Here I am on the shore of Brittany. Let the cities light up in the evening. My day is done. I am leaving Europe. . . . lost climates will tan me. . . . I will drink alcohol . . . —just as my dear ancestors did around their fires.

I will come back. . . . they will think I am from a strong race.] (*O*, 215; *CW*, 177)

Like the speaker of Apollinaire's "Zone," Rimbaud's narrator finds himself first in one place, then another. The rapidity with which verbs referring to past, present, and future pile up on one another in the above section, as elsewhere in "Mauvais sang" and *Une saison en enfer*, suggests the extent of difference between the techniques of Rimbaud's prose poetry and those of his most illustrious predecessor in the genre. Where Baudelaire had used the prose poem as a medium for the description of modern life, "drawing a disagreeable moral from each object,"[5] Rimbaud closes the brief introductory text of *Une saison en enfer* preceding "Mauvais sang" by speaking of the "absence of descriptive or discursive faculties" (*O*, 213; *CW*, 175) so characteristic of his own prose-poetic project. Rimbaud subjects the relatively conventional strategies of description and anecdotal narration which still figure prominently in the individual prose poems of *Le spleen de Paris* to severe fragmentation on all levels of the text.

Fragmentation of form in "Mauvais sang" and *Une saison en enfer* generally corresponds to the sequence's thematic emphasis on the collapse of faith in the old Christian order and discourse and the problem of constructing a new order, and an alternative mode of discourse, in an increasingly secular, materialist world. The great chain of being which, according to Christian theology, links all things in a vertical set of relations to God, corresponds on a syntactical level to the hierarchical, logical ordering of words into sentences, sentences into paragraphs, and paragraphs into extended narratives. In Rimbaud's prose poetry, by contrast, it is as if the links in this great chain of being, and with them the logical transitions we associate with coherent narration, have been severed, so that horizontal relations of mere contiguity exist

5. Letter to Sainte-Beuve, January 15, 1866, *Correspondance*, 2, ed. Claude Pichois (Paris: Gallimard, 1973), 2:583.

where there was once a single vertical thread of hierarchically ordered parts. Although Baudelaire's prose poetry offered a strong critique of received forms of lyric poetry in mid-nineteenth-century France both through its rejection of the equation of poetry with rhymed, metrical verse and its inclusion of social motifs previously considered too prosaic to be brought into a poem, the order of French prose is not itself challenged in a particularly radical way, as we have seen, *within* the individual texts of the *Petits poèmes en prose* (the coherence of the collection as a whole is another matter). Rimbaud's prose poetry represents, by contrast, a rejection not only of received verse forms—a rejection we will examine more closely in connection with "Alchimie du verbe"—but a radical departure from received prose forms as well. By means of this double rejection, Rimbaud's text offers a paradigmatic example of that "fantasy projection of total withdrawal from the orbit of the dominant" which Richard Terdiman has termed "de/citation."[6]

Although this fantasy manifests itself both thematically and formally, the text's formal struggle against the dominant is certainly its most innovative and powerful feature. Besides yielding a prose of strikingly poetic qualities, emphasizing specific verbal constellations more than logical connections, Rimbaud's narrative strategy figures, in the very deprivation of its syntactic liaisons, a fragmented world of dialogical struggle where the dominant manifests itself in Christian and secular discourses alike. Contextually situated as they are in the age of the Commune, Rimbaud's prose poems have the important function of displaying the intense dialogical struggle among these dominant discourses even as they show the actual complicity of these competing discourses in blocking the possibility of alternative discursive and social formations.[7] As his May 13, 1871, letter to Izambard again suggests,

6. Terdiman, *Discourse/Counter-Discourse,* p. 70; hereafter cited as *DCD*. With its various "techniques for the mimesis of dominant discourse and practice" (197), the related phenomenon Terdiman calls "re/citation" clearly plays a major role in Rimbaud's de/citational gesture. In "Alchimie du verbe," as we shall see, Rimbaud radicalizes the strategy of re/citation by using it to distance himself from the conventional verse forms that up to that time had dominated his *own* poetic practice. The importance of re/citation to the prose poem generally may be seen in part in the consistent preoccupation with clichés Rimbaud's work shares with that of Baudelaire (see Terdiman, *DCD*, 211), Jacob, and Ponge, among others. For a concise description of Rimbaud's break with previously accepted practices of French prose, see John Porter Houston's *The Design of Rimbaud's Poetry* (New Haven: Yale University Press, 1963), pp. 246–47.

7. Cf. Terdiman, *DCD*, pp. 69–71 and 165. In the early to mid-nineteenth century, as Terdiman points out, it became possible for description alone to serve as a counter-discourse. As a result of the increasingly complex relations between counterdiscursive

Rimbaud's conception of his own role in the construction of a new order and a new discourse out of the severely fragmented discourses of the present was profoundly ambivalent: "I will be a worker: this idea holds me back when mad anger drives me toward the battle of Paris. . . . Work now?—never, never, I am on strike" (*O*, 343; *CW*, 303). In "Mauvais sang," the possibility of a new social salvation that would replace the old Christian promise of spiritual redemption receives dubious affirmation in the speaker's "I will go into politics. Saved" (*O*, 215; *CW*, 177). In the lines that follow, the speaker's skepticism toward such salvation clearly reveals itself; the perhaps wistful, yet nonetheless ironic, even sardonic affirmation of political activism of the preceding lines yields to a most ambiguous and wryly playful expression of passive solidarity: "Now I am an outcast [*maudit*, suggesting the social role of the poet and his *main à plume*]. I loathe my country [*J'ai horreur de la patrie*, recalling the speaker's earlier confession of a "horror" of all trades]. The best thing for me is a drunken sleep on the beach [*sur la grève*, echoing Rimbaud's statement in the Izambard letter quoted above that he is "on strike," *en grève*]" (*O*, 215; *CW*, 177).

Having turned in vain for help to those interrelated but still distinguishable modes of discourse we have identified as the Christian, the scientific, the pagan, and the political, the speaker in section 4 casts about frantically for clues to a way out of his sense of desperation:

On ne part pas. . . .
Allons! Le marche, le fardeau, le désert, l'ennui et la colère. . . .
—Ah! je suis tellement délaissé que j'offre à n'importe quelle divine image des élans vers la perfection.

[You cannot get away. . . .
Let's move on! The march, the burden, the desert, boredom, anger. . . .
—Ah! I'm so alone that I offer to any divine image my desires for perfection.]

(*O*, 215–16; *CW*, 177–79)

---

formations and revolutionary political movements in the latter half of the nineteenth century, however, later counterdiscourses were forced to adopt more subtle, subterranean strategies: "The change of climate after 1848 was decisive. Direct thematic, programmatic contestation produced counter-discourse only as long as the fluidity of the social formation sustained the belief that the daily history of the society was one of *authentic* competition for control of the structure of events. It was necessary to imagine at least a potential openness to the political struggle, an absence of invisible mechanisms of control restricting the exercise of popular desire to alter the system."

When these efforts, too, end with the suggestion that secular discourses promising salvation may be as misleading as Christianity itself ("Oh my abnegation, oh my marvellous charity! here on earth, however!/*De profundis Domine,* a fool I am!" [*O*, 216; *CW*, 179]), the speaker returns in sections 4 and 5 to a sense of desolation, lack of direction, and anonymity, situating his personal history against a backdrop of cold winters, homelessness, and city life. Reviving the earlier discourses of Christian and non-Christian practices, the speaker rebels against civilization's highest representatives, both religious and secular ("'Priests, teachers, masters, you are wrong'" [*O*, 216; *CW*, 179]), and rejects Christianity, Enlightenment science, and reason in favor of the pagan ("'I have never been Christian. . . . '/Yes, my eyes are closed to your light. I am a beast, a savage. But I can be saved" [*O*, 217; *CW*, 179]). This rejection is subsequently extended to include Western civilization's commercial, judicial, military, and governmental representatives as well ("Merchant . . . magistrate . . . general . . . emperor . . . "). In contrast to these "false negroes" or "false savages" (*faux nègres*), the speaker claims himself capable of being saved precisely because he is able to see himself as a *true* savage and perceive the persistence of the pagan in a nominally Christian/scientific culture. As at the conclusion of section 2, the speaker envisions the savage state as one without language: "*No more words* [Plus de mots]. . . . Yells, drum, dance, dance, dance, dance!" (*O*, 217; *CW*, 181).

In section 6, Rimbaud continues to unfold what has revealed itself unmistakably by this point in his text to be an *internal* dialogical struggle within pagan/Western civilization: "The white men are landing. The cannon! We will have to be baptized and put on clothes and work." At this point in "Mauvais sang," the discourse of Christianity is far from a means to spiritual salvation. It is, instead, a tool of social imperialism ("I have been shot in the heart by grace" [*J'ai reçu au coeur le coup de la grâce*]) that goes hand in hand with the discourses of economic exploitation, scientific rationalism, and the salvation of a select few rather than the masses:

> . . . Le sommeil dans la richesse est impossible. La richesse a toujours été bien public. L'amour divine seul octroie les clefs de la science. . . .
> . . . Vous me choisissez parmi les naufragés; ceux qui restent sont-ils pas mes amis?
> Sauvez-les!

[. . . To sleep in the midst of wealth is impossible. Wealth has always been public property. Only divine love gives over the keys of science. . . .
. . . You choose me from among the shipwrecked. Aren't those who remain my friends?
Save them!] (*O*, 218; *CW*, 181)

After all this, when the speaker says, "Reason was born in me. The world is good. I will bless life. . . . God is my strength, and I give Him praise," his words bear perhaps a closer resemblance to forced conversion than to genuine conviction. In fact, however, the text is constructed in such a way as to render this very distinction in itself problematic.

One of the great problems in reading "Mauvais sang," in the above section as elsewhere, is that it is extremely difficult if not impossible at times to determine the standpoint from which a particular utterance is being made. Indeed, there are so many shifts of perspective, so many rapid changes in verb tenses and unmediated oscillations of position and discursive modes, so many movements back and forth and affirmations followed by negations followed by affirmations and so on, that there often seems to be no firm, enduring place to stand. In the penultimate section, however, although the speaker's discursive practice continues to be elusive, it nevertheless gives evidence of a certain demystification—itself doubtless in need of further demystification—of previous positions and discursive practices in the speaker's quest for salvation:

> . . . Je ne me crois pas embarqué pour une noce avec Jésus-Christ pour beaupère.
> Je ne suis pas prisonnier de ma raison. J'ai dit: Dieu. Je veux la liberté dans le salut: comment la poursuivre? . . .je retiens ma place au sommet de cette angélique échelle de bons sens.
>
> [. . . I do not believe I have embarked on a wedding with Jesus Christ as father-in-law.
> I am not a prisoner of my reason. I said: God. I want freedom in salvation. How can I pursue it? . . . I reserve my place at the top of the angelic ladder of common sense.] (*O*, 218; *CW*, 181 and 183)

As the phrase "angelic . . . common sense" indicates, even in his apparent attempt to be reasonable about the limitations imposed on him in his quest for salvation, the speaker ends up mingling the language of reason with the language of Christianity. In the subsequent paragraph, the speaker rejects other alternatives, including domestic happiness (the "civilized" reverse of the pagan's "dance, dance, dance, dance!") and the possibility of fulfillment through work which had been rejected in section 1. In the closed space of "Mauvais sang," the discourse of labor seems to offer no more of a possibility for salvation than the discourses of Christianity, science, reason, or pagan ritual, no more hope at the end of the text than at the beginning. Life, at the end of "Mauvais sang," is merely "the farce we all play" (*la farce à mener par tous*) (*O*, 219; *CW*, 183). The best it has to offer is not personal or social progress but merely a continuation of the same ("Enough! Here is the punishment—*Forward, march!*") (*O*, 219; *CW*, 181), not happiness but merely the habits and rewards of bourgeois culture: "—I'll get used to it./That would be the French way of life, the path of honor" (*O*, 219; *CW*, 183).[8]

"Alchimie du verbe"

"Mauvais sang" is succeeded in *Une saison en enfer* by the vertiginous downward spiral into despair that is "Nuit de l'enfer" (A Night in Hell). In that section, as in the section immediately following ("Delirium I: 'The Foolish Virgin/The Infernal Bridegroom'"), despair is again associated with a crisis of narrative and of history that manifests itself in large part as competing Christian and secular discursive practices. It is in "Delirium II: 'Alchimie du verbe,'" however, that this crisis and the dominant discursive practices we have been tracing in *Une saison en*

---

8. Cf. Jean-Louis Baudry, who describes *Une saison en enfer* in his "Le texte de Rimbaud," *Tel Quel* 36 (1969), p. 35, as a "narration of all attempts made to escape the closed space of western thought and ideology." Although Baudry is certainly right to argue that within "Mauvais sang" these attempts "only manage to repeat . . . solutions inherent to the logic proper to western history," the emphasis in subsequent sections on the ongoing degradation of human labor in existing social relations suggests that the issue of escaping from the closed space of Western societies is not to be solved finally by mere reflection on Western *thought* alone. Like Baudry, Houston (*Design of Rimbaud's Poetry*, 163–64) sees "Mauvais sang" as a kind of *Une saison en enfer* in miniature. Although "Mauvais sang" does indeed offer what Houston calls a mere oscillation back and forth, no progress as such but only the "illusion of movement," *Une saison en enfer* as a whole might rather be seen as figuring what Davies has described ("*Une saison d'enfer*" *d'Arthur Rimbaud*, 107) as a complexly progressive dialectical movement that takes "one step backward before succeeding in taking its two steps forward." There is much at stake here. The question is whether Rimbaud's important critique of oversimplified linear notions of narrative and of historical progress amounts to a reductive leveling and renunciation of *all* notions of narrative and of historical progress. My own reading is that this is not the case, despite the powerful demonstration Rimbaud offers through his own literary praxis of how difficult it can be to *make* decisions.

enfer emerge most pointedly in relation to a dialogical struggle between the discourses of prose and poetry and their *suppléments* in Rimbaud's work, the urban and the pastoral. Interspersing previously written verse poems with passages in prose, "Alchimie du verbe" bids farewell to the varied devices of rhymed, metrical verse Rimbaud had mastered before turning to prose. In the introductory prose section, summing up his previous activities as mere study (*une étude*), the speaker self-mockingly displays the eccentricity of his own former taste, his romantic, youthful dreams, and his poetic pretensions. The verse poems subsequently quoted with slight variations from the original versions, all composed in May and June 1872, represent a period of activity that looks back in its poetic program to the idea of the poet as visionary formulated in Rimbaud's letters to Izambard on May 13, 1871, and to Paul Demeny on May 15 of the same year. In their open avowal both of sympathy for the Commune ("where so many workers are dying as I write to you!" [*O*, 343; *CW*, 303]) and of impatience with received verse forms, these two letters demonstrate a clear link in Rimbaud's work between revolutionary politics and revolutionary poetry.[9] Thus, in the letter to Demeny, Rimbaud's verse poem in praise of the Commune, "Chant de guerre parisien" (Parisian War Song), is immediately followed by an attack on the anachronistic association of poetry exclusively with rhymed, metrical verse:

> —Here is some prose on the future of poetry:—All ancient poetry ended in Greek Poetry, harmonious life.—From Greece to the romantic movement—Middle Ages—there are writers and versifiers. From Ennius to Theroldus, from Theroldus to Casimir Delavigne, it is all rhymed prose, a game, degradation and glory of countless idiotic generations. . . . (*O*, 345; *CW*, 305)

As the first example in "Alchimie du verbe" from his own previous work of what he immediately thereafter labels "poetic old-fashionedness" (*O*, 230; *CW*, 195), Rimbaud quotes the poem "Larme" (Tear). An important difference between the original version of the poem and that incorporated into "Alchimie du verbe" resides in the latter's use of religious images that had not previously figured in the text.[10] Together

---

9. See Enid Rhodes Peschel, *Flux and Reflux: Ambivalence in the Poems of Arthur Rimbaud* (Geneva: Librairie Droz, 1977), p. 33.

10. For a discussion of these revisions—which include "kneeling" (*à genoux*) in line 2 (formerly "crouched," *accroupi*) and "God's wind" (*Le vent de Dieu*) in line 12 (formerly "the wind, from the sky," *le vent, du ciel*)—and for interpretations of key images at the

with the poem's movement from the pastoral landscape imaged in the first line—("Far from birds, flocks and village girls . . . " [*O*, 228; *CW*, 193])—to the corrupt urban environment of the worker imaged in the biblical and pastoral language of the last two stanzas (" . . . the city/Will paint false skies./o, for those workmen, charming/Subjects of a Babylonian king. . . . /o Queen of Shepherds,/Take brandy [*l'eau-de-vie*] to the workers . . . " [*O*, 229; *CW*, 195]), these religious images suggest a problematic that is crucial to an understanding of the prose/poetry question at issue in "Alchimie du verbe" and *Une saison en enfer* as a whole, that of the relationship between religious discourse and poetry-as-verse.

The subsequent prose section's rejection of "poetic old fashioned-ness" generally and of such "poetic" images as "a mosque in place of a factory" (*O*, 228; *CW*, 193) in particular suggests again a strong connection between form and theme, a critique of verse poetry for its tendency to replace the prosaic here and now—as in the alienation of factory labor (*ouvriers, travailleurs, usine*)—with accommodating visions of fantasy and poetic/religious harmony. As Rimbaud's denunciation of "rhymed prose" in the Demeny letter implies, it was perhaps not so much verse as the harmony of rhyme, with its promise of a "second coming" of a given sound, which Rimbaud felt to be incongruous with the more prosaic realities of life up to and including the modern. For the Rimbaud of *Une saison en enfer* and the *Illuminations*, a poetry that ignored such realities or tried to cover them over with rhyme would represent a distortion of the fundamental lack of harmony in everyday life and thus a travesty of poetry's authentically utopian impulse.

The conflict between the pastoral and the urban, the poetic and the prosaic, continues to be manifest in the alternation of subsequent verse and prose passages. Where "Chanson de la plus haut tour" (Song of the Highest Tower) nostalgically remembers "the field/Given over to oblivion" (*O*, 231; *CW*, 197), the prose that follows images a quite different, urban reality, recalling the Paris Commune under General Thiers's bombardment:

> J'aimai . . . les boutiques fanées. . . . Je me traînais dans les ruelles puantes. . . .
> "Général, s'il reste un vieux canon sur tes ramparts en ruines, bombarde-nous avec des blocs de terre sèche. Aux glaces des magasins

splendides! dans les salons! Fais manger sa poussière à la ville. Oxyde les gargouilles. Emplis les boudoirs de poudre de rubis brûlante . . . "

[I loved . . . musty shops. . . .I dragged myself through stinking alleys . . .

"General, if an old cannon remains on your ruined ramparts, bombard us with lumps of dried earth. In the mirrors of luxurious stores! in parlors! Make the city eat its own dust. Oxydize the gargoyles. Fill bedrooms with the burning powder of rubies . . . "] (O, 231; CW, 197)

In the wake of the above passage, the verse poem "Faim" (Hunger) returns to a pastoral, and at the same time a religious/Christian world and discourse now perceived as being in ruins:

> Mes faims, tournez. Paissez, faims,
>   Le pré des sons.
>   .   .   .
> Mangez les cailloux qu'on brise,
> Les vieilles pierres d'églises;
> Les galets des vieux déluges,
> Pains semés dans les vallées grises.

> [Hungers of mine, move about.
> Eat the bran of the meadow.
>   .   .   .
> Eat the pebbles that are broken,
> The old stones of churches;
> The gravel of old floods,
> Bread scattered in gray valleys.]

(O, 231; WF, 197)

In the penultimate verse poem of "Alchimie du verbe," "L'éternité," the spiritual "hunger" of the preceding continues in a hopeless hope for salvation ("My eternal soul. . . ./ . . . You fly in accord with . . . /Never any hopes" [O, 232; CW, 199]) so familiar from previous sections of *Une saison en enfer*. Here, as before, any discourse of salvation, Christian or otherwise, is unreliable, though suffering is not: "Science and patience,/The suffering is sure." Significantly, where the speaker had earlier entertained hopes of a specifically Christian salvation, the speaker's desire at the conclusion of "Alchimie du verbe" is redirected toward salvation's more secular equivalent, happiness, "Le Bonheur" (O, 234; CW, 201). In the fifth paragraph of the final long prose passage, this "happiness" is itself still conceived of, however, in Christian terms: "Over the sea, which I loved as if it were washing me of a stain, I saw the consoling cross rise. I had been damned by the rainbow. Happiness was my fatality, my remorse, my worm" (*O*, 233; *CW*, 201). As these lines and the final prose passage and concluding verse poem that follow suggest, Christ, Christian salvation, happiness, and also *verse* (reading *mon ver* as a play on *mon vers*) are virtually synonymous at the conclusion of "Alchimie du verbe," all images of a lost paradise that is fatal (*ma fatalité*) in part because it is irretrievable, impossible to recover (as the title of the next section indicates) in the prosaic, urban reality of modern life and its proliferation of competing discourses. Recalling the reference to muddy red and black cities in "Mauvais sang," as well as those images of urban life in "Alchimie du verbe" more immediately preceding this reference, the speaker exclaims: "Happiness! Its tooth, sweet to death, warned me at the crowing of the cock,—*ad matutinum*, at the *Christus venit*—in the darkest cities" (*O*, 234; *CW*, 201).

At the end of the eighteenth century, for the Novalis of *Hymnen an die Nacht*, it was still possible to figure the triumph of Christianity and love over the secular, everyday world of work and individual loneliness by concluding a sequence begun in prose with a return to the harmony of rhymed, metrical verse. Although verse still functions in Novalis's sequence as a valid mode of discourse for the imaging of an alternative world, the quoted verse poems in "Alchimie du verbe" are displayed rather as impoverished discursive objects, mere examples of a stylized discourse no longer considered adequate to the task either of representing the dialogical struggles of modern life or of figuring an alternative reality.[11] In the latter half of the nineteenth century, in a world where, in Baudelaire's words, "action is not the sister of dream," both Baudelaire and Rimbaud suggest that the poet must finally ask himself if rhymed, metrical verse has not become a mystifying anachronism. Accordingly, roughly seventy years after Novalis, following the example of Baudelaire's shift from *Fleurs du mal* to the prose poems of *Le spleen de Paris*, Rimbaud rejects rhymed, metrical verse but in favor of

11. In "Irony and the 'Order of Discourse' in Flaubert" (trans. Michael Morton, *New Literary History* 13, no. 2 [Winter 1982], p. 270; cited in Terdiman, *DCD*, 211), Rainer Warning points out that citation presupposes "a break in identity in the history of the ironic subject, a break in identity that in turn reflects a situation of fundamental historical change." By relentlessly subjecting his own past poetic discourse to such an ironic "re/citation," Rimbaud anticipates the parodic stylizations characteristic of the prose poetry of Max Jacob which will be our concern in the next chapter. On irony, the dialogic, and re/citation in nineteenth-century counterdiscursive practices generally, see Terdiman, *DCD*, pp. 76–77, 197, and 211; on the closely related concept of parodic stylization, see Bakhtin, *The Dialogic Imagination*, pp. 333 and 362–65.

prose forms much more severely fragmented than those of his predecessor. Although Rimbaud shares with Novalis the notion of a future
harmony that would be in some sense a return to the past—"This
future will be materialist [*Cet avenir sera matérialiste*]. . . .Fundamentally,
it would be Greek poetry again in a way" (*O*, 348; *CW*, 309)—there is a
decisive difference between the vision of a return of Christ, harmony
and rhymed verse at the conclusion of the *Hymnen an die Nacht* and the
images of betrayal which conclude "Alchimie du verbe." In contrast to
Novalis's *Hymns*, the verse conclusion of which figures the continuing
possibility of Christian salvation, the final verse poem of Rimbaud's
text, with its allusion to Peter's denial of Christ in the Garden of Geth-
semene (*au chant du coq* [*O*, 234; *CW*, 201]), figures the absence of
Christ and of Christian salvation, a loss of happiness ending in death:

> Salut à lui, chaque fois
> Que chante le coq gaulois.
> . . .
> L'heure de sa fuite, hélas!
> Sera l'heure de trépas.
>
> [Greetings (*salvation*) to it
> ("happiness"—Le Bonheur—but also "him,"
> Christ) each time
> The Gallic cock sings.
> . . .
> The hour of its (but also,
> again, "his," Christ's)
> flight, alas!
> Will be the hour of my death.]
>
> (*O*, 234; *WF*, 201)

In the somber, prosaic reality of the modern city, the consolations
of Christianity imaged in the "old stones of churches" (*vieilles pierres
d'églises*) of "Faim" are subject to the same fate as the "poetic old-
fashionedness" (*La vieillerie poétique*) renounced earlier and exemplified
by the symmetry, regularity, and harmony of verse in the final quoted
verse poem's refrain, "O seasons, o castles!"; both seem equally out of
place, pretty ruins from a nostalgic past. Although Rimbaud shares
with Novalis a certain nostalgia for both Christian harmony and the
rhymed verse forms with which each poet associates it, in contrast to
the *Hymnen an die Nacht*, Rimbaud's "Alchimie du verbe" ends, not with

a promise of the return of Christ and of salvation but with an image of his departure and death ("The hour of his flight"). Where Novalis's *Hymns* figure the triumph of rhymed, metrical verse over prose, Rimbaud's "Alchimie du verbe" does just the reverse: "That's over. Today I can greet [but also *save*] beauty" (*Je sais aujourd'hui saluer la beauté*) (*O*, 234; *CW*, 201). In light of the desolation of contemporary life figured in the phrase "the darkest cities" (*les plus sombres villes*)—the crucial closing words of the prose passage introducing the section's final verse poem—these last lines of "Alchimie du verbe" suggest a salutory rejection of the poetic Ideal. They embrace a salutory determination to seek happiness unsentimentally in and through the discourse of prose and the prosaic present, however difficult such happiness may be to find therein, without resorting to the harmonic discourse of rhymed, metrical verse and the nostalgia of "seasons" and "castles."

"L'éclair"

In the wake of "Alchimie du verbe," in "L'impossible," Rimbaud indicates the difficulty, faced with the prosaic reality of modern life, of sustaining the myth of youth, innocence, and purity which he, like Novalis, associates with the Orient ("Yet I never thought of the pleasure of escaping from today's suffering" [*O*, 236; *CW*, 203]).[12] Unable any longer to believe in the salvation of a pure and innocent East ("It's true, I was thinking of Eden!" [*O*, 236; *CW*, 203]) or, what amounts to the same thing, in the discourse of Christianity and rhymed, metrical verse, the speaker indicates the impossibility as well of finding salvation in the West he associates with the secular discourses of commerce, reason, science, and philosophy. For all the intensity of the dialogical struggles they are locked in with one another, Christian and secular discursive practices appear to be equally unpromising: "since the declaration of science, and Christianity, man deludes himself. . . .M. Prudhomme was born with Christ" [*O*, 236; *CW*, 203]).[13] In the following

12. For a discussion of the similar role played by the Orient in Flaubert, see "Ideological Voyages: On a Flaubertian Dis-Orientation," on Terdiman, *DCD*, pp. 227–57. Terdiman describes the Orient's presence in Flaubert's work as that of "an already-canceled utopia of free and radical counter-discourse" (255). A broader analysis of the role played by the Orient in nineteenth-century Western culture is of course provided in Edward Said's *Orientalism* (New York: Random House, 1978), from which Terdiman draws extensively.

13. With his cameo appearance at this point in Rimbaud's text, Monsieur Prudhomme (Henri Monnier) assumes his accustomed role as representative above all of the conformist behavior and cliché-ridden discourse of the nineteenth century's "good bour-

section, entitled "L'éclair" (Lightning), the speaker turns, nonetheless, to the possibility of a new, secular salvation—the materialist future announced by the "modern Ecclesiastes, that is to say *Everyone*" (*O*, 238; *CW*, 205)—which can be envisioned only as a radical departure from anything offered up to the present either by Christian or secular discourses. Significantly, the first sign of illumination, and the textual point of departure in "L'éclair," is the discourse of human labor: "Work of man! [*Le travail humain!*] This is the explosion which lights up my abyss from time to time." From time to time indeed, in *Une saison en enfer*, work appears as an (im)possible alternative to hallucinatory despair: "I loathe all trades" ("Mauvais sang"); "Poor men, workers!" ("Nuit de l'enfer"); "'I shall never work'" ("Délires I: vierge folle"). Momentarily, in "L'éclair," the notion of dignified work seems to have exploded into consciousness (*mon abîme*) as a concrete and real, in other words *possible*, alternative to the speaker's earlier despair: "Nothing is vanity; science and onward!" (*O*, 238; *CW*, 205). Like the illumination of a lightning bolt, however, that of human labor is, for the time being, short-lived.

Despite indications in "L'éclair" of an advance in the speaker's position over that of previous sections, it is important to note that the secular promise momentarily drawn from the discourses of human labor, science, and material progress continues to be formulated in part in religious/Christian terms. Although the conclusion of "Alchimie du verbe" indicates a shift in emphasis away from Christian salvation itself, the *language* of such salvation continues to inform even the most secularized hopes expressed in "L'éclair," "Matin," and "Adieu."[14] Here again, as earlier in "Mauvais sang," what appears at first to be an opposition or discontinuity between the discourse of Christianity and the discourse of reason, or science, or what might be called materialist discourse ("*Cet avenir sera matérialiste*") is complicated by the use of one mode of discourse to define the other, as in the phrase quoted above where scientific progress is spoken of as "the modern Ecclesiastes." The speaker's initial confidence in the redemptive power of work is

geois" (cf. Terdiman, DCD, 128, 195, and 211). On the counterdiscursive position toward science taken up by the prose poem as one of the dominant modes of secular/bourgeois discourse, see Terdiman, *DCD*, p. 283: "The writers of the prose poem notoriously emphasized their contempt for the rationalist, analytical, manipulative discourse of science, technology, and material production which underlay the bourgeois revolution."

14. Cf. Davis, "*Une saison d'enfer*" *d'Arthur Rimbaud*, pp. 107–12 and Hackett, *A Critical Introduction*, pp. 112–19.

immediately undermined by recalling human wickedness and sloth. In the concluding sentences of the second paragraph, the demonstrative plural "*ces*" suggests to what extent the "new" salvation (human work, whose flowering at the conclusion of "Mauvais sang" had already been identified as an "old truth") and the old Christian one share a similar utopian project: "Ah! come quickly! out there, beyond the night . . . shall we miss those future eternal rewards?" (*O*, 238; *CW*, 205).

Although the materialist alternatives of science and progress and the explosive illumination mentioned in "L'éclair" as to the possibility of dignified work ("*cette minute d'éveil*") are abandoned almost as quickly as they are proposed in that particular section of *Une saison en enfer*, the latter soon reemerges as crucially important for the sequence as a whole. If such illuminations had previously been intermittent at best and the source of only fleeting consolation, the subsequent poem, "Matin," brings with it a more enduring promise. Although the first part of the poem looks back once again to a lost paradise of childhood, the speaker is thereafter finally able to declare his account of a specifically Christian hell to be at an end: "It was really hell, the old hell, the one whose gates were opened by the Son of man" (*O*, 239; *CW*, 207). With this hell now in the background, the second half of *Une saison en enfer* projects a radical break from the alienating modes of experience and discourse to which all of history (and all histories, narratives) had previously been subjected, both the personal history of the speaker and the history of humankind. As in "Alchimie du verbe" this new beginning was prefigured in the abandonment of verse for prose, here the speaker's farewell to Christianity gives way to a welcoming of the salvation of new, nonalienated forms of labor. Once again, however, the discourse of materialist salvation draws heavily on the specifically Christian discourse it would replace.

> Du même désert, à la même nuit, toujours mes yeux las se réveillent à l'étoile d'argent, toujours, sans que s'émeuvent les Rois de la vie, les trois mages, le coeur, l'âme, l'esprit. Quand irons-nous, par delà les grèves et les monts, saluer la naissance du travail nouveau, la sagesse nouvelle, la fuite des tyrans et des démons, la fin de la superstition, adorer—les premiers!—Nöel sur la terre!

> [From the same wilderness, in the same night, my tired eyes always awaken to the silver star, although the Kings of life, the three magi, the heart, the soul, and spirit, are not moved. When shall we go beyond the shores and the mountains, to salute the birth of the new work, and the new wisdom, the flight of tyrants and demons, the end of superstition, and be the first to worship Christmas on earth?] (*O*, 239; *CW*, 207)

In the final section of *Une saison en enfer*, "Adieu," the speaker turns again to images of urban life similar to those already encountered in "Mauvais sang" and "Alchimie du verbe." Like "Mauvais sang" and the prose sections of "Alchimie du verbe," and in contrast to the poetic/pastoral qualities evoked in the verse poems of the latter, "Adieu" images the city in the most prosaic of details. A place of rotten rags and rain-soaked bread, of red and black mud, of musty shops and stinking alleys, the "harbor of wretchedness . . . under a sky stained with fire and mud" (*O*, 240; *CW*, 207), the city is itself the very personification of devouring death: "She will never be done, then, that ghoul queen of a million souls and dead bodies, *and which will be judged!*" By means of the personified city, Rimbaud's text goes on with consummate irony to associate verses (*vers*) with the prosaic other they may wish to repress, the *worms* of urban sickness, anonymity, poverty and misery: "I see myself again, with my skin eaten by mud and plague, worms/verses in my hair and armpits and still bigger worms/verses in my heart [. . . *des vers plein les cheveux et les aisselles et encore de plus gros vers dans le coeur*], lying among strangers [*les inconnus*] without age, without feeling. . . I could have died there. . . It is an unbearable memory [*L'affreuse évocation*]! I despise poverty."

Following the subsequent paragraph's contrastive images of joyous nations, celebrations, and triumphs, its recollection of the affirmative vision of "Matin" ("multicolored flags in the morning breezes"), the speaker soberly resigns himself to an unlikely role: "I, I who called myself magnus or angel, exempt from all morality, I am thrown back to the earth, with a duty to find, and rough reality to embrace! Peasant!" (*O*, 240; *CW*, 209). Although the peasant had earlier embodied, in "Mauvais sang," what the speaker most scorned ("the ploughman's hand," the "manual century"), he emerges in "Adieu" in the sober, hopeful light of the text's new morning as worthy of a respect the speaker had previously not been inclined to grant him. In this sense, as a figure of the lower classes who ends up displaying an unexpected dignity, a figure as well with whom the speaker comes to feel some degree of solidarity (however ironic, ambivalent, and problematic this solidarity remains), the peasant farmer functions much the same way in Rimbaud's text as the beggar in Baudelaire's "Assommons les pauvres!" Having said farewell to the irretrievable consolations of Christian salvation and the poetic escapism of the pastoral verses in "Alchimie du verbe" ("We must be absolutely modern") (*O*, 241; *CW*, 209), having rejected as well the prosaic deathliness and harsh realities of existing city life (*la cité énorme*), Rimbaud's speaker turns to a future built on that promise of "the birth of the new work" (*la naissance du travail nouveau*) which had been prefigured by "the work of man!" (*Le travail humain!*) in "L'éclair" and which was imaged in "Matin" as "Christmas on earth" (*Nöel sur la terre*): "Let us welcome all the influxes of vigor and real tenderness. And, at dawn, armed with ardent patience, we will enter magnificent cities" (. . . *nous entrerons aux splendides villes*).

The speaker arrives at this vision of magnificent cities to come in the concluding sections of *Une saison en enfer* only as a consequence of his rejection of verse and the poetic fantasies and harmonies associated with it in "Alchimie du verbe" and his acceptance of the more sober, prosaic view of things associated both formally and thematically with prose discourse. As the speaker says at the beginning of the final section and in lines that follow: "Yes, the new hour at least is very harsh. . . ./No hymns. Hold on to what has been gained [*Point de cantiques: tenir le pas gagné*]." *Une saison en enfer* ends, as numerous critics have noted, without entirely resolving the tension between what Edward Ahearn has recently referred to as a terrible solitariness, on the one hand, and on the other hand a continuing aspiration toward collective solutions.[15] To expect that a resolution of the fundamental individual and collective problems Rimbaud's text raises might be provided by *any* poetic text—however soberly prosaic, including Rimbaud's—*before* the advent of the birth of the new nonalienated forms of labor it projects would be to expect precisely what *Une saison en enfer* itself indicates is "impossible."[16] If what is figured as *desirable* at the text's conclusion seems clear enough—a resolution of the antinomy "individual-collective" and an alternative mode of discourse that might be able to voice this resolution—what is *possible,* or rather *im*possible at the particular moment of history in which Rimbaud was writing, in the aftermath especially of the fall of the workers' government in Paris, remains for him as it does for us a vital and vexing question, a source, finally, of frustrations and complications that are not in the text's power to resolve.

15. Ahearn, *Visions and Habitations*, p. 336. In addition to Ahearn, critics who have strongly emphasized the text's lack of resolution include Houston, Kittang, and, perhaps most forcefully, Baudry. Speaking of Robert Klein's celebrated image of *Une saison en enfer* as "the flight of a fly inside a bottle," Kittang (*Discours et jeu,* 14.) rightly emphasizes that the bottle is not of Rimbaud's making but, rather, represents the historical closure of his age.

16. This is, at least, one way of explaining why the text's concluding gesture toward accepting work is possible, in Ahearn's words (*Visions and Habitations*, 347), "only through a rejection of the effort toward visionary art and in connection with a frighteningly negative evocation of the city."

One of the strengths of the conclusion of *Une saison en enfer* from the text's own decidedly political perspective is that it does not attempt to mask unresolved contradictions. Nonetheless, though painfully aware of the difficulties of either a personal or a social transformation, Rimbaud ends the text by offering a dream of possessing "truth in one soul and one body" which remains insistently utopian. This utopian vision does not offer the alternative of a separate peace. Everything in the interrelated aspects of theme and structure in *Une saison en enfer*—especially the movement between the particular and the general, the individual and the collective exemplified in the last section's "*I* can say that victory is *mine* . . . *we* will enter magnificent cities . . . " (my emphases)—suggests that the speaker views his own struggles as inextricably linked with conflicts arising from the continuing divisions that characterize modern society.[17] For all the important differences between Baudelaire and Rimbaud, both represent such divisions, including especially that split between the individual and the collective (figured in part in the relationship between individual prose poems and the collections or sequences that contain them) which is an integral part of life in "the enormous city," whether we are speaking of Baudelaire's *villes énormes* or of Rimbaud's *cité énorme*.[18]

"Solde": The Illuminations

The dialogical struggle between verse and prose and the complex movement toward a new and dignified labor figured in *Une saison en enfer* end, by way of "Alchimie du verbe" and the momentary revelation of "L'éclair," with the notion of a radical transformation that is programmatic for the texts of the *Illuminations*. Like "L'éclair," the imagistic poems of the *Illuminations* suggest that although the debris of modern civilization continually piles up around and beneath us, everything can change radically, and in an instant: "A tap with your finger on the drum releases all sounds and begins the new harmony" ("À une raison" [To (a) Reason] [*O*, 268; *CW*, 247]); "A gust of wind blows away the walls of the hearth" ("Nocturne vulgaire"; Daily Nocturne [*O*, 286; *CW*, 235]). Taken together, both *Une saison en enfer* and the *Illuminations* suggest that any radical change that is to bring about a "new harmony" must take

17. Hackett, *A Critical Introduction*, p. 119.
18. See the passage in Rimbaud's "Adieu" quoted above as well as Baudelaire's preface to the *Petits poèmes en prose* (*OC*, 1:276; hereafter cited as *OC* followed by volume and page numbers). Other prose poems demonstrating the prominence of images of the city in Rimbaud's work include "Ouvriers" (Workers), "Les ponts" (Bridges), "Ville" (City), "Villes I" (Cities I), "Villes II" (Cities II), and "Métropolitain" (Metropolitan).

as its starting point not the anachronistic consolations of Christian salvation but the secular promise of a social transformation; not the antiquated harmony of rhymed, metrical verse but the imagistic disorder of a newly fragmented prose. The constellation of narrative dislocation and image montage which characterizes Rimbaud's prose poetry reappears and repeats itself again and again throughout modernism, including the modern prose poem. One of the more critical texts of the *Illuminations* exhibiting this constellation is "Solde" (Sale), a poem that anticipates the imagistic tendencies that have since dominated much of twentieth-century poetry and at the same time self-reflexively surpasses them *avant la lettre*. Even more perhaps than the free-verse imagist lyric with which Rimbaud was also among the first to experiment in the *Illuminations*, Rimbaud's prose poetry is emblematic, with its "crowding of images into massive blocks,"[19] of modern literature generally in capitalist society:

> A vendre ce que les Juifs n'ont pas vendu, ce que noblesse ni crime n'ont goûté, ce qu'ignorent l'amour maudit et la probité infernale des masses; ce que le temps ni la science n'ont pas à reconnaître;
> Les Voix reconstituées; l'éveil fraternel de toutes les instantanées; l'occasion unique, de dégager nos sens!
> A vendre les Corps sans prix, hors de toute race, de tout monde, de tout sexe, de toute descendance! Les richesses jaillissant à chaque démarche! Solde de diamants sans contrôle!

> [For sale what the Jews have not sold, what nobility and crime have not enjoyed, what the fatal love and the infernal honesty of the masses do not know; what time and science need not recognize;
> Revived Voices; the brotherly awakening of all choral and orchestral power and their immediate application; the unique opportunity of freeing our senses!
> For sale priceless Bodies, not belonging to any known race, world, sex, progeny! Wealth rising up at each step! Sale of diamonds with no control!] (O, 293; CW, 254–55)

Itself a "diamond" crystallization, the prose poem ironically turns out not to be as easily salable as Baudelaire had hoped. On the contrary, in the years since his death it has proven among the unsalable literary objects/commodities par excellence. "It will always be useful," Baudelaire remarked, "to show . . . what labor is required by that object of luxury called poetry."[20] In "Solde," not only is a single "jewel"

19. Cf. Houston, *Design of Rimbaud's Poetry*, p. 258.
20. Baudelaire, *OC*, 2: 343–44.

up for sale, nor even the poet's own poetic program alone,[21] but the whole jewelry store of European literature; indeed, of all of Western civilization. What is on sale in "Solde" has in fact less to do with salable "objects," in the sense of sensuous, physical, concrete, and consumable goods, than with the poverty of received ideas and discourses in the late nineteenth century. This sale extends to the "immediate possession" of the "revived (reconstituted) voices" of the second paragraph as well as to the "priceless bodies" of the third. Following the split between private and public discourse evident in the first paragraph's opposition between "fatal love" and the masses, the second paragraph's sale of the "brotherly awakening of all choral and orchestral power and their immediate application" suggests the impossibility of ever repairing this split or of realizing the dream of a univocality of meaning that would be the discursive corollary of perfect harmony between the individual and the collective. Similarly, the "unique opportunity of freeing our senses" (and of liberating meaning; *l'occasion, unique, de dégager tous nos sens*) calls attention to the disparity between the singularity of a given event or utterance (*occasion* both as "chance" or "possibility" and as a "good buy") and the plurality of meanings/interpretations (*tous nos sens*) issuing from it, as well as to the fact that the existing commodity structure mediates all events, utterances, and interpretations.

Accordingly, in the fourth and fifth paragraphs, Rimbaud turns again, as in the first paragraph, to the commodification of collective as well as individual existence:

> A vendre l'anarchie pour les masses; la satisfaction irrépressible pour les amateurs supérieurs; la mort atroce pour les fidèles et les amants!
> A vendre les habitations et les migrations, sports, féeries et comforts parfaits, et le bruit, le mouvement et l'avenir qu'ils font!

> [For sale anarchy for the masses; irrepressible satisfaction for superior amateurs; terrible death for the faithful and lovers!
> For sale dwellings and migrations, sports, fantasies and perfect comfort, with the noise, movement, and future they create!] (*O*, 293; *CW*, 255)

---

21. Jacob, p. 23. In the context of a brief discussion of Rimbaud, *bijou* (jewel) is precisely the designation Max Jacob gives the prose poem; *Le cornet à dés* (Paris: Gallimard, 1945). For an illuminating analysis of "Solde" as a "liquidation" of Rimbaud's poetic program of *voyance*, see Nathaniel Wing's *Present Appearances* (University, Miss.: Romance Monographs, 1974), pp. 31–38. See also W. M. Frohock, *Rimbaud's Poetic Practice* (Cambridge: Harvard University Press, 1963).

In the sixth paragraph, as earlier in the phrase "immediate applications," Rimbaud suggests a critique of utilitarian practicality, the impoverishment of the world to what is merely useful and consumable, immediately possessable: "For sale results of mathematics and unheard-of scales of harmony. Discoveries [*trouvailles*] and unsuspected terminologies, immediate possession." As these lines indicate, even the purest forms of intellectual and artistic activity are subject to instant commodification. Even mathematics and music, activities one might think least contaminated by everyday practicality, are subject to assimilation as commodities. Poetry too, with its imagistic discoveries, is salable, as are all the supposedly ineffable secret discourses and possessions of our most private selves: "Wild and infinite leap to invisible splendor, to immaterial delights—and ravishing secrets for each vice—and terrifying gaiety for the masses." The "wild and infinite" (*Elan insensé et infini*), the "invisible," the "immaterial" (*délices insensibles*), "ravishing secrets" (*secrets affolants*)—all the interiority of the self prized not only in Rimbaud's poetic program but also by the bourgeois amid his "perfect comforts," is subjected by the existing commodity structure to a merciless exteriorization, publication, and circulation in order to serve the "terrifying gaiety" of the collective, the masses, *la foule*.

In the last paragraph, Rimbaud suggests to what extent the unraveling of the self and of language he had advocated in his May 13, 1871, letter to Izambard merely feeds into a commodity structure in which everyone, including the poet, is reduced to a traveling salesman of his own wares: "For sale bodies, voices, the tremendous, unquestionable wealth, what will never be sold. The salesmen have not reached the end of the sale! Travelers do not have to render accounts immediately!" In the world of "Solde," there is no past or future to speak of, merely an endlessly salable present stretching out like some massive bazaar to all points of the horizon. "Solde" tells us where the beauty hailed by the speaker at the conclusion of "Alchimie du verbe" ends up in the contemporary world—alongside the other poetic *trouvailles* on the commodity rack of the world of prose and of everyday life and language; even extreme manifestations of the dialogical interaction of various modes of discourse manifest in "Solde" and Rimbaud's prose poetry generally become merely additional commodities.[22] In such a reified world, a world without a visibly different past or future, there would be little point in constructing a narrative as such, with a determinate be-

22. Cf. Terdiman, *DCD*, pp. 47, 75, and 150. In the transformed conditions of the later nineteenth century, where the world itself was "rapidly becoming a continuous

ginning, middle, and end. Thus, the sentences and paragraphs of "Sol-de" are in large measure interchangeable, like the assembly-line parts of mass production.[23] There is no history in "Solde," no progress, simply a repetition of the static infinitive "for sale" (*A vendre*) and a piling up of things, ideas, images, fragments of discourse practically any one of which could be replaced by or exchanged for another. In this respect—"*l'occasion, unique, de dégager nos sens*" echoes Rimbaud's call for a "*dérèglement de tous les sens*" in the Izambard letter quoted earlier (*O, 343; CW, 303*)—"Solde" offers a prototypical example of the antiorganic structures that inform the vast majority of the texts of the *Illuminations*. Taken both individually and collectively, these texts may be said to figure the commodity structure of society itself, in which everyone and everything, including the discursive practices of poetry and literature, are subject to the laws of exchange.

"Soir Historique"

In contrast to the role of the poet as a "multiplier of progress" projected by Rimbaud in the letter to Demeny quoted earlier, the poet in "Solde" is a multiplier of images of *no* progress. Unlike "Solde," which concludes its antinarrative by indicating that the state of commodification and reification with which the poem began will continue indefinitely, "Soir historique" (Historic Evening) carries definite traces of narrative development. With its less fragmented, more smoothly flowing syntax, "Soir historique" may seem at first merely to reproduce the bourgeois' "poetic," mystified vision of a smooth evolutionary development from the past through the present and into the future. As the text progresses, however, its sequence of verbs in the present tense carries the reader toward an unsettling vision of the future as a place of apocalyptic transformation. Beginning with the arbitrariness of "On some evening" (*En quelque soir*) and the very type of the vacationing bourgeois in the "innocent tourist" who has "retired from our economic turmoil" (*le touriste naif, retiré de nos horreurs économiques*) (*O, 301; CW,*

---

market for discourses," Terdiman argues, "the object of the counter-discourses . . . was to unmask the *fetish character* of modern forms of social domination"; "as an institution, *prose itself* seemed to refer beyond the horizon of its varied specific meanings to the practices of commerce in whose service it seemed increasingly to be employed."

23. Terdiman's descriptions of the sense of "irreducible fragmentation" and "unorganic confusion" characteristic of the daily newspaper and the department store (*DCD, 125* and *237*) might also be applied here. See also (*DCD, 301–2*) his brief discussion of Mallarmés "Etalages" (Display Windows).

251), "Soir historique" establishes as its context and background the prosaic secular reality of capitalist society so effectively displayed in "Solde."

Where the speaker of "Solde" takes us on a tour of the marketplace, however, the world of prose par excellence, the innocent, naive tourist of "Soir historique" begins by escaping from this world into the pastoral, poetic realm of the artist: " . . . the hand of the master brings to life the harpsichord of the fields. They play cards at the bottom of the lake, a mirror reflecting [évocateur]. . . ." The language of art, "the harpsichord" (le clavecin), serves the naive tourist first as a diversion, more magical perhaps than a game of cards, from the "horrors" of everyday life. Beyond this, however, the artistic discourse figured here offers an "evocative/reflective mirror" in which the bourgeoisie gets back a glorified, flatteringly deceptive aristocratic image of itself: " . . . mirror reflecting queens and favorites. They have saints, veils, weavings [also "sons," fils] of harmony." The narrator gives the naive tourist—and the naive reader—all the beautiful images he could possibly desire, a virtuoso performance right down to the most romantic of clichés, the "chromatic legends in the sunset."[24] Like the "unheard-of scales of harmony" (sauts d'harmonie inouïs) of "Solde," the poetic images of the first paragraph are part and parcel of the very "economic horrors" from which the bourgeois seeks relief and distraction. To read them otherwise is to read them naively, to attribute to artistic discourse an absolute autonomy it simply does not possess. Similarly, the apparent depth art creates by a sleight-of-hand that obscures its own discursive status ("They play cards at the bottom of the lake") may be merely the optical illusion of what is in reality only a surface reflection, a "reflective mirror" in which the bourgeois likes to reassure himself of the depth of his soul and the inaccessibility of his private life to the economic sphere.

In the second paragraph, images of art are juxtaposed to images of a less poetic nature, reminders of the ongoing struggle between high and low culture and the conflictual discursive and nondiscursive forces in the prosaic world from which art may attempt to offer refuge: "He

24. Cf. Wing, Present Appearances, p. 131, and Ahearn, Visions and Habitations, p. 341. The process of "Soir historique," Wing says, is one in which "initial strangeness is identified as tediously mechanistic." Similarly, Ahearn remarks that what "at first seems exciting" in the poem's first two paragraphs turns out to be "a tissue of literary and cultural clichés." See also Kittang (Discours et jeu, 327), who speaks of "Soir historique" as imaging "a futile game conditioned by a precise social and ideological state."

shudders at the passing of hunts and hordes. Comedy trickles on to the lawn platforms. And the embarrassment of the poor and the feeble on these stupid floor plans." The dripping comedy of these lines suggests the dissolution of the bourgeois tourist's harmonious vision of the world in the face of violence and the masses. For the bourgeoisie, evidence of the continued existence of such problems in a work of art is an obstacle to the unproblematic legendary image he wishes to have of himself. For the painted image of "these stupid floor plans" (ces plans stupides)—the project(ion) of bourgeois art and its cozily domestic view of the world ("the lake," "the lawn platforms")—the continued presence of poverty begins to seem an embarrassment. Enslaved to the image he wishes to have of himself and which he wants the discourse of art faithfully to reproduce, the naive tourist envisions a glorious and reassuring present and future: "Before his slavish vision, Germany builds itself up toward the moons; Tartar deserts are lighted up. . . . Then a ballet of well-known seas and nights. . . impossible melodies." Interspersed with these images of a grandiose ability to control the course of history, however, are more troubling suggestions of continuing problems and a less than desirable future: "ancient revolutions rumble in the center of the Celestial Empire . . . a small, white, flat world . . . is going to be erected. . . . a valueless chemistry." As these lines suggest, the bourgeois deludes himself in his hopes for building a marvelous and "poetic" future because he fails to come to terms with unresolved problems that continue from the past into the present and will continue on into the future for as long as they are ignored, whether in art or in society at large. Inevitably, the only future to be constructed on a present that seeks diversion from pressing social problems rather than solutions to them will be as "pale and flat" as an artistic/poetic discourse that seeks to isolate itself from the discourses that surround and impinge upon it. Such a future will be less an expression of chromatic legends and a bright celestial empire, however, than of the dark night of a real "historic evening" from which we have yet to awaken.

In its penultimate paragraph, "Soir historique" indicates the untenability and diseased nature of the bourgeois tourist's wistful self-image: "The same middle-class magic [La même magie bourgeoise] wherever the mail train puts us down! The most elementary physicist feels it is no longer possible to undergo this personal atmosphere, a fog of physical remorse, whose very diagnosis is already a trial/affliction." With these lines, which parody the bourgeois faith in the magic of science which is itself the reverse side of the bourgeois faith in the magic of art, the text further establishes its own resistance to the temptation to give back to the bourgeoisie the flattering image it desires in the manner of the foggy *atmosphère personnelle,* the privatistic pleasure and self-indulgence commonly associated with poetic discourse. Insisting in "Soir historique" on the historical reality and conflicting discursive and nondiscursive practices beyond the legendary world of art, the world of prose beyond the world of poetry, Rimbaud suggests that by persisting in its delusions of a grand march into the future while ignoring society's unresolved problems ("the embarrassment of the poor and the feeble"), the bourgeoisie invites disaster. To go on isolating itself and perceiving the world in this way is itself an affliction to which artists have contributed by providing the naive tourist of art with the illusion of a self-contained discourse and an agreeable diversion from real, historical problems which masks authentic dialogical struggle in such a way as to transform history into legend.

In the final paragraph of "Soir historique," Rimbaud distances himself decisively from this escapist use of art, proclaiming the apocalyptic, revolutionary triumph of history over legend and thereby affirming the value of a subversive literary form such as the prose poem which refuses any longer to ignore the world of prose and its dialogical struggles merely for the sake of creating "poetic" texts:

> Non! Le moment de l'étuve, des mers enlevées, des embrasements souterrains, de la planète emportée, et des exterminations conséquentes, certitudes si peu malignement indiquées dans la Bible et par les Nornes et qu'il sera donné à l'être sérieux de surveiller—Cependant ce ne sera point un effet de légende!

> [No! The moment of the cauldron, of seas swept away, of underground conflagrations, of the planet carried off, of resulting exterminations, certainties indicated with so little maliciousness in the Bible and by the Norns which it will be the duty of a serious man to watch.— Yet it will not give the impression of a legend!] (*O,* 301; *CW,* 251)

The negation that begins this passage, and the exclamation points and dashes that set off beginning and end, stand in relation to the rest of the paragraph like two poles of awakening. What comes in between is the sleep of legend—and by implication of literature—[25] the terrible

---

25. For a paradigmatic example of Rimbaud's use of metaphors of sleep and enlightenment-as-awakening, see the conclusion to "L'impossible" (*O,* 236; *CW,* 205).

nightmare of "exterminations," a history of the planet and of man in which the discourse of Scandinavian myth (*les Nornes*) and the discourse of the Bible are placed on the same level. Poets too, as the text up to and including the last paragraph makes clear, have participated in this mythology, which it is the purpose of "Soir historique" to explode.[26] When the "deluge" or apocalypse, or in more concrete terms the revolution, comes (with its "underground conflagrations" and "resulting exterminations"), Rimbaud suggests, its impact will not be that of legend at all but of harsh reality. The final sentence strikes with the same power as the exclamation "Work of man!" in "L'eclair." Its illumination wakes us from the image, developed most forcefully in "Mauvais sang," of history as a hallucination over which we (can) have no control.

The non-place or utopia on which *Une saison en enfer* and the *Illuminations* situate themselves is that "between" the world of prose and the world of poetry, the prosaic and the poetic, what is as well as what might be, a world, in Theodor Adorno's words, "in which things would be different."[27] With Rimbaud, the prose poem is a genre of radical negation, an expression of resistance to the pseudo-fulfillment of "bourgeois magic," whether this is presented in literary form as an uncomplicated linear narrative of history-as-progress or in the harmonies of rhymed, metrical verse. By means of this double resistance, Rimbaud carries forward the dialogical project of Baudelaire's *Petits poèmes en prose* to include a critique not only of conventional forms of verse lyric but of prose narrative as well. Through their manifest display of the discursive interpenetrations we have examined in this chapter among the varied languages of history, autobiography, the writer, farm and factory labor, materialism, science, Christianity, nationalism, colonialism, reason, madness, primitive-pagan "speech," urban and pastoral discourse, prose and verse, economic exchange, the bourgeois tourist, and apocalyptic vision, Rimbaud's texts suggest the utopian aspiration for a coincidence of desire and the fulfillment of desire, paralleling that of the individual and the collective, poetry and prose. Such a coincidence is not a given but, rather, a project that has "no

26. The Gallimard edition notes that Leconte de Lisle had evoked the Nornes in *Les poèmes barbares, Rimbaud: Oeuvres complètes,* ed. Antoine Adam (Paris: Gallimard, éditions Pléiade, 1972), p. 1013. On the striking evidence "Soir historique" provides of an "inherent connection between the poetic act and historical-political realities," see Ahearn, *Visions and Habitations,* pp. 340 and 349.

27. Theodor Adorno, "Rede über Lyrik and Gesellschaft" in *Noten zur Literatur, Gesammelte Schriften,* 2 (Frankfurt: Suhrkamp, 1978), p. 52; "Lyric Poetry and Society," trans. Bruce Mayo, *Telos* 20 (Summer 1974), p. 58.

place" in contemporary society. Through its liberation of form—a liberation that figures, as Adorno has said, "what all genuinely new art seeks . . . the liberation of society"[28]—the prose poem contributes to this project. Its aesthetic, after Rimbaud, is unthinkable apart from the notion of illumination, sudden, radical, revolutionary transformation. Yet it is also an aesthetic bound up with the failure of such transformations, in the heroic but failed attempt of the Paris Commune to put an end to bourgeois prehistory, and in Rimbaud's efforts to explode its received lyrical, historical, and narrative forms *dans tous les sens*.[29]

28. Adorno, *Ästhetische Theorie*, p. 379; *Aesthetic Theory*, p. 361.

29. The coincidence "Alchimie du verbe" displays, in particular, of a symbolic enactment of the formal decision to abandon rhymed, metrical verse, on the one hand, with, on the other hand, the allusion to the merciless bombings by General Thiers in the passage quoted earlier from that same section, suggests an integral connection between the transition in Rimbaud's poetics from verse to prose and the military/political defeat of the Commune in May 1871. On the Commune's significance for Rimbaud's poetic and political aspirations, see Peschel, *Flux and Reflux*, pp. 26–27.

PART III

The Prose Poem in
the Age of Cubism

CHAPTER 5

History as Farce: (Re)Situating Max Jacob's *Cornet à dés*

> History is one big anecdote.
> —Novalis

> "One doesn't bathe twice in the same stream," said the philosopher Heraclitus. And yet, it is always the same ones who mount the street!
> —Max Jacob, *Le cornet à dés*

The Preface: Between Baudelaire and Rimbaud

Everything that exists is most definitely *situated*, as Max Jacob remarked at the beginning of his preface to *Le cornet à dés*.[1] Although this situatedness ultimately implies extra- as well as intraliterary frames of reference, a more broadly sociohistorical as well as a more narrowly discursive horizon, Jacob's intensely self-conscious aesthetic productions suggest the extent to which the historical comes into view for the writer only as it is mediated in and through his relations to other writers' discourse. Though we may wish to insist on what Terry Eagleton has called "the irreducibility of the real to discourse,"[2] including literary/aesthetic discourse, it is nevertheless clear that the real, or history, is itself situated in and by discourse, which is at the same time our

1. Max Jacob, *Le cornet à dés* (Paris: Gallimard, 1945), p. 19; *The Dice Cup: Selected Prose Poems*, ed. Michael Brownstein (New York: Sun, 1979), p. 5. Further references will be indicated in the text by *CD* and, where translations are available, by *DC* followed by page number. Quotations appear with the permission of Editions Gallimard.
2. Terry Eagleton, *Walter Benjamin, or Towards a Revolutionary Criticism* (London: Verso Edition, 1981), p. 51. Further references will be indicated in the text by *WB* followed by page number.

principal mode of access to it.[3] In this sense, as Jacob says, "man . . . is his language" (*CD*, 19; *DC*, 5).

The language of *Le cornet à dés* itself may be situated especially with reference to the two figures we have just been considering, Baudelaire and Rimbaud, and the two major tendencies of the modern prose poem they represent. Whereas Baudelaire dialogizes the verse lyric by moving it in the direction, as we have seen, of the prose narrative or anecdote, Rimbaud's work moves in the direction of a new lyric (the free verse and prose poems of the *Illuminations*) that is intimately bound up with a radical critique of narrative and of history (*l'histoire*) as uninterrupted and continuous progress (*Une saison en enfer*). Although it is tempting to see the relationship between Baudelaire and Rimbaud as a simple diachronic progression—from Baudelaire's narrative impulse and prosification of the verse lyric to Rimbaud's illuminatingly disjunctive appropriation of both verse and prose—the evidence of Jacob's work suggests the continued importance of both orientations, the impulse to construct narratives as well as the counterimpulse to deconstruct them.

Jacob's reception of previous works of prose poetry is for him a source of unmistakable anxiety. This anxiety shows itself especially in his attempts to dismiss earlier theories and practices of the prose poem and, in so doing, to establish his own claim to the genre:

> On a beaucoup écrit de poèmes en prose depuis trente ou quarante ans; je ne connais guère de poète qui ait compris de quoi il s'agissait et qui ait pu sacrifier ses ambitions d'auteur à la constitution formelle du poème en prose. La dimension n'est rien pour la beauté de l'oeuvre, sa situation et son style y sont tout. Or, je prétends que le *Cornet à dés* peut satisfaire le lecteur à ce double point de vue.

> [Many prose poems have been written in the last thirty or forty years; I hardly know of any poet who's understood what it's all about and who's known how to sacrifice his ambitions as an author to the prose poem's formal constitution. Dimension counts for nothing in the beauty of a work; its situation and its style are everything. And, I maintain that *The Dice Cup* can satisfy the reader from this double point of view.] (*CD*, 19; *DC*, 6)

Poor cousin of the novel and narrative forms generally, bastard offspring of the verse lyric, disinherited orphan of literature, the prose

---

3. Cf. Fredric Jameson, "Marxism and Historicism," *New Literary History* 11 (Autumn 1979), p. 42: "History is not . . . itself a text or master narrative, but . . . it is inaccessible to us except in textual or narrative form . . . we approach it only by way of some prior textualization or narrative (re)construction."

poem seems constantly to require legitimation. Thus, echoing
Baudelaire's concern with the prose poem's potential "to please and . . .
to amuse," Jacob asserts the capacity of his texts to "satisfy the reader";
recalling Baudelaire's statement to Arsène Houssaye that the absence
in his texts of "an interminable and superfluous plot" allows the reader
to cut wherever he pleases, Jacob invites us to read his *Cornet* "not for a
long time, but often" (*pas longtemps, mais souvent*) (*CD*, 19; *DC*, 6). Reproducing in these important respects the preface to the *Petits poèmes en
prose*, Jacob's preface to the *Cornet à dés* is deeply marked by repressions
of various kinds. Chief among these is the repression of the prose
poem's manifest history: Baudelaire did not write prose poems, nor did
Mallarmé. Rimbaud certainly did not. Aloysius Bertrand, whose name
causes less anxiety because of a greater historical distance and lesser
fame, may perhaps have "created" the genre. Like Bertrand earlier for
Baudelaire, Marcel Schwob is too slight a figure to be considered a
threat.

Repressing a *historical* definition of the prose poem, Jacob attempts
to delimit the genre according to its "formal constitution" alone. In so
doing, paradoxically, he denies the importance of "dimension," although the prose poem's characteristic brevity is in Jacob's *Cornet à dés*
itself, as throughout the history of the genre, virtually its sine qua non.[4]
Far from offering a pedigree, the smallness of the prose poem only
serves to remind us of its family resemblance to other short forms such
as prayer or meditation, the anecdote, the epigram, the fairy and folk
tale, the short story, and the verse lyric. Well aware of these resemblances, yet determined to lay claim to the prose poem and appropriate
it as his own by excluding as invalid the claims of the genre's few major
previous practitioners, Jacob playfully reproaches Schwob for writing
"short stories [*des contes*] and not poems" (*CD*, 24; *DC*, 8), dismisses
Jules Renard's texts as mere "definitions"—a term later embraced by
another writer proclaiming himself to be in the prose poem tradition,
Francis Ponge—and asserts that the prose poem "must also avoid both
Baudelairean and Mallarméan parables if it wants to distinguish itself
from the fable" as well as from "notebooks of more or less curious
impressions" (*CD*, 22–23; *DC*, 7).

The temptation manifest in Jacob's preface to hermetically seal off

---

4. "Dimension is nothing for the beauty of the work." This claim contrasts sharply
with another only a paragraph before: "it is difficult to be beautiful for long." In his
"Max Jacob and the 'Poème en prose,'" (*Modern Language Review* 51 [1956], p. 532) S. J.
Collier points out that brevity in the prose poem was for Jacob "not merely a concession
to the reader, but an essential technique."

the prose poem from other genres is not confined to the genre's own practitioners; as Suzanne Bernard's emphasis on the need for poets to avoid the potentially "destructive effect" of mixing philosophical, moral, and didactic elements in their work suggests, it is a temptation to which the genre's commentators may succumb as well. Taken together, as we have seen, the prose poetry of Baudelaire and Rimbaud is not limited in its strategic destructions to the more conventional received forms of the verse lyric. Though the prose poem may be said to have its beginnings with Baudelaire in what I have referred to as the genre's social reinscription of the lyric and in what Barbara Johnson's calls its "deconstructive reading of the poem in verse,"[5] its project does not stop here. As the evidence of Rimbaud's texts in particular indicates, the prose poem aims, finally, *dans tous les sens*, to undermine a whole system of literary/generic classifications. Rather than attempt to isolate the prose poem from other literary genres, we may more usefully consider it as an example of intense intertextuality, a potentially explosive space where various modes of discourse gather by force of negation.[6]

A work of art, Jacob says, "has value in itself and not because it can be used for confrontations with reality" (*CD,* 23; *DC,* 7). This statement betrays what is certainly one of the most perverse aspects of Jacob's use of the term *situation,* the attempt to use it to demonstrate the *uniqueness* of the "constructed object" (the poem or "art work . . . in itself"), rather than, as one might expect, the matrix of textual and contextual relations the term so strongly implies.[7] It is indeed by their *confrontations*

5. Johnson, *Défigurations du langage poétique,* p. 48.
6. In this, the prose poem suggests a heavy concentration of what J. M. Lotman calls "minus-functions." See his *Die Struktur literarischer Texte,* trans. Rolf-Dietrich Keil (Munich: Fink, 1972), pp. 143–58, 207, 267. See also Wolfgang Iser, *The Act of Reading* (London: Routledge and Kegan Paul, 1978), pp. 207–10.
7. Thus, as Macherey has said (*A Theory of Literary Production,* 93): "the critical task is not simple. . . . To know the work, we must move outside it. . . . Conjecturally, the work has its *margins,* an area of incompleteness from which we can observe its birth and production." In his "Realism and Fantasy in the Work of Max Jacob: Some Verse Poems" (*Order and Adventure in Post-romantic French Poetry,* ed. E. M. Beaumont, J. M. Cooking, and J. Cruickshank [Oxford: Basil Blackwell, 1973], p. 149), S. J. Lockerbie speaks of Jacob's desire to place the poem at a considerable remove from everyday experience as occupying a central position in his aesthetic. In "The Poetics of *Le cornet à dés,*" on the other hand (*About French Poetry from DADA to 'Tel Quel',* ed. Mary Ann Caws [Detroit: Wayne State University Press, 1974], p. 107), Renée Hubert points out with equal justification Jacob's "deliberate attempt to break down the convention whereby mystery is alien to everyday existence and akin to remoteness." Jacob shifts, Hubert says, "from intimacy to distance and back again without warning, as though to make fun in advance of aesthetic distance."

that works of art acquire value, not only with regard to "reality" but, more specifically, with regard to other literary texts and genres. As Jacob himself says: "Two works are unequally situated. . . . Raphael is above Ingres, De Vigny above Musset. Madame X is above her cousin" (*CD*, 19; *DC*, 5). We might also say: "Rimbaud is above Jacob." For, if we read Jacob's "Madame X" as an allusion to Rimbaud's famous line, "Madame**** installed a piano in the Alps" ("Après le déluge"), we begin to get an idea of the extent of Jacob's feelings of inferiority in the face of that earlier writer. At least, this is one way of explaining the vehemence of his attacks on him.[8] Rimbaud, Jacob says, has "neither style nor situation" but is, rather, "the triumph of romantic disorder," a writer whose work is to be dismissed as thoroughly as possible as an "exasperation," "the jeweler's display window . . . not the jewel" (*CD*, 22–23; *DC*, 7).

The obsessive attacks on Rimbaud in Jacob's preface suggest the extent of Jacob's efforts to free himself from the past in order to preserve that distance or "situation" for himself in the present which would establish his own originality: "The style, or will creates, that's to say separates. The situation distances. . . ." Baudelaire and Rimbaud represent a kind of Scylla and Charybdis in the tradition of the prose poem between which Jacob's sense of his own identity as a prose poet— his "sense of closure" (*la sensation du fermé*)—is most threatened. But although it is possible for Jacob to borrow certain things from Baudelaire, such as his emphasis on surprise and shock (*CD*, 22; *DC*, 7) and the notion of a more "objective" mode of the lyric ("The more active the subject, the more intense will be the emotion given by the object; therefore the work of art must be distant from the subject"), Rimbaud's "aesthetic of discontinuity" is too close to Jacob, both historically and aesthetically, for him to acknowledge openly its impact on his own work.

Thus, Jacob defines his own situation by asserting as much distance as possible between himself and his precursors. If style is considered as "the use of materials" by a given work (*CD*, 21; *DC*, 6), then the works of Baudelaire and Rimbaud are perhaps Jacob's most intractable materials. To his credit, and despite the at times almost pathological evasiveness of his 1916 preface, it must be said that in the prose poems themselves, Jacob does not ignore the past, including his most immediate

8. Suzanne Bernard sees Jacob's "exasperation" with Rimbaud as a function of the earlier writer's reputation among Jacob's contemporaries as "the master of the prose poem, and a peerless technician."

literary heritage, indeed he *confronts* it with great directness and dar-
ing. As Friedrich Schlegel wanted to know the "chemical properties" of
literary genres in order to "melt" them down into one *Universalpoesie*,
Jacob frequently sets up generic expectations in his titles only to destroy or negate them in the texts that follow.[9] The idea of such a
procedure may well be, as Jacob said, to "transplant" (*CD*, 22; *DC*, 7)
the reader into a separate world called the prose poem, a miniature
world that would be as "complete in itself" as the work of art envisioned
by Schlegel; the effect, however, as with Schlegel's fragments, is of a
collision between and among aesthetic, historical, and discursive/ge-
neric categories, a highly concentrated dialogical struggle from which
the reader must come away each time somewhat shaken, even if all the
shock produces is undecidability.[10] Displaying that emphasis on laughter, irony, humor, indeterminacy, and semantic open-endedness which
Bakhtin has described as characteristic of novelistic discourse, Jacob's
texts are also fundamentally novelistic in the Bakhtinian sense by virtue
of their parodic stylizations of other genres *as genres* (the exposition of
"the conventionality of their forms and their language"), as well as the
capacity they demonstrate for self-critique and self-parody.[11]

"Novella"

Novella. A man has found his loved one—restlessly he dares a new
sea voyage—he seeks religion without knowing it—His loved one
dies—She appears to him now in spirit as the one looked for—At home
he finds a child from her and becomes a gardener./Life aboard ship—
Strange countries—Ocean—Sky—Weather—Stars. A gardener's life.

9. Speaking of the great interest of normative definitions of the novel for the
evidence they provide of "the novel's struggle with other genres and with itself (with
other dominant and fashionable variants of the novel)," Bakhtin explicitly mentions
Schlegel's *Lucinde* (*The Dialogic Imagination*, 9). The texts of *Le cornet à dés* and the normative definition of the genre contained in Jacob's preface are of great interest in the
history of the prose poem for similar reasons.

10. This potential may also define the genre's limitations in Jacob's hands. On the
other hand, its distancing effect, like Brechtian *Verfremdung*, may have the function Jacob
expressly disdains of "provoking reflection" as well as that he desires of giving "the
feeling of the beautiful" (*l'émotion du beau*). Says Jacob: "I put thought with the trap's bait"
(*CD*, 22; *DC*, 6).

11. See Bakhtin, *The Dialogic Imagination*, pp. 5–7; for further discussion (with specific reference to the novels of Lawrence Sterne, Jean Paul, and others) of the kind of
prototypically novelistic, parodic stylization that is carried out in such a highly condensed
space in Jacob's prose poems, see also especially pp. 309, 312, and 364.

If all literary texts are in a sense "parodies of speech-acts," Eagleton
has said, "then the modernist text might be said to be a parody of a
parody" (*WB*, 125). Looking at the above text with this in mind and
without identifying its author for the moment, we may well feel undecided as to its "modernity." In the wake of over one hundred years
of prose poetry, and against the immediate background of those parodies of parodies, the texts of Jacob's *Cornet à dés,* it is tempting, again if
it were possible to approach the text without some prior knowledge as
to its "real" or historical situation, to read it as a prose poem. The text
begins with the generic classification, "Novella," yet Jacob's prose
poems have taught us to be wary of such clues. Is what follows this
designation a prose poem masquerading as a novella or is it, on the
other hand, a mere "sketch" that the author plans to "fill in" at some
later date? Or is it a condensation of a novella with all the "stuffing" left
out? An end in itself, or a means to some "higher" and more protracted
"end"? Perhaps the author simply tired of the tedium every novel(la)
carries with it and decided to give us, instead, the very *core* of an
experience, one that presents us with many of the most familiar topoi
of the Romantics and of literature in one intense moment of reading.
Brief as it is, it is nevertheless an exhaustive text, including in the space
of a mere seven lines of prose a tragic love, adventures at sea and in
exotic far-off lands, religious quest, the reappearance of the dead loved
one as pure spirit and her (re)embodiment in the form of a child who
quite "literally" and irrationally appears, like the Christ child, out of
nowhere, ending with the no-place or utopia of life as a gardener, a lost
paradise regained. As in the poems of Emily Dickinson, dashes serve to
intensify the reading experience, connecting each phrase or sentence
like the charges of an electric current. That we may prefer to read the
text as a *poem,* an "end in itself," rather than as a mere sketch or draft
for a longer work is suggested especially by the conclusion. That affection for nouns which Jacob's contemporary, Gertrude Stein, among
others, associated with poetry, fairly explodes in the conclusion—"Life
aboard ship—Strange countries—Ocean—Sky—Weather—Stars. A
gardener's life"—in a way no novel or novella could *contain.* The names
themselves, we must feel, are enough. Everything has been said. For
what could follow this cosmic naming but—silence, no place for words.

But is the writer serious? Reading from a modernist perspective (a
certain *parodic* tradition of modernism), we may be inclined not to think
so. We cannot decide to take the text's project seriously because the
solutions it offers to our problems are passé. The simplicity of a gar-

dener's life may have been an answer for Voltaire's *Candide*, but it has no place in the twentieth century (or does it?). Parodic tissue of transparent clichés?[12] Sincere offering of imaginary resolutions to real problems? It is difficult to decide which. Has Jacob written yet another text in a style, as he was wont to say, "which is not my own"? Might we not consider the whole of literature, like the text of society, of history, as being written in a style no one of us would choose could we choose differently? Of course, once we know that the text was written between 1798 and 1800 by that arch-Romantic, Novalis,[13] we may feel inclined to declare, this time with certainty, that the text can only have been written as a sketch (not "complete" in itself), just as we can only read it as a parody or caricature of itself, of the Romantics, of literature, which is to say of ourselves, our speech and our writing. We know better. We have the prose poem "behind us."

"Roman populaire"

Against the horizon of Novalis's "Novella," we may now turn to a modernist text of a similar genre, a not so distant cousin of the former: "Roman populaire" (Popular Novel).

> Je n'en ai plus pour longtemps. Il faut que je réponde au juge d'instruction pour mon ami. Où sont les clés? elles ne sont pas au bahut. Pardon, monsieur le juge, je dois chercher les clés. Les voici! et quelle situation pour le juge! Amoureux de la belle-soeur, il était près de renoncer à s'occuper de l'affaire, mais elle est venue le prier de prononcer un non-lieu et elle serait à lui. Au fond, le juge est très ennuyé de cette affaire. Il s'attarde aux détails: pourquoi tous ces dessins? Je me lance dans un véritable cours d'esthétique. Un artiste a beaucoup d'oeuvres autour de lui pour chercher des formes. Le soir tombe; le juge ne comprend pas! il parle de contrefaçons. Des amis arrivent. La femme de l'inculpé propose une promenade générale en voiture et le juge accepte espérant que l'inculpé saura s'évader. (*CD*, 180)

12. For René Plantier (*L'univers poétique de Max Jacob* [Paris: Librairie Klincksieck, 1976], pp. 474 and 220), Jacob's work has the function of suggesting that "the experience of writing is constituted on the very ground of clichés" but also that "every cliché may be liberated." Collier, by contrast, in "Max Jacob's *Le cornet à dés*" (*French Studies* 11 [1957], p. 158) sees Jacob as "avoiding the cliché—or rather, should one say, *creating new clichés*." Clearly, an important societal as well as aesthetic problem is at stake here. The determined effort evident in Baudelaire's *Petits poèmes en prose* as well as in Jacob's *Le cornet à dés* to break through clichés and create new ones symbolically enacts on the discursive level efforts in society at large to break out of reified institutions and transform social relations.

13. Novalis, *Fragmente und Studien I*, in *Schriften*, 3: 564.

[I don't have much more to say. I've got to respond to the examining magistrate on behalf of my friend. Where are the keys? They aren't in the school. Excuse me, your honor, I need to look for the keys. There they are! And what a situation for the judge! In love with the sister-in-law, he was on the verge of renouncing his part in the whole affair, but she came to plead with him to proclaim a mistrial and then she would be all his. Actually, the judge is quite annoyed by the whole affair. He dawdles over details: why all these sketches? I'm launching into a veritable course in aesthetics. An artist has many works around him from which to choose his forms. Evening falls; the judge doesn't understand! he speaks of forgeries. Some friends arrive. The wife of the accused proposes everyone go out for a spin and the judge accepts hoping the accused will know how to escape.]

Even when additional criteria are introduced, as of course they must be for the purpose of refining generic classifications, *length* remains an indispensable initial category for establishing the possible generic identity of a given literary work, for distinguishing, for example, a novel from a novella, or a novella from a short story. The same is true, as we have noted, for the modern prose poem, which has been conceived of ever since the titular designation "Petits" in Baudelaire's *Petits poèmes en prose* as a genre scarcely identifiable by anything at all if not by a certain brevity. Novalis's text shares with Jacob's "Roman populaire" a length that indicates a possible close family resemblance—at least regarding this single, indispensable trait—to the prose poem. Like Novalis's "Novella" as well, Jacob's text bears a title that suggests that it is, in a generic sense, other than what it appears to be. Although Novalis's text appears to be only the notational sketch of a novella, in terms of length it is obviously at a far extreme from this genre. The word "sketch" is not itself, however, part of Novalis's text, and to read it as such would already be an extrapolation based in large part on how *long* we conventionally expect a novella to be. What we have, then, is an apparent contradiction between the expectation of length called forth by the generic designation "Novella" and the actual length of the text following that designation. Similarly, in Jacob's "Roman populaire," the reader's first task is to figure out how so short a text could bear as its title a generic designation that normally carries with it the expectation of a much greater length.

One plausible way of understanding the apparent contradiction between the generic designation of the title and the abbreviated form of the text itself is to see the text as an example of the procedure referred to earlier—identified by Adorno as characteristically modern—whereby the genre that is polemically eliminated by a work of art is retained by its very negation. In the two cases before us, what the title generically proposes—"Novella," "Roman populaire"—is formally negated by the very brevity of the texts that follow. Such negation is possible, however, only through the preservation in both texts of other criteria common to the genres in question. Most important, both Novalis's and Jacob's texts are printed, like novellas and popular novels generally, in prose, *en bloc* rather than *en vers*. In this second dimension of form, the mode of printing, both texts affirm a resemblance negated by the formal dimension of length. Proceeding to a third category of differentiation, the mode of narration, the first words of Novalis's text suggest a "poetic" isolation and disruption of syntactic and semantic units, whereas the more habitual punctuation of Jacob's sentences—though certainly not their semantic combination—suggests the continuity of prose.

In "The Law of Genre," a text that bears directly on central questions at issue in the prose poem generally and in Jacob's texts and "Roman populaire" in particular, Derrida points out that whenever a genre announces itself, limits are drawn carrying with them implicit laws, norms, and interdictions.[14] To the extent that what Derrida calls "the law of the law of genre" involves "a principle of contamination, a law of impurity" (*LG,* 179/59), the prose poem may be regarded as a genre that knowingly plays, to borrow Derrida's phraseology, with and against the law with the aim of disrupting previously established generic order(s) (*LG,* 182/62). By means of the resemblances and differences I have traced above, I have attempted to get at the specificity of two texts whose identities clearly have less to do with the "purity" of "prose" versus "poetic" texts than with a certain *mixing* of genres indicated initially by a contra-diction between the generic naming of the texts in question and the form (especially the length) of the texts themselves. In the case of Jacob's "Roman populaire," the contradiction is made more striking by the fact that a text labeled *novel* occurs in a collection of texts which announces itself explicitly in its preface as a collection of *prose poems.* No other genre has concerned itself more intensely with such contradictions than the prose poem, the very oxymoron of its name evoking undecidability, ambivalence, irrecon-

14. Derrida, "La loi du genre," *Glyph* 7 (1980), p. 177; "The Law of Genre," *Critical Inquiry,* p. 57. Hereafter referred to as *LG* followed by page numbers of the original French and of the English translation.

cilability, the generic conflicts within literature which are a symptomatic production of class and gender conflicts in society. The prose
poem is the literary genre par excellence of contradiction, if also, by
negation, of utopia.

Like Blanchot's "La folie du jour" (The Madness of Day), the focal
point of Derrida's analysis in "The Law of Genre," Jacob's "Roman
populaire" is largely concerned with the (im)possibility of narration.
Like Blanchot's text as well, Jacob's upsets taxonomic certainties ("popular novel," "prose poem") and calls into question not only the law of
genre but also, as we shall see, the law itself (*LG*, 183–84/63). The
prose poem's dialogizing historical function of bringing together various modes of discourse into a compact, potentially explosive space
manifests itself in "Roman populaire" in a collision of aesthetic categories with what Derrida calls "the juridical code" (*LG*, 184/63). What the
law demands, as Derrida has said, is "a faithful account of events . . . a
narrative account" (*LG*, 188/68). Such an account is also, of course,
what would be generally (generically) expected of a popular novel, yet
a logical, coherent narrative is just what Jacob's "Roman populaire"
refuses to give. From the very beginning, the reader encounters obstacles to such coherence which the unfolding of the text does little to
resolve. In the first sentence, "I don't have much more to say," difficulties arise principally because of pronouns introduced in the absence of
clear referents. Unidentifiable apart from the words he speaks, is the
mysterious speaker a popular novelist, alluding back to the only context we have up to that point, the title, "Roman populaire"? Although
situated aesthetically and historically in the age of the novel and its
popularization, Jacob's speaker is on the verge of completing what he
has to say even as he begins saying it. What he is about to offer is not,
then, a popular novel at all but, rather, a prose poem, not a long text
but a short one, not the genre that announces itself in the title but the
genre that shows itself in the form and that is announced in Jacob's
preface. Is it as a result of this initial implied contradiction, the affront
to our expectation that a popular novel will approximate a certain
length at an opposite extreme from that of the prose poem, that the
authorial "I" must respond to the magistrate? Though he claims to do
so on behalf of a friend (another writer? another writer of prose poems
in the guise of popular novels or of popular novels in the guise of prose
poems?). This claim is clearly as much a self-justification and self-legitimation, the prose poem's perennial problem, as a defense on behalf of
another.

What the law demands is the whole truth, the entire story, and hence "a competent subject who knows how to piece together a story by saying 'I' and 'exactly' how things happened to him" (*LG*, 189/69). Like "La folie du jour," however, which Derrida has said is "impossible to situate within a linear order of succession, within a spatial or temporal sequentiality" (*LG*, 190/70), Jacob's "Roman populaire" begins with what already amounts to an interruption and thus precludes the possibility of giving a complete account or of entirely accounting for itself. Taking place as it does primarily in the present tense, the text offers few alibis for its construction, nor does it propose a genealogy of events or of the formation of the "I" which would tell us how we got from the unnamed "there" of the past (the privileged locus of prose narration) to the mysterious and disjunctive "here" of the present (the privileged locus of lyric poetry). In contrast to the conventional popular novel, Jacob's text disallows the very possibility of a competent, authorial subject who can account for everything, thereby negating the logic and plot development on which the genre depends for its coherence.

The first question to which the speaker of Jacob's text must respond may be read, as the text asks to be read generally, on a self-referential level: "Where are the keys?" They are not, we are told, *"au bahut"* (school slang for "grammar school," but also, more literally and concretely, cabinet, trunk, chest, press, cupboard). *Which* keys are in question, we are not told: *romans à clés*, certainly, though other possibilities may not be excluded. Grammar schools won't give you the key to writing or understanding literature. Or then again perhaps that level of education suffices for a certain kind of "popular" novel. One of the generic laws of the popular novel is that it solves its own mysteries; the reader must be provided with the keys to such a resolution and all loose ends must be bound up neatly at the end. In mock conformity with this law, the speaker of Jacob's text responds obsequiously to the law's representative: "Excuse me, your honor, I have to look for the keys." Yet his apparent dutifulness and sense of obligation to both the laws of society (*"le juge"*) and the laws of a given genre (*"roman populaire"*) are in fact more an undermining of any possible coherence than a confirmation of it: "There they are! And what a situation for the judge!" With these words, particularly the deceptively definite pronoun of *"Les voici!,"* the text offers a radical uncertainty in the guise of certainty. The keys are said to be "here" (*voici*). Yet since we as readers are not told precisely what they are keys to (understanding? the whole story?),

we are put in the same impossible situation as the judge who is supposed to pronounce an opinion without knowing what has taken place
in the past, trying a case solely on the basis of the scant, inconclusive,
self-referential *present* evidence before us. There is no outside to which
we may appeal in order to make a decision: "In love with the sister-in-
law, he was on the verge of renouncing the whole affair, but she came
to plead with him to proclaim a mistrial [or "non-event"—*prononcer un
non-lieu*] and then she would be all his." In this sentence, which, in
contrast to the preceding, offers a terse plot summary or "key," the
judge is himself implicated in what he wants to know. The law itself is
thus not, as he represents it, as neutral or impartial as it generally
claims to be but, on the contrary, intimately *interested* in the outcomes it
produces. The interests of the law themselves determine to a large
extent which outcomes are possible or likely and which are prohibited
from the outset. The law, in short, perpetuates its own interests. The
same, of course, is true for a given genre, which has its own laws, its
own prescribed boundaries that are not to be transgressed.

The "sister-in-law" is introduced, like her predecessors, "I," "my
friend," "the keys," "the judge," with no background whatsoever. No
information is given to enable us to identify her, no past to fix her
identity for us in the present. All we know about her is that she is the
object of affection of a representative of the law. As such, she has the
power to influence the law itself, to seduce the judge into declaring the
whole affair a "non-event." What "the affair" might represent is open
to speculation"—the all too conventional and tedious love affairs of the
popular novel? the public's love affair with a genre whose laws (conventions) are "on trial" in a disjunctive prose poem bearing that genre's
name as its title, "Roman populaire"? the scandalous affairs and social
transgressions that are the shared subject matter of the popular novel
and the law itself? There is no one "correct" way to read it. The title of
Jacob's collection is, after all, *Le cornet à dés*, and in such a collection, as
Derrida has said with reference to "La folie du jour," "if an assured
and guaranteed decision is impossible, this is because there is nothing
more to be done that to commit oneself, to perform, to wager, to allow
chance its chance—to take a decision that is essentially edgeless" (*LG*,
191/71).

In Jacob's text, as in Blanchot's, an account takes place which is at
the same time no account at all, a "non-event." Whoever "the sister-in-
law" is, whether she is herself married or not, the judge's desire for her

itself implies a transgression of the marital status of an in-law, an adul-
terous mixing running counter to the law he represents. That law
determines not only what sexual combinations will be allowed, a certain
purity of sexual relations (as in the monogamous relationship between
husband and wife), but also what generic combinations are permitted
in the arts, which legal (conventional) boundaries are to be honored
and which are not. Whatever "the affair" is, the judge is bored with it,
bored perhaps with the law's insistence on *not* crossing over prescribed
boundaries of conduct (or of writing), as with the marshaling of conventions of the popular novel in which everything "adds up" to a tedious, neatly resolved plot ("He dawdles over details: why all these
designs/sketches?" [*Il s'attarde aux détails: pourquoi tous ces dessins?*]) of
the kind Jacob's text does its best to avoid: "I'm launching into a veritable course in aesthetics. An artist has many works around him from
which to choose his forms." In these sentences, the "I" of Jacob's text
virtually declares itself for the first time as a writer, an artist, and an
aesthetician. Having made his case *against* the law, the binding and
(even to the representative of the law) boring conventions of a genre
like the popular novel, the speaker finds in nearing his conclusion (*Le
soir tombe*) that the judge still does not understand that the *contrefaçons*
of which he speaks, as here in the seemingly contradictory coupling of
popular novel and prose poem, are one way out of the boredom produced by trying to maintain generic purity in gender as well as liter-
ary/aesthetic relations. If a writer has many forms to choose from,
Jacob's text suggests, why must the conventional boundaries between
them necessarily be adhered to? What law prevents them, or could
prevent them, from combining?

The "I" of "Roman populaire" is nowhere identifiable as either
male or female; this chance of being both male and female permits the
speaker, in Derrida's words, "in a more than metaphorical and trans-
ferential way, to engender" (*LG,* 196/76). At any point in his text, Jacob
is able to engender something new, to give birth out of the blue to new
characters who complicate and enrich the "story": "Some friends arrive. The wife of the accused proposes everyone go out for a spin
[*propose une promenade générale en voiture*] and the judge accepts hoping
the accused will know how to escape." If in responding to the judge on
behalf of his friend the speaker is in fact, as I have suggested, engaged
in an act of self-legitimation, then she or he is in this sense one with the
accused whom the judge hopes will find a means of escape. In this

particular case, the means of escape, the *promenade générale en voiture*, is a complete invention of the text *ex nihilo* which functions simultaneously as an image of closure and of the possibility of a liberating openness, avoiding the "prison" of an ending in which, as in the conventional novel, all loose ends are tied up. The relations between the speaker, his friend, the accused, the judge, the sister-in-law, friends, and the wife of the accused remain impossible to pin down precisely, yet the very impossibility of establishing a pure identity for each which would exclude overlap with the identities of the others (as the "I" and the accused, the sister-in-law and the wife of the accused may be one and not one), opens up the generic possibilities of a *promenade générale*, a playful sexual and literary journey of discovery situated within both genre and the law of the law of genre that has lodged within itself "the *a priori* of a counter-law . . . that would confound its sense, order and reason" (*LG*, 178/57). Like "La folie du jour," "Roman populaire" and the prose poem generally may contribute to a rereading of the history of generic (taxonomic) thinking which undermines the very principles of order, reason, and accountability such thinking shares with the law in general as well as with the kind of easily resolved (and resolvable), logically coherent, smoothly transitional, every-detail-and-convention-in-itself mode of narration gener(ic)ally expected of the popular novel.

The importance of undecidability as an active structural principle in Jacob's *Cornet* is nowhere more clearly illustrated than in the poem, "Encore le roman feuilleton" (The Serial Novel Once Again), which begins, "Robert gets lost in this park" and ends, "Robert wasn't doing anything, which is better than doing evil, and this didn't prevent him from doing badly. But let's leave Robert at Chartres" (*CD*, 128).[15] To the question: "What is to be done?" Jacob's text answers: "I can't decide." To do nothing, it is said, is better than to do evil. As Jacob goes on to remark, however, doing nothing does not prevent us from doing badly. Not to decide is to decide ("But let's leave"), to resign oneself rather than to resist. Thus, the speaker in "Poème" (*CD*, 44; *DC*, 22)

---

15. Cf. Annette Thau, *Poetry and Antipoetry* (Chapel Hill: University of North Carolina Press, 1976), p. 19. By virtue of their destruction of any sense of organic unity and coherence, their emphasis on chance occurrences and random contingency, and their playful appropriation of such constituent plot elements as meeting/parting, loss/acquisition, search/discovery, and recognition/nonrecognition, Jacob's texts bear close affinities to the Greek romance as described by Bakhtin in "Forms of Time and Chronotope in the Novel" (*The Dialogic Imagination*, 95–101).

exclaims: "Erase the heads of the Imperial generals! But they are still alive! All I can do is change their hats. . . ." Elsewhere in *Cornet*, Jacob writes sadly and mockingly of a public library "without books . . . One evening the monitor told me: 'There's something new up there.' There was something new: several characters from the revolution were seated around my table. . . ." As for the possibility of radical change or transformation of revolution, the poem's title gives its ambivalent conclusion: "We saw it but it's not possible" (*Nous l'avons vu mais ce n'est pas possible*). All that is left, as the speaker of "Poème" concludes, is a diminishing aesthetic compensation, the *Ersatz* of imaginary solutions for real problems: "When the hats of the Imperial generals were put back on their heads, everything was in its place . . . calm reigned throughout the desert of art" (*Quand on eut remis les chapeaux des généraux de l'Empire, tout se trouva à son point . . . le calme régna dans le désert de l'art*).

"Poème déclamatoire"

While such key Jacobian texts as "Roman populaire" and "Encore le roman feuilleton" carry forward the strategic destruction of narrative foregrounded earlier in the prose poetry of Rimbaud's *Une saison en enfer,* the oxymoronic title of Jacob's "Poème déclamatoire" (Declamatory Poem) (*CD,* 41–42; *DC,* 20) points to the prose poem's other principal polemical target, the verse lyric, and recalls Bernard's criticism of the "digressive" aspect of Baudelaire's *Petits poèmes en prose.* In keeping with the prose poem's fundamental dialogizing role as a genre allowing for the confrontation of various modes of discourse in a compact space, "Poème déclamatoire" calls attention to the conventional opposition between lyrical brevity and narrative discursiveness with the aim of exploding this opposition.

In the prose poem dedicated to Rimbaud entitled "Poème dans un style qui n'est pas le mien" (Poem in a Style Not My Own) (*CD,* 34; *DC,* 17), a text that overlaps in important respects with "Poème déclamatoire," Jacob writes: "The Tiny Is the Enormous" (*Le miniscule, c'est l'énorme*). Exemplifying the prose poem's characteristic strategy of overturning existing hierarchical relations, this statement is followed, significantly, by a passage that sets Rimbaud's aesthetic into direct relation with the historical/political:

> . . . celui qui a conçu Napoléon comme un insecte entre deux branches d'arbre, qui lui a peint un nez trop grand à l'aquarelle, qui a

figuré sa cour avec des couleurs trop tendres, n'était-il pas plus grand
que Napoléon lui-même. . . .

[. . . he who conceived Napoleon as an insect between two branches
in a tree; who, using watercolors, painted his nose too large; who por-
trayed his court with overly-affectionate colors: was he not greater than
Napoleon himself. . . .]

In the "camera obscura" world figured in Jacob's texts,[16] where what is
small may loom quite large and the relative importance generally attributed to the aesthetic and the political are reversed, a prose poem
may be as big as a novel. Or rather, according to the principle of
dialectical reversal at work in Jacob's prose poetry, as indeed throughout the genre's history, the prose poem may be considered a major
genre, if at all, *because* and not despite its marginal, utopian place (no
place to speak of) within literary history.

In its "humble proportions," Eagleton has said, "the miniature has a
political meaning, suggesting those 'inconspicuous and sober and inexhaustible' things with which the revolution must align; it is the heterogeneous chip that slips through the ideological net; and there is even
about it a hint of the 'monad' or compacted field of forces of Benjamin's Messianic thought" (*WB*, 56). Although Eagleton's discussion of
the miniature does not have specific reference to the prose poem, it is
highly suggestive of the prose poem's aesthetic and historical function
as a symbolic formal enactment within literature of failed revolutionary
moments (1848, 1871) within society at large. In the opening lines of
"Poème déclamatoire," Jacob images the melancholy atmosphere that
has followed in the wake of such moments:

Ce n'est ni l'horreur du crépuscule blanc, ni l'aube blafarde que la
lune refuse d'éclairer, c'est la lumière triste des rêves où vous flottez
coiffés de paillettes, Républiques, Défaites, Gloires!

[It's neither the horror of the white sunset nor the sickly dawn that
the moon refuses to illuminate, but rather it is the sad light of dreams
where you float dressed in sequins, O Republics, Defeats, Glories!]

In the early years of the twentieth century, the last hundred years
might well have seemed to have passed, in a political sense, without any
revolutionary advances, as if time had stood still and the ruins of the

16. See Marx, *The German Ideology*, in *Collected Works* (New York: International Publishers, 1976), 5: 36.

French Revolution weighed more heavily than ever, in Marx's words, "like a nightmare on the brain of the living."[17] Accordingly, Jacob invokes with mock nostalgia the consummate symbol of nineteenth-century reactionism:

> Il y a un grand calme dans l'air et Napoléon écoute la musique du silence sur le plateau de Waterloo. O Lune, que tes cornes le protègent!. . . Il y a une larme sur ses joues pâles! Si intéressant est le défilé des fantômes. Salut à toi! salut! nos chevaux ont les crinières mouillées de rosée, nous sommes les cuirassiers! nos casques brillent comme des étoiles et, dans l'ombre, nos bataillons poudreux sont comme la main divine du destin. Napoléon! Napoléon! Nous sommes nés et nous sommes morts.—Chargez! chargez! fantômes! j'ordonne qu'on charge!

> [A great stillness fills the air and Napoleon is listening to the music of silence on the plain of Waterloo. O Moon, let your horns protect him! . . . So interesting are the ghosts in their procession. Greetings to you! Greetings! The manes of our horses are soaked with dew; we are the Cuirassiers! Our helmets shine like the stars, and in the darkness our dusty battalions are like the divine hand of destiny. Napoleon! Napoleon! We are born and we die.—Charge! Charge! Ghosts! I order you to charge!]

What is promised by the left hand—the revolutions of 1789, 1848, 1871—is withdrawn by the right—Napoleon, Bonaparte, Thiers. Hence, the phantomlike parade in "Poème déclamatoire" of aesthetic/romantic clichés ("sunset," "dawn," "the moon") accompanied by and *in light of* ("la lumière triste") historical/political glories and defeats. The very Romantic (utopian) idea of revolution itself is subject to the "ridicule" of Napoleon's counterrevolution, which is then canceled and ridiculed in its turn:

> La lumière ricane: les cuirassiers saluent de l'épée et ricanent; ils n'ont plus ni os, ni chair. Alors, Napoléon écoute la musique du silence et se repent, car où sont les forces que Dieu lui avait données?

> [The light sneers: the cuirassiers salute, their swords drawn, sneering; their flesh and bones are gone. So, Napoleon listens to the music of silence and repents, because where is the power that God had given him?]

In Jacob's poem to Rimbaud, Napoleon the defeated general appears, as we have seen, as the young poet's inverted Other, as great as

---

17. Marx, *The Eighteenth Brumaire of Louis Bonaparte*, in *Collected Works*, 11: 103.

Rimbaud is small, as "tiny" as Rimbaud is "enormous." Taken together, these two figures emerge in "Poème dans un style qui n'est pas le mien" and "Poème déclamatoire" as disturbing reminders of the joint aesthetic, historical, and political failures of the nineteenth century. Just when the whole situation appears at its bleakest, however, again according to the prose poem's instinct for dialectical reversal, the *farce continuelle* of history and of art is suddenly transformed in a manner recalling both Baudelaireian shock and Rimbaldian illumination:

> Mais voici un tambour! C'est enfant qui joue du tambour: sur son haut bonnet à poils, il y a un drap rouge et cet enfant-là est bien vivant: c'est la France! Ce n'est ici maintenant autour du plateau de Waterloo, dans la lumière triste des rêves où vous flottez, coiffés de paillettes, Républiques, Défaites, Gloires, ni l'horreur du crépuscule blanc, ni l'aube blafarde que la lune refuse d'éclairer.
>
> [But here is a drum! A child beating a drum: over his tall woven cap there is a red flag, this child really is alive: it is France! Now it is not across the plains of Waterloo where you float, dressed in sequins, in the sad light of dreams, O Republics, Defeats, Glories, nor the horror of the white sunset, nor the sickly dawn that the moon refuses to illuminate.]

The child who suddenly appears in this closing passage of "Poème déclamatoire" strongly suggests an allusion to Rimbaud, that child-poet who wrote: "A tap with your finger on the drum releases all sounds and begins the new harmony" (*O*, 268; *WF*, 247). Yet is what he brings with him, and what Jacob transmits to us, truly a radical transformation, as implied by the failed drum and red flag of a revolutionary France, or a mere repetition of Napoleonic ambitions (*"Ce n'est ici maintenant autour du plateau de Waterloo"*) and romantic clichés, Novalis's "Life aboard ship—Strange countries—Ocean—Sky—Weather—Stars. A gardener's life" become Jacob's "white sunset," "sickly dawn," and of course, "the moon"? Do even Rimbaud's *Illuminations*, finally, "refuse to illuminate" or "enlighten"? Jacob's "Poème déclamatoire" is as rigidly circular, marking a teleological return to the text's point of departure, as Novalis's "Novella," even more so. True, Jacob gives us the clichés of Romantic art by a double negation (*"Ce n'est ici maintenant . . . ni . . . ni . . ."*). Still, we may wonder: can even the negation of the negation rescue us from the shared nightmare of our (the reader's, Jacob's, Rimbaud's, Baudelaire's) historical and aesthetic *situation?*

If artistic events and personnages occur, as Marx said of historical ones, "twice . . . the first time as tragedy, the second time as farce,"[18] then Jacob's situation is to a large extent that of a farcical Rimbaud. His *tragedy*, as the attitude expressed toward his illustrious predecessor in the preface to *Cornet à dés* suggests, is that he himself perceived as much. Yet although Jacob's personal, aesthetic, and historical situation, not unlike that of Rimbaud, was one of devastating defeat, he displayed this situation in his prose poems with a courageous humor that contrasts markedly with the more embittered tone of Rimbaud's own statement in *Une saison en enfer* that life is a "farce we all play" (*la farce à mener par tous*).[19] Farcical as it may sometimes seem, history nevertheless remains the "afterlife," in Eagleton's words, "of a continuous tragedy, in which, as with the afterlife of the artifact, we have a revolutionary chance to redeem the past by imbuing it through political action with retroactive meaning and value" (*WB*, 101). The aesthetic, like the miniature, has its political meaning. In Jacob's *Cornet à dés*, this meaning is characteristically proffered, as we have seen, by *negation:* "The tiny is the enormous." What better ironic homage to the heroic era of the prose poem in the nineteenth century, to Baudelaire and Rimbaud, as well as to that "slight" figure of the literary canon of the twentieth who tragically fought for the genre's *legitimation*, that assimilation which Jacob knew was to be resisted, yet which neither he, nor the prose poem, could resist?[20]

18. Ibid.

19. Writing in his *Max Jacob and the Poetics of Cubism* (Baltimore: Johns Hopkins University Press, 1971) of the "preoccupation" Jacob shared with other cubists for "proletarian values," Gerald Kamber has remarked (49): "The most intense and determined subversion of all is that of bourgeois social values, or . . . of all received collective values. In an epoch that had recently witnessed the ultimate triumph of the bourgeoisie . . . the chief practitioners of cubism lived in ostentatious indigence . . . Max Jacob and the other cubists were notably, fantastically, and laughably inept at money making."

20. See Collier, "Max Jacob and the 'Poème en prose,'" p. 526: "The *poème en prose* now stands alone as probably the most treacherous of all literary forms . . . The prose-poet must walk a precarious tightrope: a false step and he falls into the prosaic; a moment of hesitation . . . and he must . . . amuse . . . with a cheap display of card tricks." Having even less of an audience than other "serious" literary genres, the prose poem has become, Collier says, "a connoisseur's piece, its wider appeal diminishing in proportion to its rise as an esoteric art-form." With the prose poems of a Mallarmé or a Jacob, the prose poem has clearly come a long way from Baudlaire's relative democratization of the verse lyric.

CHAPTER 6

The Violence of Things: The Politics of Gertrude Stein's *Tender Buttons*

Critical responses to *Tender Buttons* have tended to focus on either its form or its content, its technical and stylistic innovations or its meanings, its sense or its nonsense. The vitality of Gertrude Stein's texts surely resides, however, in the interplay of these rather than their mutual exclusion. The willingness apparent in a number of commentaries to give up rather quickly on the sequence's extraordinarily difficult semantic dimension, in particular, has tended not only to leave largely untapped one important aspect of the text's potential pleasure but also to leave unexamined an intense appeal in the text which is to a certain extent concealed, although this concealment is itself at times, as William Gass has pointed out, "excessively discreet" and "overclued."[1] Yielding to the text's putative "openness," such commentaries fail to heed its call to *resistance;* rejecting the risks of close interpretation, they miss the possibility of a convincing critical intervention.[2] Given that the

1. William Gass, "Gertrude Stein and the Geography of the Sentence," *The World within the Word* (New York: Alfred A. Knopf, 1971), pp. 87 and 89.
2. Studies that convincingly argue the importance of *Tender Buttons* by close examinations of its semantic possibilities include, in addition to that of Gass, Robert Bridgman, *Gertrude Stein in Pieces* (New York: Oxford University Press, 1970) and Pamela Hadas, "Spreading the Difference: One Way to Read Gertrude Stein's *Tender Buttons,*" *Twentieth Century Literature* 24, no. 1 (1978). Less semantically oriented studies include John M. Brinnin, *The Third Rose: Gertrude Stein and Her World* (1959; reprint, Gloucester, Mass.: Smith, 1968); Michael J. Hoffman, *The Development of Abstractionism in the Writings of Gertrude Stein* (Philadelphia: University of Pennsylvania Press, 1965); Donald Sutherland,

meaning of a word is none other, as Ludwig Wittgenstein says, than its use in the language, to ignore a text's semantics is also to neglect its potential uses.[3] To disregard or undervalue the semantic dimension of *Tender Buttons,* in particular, is above all to risk foreclosing its considerable political urgency. In order to reactivate this sense of urgency in Stein's text and restore as far as possible its potential political force, the reading I shall offer in this chapter will therefore consider especially the semantic inferences of both its content and its form.

What Adorno has said of the relation between form and content generally is of particular relevance to Stein's text:

> While in art formal characteristics must not be interpreted in directly political terms, they do have substantive implications (*inhaltliche Implikate*) including political ones. All genuinely new art seeks the liberation of society, for form—the aesthetic complex of particulars—represents the relation that the work of art has to society. No wonder that the liberation of form is anathema to the status quo.[4]

Literary texts, like all utterances, have their contexts, and *Tender Buttons* responds to its context with extraordinary force, even violence. If Stein is to be saved from remaining, or further becoming, a mere curio of literary history, the political nature of her work needs to receive its due emphasis. Such a task, to which especially Gass and, more recently, Marianne De Koven have already contributed significantly,[5] appears particularly necessary given the relative lack of politically oriented writ-

---

Gertrude Stein (Westport, Conn.: Greenwood Press, 1971); and Norman Weinstein, *Gertrude Stein and the Literature of Modern Consciousness* (New York: Frederick Ungar, 1970). Allegra Stewart's *Gertrude Stein and the Present* (Cambridge, Mass.: Harvard University Press, 1967), is another matter; for an even-handed assessment of her etymological Jungian approach to *Tender Buttons,* see Gass, *World within the Word,* pp. 85–86 and 103. Two additional studies of Stein's work which fit somewhat less neatly into the above categories also deserve mention: Majorie Perloff, "Poetry as Word System: The Art of Gertrude Stein," *The American Poetry Review* 8, no. 5 (1979), pp. 33–43, and Neil Schmitz, "Gertrude Stein as Post-Modernist: The Rhetoric of *Tender Buttons,*" *Journal of Modern Literature* 3, no. 5 (1974), pp. 1206–18. Perloff's survey of Stein's work devotes only brief attention to *Tender Buttons* in its concluding pages; Schmitz's essay discusses the text's rhetoric at some length in terms of self-referential modes of discourse. Although both Perloff and Schmitz do consider the text's semantic potential, neither addresses the sequence's political implications. Perloff emphasizes especially the text's aberrations from descriptive referentiality; Schmitz describes the text as "the telling of what happens in each successive moment of happening" (1217).

3. Ludwig Wittgenstein, *Philosophical Investigations,* trans. G. E. M. Anscombe (Oxford: Basil Blackwell, 1963), p. 43.

4. Adorno, *Ästhetische Theorie* p. 379; *Aesthetic Theory,* p. 361. Hereafter cited as *AT.*

5. Marianne De Koven, "Gertrude Stein and Modern Painting: Beyond Literary Cubism," *Contemporary Literature* 22, no. 1 (1981), pp. 81–95.

ers in the past and present of the North American (United States) literary tradition. Yet although from a political perspective Stein's aggressive feminism offers a potentially important model that is without any doubt worthy of more serious attention than it has by and large received (especially from male critics), one thing becomes increasingly clear: however radical the politics of Stein's texts in some respects, they nevertheless display contradictions and unresolved ambivalences that hinder one's ability to reclaim them as unproblematic models for feminist or other revolutionary literature. There are, as Stein's real affinities to the cubists suggest, two sides and more to practically every issue, word, object, and image, and the position of her text is most often a complication rather than a reduction of political alternatives.

Tender Buttons offers the reader both choice and change, or rather, choices and changes. "The use of this," Stein says, "is manifold."[6] Though the radical semantic "openness" of *Tender Buttons* has received repeated confirmation in Stein criticism, we may usefully ask ourselves in what ways this openness also implies closure and to what extent Stein's apparent liberation of meaning brings with it its own restrictions.[7] If few texts are more satiated or overly full of meanings than Stein's, equally few are less totalizable. Nevertheless, we may continue to be intrigued, as Pamela Hadas has put it, "by the suggestion that there is a 'story' connected with the fragments of sensibility called *Tender Buttons*."[8] Many stories are possible, many narratives and uses

6. Gertrude Stein, *Tender Buttons*, in *Selected Writings*, ed. Carl van Vechten (New York: Random House, 1962; copyright, 1945, 1946, © 1962, by Random House, Inc. Copyright 1933, 1934 by Gertrude Stein), p. 466; hereafter referred to as *SW* and quoted by permission of Random House, Inc. The following abbreviations will be used to indicate other works by Stein: *GS* for *Gertrude Stein: Writings and Lectures 1911–1945*, ed. Patricia Meyerowitz (London: Peter Owen, 1967); *HW* for *How Writing is Written*, ed. Robert B. Hass (Los Angeles: Black Sparrow Press, 1969); *N* for *Narration* (1935; reprint, Chicago: University of Chicago Press, 1969).

7. One use of Stein's text has been to consider it as, in Norman Weinstein's words (84), "a reduction of meaning . . . to nil," although in so doing Weinstein also observes, and more justly (64), that "playing with concealing semantic correspondence stands at the core of *Tender Buttons*." If it is true, as I believe it is, that the text displays an "emptying of the words contained in the 'linguistic moment'" (Weinstein, *Stein in Pieces*, 62), it may also be considered as, at the same time, "'overburdened with apprehensible content'" (Oscar Cargill, as quoted in Bridgman, *The Literature of Modern Consciousness*, 125). As Bridgman has suggested (125), it is rather that each piece has too much meaning than too little. One of the conclusions to be drawn from *Tender Buttons* (and one that Stein herself acknowledged) is that it is impossible, as Allegra Stewart has said (*Gertrude Stein and the Present*, 50), "to write words in such a fashion that meaning is absolutely absent." As Bridgman points out (481) with reference to Stein's work, "the moment any word was put down, meaning had been restricted."

8. Hadas, "Spreading the Difference," p. 61.

may be (re)constructed from the text; indeed, this manifold use is characteristic of its irreducible specificity. But then there is the question, which the text poses repeatedly, of *choice*. It is perhaps most useful, I think, to read *Tender Buttons,* as Hadas has done, *against* the grain of its discontinuity, to confine and thus even to violate, in a sense, its infinitely dense discourse, to see what can be done with it beyond wide-eyed celebration. Alongside the predominantly personal story Hadas constructs from *Tender Buttons* concerning the relationship among Gertrude, her brother Leo, and Alice B. Toklas, another narrative may be constructed that displays the urgency of certain aesthetic and socioeconomic attitudes and crises.

"Poetry and Grammar"

Coming at the end of the eighteenth century, a collection of texts such as Schlegel's *Athenäums-Fragmente* radically calls into question, as we have seen, the neoclassical emphasis on unity, continuity, and linearity. Such fragmentation, occurring in a work written near the beginning of the twentieth century, such as *Tender Buttons,* though extreme should perhaps surprise us less than the possibility of reconstructing from it a "concealed" or "latent" narrative, however severely fissured. Such a reading, which requires us to consider the text's evident fragmentation while at the same time focusing on the ideological conflicts it opens before us, may be of some use in demonstrating to what extent the text recounts a "story" (history) even when it seems not to want to do so. Of the possible stories to be retold from *Tender Buttons,* the most urgent concern intense reification, oppression, and violence. The section entitled "Objects" illustrates how these threads of meaning and narrative converge and also points to certain contradictions that the text itself does not resolve. The five texts from this section which I chosen to highlight might be described as "knots" within the "Objects" section, or perhaps I should say "knotholes," behind or through or by the aid of which we may gain insight into Stein's textual production, the ways it simultaneously conceals and reveals a historical, social, and economic matrix that we may call "Victorian," or "bourgeois/patriarchal."

On one level, *Tender Buttons* is a text about the impossibility of a private language or of any wholly private sphere or object freed and/or cut off from its sociolinguistic context. Though Stein certainly succeeds, by virtue of her extremely eccentric syntax and unexpected juxtapositions, in composing many passages of virtually impenetrable density, the fundamental elements (words) of her texts cannot entirely detach themselves from the everyday sociohistorical contexts and uses in which they are embedded. The reader who stays with *Tender Buttons* discovers there among other things what in Bakhtinian terms may be called "a sharpened dialogic relationship to the word," an acute awareness of the extent to which any word, any object, any concrete discourse or utterance is, in Bakhtin's words, "always entangled in someone else's discourse about it . . . already present with qualifications, an object of dispute . . . conceptualized and evaluated variously, inseparable from the heteroglot social appreception of it."9 One of many possible ways of getting into the intensely *social* texts of *Tender Buttons,* and one that up to the present has been only minimally utilized, is through the opposition of poetry and prose. Yet this means of access must be used with caution. In the essay "Poetry and Grammar," Stein writes: "What is poetry and if you know what poetry is what is prose" (*HW,* 123). From this first sentence on, the reader familiar with Stein knows better than to expect her to "get us somewhere" or to answer the question with other than a kind of rhetorical resignation— no question mark. There will be qualifications, decisions, and revisions we will have ample time to reverse. Oppositions will be dismantled and reconstructed. We will know and not know, decide by not deciding. Such, Stein might say, is life, and this her mimesis of it. We can do nothing given such a situation—and then again, we may *resist.* But resist what? "change"? the status quo? both at once? neither? The sense of options in Stein's text dissolves as rapidly as it proliferates.

Slang, with which *Tender Buttons* abounds, exists, Stein says, "to change the names which have been names for so long" (*HW,* 126). A great deal of Stein's work, and *Tender Buttons* in particular, might be explained with reference to two lines by Shakespeare: "What's in a name? A rose / By any other name would smell as sweet." Hence, for example, Stein's "hostility" to nouns. According to the chain of associations Stein develops in "Poetry and Grammar," *nouns* are synonymous with the petrified status of both women and poetry. *Tender Buttons* was thus an attempt, Stein said, to rid herself of nouns: ". . . in doing very short things I resolutely realized nouns and decided not to get around them but to meet them, to handle them in short to refuse them by using them and in that way my real acquaintance with poetry was begun" (*HW,* 134). If we read Shakespeare as the arch author(ity) of a certain

9. Bakhtin, *The Dialogic Imagination,* pp. 352 and 330; see also pp. 276, 278, 283, 294, and 300.

patriarchal literary tradition, one dominated, that is, by men generally and by no single author in English literature more than by Shakespeare, we can see better the polemical significance of Stein's famous phrase: "A rose is a rose is a rose is a rose." If one is not to "get around" the tradition (and there is, as Stein saw, no way around it), we may choose the path of confrontation, insistence, struggle. Stein's simple phrase marks, among other things, the struggle to tear a rose, a single woman, all women, their names, and all nouns—in short poetry—away from patriarchal control, "to meet it," to manhandle it, "to refuse . . . by using." For her own literary production, it is a matter of life or death. Shakespeare, synecdochic of the entire male tradition at its best (strongest, most tempting), has so indelibly left his mark on the word "rose" that to erase it requires extraordinary energy and emphasis. Repetition is a form of struggle. It is also a form of resignation. Using by refusing nouns, Stein's *Tender Buttons* displays a Janus-faced ambivalence in which prose and poetry, verbs and nouns, men and women cannot be dislodged from each other however hard she, and we, may try.

For Stein, there is nothing in grammar which does not also imply *genre*, that sexual difference which may be also more than difference, namely, opposition. Commas, for example, "are servile they have no life of their own they are dependent upon use and convenience and they are put there for practical purpose" (*HW*, 129). This description of the comma, which conforms to one of many stereotypes about women and suggests a "manly" disdain for them, is matched by an admiration for periods, which "did not serve you in any servile way as commas" (*HW*, 128). Verbs and periods are strong and masculine; nouns and commas, on the other hand, are feminine, infinitely manipulable and accommodating, and so worthy of our disdain: "As I say commas are servile . . . and their use is not a use" (*HW*, 129). Commas and nouns, like women and poetry, have only a servile use within society. They show no resistance or mobility such as do periods and verbs, prose and men. *Tender Buttons* is, among other things, a direct confrontation of such oppositions, which are not conceived of merely as an internal affair of grammar or language in the narrow sense. What Stein gives us is a grammar highly suggestive of social relations.

The internal relations, or politics of grammar, of language, and of literature, as of society, are characterized by an intense and undecidable ambivalence:

> Poetry is concerned with using and abusing, with losing with wanting,
> with denying with avoiding with adoring with replacing the noun. . . .
> Poetry is doing nothing but using losing refusing and pleasing and
> betraying and caressing nouns . . . you can love a name and if you love a
> name then saying that name any number of times only makes you love it
> more, more *violently* more persistently more tormentedly. (*HW*, 136)

Stein's conspicuous omission of commas in the above passage develops
her project of getting prose moving again by eliminating its weak links,
the indecisive "feminine" pauses (in contrast to the period's decisive
"masculine" pause) that stand as obstacles to the narrative force she
seeks to establish. Appropriately, since Stein explicitly associates both
commas and nouns with female passivity and poetry, the absence of
commas coincides with Stein's emphasis on getting rid of nouns as well.
As the passage suggests, however, Stein's willful suppression of com-
mas/nouns/poetry/women is simultaneously an expression of her violent love for them, as if subjecting them to the utmost restriction were
itself the necessary means to liberating them from their currently petrified status. For Stein, prose is characterized by narrative as poetry is
not. Poetry has to do with a certain vocabulary; prose does not. As
prose represents liberation, poetry suggests restriction. In *Tender Buttons*, such distinctions confront each other as mere difference, but Stein
tells us this difference "is spreading" ("A Carafe, That Is a Blind Glass"
[*SW*, 461]). When the "Objects" section draws to a close, as we shall see,
mere differences turn into opposition. As a consequence of the crises
of Stein's textual production, a violent solution offers itself which is,
however, no solution but a resistance that invites us to continue.

"Objects"

With its violent starts and stops, both within and among its brief texts,
its abrupt changes of focus at the semantic level and its ungrammatical
shocks at the syntactical level, *Tender Buttons* offers a striking display of
the production of literary texts. In few places is literature, for the
reader, more of a conspicuous consumption, a feast yet also a famine.
Replete with all the possible everyday meanings and associations we
may have with the individual words selected, its texts are at the same
time emptied of these meanings by Stein's combinations of various
words to create syntactical and semantic incompatibilities. Stein's repetition brings us everything we could want and more, though this more

may be less, as Stein tells us in the central section called "Foods," since "so little is more" (*SW*, 483). Similarly, a method is both a method and no method, as in "A Method of a Cloak": "A single climb to a line, a straight exchange to a cane, a desperate adventure and courage and a clock, all this which is a system, which has feeling, which has resignation and success, all makes an attractive black silver" (*SW*, 464). For the reader who feels more or less at a loss—and what reader would not— by the time she or he reaches this, the ninth text of the "Objects" section of *Tender Buttons*, the "Method" of its title may offer a momentary sense of relief, a hint that we might finally find out what is going on in an otherwise mystifying labyrinth of words. To this response, however, another more unsettling one must quickly follow. Methods can be reassuring. They may provide us with a way of getting a handle on a thing, a way of making "abstract" sense of "concrete" phenomena. A method is a way of rationalizing, of drawing and holding things together. Offering a reduction of reality to manageable proportions, methods may also have a tendency to linearity, even transcendence—"A single climb to a line." In contrast to the horizontal leveling of metonymic relations based on sheer contiguity, a method may imply vertical hierarchization, metaphorical unity in diversity, as in "all this which is a system," a *poetic* (but also philosophical) quality, "which has feeling."

Tender Buttons has been called "a book of object definitions without description,"[10] yet it is not difficult to see description in "A Method of a Cloak"—the chic styling of "A single line," the "cane" as accessory, the ensemble "all makes an attractive black silver." The description here, Donald Sutherland has said,

> is of course not what everyone knows about cloaks or expects of them generally but what was actually experienced in looking directly at one once, the style of the lines and folds felt as a distinct impression—their dash and regularity at once. In this poem at least one can reconstruct closely enough what the original experience was like. The "cloak" may be a metaphor for regularity of interval in the folds, but otherwise the ordinary meaning of each word is enough to re-create the experience about as sharply as any experience of the kind can be re-created in words.[11]

10. Weinstein, *The Literature of Modern Consciousness*, p. 59.
11. Sutherland, *Gertrude Stein*, p. 75.

Sutherland's gloss reveals the text's relative accessibility to a fairly traditional kind of visualizing response. In this very accessibility, to be sure, "A Method of a Cloak" is more like the exception that proves the rule (or method) of Stein's "Objects"—its dominant, excessively discreet, overclued discourse—than the standard by which other texts of *Tender Buttons* are to be measured. Thus, "A single climb to a line, a straight exchange" is as much a ruse as a clue. It guides as much as it misleads. The text is playful, multidirectional, "cloaked" like the detective stories Stein was so fond of, "a desperate adventure" of silence and sound, of senses, directions, and meanings more than of one-sense, or non-sense. In all this it is also very much concerned, however, with "what everyone knows about cloaks" (and clocks) and what one "expects of them generally"—to play a role, for example, in mysteries—as well as with the "ordinary meaning of each word." Playing off the common association of the word "cloak," for example, with "cloak and dagger," the title suggests the deliberate, formulaic concealment of thrillers or espionage stories which exploit all the right conventions ("all this which is a system"). The stereotypical nineteenth-century detective wore a cloak, as did the spy. In the context of "a desperate adventure and courage and a clock," the preceding phrase, "a straight exchange," might well evoke a quickly negotiated, dangerous covert operation in which, as the saying goes, "time is of the essence." Exactly what is exchanged remains mysterious; "a straight exchange to a cane" points to a man's world, as does "attractive black silver." The latter suggests not only graying hair but also perhaps a tarnished, illicit financial transaction. Another kind of exchange takes place in the alliterative and semantic reciprocity of "cloak" and "clock," the concealment of a mystery and the amount of time available for uncovering it. In this case, the amount of time is limited to a very brief text, the site of a linguistic exchange between writer and reader which is at the same time an exchange of "feeling." Like the detective and the spy, both writer and reader share feelings of "resignation and success" involved in the reciprocal acts of encoding and decoding, creating and interpreting, depositing and withdrawing, concealing and revealing meaning in a text that remains to a large extent private despite our attempts to unravel the semantic potential latent in our collectively shared associations with words.

In its apparent concern with the world of men, their silver-black world of contradictions, "A Method of a Cloak" looks back especially to the second text of the "Objects" section, "Glazed Glitter" (*SW*, 461), where Stein writes: "Certainly glittering is handsome and convincing." For the most part, however, Stein's texts focus more explicitly on a world of *women,* and *Tender Buttons* is among other things an elaborate cloaking of lesbianism. The setting is domestic—(household) "Objects," "Food," "Rooms." As we have seen in looking at "Poetry and Grammar," this focus on women suggests also a focus on nouns, on poetry, in opposition to the prosaic world of men, business, and the "outside" world. As "outside" figures the world of men, so "inside" figures the world of women. The former are "worldly," the latter "domestic." *Tender Buttons* does not merely exploit these stereotypes, however; it uses them with the very definite aim of breaking them down. Thus, Stein wondered of poetry and prose "if it were possible to make even in a short sentence the two things come to be one" (*HW*, 133). As prose was characterized by sentences and paragraphs, Stein thought, so poetry by nouns. In "A Method of a Cloak," Stein does indeed meet this problem head on, constructing a literary object that cannot be better described than by that oxymoronic, ambivalently utopian designation—"prose poem."

Composed of a series of six commas and fifteen nouns in five lines, including the title and the nominalized adjectives "black" and "silver" in the final clause, "A Method of a Cloak" shows as well as any other text of *Tender Buttons* the proper concentration of Stein's approach to (her own definition of) poetry. Containing only three of the most common of verbs in a single repetition—"is . . . has . . . has . . . makes"— the text shows a woman's concern for domestic *economy* in its own sparing use of language; it offers each word as if it were hard to come by and challenges the reader to *make* the most of it, something of (apparently) nothing, sense of nonsense. In "A Method of a Cloak" and *Tender Buttons* generally, Stein not only makes "the cheapest things out of the best materials . . . a cheap product, within almost anyone's means,"[12] she also does the reverse. With the simplest, most accessible language, she constructs texts of an almost inexhaustible interest and complexity, as well as preciosity. As the strong sense of closure offered by the last clause of "A Method of a Cloak" suggests, she is as capable of fixing the object, noun, language, in *poetry* as she is of decontextualizing language, dislodging it from its habitual uses in accordance with that liberation she associates with *prose.* In the four-line, one-sentence

12. Ibid., pp. 95–96.

paragraph of "A Method of a Cloak," with its crowd of nouns, barriers between prose and poetry begin to crumble. Yet the text tends more in the direction of poetry, fixity, immobility, the arrested synchronic moment than toward diachronic narrative. It describes and is caught up in a system—linguistic/economic—that it cannot transcend and that is "both perfectly transparent . . . and perfectly opaque. . . ."[13]

As one moment in what we may call a narrative of objects, or prose poem sequence, "A Method of a Cloak" is as much a false clue as it is a key to *Tender Buttons*. Its "poetic" dimension may be seen, among other things, in its isolation of a given object/noun (Cloak) within a frozen system. Its "prosaic" dimension, by contrast, has much to do with the matrix of human relations and activities that system suggests. Although the word (product, commodity) "cloak," is perhaps most frequently associated with men even as the process of its production (weaving, sewing, etc.) is associated with women, both are equally implicated by the notion of exchange. In a later poem of the "Objects" section, "A Long Dress," Stein addresses this problem more directly:

> What is the current that makes machinery, that makes it crackle, what is the current that presents a long line and a necessary waist. What is this current.
> What is the wind, what is it.
> Where is the serene length. . . . A line distinguishes it. A line just distinguishes it. (*SW*, 467)

On a quite literal level, the "current that makes machinery" in the above lines is doubtless electricity, a source of energy, like the wind, that makes machines "crackle." The machinery in question is most likely the sewing machine that serves the dressmaker's object of creating a stylishly "long line" and "a necessary waist," that is to say a waistline and a "serene length" that seem just right, pleasing to the eye. The labor of women for women—the elegance of the dressmaker's design suggested by "A line just distinguishes it"—is as manifest in this text on the making of "A Long Dress" as the labor of women for men is concealed in "A Method of a Cloak," with its suggestion of simple but elegant styling for men's clothing in "A single climb to a line, a straight exchange to a cane . . . all makes an attractive black silver."

To speak of "exchange," "current," or "machinery," is to speak also

13. The phrase is from Macherey, *Theory of Literary Production*, p. 34.

of language, of capital and the commodity structure ("a system"). Elsewhere, Stein writes, in ironic, perfectly regular verse:

> Money is what words are.
> Words are what money is.
> Is money what words are.
> Are words what money is.[14]

The word, Sutherland says, commenting on this passage, "must be
capable of a great range of applications, as the banker's dollar is capable of a great range of exchanges."[15] In *Tender Buttons,* Stein experi-
ments with the isolation and currency of language, of poetry and prose.
In so doing, she is drawn into a style of writing that offers more contradiction than resolution. With their obsessive repetitions, Stein's texts
suppress use (meaning) as much as they encourage, on the other hand,
a resistance to meaninglessness and a reconstruction of the meaning(s)
they themselves refuse. At times, any such reconstruction seems an
impossible task. Nevertheless, there are texts in *Tender Buttons* which
suggest the possibility of narrative development; to leave these lying
unattended represents, I think, a betrayal of Stein's texts, or at least of
some of its most urgent "objects"—reifications, oppressions, and re-
sistances. One such narrative may be reconstructed from the poem "A
Plate" (*SW,* 466): "An occasion for a plate, an occasional resource is in
buying and how soon does washing enable a selection of the same thing
neater. If the party is small a clever song is in order." These lines not
only bring us back to the notion of a domestic economy ("buying")
already encountered in "A Method of a Cloak" and "A Long Dress,"
they also provide a narrative strand ("the party") that runs through
Tender Buttons from beginning to end, though it is often submerged like
a whisper by the noise of other conversations. As Hadas has said: "The
surrounded and surrounding, the entering and entered, the contained
and containers—all add up to a house in significant disorder, but it is
not impossible to attend its Saturday night salons—the echoes of them
anyhow."[16] Of course, nothing ever happens at a party, or only "on
occasion." The party is thus, as it was for Virginia Woolf in *Mrs.
Dalloway,* a well-suited topos for a narrative that does not want to be a
narrative, where nothing happens and everything happens, a narrative

14. Quoted from Stein's *Geographical History of America,* in Sutherland, *Gertrude Stein,*
p. 89.
15. Ibid.
16. Hadas, "Spreading the Difference," p. 50.

of objects and of the people who possess and are in a sense possessed by them.

It is also a cause for anxiety: "Plates and a dinner set of colored china. Pack together a string and enough with it to protect the centre, cause a considerable haste and gather more as it is cooling, collect more trembling and not any even trembling, cause a whole thing to be a church." Traditionally it is the woman more than the man who has been responsible for taking care of the domestic details involved in planning and giving parties. Thus, the harried voice and notational style of the above lines suggest a hostess (not, probably, a host) frantically preparing for the arrival of guests: setting the table ("Plates and a dinner set of colored china"); trussing a chicken or turkey and attending to it fresh from the oven ("Pack together a string and enough with it to protect the centre . . . as it is cooling"); getting nervous ("trembling"), yet trying to overcome last minute jitters and clean up as much as possible ("gather more . . . collect more") in order to create an atmosphere of serenity and propriety (as in the French "propre," meaning cleanliness, next to godliness), a strong sense of order and belonging ("cause a whole thing to be a church"). In their semantic insistence on what is proper, just right, even necessary, these lines are representative, like "a necessary waist" or "A line just distinguishes it," of the extent to which the first half of "Objects" is dominated by an emphasis on decorum that the second half gradually comes to reject in a violent manner and which Stein's undecorous disruptions of syntax implicitly oppose throughout the whole of *Tender Buttons*. In "A Plate," this emphasis is already a source of great tension: "A plan a hearty plan, a compressed disease and no coffee, not even a card or a change to incline each way, a plan that has excess and . . . shows filling." Whereas "A plan a hearty plan . . . no coffee" suggests again the anxiety connected with wanting to provide for all the needs of party guests ("a plan that has excess and . . . shows filling"), "not even a card or a change to incline each way" may allude to invitations given or withheld, accepted or declined. To "protect the centre" is to care for "a compressed disease," to avoid, probably, a heart attack. The pressures of *serving* are great; the servants, of course, are women; men, the absent "centers" of attention, demand to be served. As the following text object, "A Seltzer Bottle," tells us: "Any neglect of many particles . . . any neglect of this makes around it what is . . . certainly discolor in silver." Neglecting important details, or even minor ones ("many particles"), may well cause displeasure ("discolor") among the male guests, especially when we recall that silver, according to Stein's operative network of associations—"glittering," "handsome," "cloak," "cane"—is a man's color, a *property* of men which women polish.

In *The Origin of Family, Private Property and State*, Friedrich Engels points out that in Euripedes "the wife is described as *oikurema*, a *thing* for housekeeping" (my emphasis).[17] Decorum, propriety, property, monogamy, all these may contribute, as Stein passionately suggests in the text called "A Chair" (*SW*, 468), to the oppression of women:

> A widow in a wise veil and more garments shows that shadows are even. It addresses no more, it shadows the stage and learning. A regular arrangement, the severest and the most preserved is that which has the arrangement not more than always authorized.
>
> A suitable arrangement, well housed, practical, patient and staring, a suitable bedding, very suitable and not more particularly than complaining, anything suitable is so necessary.
>
> A fact is that when the direction is just like that, no more longer, sudden and at the same time not any sofa, the main action is that without a blaming there is no custody.

The shadow the husband's death casts over the widow he leaves beind is figured in Stein's poem by a veil that is "wise" because it follows convention. Like "more garments," "even" shadows, and a "regular arrangement" (heterosexual, monogamous), "wise veil" suggests a conventional, "straight," socially respectable response to the husband's death. Yet this conventional wisdom, which implies that the widow should hide herself away and be chaste in honor of her dead husband, is no longer helpful, if indeed it ever was, for the woman involved. Such conventional wisdom has nothing to say to women: "It addresses no more." Instead, it limits a woman's ability to realize her full potential: "it shadows the stage and learning." Like "even" shadows and the "regular arrangement" as well, "the severest and the most preserved . . . not more than always authorized" suggests the longevity and restrictiveness of the patriarchal culture that keeps women in their place. That place, as the next paragraph implies, is in the home, "well housed, practical, patient and staring." According to conventional male wisdom, the woman's confinement to the home is a "suitable arrangement . . . a suitable bedding, very suitable," an arrangement so suitable it has come to seem "necessary." The woman's place is simply to accept this situation ("not . . . complaining") even though, as the next paragraph suggests, it may leave her at her husband's death suddenly without any more property than the chair

---

17. Friedrich Engels, *The Origin of Family, Private Property and State*, in *The Marx-Engels Reader*, ed. Robert C. Tucker (New York: Norton, 1978), p. 738.

she sits in ("no more longer, sudden and at the same time not any sofa"). Given this state of affairs ("when the direction is just like that"), the husband dead and the woman without any property of her own, the widow has no choice but to rebel against social convention and claim her rights, including property and children ("without a blaming there is no custody"), or acquiesce to the ascetic values (the "wise veil") and decorum of a "regular" arrangement, sexual and otherwise, that may be "very suitable . . . a suitable bedding" for men but that for women is merely "the severest and the most preserved . . . not more than always authorized" of existing social conventions. The death of the married man leaves the widow, in a society opposed to women remarrying, still under the long and "even" (conventional, regular) shadow of Victorian values, alone, condemned to a life without the joys of sexual companionship. In a less literal sense, any woman constrained to continue in an alienated marriage, unable for propriety's sake to seek divorce, might also be considered a "widow"; in both cases, the woman has had her *singular* pleasure, and that is supposed to be enough.

To marry and accept the *rule* of monogamy (one partner, one life) is to accept an "arrangement" or order that is at once patriarchal, male-centered, and bourgeois. In the final lines of "A Chair," Stein calls on women for solidarity and resistance to that order:

> . . . shine in the darkness necessarily.
>   Actually not aching, actually not aching, a stubborn bloom is so artificial and even more than that, it is a spectacle, it is a binding accident, it is animosity and accentuation.
>   If the chance to dirty diminishing is necessary, if it is why is there no complexion, why is there no rubbing, why is there no special protection.

This conclusion to "A Chair" carries with it unmistakable suggestions of sexual deprivation. The repeated phrase, "Actually not aching, actually not aching," in fact suggests its opposite. Without a man to satisfy her needs, the widow must "shine in the darkness necessarily," pretend, in other words, that she is unaffected in the midst of her loneliness, attempt repeatedly to convince herself and others that she is actually *not* aching when she is actually aching very much, both sexually and emotionally. A "stubborn bloom," she must willfully act *as if* she were happy, cheerful, in full blossom, although in so doing she succeeds only in being "artificial" and making a "spectacle" of herself, causing "animosity" and accentuating her own sense of deprivation. There is no good reason, the text implies, that a woman should remain sexually and otherwise alone just because of a "binding accident," because one person she has been committed to by law has died and left her.

Throughout *Tender Buttons,* running counter to its emphasis on propriety, cleanliness, and decorum and in accordance with stereotypical Victorian, bourgeois/patriarchal values, lovemaking is imaged as something "dirty." The word is also subject to a reversal throughout Stein's text, however, which places it in a more positive light. Thus, "if the chance to dirty diminishing is necessary . . . why is there no rubbing" may be rewritten as follows: if the widow's opportunities for lovemaking ("the chance to dirty") necessarily diminish following the husband's death because she is not supposed to remarry, why does she not look to other *women* for sexual gratification ("dirty . . . rubbing") and companionship. The quirkiness of Stein's syntax in the above line seems designed in large part to deliberately cloak this lesbian content, although the elliptical omission of a logical connective between dirty and diminishing may be plausibly explained on more "aesthetic" grounds by the desire to highlight the alliterative shock of "dirty diminishing." In any case, since a widow is usually an older woman, her chances of attracting another man are likewise diminished, and she has all the more reason to look elsewhere. Although this too seems necessary given the circumstances, few women, Stein suggests, know to take advantage of it.

"Arrangements," in *Tender Buttons,* are not only linguistic ("an arrangement in a system to pointing"), but also, and necessarily, social and sexual. Thus, in another text from "Objects" called "In Between," Stein writes: "In between a place and candy a narrow foot-path that shows more mounting than anything. . . . A virgin a whole virgin is judged made . . . and a perfectly unprecedented arrangement between old ladies." If it is amusing to visualize Gertrude writing these lines (and Alice over her shoulder—laughing? blushing?), it is also not difficult to understand why many (especially male) critics might be inclined to move so quickly "beyond semantics" in reading *Tender Buttons.* Even after the "sexual revolution" in America, Stein's work has in it the potential to challenge deep-seated norms. With eloquent humor and courage, Gass has spelled out the sexuality of Stein's text as no one before him dared to, though it would be remarkable if earlier critics had not perceived it. Sexual semantics are written all over *Tender Buttons,* and this sexuality, as Gass rightly observes, is not only a joke. Sexual relations enter *Tender Buttons* under the sign of oppression, and one of the text's secret and not so secret messages is the need for women to *get out from under.*

One of the manifestations of such oppression, prostitution, is hinted at in the text near the conclusion of the "Objects" section entitled "Suppose an Eyes":

> . . . A white dress is in sign. A soldier a real soldier has a worn lace a worn lace of different sizes that is to say if he can read. . . .
>   Go red go red, laugh white. Suppose a collapse in rubbed purr, in rubbed purr get.
>   Little sales ladies little sales ladies little saddles of mutton. Little sales of leather and such beautiful beautiful, beautiful beautiful.

That this is an *obscene* text is beyond question. Why it is obscene is not. In the space of a very few lines, Stein brings together virtually all forms of sexual relations: "A white dress" suggests virginity and marriage, a "sign" of complicity and/or acquiescence to the existing order like "the sign" of "A Chair"; "soldier a real soldier . . . if he can read" points to the stupidity of male violence and the patriarchal institution of marriage where the virgin is raped ("a worn lace a worn lace of different sizes") and adultery is not exceptional. Certainly the most difficult expressions to interpret in the passages are "A white dress is *in sign*" (my emphasis) and "Go red go red, laugh white." The former may suggest that a white dress is modish, as in "in fashion," but also perhaps that it is put on display to attract attention. What a white dress attracts, of course, is men, whether as future husbands or as paying customers. The implied opposition of "go red, laugh white" is even more obscure but may imply the hypocrisy of doing one thing and saying another. Red suggests the prostitution of female sexuality (as in the "red light" districts frequented by soldiers) in contrast to the implied purity of whiteness. Taken together, all this may point to the double standard of men who go to one kind of woman for sex and to another for marriage. Commenting on the above passage, Gass has construed "little sales ladies" as "little *dirty* ladies,"[18] thus suggesting the lesbian motif we have already encountered more than once. Yet although "sales" is certainly a pun on the French "dirty," its English meaning is equally important here, echoing "a sold hole" in the poem "Red Roses" (*SW*, 472). "Suppose a collapse," "rubbed purr," "saddles of mutton," "sales of leather"—the sexual connotations of all these phrases taken together virtually spell themselves out. What is perhaps most interesting about the phrase "little sales ladies" is that it brings together lesbianism,

18. Gass, *The World within the Word*, p. 101.

marriage, and prostitution in a single "dirty" image, as if the condition of the most degrading exploitation of women by men were also and at the same time the condition for their potential *liberation* by and for women.

In the texts that follow in the "Objects" section—"A Shawl," "Book," "Peeled Pencil, Choke," "It Was Black, Black Took," and "This Is This Dress, Aider," this apparent paradox is developed to an explosive conclusion. The final poem, especially, deserves attention in this regard:

> Aider, why aider why whow, whow stop touch, aider whow, aider stop the muncher, muncher munchers.
> A jack in kill her, a jack in, makes a meadowed king, makes a to let.
> (*SW,* 476)

The reader interested in a detailed explication of these lines can do no better than refer to Gass's gloss of it. The title, as he observes, despite its and the poem's humorous side, must be read as an urgent appeal that is not to be taken lightly: "This Is Distress, Aid Her." "Aider" is, as Gass says, "only a sound shadow for aid her and a muffled form of 'Ada,' one of Gertrude's code names for Alice, . . . also the original French root, meaning to give pleasure to." Beyond this, however, it is important not to overlook the word's purely grammatical status. In the final text, Gass continues, "the square off of male vs. female, the balance of pleasure and pain with rescue and reward, is perfect."[19] In a narrowly aesthetic sense, we may well agree with this reading. From a more political perspective, however, to consider the conclusion of "Objects" as a "perfect balance" begs perhaps the most urgent question of the text, one that Stein decidedly leaves open for us to decide: What is to be done?

What Marx refers to as the "violence of things" or rule of "material forces" in bourgeois society,[20] the contingency ("a binding accident") and mere appearance of freedom which have as their concealed underside a violent closure and the "severest" order, shows itself unmistakably in the progress of Stein's "Objects." Not only does this section have

19. Ibid., p. 102. Schmitz's neglect of the political dimension of the "Objects" section leads him to explain "This Is This Dress, Aider" as "estrangement . . . resolved in lovemaking, a scene rendered with Rabelaisian vigor." He thus interprets the destructive violence of the phrase "jack in kill her" merely as an indication of mutual satiation in orgasm!

20. Marx, *The German Ideology,* in *The Marx-Engels Reader,* p. 199, and in *Collected Works,* 5:79.

narrative threads we may pick up if we choose, it has a very definite telos that is defined as much by violence as by negation. Women as "objects," prostitution, oppression, male violence: these prominent motifs of *Tender Buttons* converge in the concluding text of the "Objects" section in a single word, a precise pont of resistance: "Aider." As the grammatical ambivalence of the verb suggests, this text depends, like any text, on its readers to carry out, to carry on, its resistance, to turn its meanings to use. The uses and meanings of a text, however, are "manifold." Thus, "Aider" may be frozen as an infinitive, static, inviting us to an act it cannot itself accomplish, or it may be read, and if we read it so *must* be read, as an imperative, urgently calling for a solidarity of women (and men) to resist all forms of sexual and societal violence and oppression, including the rape and murder suggested by the phrase "A jack in kill her" and the absolute sexual power of the male implied by Stein's image of a "meadowed king," a bull or stud horse.

"Rooms"

How to resist is, of course, another question. On the point of resistance itself, *Tender Buttons* seems at first unequivocal, but as the text moves forward from the end of "Objects" through the rituallike "Foods" to the concluding "Rooms," there is evidence of a gradual dissolution of the text's resolve, ending in a qualified acceptance of and resignation to the status quo. This change, certainly, has to do with violence, the question of violent resistance as a means to a nonviolent end. "Objects" suggests that the only way to overcome the oppression of women is by confronting it head on; its texts are remarkable not least of all for confronting male violence, the reification and oppression of women, with a violent use of language. If such a procedure is revolutionary, it is so by an obsessive complicity, as if by heating up the text over and over again to the point of crisis one could eventually break through into a new language. "Objects" presents a continuous yet at the same time violently disjunctive series of crises that have a consummation of sorts in the manifestly thematic violence of the last poem's "A jack in kill her . . ." Confronted with such violence, we may well decide that any attempt to meet it nonviolently will only result in complicity with the status quo. On the other hand, the conclusion of "Objects" suggests that to meet violence with violence may be to involve oneself in another kind of complicity that only reproduces already existing relations of domination. Thus, the text leaves us, as it were, without a strategy of resistance, as if between a theory and a praxis: "Aider" as helpless infinitive and "Aider" as an urgent imperative.

On this much, if on little else, Stein and Marx could agree: "the real point aimed at is to do away with the status of women as mere instruments of production [and reproduction, women as domestic, household objects]. . . . the abolition of the present system of production must bring with it the abolition of the community of women springing from that system, *i.e.*, of prostitution both public and private."[21] As other of her writings make clear, particularly those on money, Stein is in certain fundamental respects far from a revolutionary in any Marxist sense. Her ideology is intensely American: "I don't envisage collectivism. There is no such animal, it is always individualism, sometimes the rest vote and sometimes they do not, and if they do they do and if they do not they do not" (*HW*, 53). If Stein's texts present a challenge to "patriarchal/logocentric thought,"[22] it is nevertheless difficult to reconcile a radical revolutionary feminism with statements such as the following: "So, now please, everybody . . . is money money, and if it is, it ought to be the same whether a father of a family earns and spends or a government, if it isn't sooner or later there is a disaster" (*HW*, 107). When it comes to economics, Stein's politics border unmistakably on the paternalistic, the patriarchal, the ultraconservative, not to say reactionary: "One thing is sure until there are rich again everybody will be poor and there will be more than ever of everybody who is even poorer" (*HW*, 112).

All of which brings us back to the center, change and resistance, opposition and difference, ambivalence, undecidability. Moving chronologically through *Tender Buttons:*

> . . . The change has come. There is no search. But there is, there is that hope and that interpretation and sometime, surely any is unwelcome. . . . (*SW*, 461)
>
> . . . Does this change. It shows that dirt is clean when there is a volume. . . .
> . . . Supposing you do not like to change, supposing it is very clean that there is no change in appearance, supposing that there is regularity and a costume is that any worse than an oyster and an exchange. . . .
>   . . . Some increase means a calamity and this is the best preparation for three and more being together. A little calm is so ordinary. . . . (*SW*, 462)

21. Marx, *Manifesto of the Communist Party,* in *Collected Works,* 6:502.
22. De Koven, "Beyond Literary Cubism," p. 94.

This is no dark custom and it even is not acted in any such way that a restraint is not spread the centre is in standing. (*SW*, 468)

The meaning of this is entirely and best to say the dark, best to say it best to show sudden places, best to make bitter. . . . (*SW*, 471)

. . . a single financial grass greediness. . . .
. . . A change, in a change that is remarkable there is no reason to say that there was a time. (*SW*, 471)

The change the dirt, not to change dirt means that there is no beef-steak and not to have that is no obstruction, it is so easy to change meaning, it is so easy to see the difference. (*SW*, 477)

. . . The difference . . . does mean that meadow is useful and a cow absurd. (*SW*, 477)

A change, a final change. . . . There is no authority for the abuse of cheese. What language can instruct any fellow. . . .
A sudden slice changes the whole plate, it does so suddenly. . . .
. . . What is the custom, the custom is in the centre. (*SW*, 483)

The center is custom, propriety, to be followed in the first line of "Rooms" by an instruction: "Act so that there is no use in a centre" (*SW*, 498). But is there, or isn't there? Is there use? A center? Is there "use in a center"? "Act," so that there is none. Turn aside from it and pretend not to see? Or look it in the eye and face up to it? Behave so as to decenter? Or is this change "already here," so that "There is no search" ("but there is that")? Or has there never *been* a center? Stein's instruction is of such "manifold" use as to border on the useless—*as instruction*. It is so multidirectional as to have no direction (*sens*, meaning). Yet the end of "Objects" shows us a high degree of urgency: "Aider." Change is needed but never comes, stranded in the infinitive. How should we respond to "if the persecution is so outrageous that there is nothing solemn is there any occasion for persuasion" (*SW*, 484)? What are we to do with her words: "Take no remedy lightly, take no urging intently, take no separation leniently. . . ." (*SW*, 485), and, regarding *Tender Buttons*, "A work which is a winding a real winding of the cloaking of a relaxing rescue" (*SW*, 485)? Insofar as *Tender Buttons* addresses the potential liberation of women from traditionally pre-scribed modes of behavior which reduce them to the status of domestic objects or domestic servants, the "relaxing rescue" the work proposes paradoxically seems possible only as a consequence of an extreme ten-sion and strategic concealment, both syntactic and semantic, in the redemptive project itself, "a real winding of the cloaking." Sometimes Stein seems to suggest that we, men *and* women, have already been

saved, and there is nothing to be done after all: "Choose the rate to pay
and pet pet very much. . . . Cuddling comes in continuing a change. . . .
A cow is accepted" (*SW*, 486). Such statements as these are not easily
understood in part because it is unclear to what extent they are to be
read ironically. Whereas "Choose the rate to pay and pet pet very
much" suggests acquiescence to the existing economic order and to the
prostitution/commodification of affection, "cuddling comes in continuing a change" implies that true affection manifests itself in a resistance to the existing order of things which is, nevertheless, more
reformist than revolutionary, more intent on continuity than disruption. The phrase "A cow is accepted" may suggest that women currently have no reason to feel alienated or exploited, or that if "things"
continue to change they will eventually arrive at a state of acceptance;
on the other hand, if we read it ironically, the phrase suggests that a
woman is accepted only to the extent that she fulfills our conventional
expectations of women's behavior.

In the latter case, women still have much to overcome: "Why is a
cup a stir and a behave./Why is it so seen" (*SW*, 489). Like "cow," "cup"
may be read as a conventional symbol for woman, a particular image of
how women are viewed in society ("Why is it so seen"). Like the cup,
which is a "stir and a behave," a woman is supposed to offer something
stimulating but decorous, to see to it, as a hostess, for example, that
things are lively, "stirred up," but also under control, properly be-
haved. As long as women were (are) seen in such a way, Stein suggests,
they "had no change. They were not respected. . . . Any change was in
the ends of the center. . . . There was no change" (*SW*, 498). If custom
is the center and the center is a bourgeois/patriarchal, Victorian order
in which women "were not respected," what was to be done? "The
truth has come. There is a disturbance. . . . There is a use, they are
double" (*SW*, 498). Painfully aware of the reified status of women in
society and of the double standards or uses society holds for them (as,
for example, "stir *and* . . . behave"), Stein adopts the ends of the patriarchal order she opposes, offering the disturbance of a certain playful violence, a violent use of language and of poetry, to achieve new
ends, a new feminist language of nonlinear prose. Linearity ("A single
climb to a line, a straight exchange to a cane"), the center, ends, all
these are for Stein typical male emphases, in contrast to the nonlinear,
decentered, nonteleological female project implied in statements such
as "The difference is spreading" (*SW*, 461, near the beginning of "Objects") or "Act so that there is no use in a centre" (*SW*, 498, the first

sentence of "Rooms"). Stein's prose/poetry is not, as we have seen, devoid of linearity, though its procedure of refusing by using does aspire to "manifold" ends/uses. The fact of this aspiration, however, still leaves open the question of radical change.

In "Rooms," Stein tends toward a politics—no less a male alternative in its way, certainly—that would rather rearrange the furniture than condemn and violently destroy existing structures, whether of commodity or sexual relations. "Rooms" is as much a work of the vehement accommodation of differences as "Objects" is a work of emphatic confrontation and opposition. "If the centre has the place," "Rooms" says, "then there is distribution. That is natural" (SW, 499). It is "natural," although "the persecution is outrageous," and as Stein goes on to say: "There is a contradiction" (SW, 499). Time and again, whether it is a question of verbs or nouns, prose or poetry, men or women, violence or nonviolence, change or no change, Stein's texts become entangled in ambivalence. Of course, this ambivalence is also to a large extent the motor of her textual production, and thus it is understandably not something she would give up lightly ("Take no remedy lightly"). Similarly, the reified roles of women, like the intransigent fixity of nouns in the language, are in themselves cause not only for refusing but for using, for a passionate rejection as well as for a passionate affection: "Any force which is bestowed on a floor," Stein says, "shows rubbing" (SW, 499), as a woman scrubbing a floor may show a real affection by so doing. And yet: "That is so nice and sweet and yet there comes the change, there comes the time to press more air. This does not mean the same as disappearance" (SW, 499). In other words, although there may be much in currently accepted modes of female behavior that is "nice and sweet," the time has come for women to alter the situation for the better, that is, to claim more space and expand their role within society. Doing so, however, need not necessarily entail the "disappearance" of the "nice and sweet" characteristics one conventionally associates with women. What "Rooms" offers on a thematic level is the hope of spreading "feminine" virtues without maintaining feminine roles as such in contemporary society. Since "The whole arrangement is established," however, "The end . . . is that there is a suggestion . . . that there can be a different whiteness to a wall" (SW, 499). The walls of "Rooms," of social and sexual oppression, are not to be torn down, then, as one may have expected them to be at the end of "Objects"; they are, instead, to be *whitewashed*.

The isolated fragments in the "Objects" section of *Tender Buttons* exemplify the avant-grade project articulated in Adorno's *Ästhetische Theorie* of saving works of art through the dismantling (*Demontage*) of the claim that they "might indeed be what they cannot be and nevertheless must want to be" (*AT*, 283/271). The work of art which pretends to offer some transcendence or liberation from the reification that surrounds it may in fact be more subject to it, Adorno argues, than the art work that offers itself as evidence of continued nontranscendence and nonliberation; it is thus "only qua things," only by displaying their own thinglike status, "that art works become the antithesis of the reified social order" (*AT*, 250/240). Accordingly, by virtue of their conspicuous fragmentation at the level of form, the discrete, monadic, objectlike texts in the "Objects" section violently resist any totalization that might imply existing conflicts have already been resolved. "Rooms," by contrast—with its much smoother flow of language, the absence of titles to break up discrete texts such as one finds in both "Objects" and "Food"—suggests an aspiration toward the unbroken continuum of prose, or what in Adorno's terms might be called a "non-violent integration of divergences" (*AT*, 283/272). The suggestion of the possibility of a nonviolent integration, so radically called into question by the end of "Objects," is a part, we cannot help feeling, of the whitewash of "Rooms," which promises a reconciliation of differences as if at times it were already accomplished, or as if there were no oppositions or antagonisms, no center in need of decentering. "Objects" is as much a section of *prose poems* as "Rooms" is a section of *poetic prose*—the one implying opposition, interruption, sudden change; the other difference, continuity, gradual change. Whereas the former calls for destruction and leveling, the latter asks only for rearranging. The one leads to a radical telos, a confrontation with death and violence which is also an orgasmic sexual release, the coupling of eros and thanatos in "A jack in kill her"; the other avoids *an* end in favor of *ends*. Where "Objects" problematizes the notion of a nonviolent integration, "Rooms" tells us that "Harmony is essential" (*SW*, 500).

Relations that appear at one time to be those of mere quantitative difference may in times of crisis easily take on both the appearance and the reality of opposition. "Some increase," Stein says, "means calamity" (*SW*, 462). In such cases, it may well be that, as Stein also remarks, "The best slam is utter" (*SW*, 489). The tendency of "Rooms" to dissolve opposition into difference shows, however, a tendency toward non-violence and resignation which contrasts sharply with the spirit of violent resistance in the latter half of "Objects": "All along the tendency to deplore the absence of more has not been authorized. It comes to mean that with burning there is that pleasant state of stupefication. Then there is a way of earning a living. Who is a man. . . . so much resignation, so much refusal . . . so much and yet more silence" (*SW*, 501). Whereas "Objects" stresses the importance of rising up against the male stricture not to "deplore the absence of more," the severely limited, largely domestic roles of women in society ("without blaming there is no custody"), and the expectation that women would simply "behave" despite outrageous persecution, the above passage suggests that in "Rooms" the "burning" desire for change gives way to a numb acceptance ("a pleasant state of stupefication") of modes of behavior dictated by men (". . . a way of living. Who is a man.").

Under these circumstances, the wish for harmony goes unrealized, in *Tender Buttons* as in society at large: "There was a whole collection made. A damp cloth, an oyster, a single mirror, a mannikin. . . . This shows the disorder" (*SW*, 502–3). In the prosaic, disordered world of the present, a whole collection is not whole at all but a collection of fragments, assorted reminders of society's tendency to exploit women as objects of household labor, sexual gratification, vanity, and commodification ("A damp cloth, an oyster, a single mirror, a mannikin"). What is concealed or cloaked in such images is the extent to which women themselves accept their objectlike status without question, becoming the very products a male-dominated society wants them to be. Accordingly, Stein asks: "Why is there so much resignation in a package, why is there rain, all the same the chance has come, there is no bell to ring" (*SW*, 502). Instead of rebelling, blaming, deploring, women resign themselves to the manufactured, "packaged" uses men project onto them, although, as the phrase "there is no bell to ring" suggests, women must wake themselves up on their own if they are to make a change. History, oppression, resignation, all these may come to seem as inevitable and out of control as the weather, so that even when "the chance has come," the moment passes by without our seizing it. What is the point, Stein suggests, of politics: "Is there any use in changing more doors than there are committees" (*SW*, 504).

Implicitly renouncing the violence figured earlier in the "Objects" section, "Rooms" concludes Stein's text by moving in a fairly conventional direction:

> A religion, almost a religion, any religion . . . a service in indecision . . . and a question and a syllable in answer . . . and a single set of

sisters and an outline . . . and the centre . . . and yet solid quite so solid
and the single surface centered and the question in the placard and the
singularity, is there a singularity, why is there a question and the singularity why is the surface outrageous, why is it beautiful. . . . (*SW*, 505)

The oppression of women is, as "Objects" shows us, "outrageous," yet
they are still "beautiful, beautiful beautiful beautiful" (*SW*, 475) in a
severely restricted way, like caged birds singing. Loving women as she
does within these reified yet beautiful roles, Stein shows something of a
man's reluctance to see them change.[23] Thus, the division of roles and
of labor itself remains unchallenged: " . . . obligingness leads to a harmony in hesitation" (*SW*, 506). Respect grows, in "Rooms," for the way
things have been and continue to be ("what is ancient is practical") to
such an extent that in the end the speaker comes to seem almost
ashamed for having resisted in the first place ("nonsense more nonsense is sullen"), all but retracting her earlier polemic against such
"male" emphases as the center, order, and measure ("centre no distrac-
tor, all order is in a measure"). Though there continue to be nagging
doubts, even these are expressed in coy, evasive double negatives; in
contrast to the earlier urgency of "Aider," we now have "why is not
disturbing a centre no virtue. . . . No change is not needed," followed
by the fatalism of "Why complain at all when it is all arranged that as
there is no more appeal and not even any more clinching that certainly
now some time has come" (*SW*, 507). In place of an urgent call for help,
there is the equivocal "secure the steady rights" (*SW*, 508), as if all the
necessary rights had already been obtained and needed only to be tied
down or enforced. Rather than a clear challenge to the very principles
of domination and submission, the reader is advised simply to "translate more than translate the authority, show the choice and make no
more mistakes than yesterday." Although there is "more craving than
there is in a mountain," we get used to it: "This does not seem strange
to one, it does not seem strange to an echo. . . ." The echo of "Aider,"
the intense reification and oppression of "Objects," has faded here to a
pair of rhetorical questions: "Why is there so much useless suffering.
Why is there." Nothing, apparently, or little, is to be done. Instead of a
revolutionary dislocation of the center, there is merely a troubled ac-

23. See Gass, *The World within the Word*, p. 104: "If the appropriate joke about the
women's movement is that it needs a good man to direct it, the attitude of Gertrude Stein
was that although the male role was the one worth playing, the only good man was a
woman."

ceptance, an anguished resignation, more an effort to assimilate than to destroy: "a wideness makes an active centre."

Thinking of the central section called "Food," which is a rituallike prelude to this conclusion, we may recall the worker in bourgeois society for whom Marx says "the thing which *stands opposite* him has . . . become the *true community* [*Gemeinwesen*], which he tries to make a meal of, and which makes a meal of him."[24] The same, of course, may be applied to women aspiring to integrate themselves nonviolently into a man's world, the bourgeois/patriarchal society of the early and not so early twentieth century. Given such a society, as Stein says:

> What was the sensible decision. The sensible decision was that notwithstanding many declarations . . . not even notwithstanding the choice . . . notwithstanding . . . being overbearing . . . not even with drowning and with the ocean being encircling, not even with . . . terrific sacrifice of pedestrianism and a special resolution, not even more likely to be pleasing. The care with which the rain is wrong . . . the care with which there is a chair. . . . The care with which there is incredible justice and likeness, all this makes a magnificent asparagus, and also a fountain. (*SW,* 509)

"All this makes," as at the end of "A Method of a Cloak," "an attractive black silver," more a man's world than a woman's, at the very best an androgynous imbalance tipped, in the conclusion's sexually evocative images, in favor of the masculine—"asparagus, and also a fountain." At the risk of abandoning a strongly held position of solidarity with women ("many declarations . . . a special resolution"), the "choice" to actively encourage change on their behalf (the frozen infinitive, "Aider"); at the risk of adopting typically male character traits ("being overbearing") and being insensitive to the suffering of those around her ("drowning and the ocean . . . encircling"); at the risk even of accommodating herself to nonthreatening mediocrity ("terrific sacrifice of pedestrianism . . . not . . . more . . . pleasing") for the sake of greater communication—an accommodation formally suggested in the text by the more readable, continuous syntax of the "Rooms" section itself compared to the two preceding sections—and resigning herself to a fatalistic "why is there rain" philosophy that echoes the worried helplessness of the conventional widow ("The care with which the rain is

24. Marx, *The Grundrisse,* in *The Marx-Engels Reader,* p. 262.

wrong . . . the care with which there is a chair . . ."); at the risk of all this, Stein apparently decides to play along with the status quo, "notwithstanding" a dozen qualifications. Against her provocative advice to the widow in "A Chair" and the violent rejection of sexual and social decorum at the end of the "Objects" section, Stein decides to be "sensible." Further whitewashing the "outrageous" surface, the radical difference of "so much useless suffering," she ends her text, not with a call to violent resistance to injustice but with an emphasis on the "incredible justice and likeness" of things as they are.

Of course, we could say in defense of Stein's conclusions that she is merely acting as the literary architect of a new nonpatriarchal order, and that the "rooms" she sketches are *yet to be*. The closure provided by "Rooms," however, cannot negate or nullify the lessons of "Objects." As Stein says: "A lesson is of consequence" (*SW*, 500). The conciliatory poetic prose of "Rooms," with its emphasis on continuity and the flow of language, cannot simply smooth over the memory of the painfully disruptive prose poetry of "Objects." On the contrary, the latter remains evidence of a fragmentation that will not be assimilated into an unbroken continuum. The alternatives these two sections offer do not appear only to be exploded, or resolved, or dissolved "once and for all." They are, in this sense, coterminous, like the options of violence and nonviolence, sudden and gradual change, which daily confront us and which are part of the very subject matter and urgency of *Tender Buttons*. Stein's work has survived, as much as for any other reason, because it offers a certain resistance. But this resistance would itself be useless if readers simply ignored the semantic urgency it figures. The *Appellstruktur*[25] of *Tender Buttons* is thus (at least) double. On the one hand, it calls for resistance to the habitual meanings/uses of language in contemporary society, ours and hers. On the other hand, it also calls for resistance to an uncontrolled play of meaning whose deceptive "openness" would cancel or taboo any meaning or use whatsoever from the text.

By means of its form, *Tender Buttons* invites us more to brush against the grain (a kind of affection, "rubbing") than to "go along," though "Rooms" tends in the latter direction. The pact Sartre speaks of between text and reader calls us,[26] in Stein's case especially, as much to

25. See Wolfgang Iser, *Die Appellstruktur der Texte* (Konstanz: Universitätsverlag, 1970).

26. Sartre, *Qu'est-ce que la littérature?*, pp. 70–79.

confrontation as to cooperation. We will inevitably want to "go along" with the text in some things, *resist* it in others. To respond in this way doubtless involves what Derrida has described, with reference to his own critical activity and criticism generally, as "a brutal and mercilessly depleting selectivity . . . a certain kind of police brutality [that] is perhaps an inevitable accomplice to our concern for professional competence. . . ." What Derrida goes on to refer to as the "calculated risk of flattening out the unfolding or coiling up" of the text may indeed seem at times "an act of unjustifiable violence."[27] It may also be, however, as Derrida's own example makes clear, a way of exercising a certain political and textual praxis, of self-consciously using the text as a pretext for politico-critical intervention that is perhaps not altogether unjustifiable after all. Far from being superfluous or tangential to Stein's *Tender Buttons,* such an intervention is, in any case, just what it asks for: "Aider." The task of such a reading is to unravel a tightly woven text like Stein's ("A work which is a winding a real winding") in order thereby to salvage vital yet otherwise inaccessible or neglected semantic content from its syntactic concealment (the "cloaking" of a "rescue"), to de-reify a potentially frozen text, to set it in motion, re-mobilize it—"if necessary," to borrow Eagleton's phrase, "by hermeneutic 'violence' "— in a struggle to transform its subject matter, its "objects," within a wider political content.[28]

Since one of the central aims of this chapter has been to contribute to such a transformation, to show Stein's text as an "intersection of meaning and force" (*WB,* 119), any preemptive or totalizing conclusions as to Stein's politics would be counterproductive. Certainly, I have tried to show that, despite undeniable textual innovations, Stein's position as a feminist "revolutionary" (would she herself have accepted the designation?) is at the very least a complicated one. Although we may not want, in Macherey's words, "to interpret . . . multiplicity as equivocation,"[29] it seems equally important to locate and call attention to equivocation where it exists. Stein's repetition, for example, displays a characteristic ambivalence. On the one hand, it suggests a revolutionary attention to the critical problems of society: How can we go on? How can we *change* directions (meanings, *sens*). On the other hand, it

27. Derrida, "The Law of Genre," *Critical Inquiry,* pp. 66 and 68.
28. Eagleton, *Walter Benjamin, or Towards a Revolutionary Criticism,* p. 90; hereafter cited as *WB.*
29. Macherey, *A Theory of Literary Production,* p. 124.

also suggests a mere ritualistic reproduction of what has already been and what already is. Stein's "continuous present" is as much a repression of history and oppression as it is a strategy of ongoing resistance to it.

In my own reading of *Tender Buttons,* I am continually drawn back to the "Objects" section, the point of greatest resistance, to the question of violence and of radical change, the suddenness of poetry and the gradualness of prose. In "A Method of a Cloak," as elsewhere, we have seen how prose and poetry may be brought together in a harmonious way. "This Is This Dress, Aider," by contrast, with its "jack in kill her," suggests the extent to which they can be exploded apart. The violence manifest in the "Objects" section of Stein's text is followed, in any case, by a gradual lessening of resistance. *Tender Buttons,* Stein said, "did not decide anything for me but it did help me in my way" (*HW,* 143). Similarly, we may ask ourselves not only of Stein's text but of the modernist tradition of the fragment and the prose poem generally: Is it still a "help," or has it become in some sense an obstacle? Probably, it is still both, depending on how we *make use* of it. We may still ask ourselves as well, as Stein said, "if eventually prose and poetry were one or not one" (*HW,* 143), and if they were one, what meaning or use a unity between them might imply, whether liberating or restrictive. There is always the unavoidable danger of complicity with social and/or textual givens, whether through violence or nonviolence—Stein cannot help reproducing the grammars of language and social relations even as she attempts to undermine them. "Refusing by using," she furthers the opposition of poetry and prose as much as she subverts it.

There is no present sense, Stein says, "that anything is progressively happening" (*N,* 17): "Perhaps it is not going to be prose and poetry again. Nothing really changes everything is as it was but perhaps it is not going to be prose and poetry again perhaps it is not poetry and prose now in spite of anything and everything being always having been what it was. So to begin again about what prose and poetry have been" (*N,* 21). The prose poem, as Stein's *Tender Buttons* demonstrates, can be as much a utopian genre as a genre of ambivalence. In this sense, perhaps, it may be regarded as a kind of self-conscious and explosive condensation of literature generally. The points at which literature and history, or poetry and prose, meet, is a question Stein was fond of considering: ". . . perhaps history will repeat itself and it will come to be done. Perhaps no perhaps yes anyway that is all I know at present" (*N,* 62). Literature has in common with all art, Adorno has said, the desire for that which never was yet everything it is has already been: "What has not yet come into being, however, is the concrete. . . . The concrete, however, can scarcely be named even by works of art other than by negation. Every work of art is a utopia insofar as it anticipates by means of its form what it itself might be after all" (AT, 203). In keeping with the prose poem's historical function as a form that anticipates a concrete, utopian, genreless literature via polemical negations of other genres (especially the novel and the verse lyric), and by virtue of its dialogization of poetry and prose and its fragmented presentation of women-as-objects, Stein's *Tender Buttons* anticipates a society without relations of domination based on gender. In the "Objects" section, in particular, Stein's approach to the concrete takes the form of a violent verbal abstraction, so that what "hasn't yet been" can appear only as the dazzling negative image of everyday uses of language, as is also true for women. Adorno writes: "Even though every work of art becomes *a priori* helpless by its very gesture of self-legitimation, itself a thing that negates the world of things, it cannot simply refuse that legitimation before the world of things for the sake of its own *a priori* status" (AT, 182). Illegitimate literary genre par excellence, the prose poem typically seeks its legitimacy not by trying to get around reification but by meeting it head on. By means of its very objectlike appearance *en bloc* on the page, the prose poem suggests that passing through the condition of reification—being treated like an object— first of all requires taking on the *form* of an object. The prose poem neither retreats into the false security of a facile poetic harmony nor shies from the challenge of prosaic reality. In Stein's *Tender Buttons*, especially in the first section, "Objects," both the utopian impulses and the deep-seated ambivalences of the genre converge in explosive fashion, with political implications that are as lively today as they were in 1912.

Through the conflicts of genre, gender, and class which take place at various levels in *Tender Buttons,* both within and among its various parts, Stein invites us to consider the extent to which things are connected to things, or words to words, not only "by virtue of their difference,"[30] but also by force, oppositions, violence both manifest and concealed, as by "A Method of a Cloak." Of the English language Stein wrote: " . . . we are changing grammar and punctuation and shoving it around and putting pressure upon it but there it is . . . it has come to

---

30. Hadas, "Spreading the Difference," p. 62.

stay" (*N*, 12). As this statement suggests, Stein's playful violence toward language is not immune to a certain linguistic fatalism. Yet Stein herself offers a powerful example through her life and work of various ways in which the grammars of language, as also of sexual and social relations, may be changed. The question is *who* is going to do it and *how* it will be done ("whow"). As Stein might say: "Everybody has to think about that" ("Still More about Money" [*HW*, 109]).

PART IV

The Other Side of Things

CHAPTER 7

Self-Reflexive Fables: Ernst Bloch's *Spuren*

Never has a work of art that counts corresponded exactly to its genre.

—Adorno, *Ästhetische Theorie* (297/285)

When Ernst Bloch's *Spuren* (Traces) first appeared in 1930, at a time when the order and class structure of Western industrial societies had been severely shaken by economic crisis, Bloch's contemporaries did not know what to make of it.[1] Philosophical essays, critical reflections, parables, short stories, fables, fairy tales, anecdotes, *Mischformen* (mixed forms), *Denkbilder* (thought-images), models of a prose form that transgresses the usual literary boundaries, all these terms have been used to describe Bloch's collection.[2] Although the texts of *Spuren* undoubtedly have much in common with these various modes, they bear an especially close though hitherto neglected family resemblance as well, both formally and functionally, to Friedrich Schlegel's fragments and the hybrid texts of prose poem collections from Baudelaire and Rimbaud to the present. Distinguishable, like the prose poems we have considered thus far, by their fundamental brevity and condensation and their appearance in prose, *en bloc,* on the page, Bloch's texts are also, like these earlier examples, concentratedly novelistic in the

1. Hans Meyer, "Ernst Blochs poetische Sendung," in *Ernst Bloch zu ehren,* ed. Siegfried Unseld (Frankfurt: Suhrkamp, 1965), p. 23.
2. In addition to Meyer, see Heinz Schlaffer, "Denkbilder," in *Poesie und Politik,* ed. Wolfgang Kuttenkeuler (Stuttgart: W. Kohlhammer, 1973), p. 138; Jameson, *Marxism and Form,* pp. 123–24, subsequently referred to as *MF;* and Günter Witschel, *Ernst Bloch: Literatur und Sprache, Theorie und Leistung* (Bonn: Bouvier Verlag Herbert Grundmann, 1978), p. 9.

211

212   THE OTHER SIDE OF THINGS

Bakhtinian sense, with each individual text offering a highly charged matrix or point of intersection for the interanimation of various modes of discourse.[3] Composed in an era of intense political activism, *Spuren* is manifestly dialogical in the contribution it makes toward what Ricoeur refers to in conjunction with specifically *poetic* discourse and its "rule of metaphor" as a "decategorization of our entire discourse."[4] In its undermining of the reciprocal exclusions of various discursive practices—which are for Bloch in particular not merely a question of prose and poetry, or of the aesthetic and the philosophical, but a question most fundamentally of the social and the political—*Spuren* may be regarded as both an extension and a transformation of the prose poem's fundamental historical project as a norm-breaking, genreless genre.

What most distinguishes Bloch's *Denkbilder* from the prose poem generally is their greater, or rather, more direct concern with reflection, philosophy, "metalanguage," *Denken*. In this sense, and despite the explicit allusion to Rimbaud contained in "Montagen eines Februarabends" (Montages of a February Evening), *Spuren* is closer to Baudelaire's *Petits poèmes en prose* than to *Une saison en enfer* or the *Illuminations*.[5] More or less explicit allusions to Baudelaire are scattered throughout Bloch's short texts, from mention of "La passante" (The woman passing by) in the text with the Browningesque title, "Pippa geht vorüber" (Pippa Passes over) (*S*, 82) to the "lighted window" of "Gruss und Schein" (Greetings and Appearances) (*S*, 175) to the text entitled, "Ein verquerender Flaneur" (A Frustrated Flaneur) (*S*, 108). Close to Baudelaire as well is the allegorical, anecdotal, narrative struc-

---

3. The conspicuous textual/generic interaction provided by Bloch's texts both individually and collectively has been noted in some fashion in virtually all previous commentaries, though without reference to either Bakhtin or the prose poem. For a discussion of the relationship of the prose poem to other short prose forms such as the parable and the essay, see Fülleborn's *Das Deutsche Prosagedicht*, especially pp. 23–30. For the importance of the graphic element or mode of printing in distinguishing poetry and prose, see Lotman, *Die Struktur literarischer Texte*, p. 156: "The graphic form does not appear here as a technical means for fixing the text, but as a signal of a structural nature, according to which our consciousness perceives the text presented to us as already 'built in' to a certain extratextual structure."

4. Ricoeur, *The Rule of Metaphor*, p. 305, hereafter referred to as *RM*. Cf. Witschel, 143), who describes the language of *Spuren* as "metaphorically satiated."

5. Ernst Bloch, *Spuren* (1930; reprint, Frankfurt: Suhrkamp, 1959), p. 166, hereafter cited as *S*. I quote from this work with the permission of Suhrkamp Verlag, the owner of the rights. The following abbreviations are used to refer to other of Bloch's texts from Suhrkamp: *PH, Das Prinzip Hoffnung*, 1959; *SO, Subjekt-Objekt*, 1962; *TE, Tübinger Einleitung in die Philosophie*, 1964.

ture that dominates the collection. If the relationship between *Spuren* and the *Petits poèmes en prose* may be conceptualized as the difference between *Denkbild* and prose poem, philosophical poetry and prose poetry, it is nevertheless clear that the Schlegelian project of a fusion of genres is fundamental to both. *Denkbild* and prose poem also bear a crucial family resemblance to each other, as I have indicated, by virtue of their metaphorically satiated language: "To apprehend or perceive, to contemplate, to see similarity," Ricoeur writes, "—such is metaphor's genius-stroke, which marks the poet naturally enough but also the philosopher" (*RM*, 27). If mimesis is to poetry, as Ricoeur says, what persuasion is to prose (*RM*, 36), then Bloch's "traces" do their best to erase the difference between these; to be mimetic and persuasive at once, both poetry *and* prose; to leave the *mark* of the poet no less than of the philosopher.

In "Das Merke" (Mark Well) (*S*, 16–17), a text that is as programmatic for reading *Spuren* as Baudelaire's preface, "L'étranger," and "Le thyrse" are for the *Petits poèmes en prose*, Bloch announces this intention directly:

> Kurz, es ist gut, auch fabelnd zu denken. Denn so vieles eben wird nicht mit sich fertig, wenn es vorfällt, auch wo es schön berichtet wird. . . . Aus Begebenheiten kommt da ein Merke, das sonst nicht so wäre; oder ein Merke, das schon ist, nimmt kleine Vorfälle als Spuren und Beispiele. Sie deuten auf ein Weniger oder Mehr, das erzählend zu bedenken, denkend wieder zu erzählen wäre. . . . Manches läßt sich nur in solchen Geschichten fassen, nicht im breiteren, höheren Stil, oder dann nicht so. Wie einige dieser Dinge auffielen, wird hier nun weiter zu erzählen und zu merken versucht; liebhaberhaft, im Erzählen merkend, im Merken das Erzählte meinend. Es sind kleine Züge und andere aus dem Leben, die man nicht vergessen hat; am Abfall ist heute viel. Aber auch der ältere Trieb war da, Geschichten zu hören; gute und geringe, Geschichten in verschiedenem Ton, aus verschiedenen Jahren, merkwürdige, die, wenn sie zu Ende gehen, erst einmal im Anrühren zu Ende gehen. Es ist ein Spurenlesen kreuz und quer, in Abschnitten, die nur den Rahmen aufteilen. Denn schließlich ist alles, was einem begegnet und auffällt, dasselbe. (*S*, 16–17)

> [In short, it is good also to think in fables. For so much is left unresolved when it occurs, even when it is beautifully reported. From events there comes a kind of attention that otherwise wouldn't be as it is; or a kind of attention already there takes small occurrences as traces and examples. They point to a less or more that would be reflected on in the act of narrating, narrated in turn in an act of reflection. . . . Some things can only be grasped in such stories, not in a more expansive,

higher style, at least not exactly. The following are attempts to further narrate and call attention to how a few of these things came to be noticed; in a loving way to notice while narrating, to suggest narrative in the act of taking notice. They are small traits and other things out of life that haven't been forgotten; today there is much value in waste. But there was also the older impulse to hear stories; good, brief stories in various tones, from various years, remarkable stories that come to an end if they do so at all only once they have touched you. It is a reading of traces in all directions, in segments that only divide up the frames. For, finally, everything that meets you and occurs to you is the same.]

In a text called "Die Perle" (The Pearls) (*S*, 219–20), which was added to the second edition of *Spuren* as its conclusion in 1959, the final sentence above is emended to avoid, or correct, possible misunderstanding: "Only very far in the distance is everything that meets you and occurs to you the same" (*S*, 220). This line and the text of "Die Perle" in its entirety, to which we will return at the conclusion of this chapter, are of crucial importance not only to *Spuren* but to Bloch's philosophy generally. For the moment, however, I would like to emphasize certain aspects of "Das Merke." The phrase, "reflected on in the act of narrating, narrated in turn in the act of reflection," in particular, suggests Bloch's resistance to any idea of a "system," whether literary or philosophical, that would seek to maintain, as Ricoeur tends to do, an ultimate distinction between philosophical and poetic discourse. In its attempt to show these not as reified opposing terms but as terms of a potential and actual dialectical interpenetration, Bloch's *Spuren* typifies Bloch's philosophical outlook. Like Schlegel's project of a *Universalpoesie* and like the prose poem, Bloch's texts are concerned with setting various modes of discourse into relation with one another. Also like the prose poem, Bloch's texts often deal with everyday experiences usually ignored or overlooked, special acts of attention to or awareness of details, those "small traits . . . out of life" in which quantity may be subject to a dialectical reversal in the manner of Max Jacob's "The miniscule is the enormous!" Thus, the quantitative modifiers "less and more," in "Das Merke," take on the qualitative character of nouns—"ein Weniger oder Mehr."

"You pay attention precisely to small things, go after them." This statement, also from "Das Merke," suggests an ethic of Bloch's *Spuren* and also of the prose poem. "Things" may refer both to events and physical objects. This double significance points, on the one hand, to a more explicitly narrative perspective such as we will see in "Spielformen,

Leider" (Forms of Play, Unfortunately) (*S*, 22–27); and on the other hand to the more lyrical attention of a text such as "Der Rücken der Dinge" (The Other Side of Things) (*S*, 172–75). Both emphases, as the different "rules" of metaphor in Baudelaire and Rimbaud demonstrate, are at home in the prose poem. Like the small events and inconspicuous objects the prose poem so often takes as its subject matter, Bloch's texts, as we have noted, are generally brief and condensed, presenting a passing impression in the hard outline of a poem-object. Thus, the simple word *Eindruck* (imprint, impression) occurs three times in the single page of "Das Merke." The ambitions of Bloch's "Merke," however, are greater than the text's humble dimensions at first lead us to suspect; a small pleasure (*Vergnügen*) is intended, certainly, but a subversive one: "An imprint on the surface of life so that, perhaps, life tears apart" (*S*, 16).

"Spielformen, Leider": Bloch as Storyteller

The "traces of the storyteller," Walter Benjamin writes, "cling to the story the way the handprints of the potter cling to the clay vessel. Storytellers tend to begin their story with a presentation of the circumstances in which they themselves have learned what is to follow, unless they simply pass it off as their own experience."[6] Thus, Benjamin notes of Leskov, his exemplary storyteller, "his tracks are frequently evident in his narratives, if not as those of the one who experienced it, then as those of one who reports it" (ST, 92). Not coincidentally, in the same essay, Benjamin alludes explicitly to Bloch and his notion of a "hybrid between fairy tale and legend" (ST, 103). The difference of point of view between the one who experiences and the one who reports may be structurally articulated, of course, as the difference between first and third person. Depending in part on the density and length of the text in question, this difference may also correspond to the distinction between "lyric" and "narrative."

Situated on a sliding scale between these two poles, the *anecdote* is a form that lends itself to both lyrical and narrative emphases within a compact, potentially "explosive" space. As such, it figures prominently in both the *Petits poèmes en prose* and *Spuren*. Like Baudelaire, Bloch often begins with a bald statement or brief declaration suggesting a verbal detonation. Thus, Baudelaire's "Un plaisant" (A Joke) begins:

6. Benjamin, "The Story-Teller," in *Illuminations*, p. 92. Hereafter referred to as ST followed by page number.

"It was the explosion of the new year."[7] Like Bloch's "Spielformen," Baudelaire's poem is intensely occasional: its subject matter is the catalytic intersection of everyday chance experience and festival. As Baudelaire's poem has as its setting the celebration of the new year, so Bloch's is set on the French Bastille Day, July 14. But we are getting ahead of ourselves, for at the beginning of Bloch's "Spielformen" there is no indication of the explosion—other than the punch of the sentence itself—that will be explicitly thematized only in the concluding third section. On the contrary, the poem begins precisely with the sad uneventfulness of the everyday: "The day today [*der Tag heute*] didn't look like much" (*S*, 22). Especially noteworthy in this first sentence, in addition to its characteristic brevity and its casual oral quality—the latter an important dialogical feature typical of Bloch's style throughout *Spuren*—is the emphasis it receives by being set off typographically as a paragraph of its own. With its past tense, *sah*, and its setting in the present, the sentence suggests both the morning's expectations of a new day and the retrospection of the day's end. We expect what follows to relate something of the day's events, yet we cannot say, despite the title's "Unfortunately," whether it will offer us more of disillusion, despair, fulfillment, or hope. Every epoch, Karel Kosik has remarked, "is a nodal point of the three-dimensionality of time: with its preconditions it reaches back into the past, with its consequences it reaches forward into the future, and by means of its structure it is anchored in the present."[8] In their movement toward establishing a relation between an unstable present and future, on the one hand, and, on the other hand, between that same present and a concrete, lived past that is both "experienced" and "reported," the three sections of Bloch's "Spielformen" constitute an attempt to move "beyond the historical suddenly to real presence" ("Fall ins Jetzt" [Fall into the Now]). As such, they are profoundly historical as well as anecdotal, both lyrical and narrative.

Traces of personal experience cling to Bloch's "Spielformen" most visibly in the two-sentence second paragraph and the first two sentences of the third. This is also the place where the pretext of the lyrical "I" yields to prosaic reality and to narrative:

7. Baudelaire, *Petits poèmes en prose*, in *Oeuvres complètes*, 1: 279; subsequently referred to as *OC* followed by volume and page number. Translations by Louise Varèse in *Paris Spleen* will be cited as *PS*.

8. Karel Kosik, *Die Dialektik des Konkreten* (Frankfurt: Suhrkamp, 1967), p. 234; hereafter cited as *DK*.

Kein Geld, auch Paris wird dann kleiner. Ging in die alte Ar-
beiterkneipe, es gibt schlechtere, die nicht billiger sind.
  Da sah ich aber einen, der ging auf. So richtig, so schuldlos genieß-
end, wie es sich gehört. (S, 22)

[No money, Paris too grows smaller. Went into the old worker's pub;
there are worse that are not cheaper.
  There I saw a man getting high. So properly, so guiltlessly enjoying,
the way it should be.]

Like Baudelaire's *flâneur*, Bloch takes a special interest in cafés. In
contrast to a speaker such as that in the prose poem "Les yeux des
pauvres," however, a speaker who distances himself from what Marx
called the "'dangerous class,' the social scum, that passively rotting
mass thrown off by the lowest layers of old society,"[9] Bloch's speaker
deliberately mingles with its members, preferring them to the bourgeois who, he says, "calls himself, not only comfortably, but proudly, a
man of independent means [*einen Rentier*]" (S, 23). In contrast to
Baudelaire and without the least ambivalence, Bloch's speaker aligns
himself, not with the bourgeois of open air cafés, but with the workers
in their dingy pubs:

Der Mann mir gegenüber hatte Hummer in den verschafften Fäusten,
biß und spuckte rote Schale, daß der Boden spritzte. Doch dem zarten
Wesen darin sprach er fröhlich zu, als er es einmal hatte, still und
verständig. Endlich war hier ein Gut nicht mehr durch genießende
Bürger geschändet; der Schweiß der Entbehrenden, die Schande der
Kapitalrente schmeckte diesem da nicht mit. (S, 22–23)

[The man across from me had lobster in his misshapen fists, bit and spit
out red shell that sprayed the floor. Yet to the tender substance inside
he addressed himself gladly, once he had it, quietly, sensibly. Finally
here was a commodity no longer disgraced by bourgeois enjoyment; he
did not taste along with it the sweat of the one who makes do without,
the shame of unearned income.]

Given the close family resemblance between the *Denkbilder* of
Bloch's *Spuren* and the prose poems of Baudelaire's *Petits poèmes en
prose*, we may well say that, as Eagleton has remarked with reference to
bourgeois revolutions, literary and otherwise, "the 'contents' are new
but the 'forms' are not."[10] Hence, Bloch's title, "Spielformen, *Leider*,"

  9. Marx, *Manifesto of the Communist Party*, in *Collected Works*, 6:494.
  10. Eagleton, *Walter Benjamin, or Towards a Revolutionary Criticism*, p. 165; hereafter
cited as *WB*.

for the question the text poses is very much one of revolution, both in literature and in society. Sometimes, Eagleton says, people *"seem* engaged in revolutionizing themselves, though this is in fact a ritual repetition of the old; yet even so these are 'periods of revolutionary crisis.' Are they, then 'genuinely' revolutionary or only apparently so? How can their *apparent* 'creating of something that has never existed' be reconciled with the fact that this is indeed 'a new scene of world history'? Is it really new or not?" (*WB*, 165). The revolutionary impetus of the prose poem, manifest in Baudelaire over a decade too late for the failed revolution of 1848 and again in Rimbaud roughly contemporaneous with the Commune in 1871, repeats itself with the *Denkbilder* of Bloch's *Spuren,* this time in anticipation and retrospection of a period of revolutionary crisis which was indeed to bring only a ritual repetition of past failures to transform literature and society.[11] Set on July 14, 1928, the year before the economic and social crisis that might have spelled an end to bourgeois prehistory, the first two sections of "Spielformen, Leider" rehearse the production of new forms under the spotlight of past history: "In the worker with the lobster something else was recalled, from the great break-in long ago. Only there did a certain afterwards shimmer up where money no longer barks after goods or wags in them. Where the utterly foolish choice is spared between pure conviction and pure enjoyment" (*S*, 23).

Though the political content of Bloch's *Spuren* is at once more explicit and more concrete than in the works of either Baudelaire or Rimbaud, with an active proletariat as a specifically localizable point of reference, what Bloch would call a utopian *tendency* is clearly shared by all three. As much as the first line of the first section suggests a dreary identity, a day like any other, the opening of the second and central section suggests difference. Where the focus of the first section, from the point of view of an observing "I," is on a solitary worker, the second is dominated by the collective, "impersonal" first-person and third-person plural: "One didn't just go out on this evening as on any other. Didn't form chains in front of the street, its center, on which the cars roared, left this way, right that way, sharp and against us" (*S*, 23). As the speaker of Baudelaire's "Perte d'auréole" (Loss of Halo) loses his

11. Schlaffer, "Denkbilder," p. 153, rightly speaks of a "double poetry" in Bloch's *Denkbilder* and in those of Adorno and Benjamin as well: "the poetry they wanted to use as preparation for political action and the poetry that belongs to all past hope, which was no fulfillment." What Schlaffer says of the *Denkbild* is equally true of the prose poem: "The historical misfortune of this form determines its contemporaneity."

poetic "aura" in the mud of a crowded, bustling, prosaic city street—
"you know my terror of horses and cars" (*OC*, 1:352)—so Bloch's
speaker is carried, as it were, by the irresistible movement of things
(people, objects, events) into the center of the *mass*, which is not static
but a living, dynamic force: "finally this center was alive, yes, something grew on it." The city street—which was for Breton "the only valid
place of experience" as it was for Baudelaire a kind of modern testing
ground of the poet's skills (see especially "Le soleil"), the place of significant chance encounters—is for Bloch the site of a class struggle that
his *Denkbilder*, like the prose poem, figure in explosive literary form.
Unlike the autobiographical speaker of Baudelaire's "A une heure du
matin," however, who retreats into his room at the end of the day
turning a key he says he hopes will increase his solitude and strengthen
the "barricades" that separate him from the world (*OC*, 1:287), the
speaker of Bloch's text goes out in the evening to brave the "artillery of
the occupying traffic" and share in the present celebration and anticipation of past and future revolutions.

> Das ist Pariser Straße am 14 Juli, dem großen Tag. Auch als die
> Bastille erstürmt wurde, hat das Volk getanzt . . . freilich tanzte man
> damals anders nach der Natur. Aber haben sich die Revolutionäre auch
> beruhigt . . . so schießt doch durchs "Nationalfest" zuweilen noch ferne
> Erinnerung . . . ohne Frieden mit dem gekommenen bourgeois gen-
> tilhomme. (*S*, 23)

> [That is Paris street on July 14, the great day. When the Bastille was
> stormed the people danced then as well . . . though to be sure they
> danced differently, naturally. But if the revolutionaries too have settled
> down . . . still at times there shoots through the "national celebration" a
> distant memory . . . not at peace with the arrival of the bourgeois
> gentilhomme.]

The traces Bloch's speaker reads in the Bastille Day celebration
extend forward into the future as much as backward into the past. The
present, characteristically for Bloch "a hollowness, an insufficiency"
(*MF*, 135), is the site on this one day of something of that utopian
aspiration or potential or tendency Adorno associates with the lyric.[12]
This potential, referred to elsewhere by Bloch as "poetry in empty
space" (*Poesie im Hohlraum*) is revealed for the speaker through the
most prosaic of incidents: "For on July 14, 1928, as a car driven by a

12. Adorno, "Rede über Lyrik und Gesellschaft," p. 52; "Lyric Poetry and Society,"
p. 58.

gentleman in a straw hat attempted to push through one of these dance streets, the people wouldn't make room, although no one was dancing at that moment and mere taxis had gone through in droves" (*S*, 23–24). What follows is as interesting for how it is told as for what it tells. The speaker "reports" the ensuing sequence of events "as they happened": the driver's impatience to get through the crowd; the twenty fists that landed on the car and hindered its progress; the bold defiance of a young girl who leaped melodramatically in front of the car, dancing, "laughing and fearless, a flower in her hand, later in her mouth"; the angry words of the driver and the tense moments in which the car was almost overturned before it escaped from the scene; the straw hat knocked from the car owner's head left behind for the revelers to toss among themselves. What is perhaps most surprising in this text, the source even more than the events themselves of much of its pleasure, a strength as well as, possibly, a weakness, is its tight interweaving of event and interpretation, "experience" and "report," storytelling and explanation. The meaning of history, Kosik has said, lies *in history*: "in [history] man explains himself, and this historical explanation, which is identical with the formation [*Bildung*] of men and of humanity, is the only meaning of history" (*DK*, 234). From that "nodal point" of three-dimensional time which is the present, Bloch's text offers, as we shall see, an interpretation of its own story, its own history, its own anecdote. Unable as we are to transcend our own historicity in any absolute sense, the human task in a sense always remains, as Kosik suggests, to realize outselves from *within* history, to interpret and so to *make use* of "things," even and especially the small things, *Denkbilder*, prose poems, anecdotes, "minor" incidents: "And so the straw hat was never even entered in a police report, much less then in history, but only in this small, waiting story" (*S*, 25).

The "truth content" of the work of art, Adorno has said, "cannot actually be nailed down except by philosophical reflection. This alone is what legitimates aesthetics. . . . Actually, art works, notably those of the highest calibre, are waiting to be interpreted. If one accepted the assertion that there is nothing in art to interpret and that art merely has being, one would expunge the line of demarcation that separates art from non-art" (*AT*, 193/186). Some "things," in all the senses mentioned above and including literary texts, seem to call out more urgently than others, to "wait," as both Bloch and Adorno suggest, upon their interpretation. What is perhaps most unusual about Bloch's *Spuren* is its simultaneous gesture toward narrative and critique. Thus, interwoven with the incidents merely reported in the second section of "Spielformen, Leider" are interpretations of the straw hat as a "symbol of the ruling class," of the Paris street as the very type of "a street of rebellion," the whole incident explicitly summed up as a "Civil War," the hat finally ending up "on the ground . . . levelled and trampelled, a very small, very allegorically crushed representative of the Bastille" (*S*, 24). In the middle of the narrative, the speaker offers a concise "moral of the story," its ethics or politics:

> Hier hätte sich nun der Fahrer wirklich zurückziehen lassen sollen, aber die herrschenden Klassen kapitulieren auch noch schief, abstrakt und undialektisch; kurz, statt die Lage zu fassen und sich in ihr aufzuheben, verwandelte der Provokateur die Kraft seines Vorstoßes in eine nicht minder anmaßende des Rückzugs, drehte um, fuhr bei dem schweren und falschen Manöver nun wirklich in die Masse hinein. (*S*, 24)

> [Now here the driver really should have let himself be drawn back, but the ruling classes even capitulate wrong, abstractly and undialectically; in short, instead of grasping the situation and cancelling, preserving, raising himself in it, the provocator transformed the power of his push forward into a no less presumptuous retreat, turned around, and now really drove as a result of the difficult and mistaken manoeuver right into the crowd.]

Nothing here of that storyteller "who could let the wick of his life be consumed completely by the gentle flame of his story" (ST, 108–9). Like Benjamin's storyteller, however, Bloch does want to offer "something useful . . . a moral . . . some practical advice . . . a proverb or maxim" (ST, 86), "counsel—not for a few situations . . . but for many" (ST, 108). In this, the texts of *Spuren* doubtless have an "old-fashioned ring" (ST, 86), though this ring carries with it an element of surprise which keeps faith with a kind of "naive poetry" (ST, 97), the older and more collective forms of fairy tale and fable, without being confined by them.

Following such violently disruptive modernist texts as those of Rimbaud, Jacob, and Stein, the first surprise of *Spuren* may well be its unabashed emphasis on reflective, descriptive, and narrative continuity. Certainly, this continuity is to be found, as in Baudelaire's *Petits poèmes en prose,* more within individual texts than in the more modernist "montage" of the texts qua collection. Such continuity itself, however, is scarcely grounds for dismissal. As Eagleton has pointed out:

Narrative . . . far from constituting some ruling-class conspiracy, is a valid and perhaps ineradicable mode of human experience. . . .

. . . Narrative continuities do not merely orchestrate into momentary cohesion and a cacophany of historical noises. For there *are* real historical continuities, and it is a dismal index of our theoretical befuddlements that one needs to assert anything so obvious in the first place. (*WB*, 72–73)

In *Spuren,* Bloch takes up the age-old task of retelling a story and so infusing it with new meanings. In the collection's predominantly narrative tone, Adorno remarks, Bloch offers "the paradox of a naive philosophy; childhood, unravaged through all reflection, transforms the most mediated into the most immediate, that is reported." If the texts of *Spuren* are without the denotativeness of the parable, it is nevertheless true, says Adorno, that the interpretations of narrative Bloch offers remain often "far behind the narrative itself, an antinomian sermon on the text."[13] The danger is clear enough. "Counsel woven into the fabric of real life," says Benjamin, "is wisdom," but such counsel is "less an answer to a question than a proposal concerning the continuation of a story which is just unfolding. To seek this counsel one would first have to be able to tell the story" (ST, 86–87). In *Spuren,* Bloch plays two roles, that of the storyteller (or poet, *Dichter*) and that of the critic. If there is a *poverty* to the texts, it is certainly that, in Benjamin's words, events (and objects) come to us "shot through with explanation" (ST, 80). Yet if it is "half the art of storytelling to keep a story free from explanation as one reproduces it" (ST, 89), there is also often an undeniable pleasure to even those narrative/critiques where Bloch's speaker seems to settle on a single meaning, the pleasure of counsel as well as of stories, of interpretation as well as of use, a kind of integrity of these moments which has at least as much *Vor-schein* (of what might be) as *Schein* (of what is). Like Benjamin's chronicler, whose interpretations share both the historian's impulse to explain and the storyteller's desire to display, Bloch is concerned, as his title indicates, with *traces,* not so much "with an accurate concatenation of definite events'" as with "the way these are embedded in the great inscrutable course of the world" (ST, 90). He has at once the chronicler's "eschatological orientation" and the storyteller's "profane outlook," so that in a number of his texts, "it can hardly be decided whether the web

13. Adorno, "Blochs Spuren," in *Noten zur Literatur, Gesammelte Schriften,* 2:235 and 243.

in which they appear is the golden fabric of a religious view of the course of things, or the multicolored fabric of a worldly view" (ST, 96).

At the crux of this problematic stands allegory. The allegorical, Bloch says, "keeps the metaphorical circulating; the symbolic tries metaphorically to land" (*TE*, 144). The straw hat of "Spielformen, Leider" offers in this sense a good example of a Blochian "allegorical symbol": allegorically tossed around in the air from hand to hand, it settles to earth, as we have seen, as a symbol of the ruling class and its downfall. In "Montagen eines Februarabends," for example, after alluding to "widely scattered elements brought together in plain view, as in the delicious, strange Syzygian of a poem by Rimbaud" (*S*, 166), Bloch writes that there is "everywhere an echo of allegorical meanings" (*S*, 167). Like the notion of "traces," these allegorical meanings refer to past, present, and above all for Bloch, future. As re-ligious (tying together) as it is profane, allegory both preserves and destroys, paradoxically "kills" in order to "save" meaning (Benjamin). As such, it may be used at times for the purest deconstruction, but also, in the hands of a Bloch, with the aim of a reconstruction of utopian potentiality in the sense implied by Adorno when he says of Bloch: "He is one of the very few philosophers who do not shrink back from the thought of a world without domination and hierarchy."[14]

Roughly fifty years after the first publication of *Spuren* in 1930, Douglas Kellner and Harry O'Hara concisely situate Bloch's importance in this regard: "Crucial is Bloch's claim that what could have been can still be: for Bloch, history is a repository of possibilities that are living options for future action."[15] What action seems called for depends inevitably on how, and what, we read. If *Spuren* calls on us to read "small things," to read them *allegorically*, the nature of such reading remains to be explored. Among other things, such a reading might be, in Irving Wohlfarth's words, "a mythical, ideological activity synonymous with the guilt and distortion of missed opportunities."[16] In the third section of "Spielformen, Leider," set in 1926 (two years earlier than the first two), Bloch reveals exactly this. In contrast to the worker's bar of the first section, the third is set, like Baudelaire's "Les yeux des pauvres," in a café. The tone is impersonal, uninvolved, a

14. Ibid., p. 249.
15. Douglas Kellner and Harry O'Hara, "Utopia and Marxism in Ernst Bloch," *New German Critique*, no. 9 (Fall 1976), p. 28.
16. Irving Wohlfarth, "Walter Benjamin's Image of Interpretation," *New German Critique*, no. 17 (Spring 1979), p. 91.

retreat from the more engaged mingling with the masses in the second section: "He [a quiet man] sat in front of a green schnapps; occasionally he read. The café at that hour was very busy, the conversations likely, political unrest lay in the air" (*S*, 25). What the man is reading takes him "far from the rising price of bread and the fall of the franc," thirty years back to the fin de siècle, that mythical escape from the modern world when everything was in full bloom and the West was not yet in decline. What this version forgets, of course, is how politically unsettled the peaceful "gay nineties" were. Bloch's café guest finds in his reading a reminder of "anarchistic bombing attempts in Paris," "fear inducing names," in a time "of dynamite and the most concealed threat to bourgeois society and custom" (*S*, 25). In short, a connection is established between the past and the present which would collapse these into one revolutionary moment.

Reading may be used to reveal, among other things, the traces of a revolutionary potential that waits to be released, to be interpreted, and thus to be used for revolutionary purposes; on the other hand, these traces may pass by, as with Bloch's café reader, without being apprehended. Elsewhere, in *Subjekt-Objekt*, Bloch speaks of "grasped history" ("*begriffene Geschichte*") (*SO*, 82), and in another text in *Spuren* of a man who was "right in the middle" of a story he could "almost read . . . /Where it leads? Certainly to a kingdom of poetic meaning, even if it has not yet been determined where that lies" ("Der Zweimal Verschwindende Rahmen" [The Twice Disappearing Frame]) (*S*, 149). Crucial to Bloch's project of apprehending traces in history, stories, anecdotes, narratives, in *reading* generally, is the notion of *interruption*. Thus, the second paragraph begins: "Here the guest had to be interrupted, for a young couple that had sat down at his table was talking" (*S*, 20). Looking perhaps, for an escape from prosaic reality in the auratic, reassuringly poetic atmosphere of fin de siècle France, the speaker had found instead a world of violence and destruction. Here, by contrast, as if by some *trompe l'oeil* that would deny the very existence of such all-too-contemporary problems as "the rising price of bread and the fall of the franc" (*S*, 25), an "elegant" couple enters the scene, "the way the 'lady,' the way the 'gentleman' imagine themselves dressed in Paradise" (*S*, 26). For such as these, it may seem as if the "kingdom of poetic meaning" were no pipedream, nor, as for Bloch, a "concrete utopia" awaiting realization but, rather, a present already realized. What follows in the narrative is a further interruption in which, literally and figuratively, the tables are turned (*Tische umfielen*), both on the elegant couple and on the "quiet reader." As the latter gets up to buy some cigarettes, thinking no longer of the "panthers of Batignolles" (a fin-de-siècle group of violent anarchists), a "horrible explosion" occurs for which he is himself responsible: "The reader's knees trembled, yet on the whole he was unhurt, as was the couple by the way as well, which was nevertheless pure chance. For how easily the splinters of the seltzer bottle the café guest had knocked over as he went to get himself cigarettes could have wounded."

"Play-forms, Unfortunately." Following the reading of his "very historical dynamite book," the café customer reproduces the playful violence—no one is really hurt, but also nothing radically changes—of the anarchists thirty years earlier. What he does so unsuspectingly (*ganz ahnungslos*) suggests, on the one hand, that the missed opportunities of previous history may be seized, half-unconsciously, by a Freudian slip—and not just of the reading eye or of the speaking tongue—that reveals a latent utopian intention. On the other hand, the accidental nature of the violent interruption suggests an anarchistic adventure, as opposed to Bloch's "grasped history." The moment is not so much seized, in this case, as experienced; its potential meaning is not grasped until later, when it has the polished ring of truth. Having paid for damages, the guest leaves the café ("almost ashamed to have come away so harmlessly") for his usual restaurant, where he tells "the heroic story, wherein out of bad luck an assassin, the Day of Judgment [*Weltgericht*] had appeared out of a seltzer bottle." The comfort of legend and of literature, however, has its limits, and revolution may be reduced by it to a tale of Aladdin's lamp, a fairy tale:

> Rasch hatte sich der Geist [but also "*der Gast*"] wieder in die Flasche zurückgezogen; doch die dunkle Scham des Manns, der Ärger des Paars an seiner Strafe standen noch fühlbar in der Luft. Betroffenheit des Literaten, Erberinnerung der Bourgeoisie: beides spielte über dem *unfähigen Ereignis* [my emphasis]. Spielte eine Vergangenheit nach, die nicht verging, eine Zukunft vor, von der sich selbst der Pariser Bürger nicht losgesprochen fühlt. Was ein Fest wurde wie der 14 Juli, ist gewesen; aber die Furcht, die einmal darin war, ist noch frisch. Speisten alle Arbeiter Hummer, so ritzten die Splitter der Syphonflasche keine Gefühle. (*S*, 26–27)

> [Soon the spirit [but also the café customer, "*der Gast*"] had drawn back into the bottle; yet the dark shame of the man, the anger of the couple at his punishment still remained palpably in the air. Perplexity of the man of letters, memory of the inheritance of the bourgeoisie: both played over the *impotent event* [my emphasis]. Played on a past that

didn't go away, a future from which even the Parisian bourgeois himself does not feel himself absolved. What became of a celebration on the 14th of July is past; but the fear that was once there is still fresh. If all workers dined on lobster, the splinters of the seltzer bottle wouldn't cut open any feelings.]

In this conclusion, the literary text functions as compensation for a deep-seated social impotence to correct the wrongs of past history. As such, it is the symptomatic presentation of an "impotent event." Yet it is also, and this is the crucial point for Bloch, a promissory note insofar as it reminds us of our debts and obligations to both past and future. It is only through the arresting present moment of revolutionary praxis, however—what Bloch and Benjamin have both called the *Jetztzeit* or "time of the now"—that these debts and obligations can begin to be met and absolved, "described, explained, cancelled, preserved, and raised (*aufgehoben*) at one stroke" ("Der Schmutz" [The Dirt]) (*S,* 21). Such is the specifically *lyrical* intention of Bloch's "Spielformen," as of *Spuren* generally—in the sense Adorno gives to the lyric as expressing the "dream of a world in which things would be different"—to provide impetus for an intensely *active* reading that would not divorce interpretation from use: "The here and now of men, without action, tastes flat; not least of all because it could be so splendid and is not" ("Stachel der Arbeit" [Thorn of Work]) (*S,* 103). Bloch's "grasped history" does not necessarily posit a *Jetztzeit* of *absolute* presence; it does however posit one of historical awareness and action *toward* the future, mindful not only of continuity but also of the chance for a "revolutionary change that contains an eruption of novelty, a break with the past, the qualitatively new."[17] This possibility, which Bloch will refer to much later in his astoundingly consistent oeuvre as *Novum*, appears in *Spuren* under a more concrete name: "Der Rücken der Dinge" (The Other Side of Things).

Objective Transformations: *Schein* and *Vor-Schein*

The "primacy of the object" Adorno describes as a constitutive feature of modern art is only able to preserve itself, Adorno says, in the form of unconscious history writing, "anamnesis of what has been vanquished or repressed, perhaps an anticipation of what is possible" (*AT,* 384, 366). Certainly it is possible, as Stein's *Tender Buttons* demonstrates, to

17. Kellner and O'Hara, "Utopia and Marxism," p. 33.

construct a narrative or history of objects no less than of events. The latter suggests the anecdotal structure so prominent in Baudelaire's *Petits poèmes en prose* as well as in Bloch's "Spielformen, Leider." Like Baudelaire's collection, however, Bloch's *Spuren* ranges freely from a focus on events to a focus on physical objects, "things" in the other primary sense indicated above. Like Baudelaire, Bloch has a fondness for lyrical mediation as well as for a concise, well-told story, for poetry as well as for prose, both poetic and speculative thought:

> Ob es die Rose weiß, daß sie eine Rose ist, diese Frage ist nicht nur ein später Witz des Verstands, sondern sie liegt bereits Kindern nahe, grade weil sie sachlich sind und jedes Wort in bar haben wollen. Ganz einfach, ganz früh hingesehen: was "treiben" die Dinge ohne uns? wie sieht das Zimmer aus, das man verläßt? (*S*, 172)

> [Does the rose know that it is a rose? This question is not only a later witticism of understanding; it also already lies close to children, precisely because they are down-to-earth and want every word in cash. Quite simply, looked at quite early: what do things "do" without us? How does the room look in our absence?]

Having begun with a decidedly prosaic object ("the towel is rough to the skin, coarsely woven"), in the above passage Bloch then moves to the most poetic of objects, the rose, with all its weight of allegorical and symbolic meaning. The text's intention is to be down-to-earth, objective (*"sachlich"*), to approach "things" concretely, and clearly this orientation carries with it a speculative element that is "naive." Bloch's naiveté, however, like that of Benjamin's storyteller, is deliberate. Its purpose, as the questions that end the above passage suggest, is to restore that state, or rather, *activity* of astonishment (cf. "Das Staunen" [*S*, 216–18]) which for Bloch provides perhaps the most visible and important trace of a unity between philosophy and poetry. In contrast to Ricoeur, Bloch will not acknowledge a final separation between these two modes of discourse. Their relationship is, instead, a fluid one, their interpenetration to be encouraged. If philosophy has as its task, as Ricoeur says, the disruption of old categorization and the establishment of "new logical frontiers on the ruins of their forerunners" (*RM*, 197), it is allied in its endeavor with poetry. In this sense, Bloch's "naive" but also self-consciously metaphorical question, "what do things 'do' without us?", provides a bridge between the philosophical and the poetic, the speculative and the lyrical, "abstract" and "concrete" thinking.

"To present men *'as acting'* and all things 'as in act,'" Ricoeur says, "such could well be the ontological function of metaphorical discourse, in which every dormant potentiality of existence appears *as* blossoming forth, every latent capacity for action *as* actualized" (*RM*, 43). Certainly, this is one of metaphor's intended functions in Bloch's *Spuren*, its *object* in the phenomenological sense. Like Rimbaud, Bloch is concerned with children, with a sense of wonder and an accompanying openness to the possibility that things might be different than they are. Baudelaire too is no stranger to the "hidden" potential of the inanimate:

> Les meubles ont des formes allongées, prostrées, alanguies . . . on les dirait doués d'une vie somnambulique, comme le végétal et le minér-al. Les étoffes parlent une langue muette, comme les fleurs, comme les ciels, comme les soleils couchants.
>
> [Every piece of furniture is of an elongated form, languid and pros-trate . . . endowed, one would say, with a somnambular existence like minerals and vegetables. The hangings speak a silent language like flowers, skies, and setting suns.] (*OC* l, 280; *PS*, 5)

Responding to Adorno's definition of the lyric as the dream of a world in which things would be different, Hans Robert Jauss has remarked that the lyric's appeal is not in this regard, as Adorno claims, "a recent phenomenon, namely a formal response to the reification of the world and thereby 'thoroughly modern,'" but a demand ("*Forderung*") of older lyrics as well.[18] For Bloch, indeed, this characteristically utopian demand is shared, like metaphor, by both philosophy and poetry.

It is in the lyric, however, and in modern times in that consummate poem-object, the prose poem, that this dream finds its most concise if not also its most tangible form. From the passage of Baudelaire quoted above to Rimbaud's *Illuminations* to the "Objects" of Stein's *Tender Buttons* to Francis Ponge's *Le parti pris des choses* (Taking the Side of the Things), the history of the prose poem displays an extraordinary pre-occupation with material objects. For this reason too it seems appropri-ate and useful to consider the *Denkbilder* of Bloch's *Spuren*, the last section of which is called "Dinge" (Things), in terms of the prose poem problematic. That a pronounced focus on the world of material objects has clear philosophical as well as poetic—Bloch would also say *uto-pian*—potential is evident in a work such as Wittgenstein's *Philosophical Investigations*. Indeed, much of the energy of the latter work may be

18. Hans Robert Jauss, *Ästhetische Erfahrung und literarische Hermeneutik* (Munich: Fink, 1977), 1:338.

attributed to "naive," in other words *fundamental*, questions such as those in the Bloch passage above which convey, like the texts of *Spuren* generally, a sense of wonder and astonishment at once "philosophical" and "poetic." In this sense especially, Bloch's *Denkbilder* may be said to extend the range or grasp of the prose poem's metaphorically highly charged, compact space from its more typical attention to prosaic and poetic images (*Bilder*) to a more explicit focus on philosophical issues (*Denken*) as well. From the "astonished" point of view of both philosophy and poetry, nothing is proven, everything open, full of potentials yet to be released, all science heuristic, all things bracketed by a phenomenological uncertainty as unsettling as it is promising:

> Das Feuer im Ofen . . . was die Möbel während unseres Ausgangs taten ist dunkel. Keine Vermutung darüber ist zu beweisen, aber auch keine, noch so phantastische, ist zu widerlegen. Eben: Mäuse tanzen auf dem Tisch? Grade, daß alles bei unserer Rückkehr wieder dasteht, "als wäre nichts gewesen," kann das Unheimlichste von allem sein. . . . Wird der Tisch notwendig immer als Tisch geglaubt und daß er sich nicht genug darin tun kann, ein Tisch zu sein—nur nach der scheinenden Vorderseite, die er dem Blick zuwendet, sobald wir auf ihn blicken? Die Welt als bloße Vorstellung . . . ist ein sehr natürlicher, ganz vorwissenschaftlicher Schreck; Berkeley, sozusagen, ist heutigen Menschen ihr primitiver Zustand. (*S*, 172–73)

> [The fire in the oven . . . what the furniture did at our departure is dark. No speculation thereon may be verified, but also none, even the most fantastic, may be refuted. For example: Mice dancing on a table? The very fact that everything is there again at our return "as if nothing had happened" can be the most unsettling of all. . . . Is the table always necessarily believed to be a table, as if it couldn't be happier being a table—only from the front side that appears to us, that it turns to our gaze as soon as we glance at it? The world as mere representation . . . is a very natural, quite pre-scientific fright: Berkeley, we might say, is contemporary man in his primitive condition.]

Beginning here with an example that recalls the domestic magic of a fairy tale, mice dancing on a table, Bloch moves through observation and reflection to one of the most persistent of modern philosophical problems: "The world as mere representation." This procedure is typical of Bloch, for whom real philosophizing begins, like real poetry, with what Jameson has called a "renewal of thought in astonishment . . . a concrete working out of the astonishment we feel before the world itself" (*MF*, 122–23).

The texts of *Spuren*, those "glowing emblems," are, says Jameson, "dramatic rather than lyrical, involving not a contemplative perception of . . . some central object at rest, but rather a convulsive stirring within objects, a stirring which unfolds itself in time" (*MF*, 123). Certainly, the notion of a "convulsive stirring within objects" is an important element of Bloch's texts.[19] To identify Bloch's compositional strategy as "dramatic rather than lyrical" or "contemplative," however, is to underestimate the lyric's own dramatic potential, which is evident in the modern "prose lyric" or "prose poem" as well as in older lyric forms.[20] Bloch's *Spuren*, Baudelaire's *Petits poèmes en prose*, *Denkbilder*, and collections of prose poems generally suggest the extent to which narrative, dramatic, meditative, and lyrical moments may be drawn together so energetically and interestingly in a compact space that the barriers between them begin to fall:

> Ein Andres macht die Dinge sogar bedenklich, während sie unter unserm Blick stehen. Ist man im Theater und brennen etwa die Kerzen im letzten Akt Wallenstein auf dem Tisch und Wallenstein unterschreibt den Vertrag mit Wrangel: so sind die Kerzen und der Tisch wirklich Kerzen und Tisch, Schauspielern nicht . . . wieso entsteht also kein Riß, wieso fühlt der Zuschauer, Illusion hin oder her, keine verschiedenen Ebenen des Ernstes? *Schauspielern denn auch die Dinge?* (*S*, 173)

> [Another makes things seem doubtful even while they stand right before our eyes. In the theater where the candles on the table burn, for example, in the last act of *Wallenstein* as Wallenstein signs the agreement with Wrangel; are the candles and the table then really candles and table, not actors . . . how is it that there is no split, how is it the spectator, illusion here illusion there, feels no variety of levels of seriousness? *Are things then actors too?*]

19. The sections of *The Dialogic Imagination* on the relationship between words and objects cited in the previous chapter with reference to Stein's *Tender Buttons* are of great interest here as well. In a passage, for example, that offers a potentially helpful sociolinguistic contextualization of what is involved in Bloch's project of exploring the other side of things, Bakhtin writes (277): "The way in which the word conceptualizes its object is a complex act—all objects . . . are from one side highlighted while from the other side dimmed by heteroglot social opinion, by an alien word about them." Using language that is close in a number of key respects to Bloch's own, Bakhtin goes on to speak of the "intention" of the dialogized word ("its directionality toward the object") in terms of a refracted ray of light that illuminates "the social atmosphere of the word, the atmosphere that surrounds the object."

20. For Aristotle, as Ricoeur points out, the "dramatic" power "'to represent things as in a state of activity' does not concern tragic poetry alone . . . it applies to lyrical mimesis as well . . ." (*RM*, 307).

The "masks" of things, their "aura," is constituted for Bloch by both *Schein* and *Vorschein*. The former, roughly the equivalent of ideological projection, is for Bloch, as it is also for Benjamin in "The Work of Art in the Age of Mechanical Reproduction," the intended *object* of a concerted and deliberate destruction, the "counter-face" or counterfeit of *Vor-Schein*. Like the aura of Benjamin's storyteller, *Vor-Schein* is something worth preserving, the promise of a future "concrete utopia" where a new, collective *use*-value may succeed the current hegemony of exchange, where "money no longer barks after goods . . ." (*S*, 23) and we may have what Bloch says the child wants, "every word in cash" (*S*, 172). Such, in a sense, is the tendency of Bloch's and Benjamin's notion of allegorical reading, which risks "killing" the text in order to turn it at least to new uses. The uses Bloch envisions would be a radical departure from current usage, the "other side" or "back" of it, "beyond use" (*jenseits des Gebrauchs*) (*S*, 173), "not an *Aufhebung* of the object per se, but simply . . . *Aufhebung* of the object as it is alienated from the self" (*SO*, 107–8), a liberated use opening, in Jameson's words, "onto otherness or difference" (*MF*, 146). Thus, in "Der Rücken der Dinge," we catch a glimpse of that "transformation of objects in the world to come" which Jameson has associated with "lyrical expression generally," and we do so precisely, as so often in the prose poem, through a focus on "humbler artifacts." The making of the latter, including the making of *Denkbilder* and prose poems, may well embody one of the more authentic ways "in which man attempts to rejoin himself through the things around him . . . the heart of lyric expression" (*MF*, 149). Such a view is, in any case, eminently compatible with the materials of Bloch's text:

> Obst, Rosen, Wälder . . . die Kerze aus Stearin, selbst aus Wachs, der schöne Schrank aus Holz, gar aus Eisen, das steinerne Haus, die Glut im Ofen, gar in der elektrischen Birne gehören einer andern Welt, einer in die menschliche nur eingesprengten. (*S*, 174)
>
> [Fruit, roses, woods . . . the candle made of stearin, even of wax, the beautiful cabinet made of wood, even in iron, the stone house, the glow in the oven, even that in the electric bulb, all these belong to another world that is merely interspersed in the human.]

Sometimes, Bloch's objects are more distant or more spectacular: "The sea . . . the lightning whose light comes down onto the writing table" (*S*, 174). In accordance with the notion that the everyday is, in Kosik's words, "a phenomenal world, in which reality manifests itself in a certain way and simultaneously conceals itself" (*DK*, 75), Bloch consistently sets into relation distance and nearness, the extraordinary and the everyday:

> Deshalb könnte sich auch der Jugendeindruck von Wallensteins Kerzen und Tisch mit einem ganz andern "Phantasma" leicht verbinden, mit einem Märchen jenseits des Theaters, in der weiten Welt selbst, die wir bewohnen, mit dem Märchen Sindbads des Seefahrers und einem Motiv seines Unsterns. Hier markierte sich das abgewendete Gesicht der Dinge, ihr noch "irrationales" Eigenleben sogar drohend als das X, das es jenseits der Gebrauchsmasken ist. (S, 174)

> [This is why the youth's impression of Wallenstein's candles and table may be easily linked to a completely different "phantasm," with a fairy tale beyond the theater, in the wide world that we live in, with the fairy tale of Sinbad the sailor and the theme of his misfortune. Here the face of things that is turned away from us, the still "irrational" life showed itself as perhaps even a bit threatening, the X that exists beyond the masks of use.]

Wearing the double mask of present appearance (*Schein*) and anticipation (*Vor-Schein*), Bloch's "things" suggest the potential of both eros and thanatos; if they "point" to anything, they cannot escape doing so ambiguously. Thus, Bloch goes on to retell the tale of Sinbad's shipwreck, where the captain and some of his sailors rescue themselves on an island "full of fruits, cocopalms, birds, and huntable animals, with a spring in the wood." This utopian salvation soon turns into an apocalypse, however: as the survivors light a fire toward evening, it turns out the island is the back of a dragon who, after sleeping peacefully for many years, is wakened by the fire and dives under, taking with him not only the crew members but also all the ships in the surrounding water. Bloch's *Vor-Schein* is thus not so harmlessly alluring as it may appear. The utopian dream implies risk, the possible destruction of much that may seem worth preserving, and with no guarantees as to the outcome:

> Manche dieser und noch andre, vielleicht weniger unheimliche, doch ebenso sprengende Möglichkeiten stecken in der Vexierfrage, wie das Zimmer aussieht, wenn man es verläßt. Vorn ist es hell oder hell gemacht, aber kein Mensch weiß noch, woraus der *Rücken* der Dinge besteht, den wir allein sehen, gar ihre *Unterseite* und worin das Ganze schwimmt. Man kennt nur die Vorderseite oder Oberseite ihrer technischen Dienstwilligkeit, freundlichen Eingemeindung; niemand weiß auch, ob ihre (oft erhaltene) Idylle, Lockung, Naturschönheit das ist, was sie verspricht oder zu halten vorgibt. (S, 174–75)

[Some of these and still other, perhaps less uncanny yet equally explosive possibilities lie in the vexing question as to how the room looks in our absence. In front of us everything is bright or made bright, but nobody knows what makes up the *back* of things that we alone see, much less their *underside* and what everything is swimming in. We know only the front side or the top side of their technical willingness to serve, friendly incorporation; no one knows either whether their (oft maintained) idyll, enticement, natural beauty really is what it promises or pretends to hold.][21]

"Die Perle": Traces of an Open System

In the texts from *Spuren* we have examined thus far, the relation of reading to praxis is clearly a major problematic;[22] actions are shown to be inextricably linked to our interpretations of "things," whether of physical objects ("Der Rücken der Dinge") or events ("Spielformen, Leider"). As the counsel of Benjamin's storyteller suggests, these complementary lyrical and narrative emphases may have a practical dimension. In the text called "Die Perle," Bloch reaffirms literature's potential for contributing to a utopian praxis that would be beyond mere utility (*jenseits des Gebrauchs*): "And the advice, 'Leave everything and you will find everything,' is not only false in itself but also for action" (*S*, 219). The counsel of literature, to be sure, may be double-edged. Bloch goes on to retell a tale from India about a king who has lost a very beautiful pearl and has his subjects search far and wide for it, until one day he discovers it himself. Like the café guest in "Spielformen, Leider" who unsuspectingly causes a harmless explosion, the king makes his discovery "on the path of purposelessness" (*auf dem Wege der Absichtslosigkeit*) (*S*, 219). As so often in *Spuren*, Bloch follows immediately with a summary, a moral of the story: "Precisely the do-nothing then, who perhaps forgot his desires and who was no longer driven on by them saw them fulfilled" (*S*, 219). To be content with this interpretation, however, would be to accept the kind of essentially contemplative approach to literature Bloch expressly rejects. Thus, he continues, not

21. "The true utopia," Bloch says (*PH*, 133), "has nothing to fear from the demystification which has taken place, but can only learn from it and vice-versa; thus there is also a birth of utopia from the spirit of destruction and vice-versa."

22. Writing on another text from *Spuren* entitled "Armer und Reicher Teufel," Witschel has remarked (*Literatur und Sprache*, 136) that although the action is closed, the text as a whole remains open, "for what reader would not feel himself called upon to reflect on the figures [*Chiffren*] in his life in which highly conscious moments came into correlation and opened up to him an anticipatory mode of thought like a bolt of lightning" (translation mine).

with a further illustration or collaboration of the tale's manifest thesis but with a critique of it:

> Soweit die alles zeithafte Handeln verlassende Fabel, gleich wie wenn das Draußen schon soweit wäre, daß es das Unsere von selber gibt. Und es nur dann schenkt, wenn wir nichts dazu tun; was entschieden zu schön wäre, um wahr zu sein, und zu steril, um Frucht zu entwickeln. (*S*, 219–20)

> [So it is according to the fable that abandons all time-bound action, as if what is outside us were already so far along that it gives us what is ours on its own and does so of its own accord; all of which would be decidedly too good to be true and too sterile to bear fruit.]

To *interpret* the world "in various ways," Marx's famous dictum goes, is to do what philosophers have always done, "the point, however, is to *change* it."[23] Like Marx—one thinks also of Rimbaud's *changer la vie* and of the reiteration of this project (*transformer le monde*) by Breton, Bloch's surrealist contemporary—Bloch wants to see words put into action. Flying in the face of art-for-art-sake's capitulation to the impotence of art in the modern world, Bloch insists on literature's potential to have a significant part in effecting radical change. Hence the desire for "grasped history," which is acted out in *Spuren* ("Spielformen, Leider") by the dialectical interplay of lyrical, narrative, and reflective moments, of interpretation and critique. "Here too one sees how there is no true path without a goal, and also no goal without the power of a path to arrive there, indeed a path itself preserved in the goal" (*S*, 220). For Bloch, the goal of literature as well as of philosophy is always "action" (*Handeln*). The first word said of a literary text, as of anything else, establishes a direction or meaning, a *sens* that is also, inevitably, a limitation. To interpret, to "give" meaning, however, is simply, as Wittgenstein observes, to *use* language. Granted that any one concretization of a given text's "structural possibilities" (*Strukturierungsangebot*) runs, as Wolfgang Iser has said, "against the openness of the text," carrying with it a "part of illusion" (*Illusionsanteil*) which corresponds to its degree of closure,[24] Bloch would still find it crucially important that even the "depragmatizations" characteristic of imaginative literature be

---

23. Marx, "Theses on Feuerbach," in *Collected Works* (New York: International Publishers, 1976), 5:8.

24. Wolfgang Iser, *Der Akt des Lesens* (Munich: Wilhelm Fink, 1976), pp. 202–3. The passage quoted here is not available in the book's English translation; see *The Act of Reading*, p. 124.

turned to new uses (the other side of things), that the wealth of potentiality "in" literary texts not be left unrealized, paradoxically encaged by an openness that is at least as much *Schein* (to be disclosed) as *Vor-Schein* (to be reopened).[25] Interpretive intervention alone may not be capable of changing life, but neither is it something to be dispensed with in the hope that "things" will "turn out" alright, or as if they already had: "Something of the kind was further maintained, not for temporal action but for the prior spatial existence of the external world in and of itself and its scattered juxtapositions, in a manner making it seem "as if such a thing as diffusion didn't even exist" (*als ob es gar nichts Zerstreutes wäre*) (*S,* 220).

Zerstreutheit (distraction, the scattered state of things), we may recall, is one of Hegel's characteristic terms for designating the world of prose he considers so fundamentally opposed to the "oneness" (*Einheit*) demonstrated by both philosophy and poetry.[26] For Bloch, Hegel is above all the philosopher of becoming (*Werden*), on the one hand, and, on the other hand, of the closed system:

> So gibt es die Geschichte von einem sehr weisen Mann, dem die Welt bereits derart zu sich gekommen und aus dem Schneider der Vielheit heraus war, daß er, wie gemeldet wird, immer von Zeit zu Zeit eine Brille aufsetzen mußte, sonst sah er alle Dinge als Eines. Nun aber, es wird einem auch diese Perle nicht geschenkt, schon deshalb nicht, weil neben ihr dann ja überhaupt nichts mehr als diese Eine wäre. Wenigstens nach mystischer Meinung, wie sie freilich auch die banalsten Ableger in pensionierten Ruhewünschen oder auch der Wiederkehr des immer Gleichen aufweisen kann. Doch wie höhnisch oft und gerade wieder wie zahlreich sieht sich der Wunsch nach Ende des Treibens, der Zerstreutheit, Zerstreuung nicht durchs Eine, sondern nur durchs Eintöniges erfüllt, also nicht verneint, sondern betrogen. (*S,* 220)

> [Thus there is the story of a very wise man for whom the world had already come to itself so completely, was so beyond diversity, that he reportedly had to put on a pair of glasses every now and then; otherwise he saw all things as one. Well now these pearls too are not just going to be given to you, certainly not because besides them there is indeed absolutely nothing else but this oneness. At least according to mystical opinion, as surely the most banal scions can demonstrate in the

---

25. Ibid., p. 355. Iser writes: ". . . if there is not *one* specific meaning of a literary text, this 'apparent lack' [*Mangel*] is in fact the productive matrix which enables the text to be meaningful in a variety of different contexts." For Iser's discussions of the concept of depragmatization, see pp. 61, 79, 93, 109, 184, 212.

26. See Hegel, *Ästhetik,* 3:254–55.

longings for rest of those in retirement or the eternal return of the
same. Yet how scornfully often and precisely again how frequently the
desire for an end to activity, distraction, diffusion is realized, not
through oneness, but through one-dimensionality, not, that is, negated,
but defrauded.]

In *Subjekt-Objekt*, which was first published in 1951, some twenty years
after the first edition of *Spuren,* Bloch portrays Hegel's limitations precisely as those of this "very wise man to whom the world had already
come to itself" so completely that the philosophy of becoming had
ended in a philosophy of "what had already been" (*Gewordensein*).
Hegel's system is "one that is already completed rather than one of an
ongoing utopian process" (*SO,* 144). The latter, of course, is Bloch's
view of the Marxian corrective: "The whole world is here an open
system working through a dialectical process of enlightenment. Its
point is a humanity no longer objectively alienated from itself among
objects that are themselves no longer alienated. That is Hegel's life in
Marx" (*SO,* 416). System, Bloch says, is a *"utopian-concrete whole"* (*"uto-
pisch-konkretes Totem"*) (*SO,* 470), not Hegel's "bookish closure" (*Buch-
Geschlossenheit*), his idealistic "seamless coherence, hung onto a fixed
beginning or fixed end" (*SO,* 472). *Spuren* itself, as the second edition
of 1959 suggests, is an *open* book. Both its beginning text, "Zu Wenig"
(Too Little) and its concluding one, "Die Perle," were absent from the
original edition. In between, some nineteen other new texts have been
added. But does *Spuren* illustrate or exemplify that interruptive yet
"systematic openness" Bloch associates with materialism?

   Both terms, "systematic" and "openness," are problematic. Egenolf
Roeder von Diersburg has described Bloch's mode of thought as "utterly unsystematic,"[27] and Jürgen Habermas has described Bloch's philosophy as a form of "speculative materialism": "A utopia that grasps
anew the dialectic of its own realization in a utopian manner is not so
concrete as it might claim to be."[28] One of the major problems with
Bloch's project of "reflecting in the act of narration, narrating in the
act of reflection" is that of the relation between philosophy and poetry,
which is also the problem, as we have seen, of metaphor. As Habermas
says: "a residue of metaphor always clings to utopia."[29] And not just to

   27. Egenolf Roeder von Diersburg, *Zur Ontologie und Logik offener Systeme* (Hamburg:
Felix Meiner, 1967), p. 49.
   28. Jürgen Habermas, "Ein Marxistischer Schelling," in his *Über Ernst Bloch* (Frankfurt: Suhrkamp, 1968), p. 78.
   29. Ibid., p. 81.

utopia either, but also, as Jacques Derrida has argued, to *philosophy*, as well as poetry.[30] *Spuren* situates itself through the interpenetration of the philosophical and the poetic in such a way as to suggest, like the prose poem, a dialogized "non-generic unity" (*RM*, 272) among various modes of discourse. For Bloch, however, unlike for Hegel, such a unity is conceived as a continually open process, driven by "the thorn of ever new contradictions, ever new solutions and contradictions" (*SO*, 65), by the "thorn of work" ("Stachel der Arbeit") (*S*, 99–103). In place of "certainty, well-orderedness, closure, those three image criteria of the closed system, the open system has only one: expedition, forwarding." If Bloch's notion of "Expedition" recalls that "eternal becoming" (*ewig nur werden*) Schlegel associates with the novel and with *Universalpoesie*,[31] the popular, serialized novels of the nineteenth century and the best sellers of the twentieth century seem closer to Bloch's three criteria for a *closed* rather than an open system. Nearer to the latter is not only the more fragmented structuring of innovative novels in the nineteenth and twentieth centuries but also the tradition of the prose poem qua collection, the open system of a collection such as Baudelaire's *Petits poèmes en prose* which anticipates in fundamental respects, as we have seen, the form of Bloch's *Spuren*.[32]

Though the comparative openness of Bloch's collection is relatively clear, its status as "system" (call it "philopoetic") seems more questionable. If the work of art that believes it can possess its own content is, as Adorno says it must be, "naive and rationalistic in the worst sense of the word" (*AT*, 47/40), what then of Bloch's "grasped history" and his mode of apprehension, namely allegory? Does the latter, itself a rationalizing procedure, hinder or assist an openness that would be, in Schlegel's words, "not linear, but open to all sides"?[33] Does Bloch's procedure of offering a text followed immediately by his own interpretation of that text close off more potential than it liberates? Certainly it risks, as we have seen, limiting the text in order to help "turn it" to new uses, risks being (mis)understood as an attempted totalization in order to move toward some apprehension of a totality which is not

30. Derrida, *White Mythology*, passim.

31. Schlegel, *Athenäums-Fragmente, Kritische Ausgabe*, p. 183. See also Iser on the novel and "discovery" in *The Implied Reader* (Baltimore: Johns Hopkins University Press, 1974), p. xiii, passim.

32. Among important works for the *rapproachement* of prose poetry and a twentieth-century style fragmentation of the novel, Lautréamont's *Les chants de Maldoror* is doubtless the most striking early example.

33. von Diersburg, *Zur Ontologie*, p. 2.

given, but to be *constructed*.[34] Just as certainly, Bloch's allegorical "Al-teritas" aspires to a symbolic "Unitas," a "significant increase in 'mean-ing'" (*bedeutend 'Mehrdeutige'*) (*TE*, 144) that would be distinguished, as is Ricoeur's "*Mehrdeutigkeit*," "from pure and simple dissemination—from *Vieldeutigkeit*" (*RM*, 311). Bloch, to be sure, would not entirely agree with Ricoeur that "in confronting this polysemy of being, philos-ophy confirms that thinking is not poeticizing" (*RM*, 311). If his con-cerns are, like Ricoeur's, manifestly religious in their focus on unity, they are in other senses quite different. To the extent that metaphor may be said to present "in an open fashion, by means of a conflict *between* identity and difference, the process that, in a *covert* manner, generates semantic grids by fusion of differences *into* identity" (*RM*, 198), Bloch sees in the use of metaphor, whether "philosophical" or "poetic," a possibility for political praxis.

What Ricoeur calls "the 'search' for a non-generic bond of being"—a search fundamental, as we have seen, to the prose poem's own project as genre—is inseparable for Bloch from the idea of establishing a class-less society. What for Ricoeur remains "a task for *thought*" (*RM*, 272; my emphasis) is for Bloch, as it was for Marx, not just a question of interpretation or thought at all but one of actively changing the struc-ture of a contemporary society that remains in many vital respects, despite certain "traces" of an open system, decidedly more closed than open, more restrictive than liberating. To quote Ricoeur once again: "Destruction of the metaphorical by the conceptual in rationalizing interpretations is not the only outcome of the interaction between dif-ferent modalities of discourse. One can imagine a hermeneutic style where interpretation would conform both to the notion of concept and to that of the constitutive intention of the experience seeking to be expressed in the metaphorical mode" (*RM*, 303). *Spuren*, certainly, gives traces of such a project, but its "goal," as "Die Perle" puts it, is not just a more open "hermeneutic style" but an open society.

At the heart of this project, there is a deep and perhaps irreconcil-able tension; *Alteritas*, the "Real-Allegorien" of art, and *Unitas*, the "Real-Symbolen" of religion (*TE*, 146)—*Spuren* wants to have both and at the same time to infuse these with a political significance, a political

---

34. Such a totality is referred to by Harold Steinhagen as "a coherence, a hidden—not yet existing—order, to which they ['things'] point as allegorical fragments while at the same time testifying to its nonexistence" ("Zu Walter Benjamins Begriff der Alle-gorie," *Formen und Funktionen der Allegorie*, ed. Walter Haug [Stuttgart: Metzler, 1979], p. 672).

use.[35] Like Benjamin, Bloch preserves the image of "an almost messianically selective hand to bring things out of their scattered state," a hand to be coordinated with the eye in a sudden "leap of the lucky glance" that would bring out traces of utopian desire from their submersion in the past and present for a redeeming future ("Die glückliche Hand" [The Lucky Hand]) (*S*, 201–2). In attempting to bring out such traces, Bloch's *Denkbilder* may be said to develop characteristic "minus functions" of the prose poem,[36] infusing the form with an explicit philosophical and political content that illuminates the utopian tendency the genre already displays in the hands of Baudelaire and Rimbaud.

Like the texts of Baudelaire's *Petits poèmes en prose*, which oscillate between everyday ennui and the unattainable ideal ("Spleen et idéal"), Bloch's *Denkbilder* tend to argue in a manner described by Adorno as "at once utopian and dualistic."[37] The indispensable emphasis on praxis as a mediation and a cure for dualistic thinking which is both forwarded and problematized in Baudelaire's "Assommons les pauvres!" remains, as Bloch's own texts suggest, an "impotent event" so long as readers do not *act:*

> Sehe man drum jetzt und hier sich um, mit tätig gesetzter Zeit im tätig umgebauten Raum, die Spuren des sogenannten Letzten, ja auch nur wirklich Gewordenen sind selber Abdrücke eines Gehens, das noch ins Neue gegangen werden muß. Erst sehr weit hinaus ist alles, was einem begegnet und auffällt, das Selbe. (*S*, 220)

> [If you look around here and now, with actively posited time in actively restructured space, the traces of the so-called last thing, indeed of what has also actually already been, are themselves imprints of a

35. Bloch's position, in contrast to that of Ricoeur, recalls Marx's affirmation in the important Amsterdam speech of September 8, 1872, of the possibility of nonviolent revolution (*The Marx-Engels Reader*, 523): "Someday the worker must seize political power in order to build up the new organization of labor; he must overthrow the old politics which sustain the old institutions, if he is not to lose heaven on earth, like the old Christians who neglected and despised politics." Von Diersburg summarizes Bloch's perspective nicely when he says (*Zur Ontologie*, 6) that for Bloch: "The single function of 'openness' is to create a space for the social utopia; its only meaning is to offer this utopia a home."

36. For general discussions of the concept of the "minus-function," see Iser's *The Act of Reading*, pp. 207–10, and Lotman, *Die Struktur literarischer Texte*, pp. 143–58, 207, and 267.

37. Adorno, "Blochs Spuren," p. 241. For further analysis of Bloch's mode of argumentation see Renate Kubler's "Die Metapher als Argument. Semiotische Bestimmung der Blochschen Sprache," in *Ernst Blochs Wirkung* (Frankfurt: Suhrkamp, 1975), pp. 271–83.

passing that must still have gone into the new. Only very far in the distance is everything that meets you and occurs to you the same.]

These final sentences of "Die Perle," which are at the same time the "conclusion" of *Spuren*, offer a correction, as we noted near the beginning of this chapter, of the conclusion of "Das Merke." Bloch's concept of "the same" (*das Selbe*), the identity of identity and difference—not "one-dimensionality" but "oneness"—is not a *fait accompli* but a *project* not yet realized. Its emblem, the pearl, suggests the allegorical variety and multiplicity of the baroque, an extravagant wealth or potential some have to work (dive) for which is taken for granted (given) by others, eros (a lover's gift) but also thanatos ("Those are pearls that were his eyes"), a small jewel (Jacob's definition of the prose poem) that may be strung together with others of its kind (or genre) in a variety of ways. Like collections of *Denkbilder* and prose poems, pearls may be strung in linear, circular, arabesque, and other arrangements (Baudelaire's "Thyrse," Bloch's "Rokoko"), arranged and rearranged; always open to one or many others of their kind, paratactic, compact, hard and resistant, enduring yet simple, they are at once opaque and luminescent. But is Bloch's "Newness" (*das Neue*) "of the so-called last thing" a utopia, an apocalypse, or both at once? "The true beginning [*Die wirkliche Genesis*]," Bloch writes in the famous passage at the conclusion of *Das Prinzip Hoffnung* (The Principle of Hope) "is not in the beginning [*am Anfang*], but in the end . . . grounded in real democracy, . . . something that appears to everyone in childhood and wherein no one has ever been: home" (*PH*, 1628). "In the end," the concrete utopia of Bloch's *Spuren* remains a "waiting story," both utopian and dualistic, gesturing like the prose poem generally qua collection toward an open system in the empty space (*Hohlraum*) of society's missed opportunities.

"Idealism," Bloch says, "is what continues running on and on within itself . . . materialism, by contrast, is interruption" (*SO*, 135). Without the interruptive mediation of an effective and concrete—namely collective—political praxis, Bloch's dialectical materialism falls, as Irving Fetscher has pointed out, "to a large extent together with Hegel's dialectical idealism."[38] Although *Spuren* gestures toward the realization of an open system, the possibility of a utopian collective praxis seems, at

---

38. Irving Fetscher, "Ernst Bloch auf Hegels Spuren," in *Ernst Bloch zu ehren*, ed. Siegfried Unseld (Frankfurt: Suhrkamp, 1965), p. 94.

least for the present, to be closed. Thus, Bloch places his "home" on the horizon, not, like Novalis, in the past (*immer nach Hause*), nor, like Hegel, in the present, but in the future.[39] A "concrete" dialectic, Kosik has said, can grasp the totality not "as a complete or formalized whole" but only through the genesis and development of its parts (*DK*, 53). But is this totality *Schein* or *Vor-Schein?* For Bloch, to be sure, it is both, accessible, if at all, only through its fragments. As poetic and philosophical fragments, utopian "wish-forms" ("Fall ins Jetzt" [*S*, 99]) par excellence, *Denkbild* and prose poem share a tendency toward the concrete. This tendency manifests itself above all in their objectlike density and compactness *as forms*. To some extent also, it shows in what Bloch calls the "dialectically aimed, systematically open and penetrating glance into the form-building tendencies of matter" (*PH*, 1627), the shared thematic focus on "small things"—inconspicuous physical objects and everyday events—as emblems of the prosaic, reified existence of people-as-things, as well as of the poetic potential for a world in which things would be different.

39. Although *Spuren* displays an acute awareness of what Bakhtin calls the "inconclusive present" and develops the process of a "reorientation toward a real future" Bakhtin associates with novelistic discourse (*The Dialogic Imagination*, 39–40), Bloch's utopian notion of a "final goal" remains problematic. As Wohlfarth has asked, speaking in the context of Walter Benjamin's "Image of Interpretation": ". . . would not such a final resting-place amount to the reinstatement of identity [Bloch's *das Selbe*], to death warmed up as utopia?"

CHAPTER 8

Fragments of a World Restored: Francis Ponge's "Rhetoric by Objects"

"Aurait-on réussi, LE GRAND RECUEIL, alors, serait un livre. Mais enfin, lecteur, je t'y laisse. Promène-toi au petit bonheur. Va et viens" (Had we succeeded, THE GREAT COLLECTION, then, would be a book. But never mind that, reader, I'll leave you there. Stroll about as you please. Come and go).[1] With these remarks at the conclusion of a brief introductory note to *Lyres*, the first of the three volumes that make up his largest collection to date, Francis Ponge addresses two characteristic concerns of the modern tradition of the prose poem within and against which he has consistently placed his work—the relation of the individual text to the collection "as a whole," and the active participation of the reader in constructing textual and intertextual coherence. From Baudelaire to Jacob to Ponge, the preface and the occasion it allows for a direct appeal to the reader have played an important role in the prose poem's history. The introductory remarks given above recall especially the preface to the *Petits poèmes en prose* ("We can cut wherever we please, I my dreaming, you the manuscript, the reader his

1. Francis Ponge, *Le grand recueil I, Lyres* (Paris: Gallimard, 1961), p. 3; hereafter cited as *GRL*. Other references to Ponge's work will be indicated as follows: *Le grand recueil II, Méthodes* (Paris: Gallimard, 1961), *GRM; Tome premier* (Paris: Gallimard 1965), *TP; Nouveau recueil* (Paris: Gallimard, 1967), *NR; Le savon* (Paris: Gallimard, 1967), *LS; Soap,* trans. Lane Dunlop (London: Jonathan Cape, 1969), *LD*. All quotations appear with the permission of Editions Gallimard. Quotations from *Soap* appear with the permission of Jonathan Cape Limited.

reading . . . "), with Ponge's "Had we succeeded" echoing Baudelaire's description of his own collection as "an accident of which anyone else but me would be proud. . . ." Although the prose poem as a genre grew largely out of a sense of the impossibility of a seamlessly coherent work or oeuvre, it nevertheless displays an aspiration over the course of its relatively brief history, already evident in Baudelaire but most intensely and self-consciously apparent in Ponge and before him in Mallarmé, to offer something more than a mere collection of disparate texts such as one associates with the verse lyric, to offer, instead, the possibility of a previously unrealized and newly constructed unity, a new kind of *Book*.

The history of the prose poem is, among other things, a history of failures to realize such a project, even if or although, in Ponge's optimistic phrase, "the failure is never absolute" (*TP,* 206). Once again, Baudelaire's collection provides the first example: "neither head nor tail . . . at once head and tail. . . . Chop it into numerous fragments and you will see that each one can get along alone." Divided up as it is into fragments that depend on the reader to an unusual degree for whatever coherence it is to have among its parts, Baudelaire's "whole serpent" resonates in the conclusion of Ponge's *Le savon* (Soap): "As for the paradise of this book, what is it? What else could it be, if not, reader, *your reading* it [*ta lecture*] (how it does bite its tail in these last lines)" (*LS,* 128; *LD,* 97). As this juxtaposition suggests, Ponge views himself as completing a circle begun with Baudelaire, the gesture collections of prose poems make toward the unity of a book. However, Ponge wants to complete the circle not only of the prose poem but of literature itself. "It seems to me," Ponge says with reference to Malherbe, Boileau, and Mallarmé, "that it is enough for me to add myself to them in order for literature to be complete./ Or rather: the difficulty is for me to add myself to them in such a way that literature would be complete" (*TP,* 166). A small form with large ambitions, the prose poem is merely Ponge's chosen medium, his particular *parti pris* for bringing about an end to literature, a utopian genreless genre or genre to end (realize) all genres. Baudelaire, Ponge writes, refers to his "small work" (*petit ouvrage*) as a "description of modern life": "What I shall attempt to do then will be on the order of the definition-description-literary artwork" (*GRM,* 14).

In the wake of Mallarmé and Lautréamont, however, and in defiance of the characteristic brevity otherwise associated with the prose poem, Ponge resists that very "*small* happiness" (*petit bonheur*) to which

the individual prose poem may seem confined: "Chosen genre: definition-descriptions./Limits of this genre: its extension. From the formula
(or concrete maxim) to the novel à la *Moby Dick*, for example" (*GRM*,
20). With this definition, Ponge challenges "the presumed hierarchy of
genres" (*TP*, 231) and generic distinctions generally, as well as one of
the most basic distinguishing features of texts we might like to consider
prose poems, namely brevity. Situating himself "between the two genres (definition and description)" as Baudelaire had previously situated
himself between poetry and prose, Ponge demands "infallability," "in-
dubitability," and "brevity" on the one hand, concreteness and a "respect for the sensory aspect of things" on the other (*GRM*, 11): "We
must work," Ponge writes, "from the *discovery* made by Rimbaud and
Lautréamont (of the necessity of a new rhetoric)" (*GRM*, 42).

Ostensibly, the dialogization or mixing of genres Ponge calls for
and the new rhetoric he seeks to establish on the basis of such a procedure would be on a smaller scale than that called for in Schlegel's
classic formulation. Philosophy, Ponge says, is just one among many
genres of literature, to which he prefers others: "Less voluminous. Less
tomely. Less severalvoluminoustomely [*volumenplusieurstomineux*] . . . /
Remains that I must remain a philosopher *in petto* [*Reste qu'il faut que je
reste* in petto *philosophe*]" (*TP*, 221). Yet although Ponge's early career is
marked by the brief, prose-poetic texts of *Le parti pris des choses* and by
frequent claims of antipathy to philosophy, in practice, as the title of
the second volume of *Le grand recueil*, *Méthodes*, suggests, Ponge's work
has moved increasingly in the direction of longer, more reflexive, metapoetical texts. Indeed, the tripartite division of the collection itself
plays on the speculative trope of a dialectical movement from poetry
(*Lyres*) to philosophy (*Méthodes*) ending in the failed synthesis, the fragmentation, of *Pièces*. The shift in focus between Ponge's first two collections, *Le parti pris des choses* and *Proêmes*, anticipates this movement as
well, with the former more "poetic," the latter more "philosophical."

In "Natare piscem doces," Ponge writes: "No, there is no possible
dissociation of the creative personality and the critical personality" (*TP*,
148). Although it has been Ponge's acknowledged ambition to create "a
classical work (. . . according to the genres)" (*TP*, 227), the evidence of
his writings, his "definitions that establish uncommon relationships,
upset the usual classifications" (*GRM*, 18), suggests a contrary "Romantic" tendency in the manner and spirit of Schlegel's fragments. "Nostalgia for Unity, you say," Ponge writes in response to Camus' reading of
his work, "No: for variety" (*TP*, 225). And again in "Tentative Orale":
"It's not unity I seek but variety" (*GRM*, 253). Despite these denials,

Claudine Giordan is certainly right to insist not only on Ponge's "desire for absolute unity" but also on the relation of this desire to the Bible.[2] More than any other, the Bible represents the Book of books, the unity of diversity that incorporates "classical" as well as "romantic" impulses. Like Friedrich Schlegel's *Universalpoesie*, Ponge's texts carry with them a "nostalgia for the absolute" (*TP*, 207) from which they cannot finally be detached, however much Ponge might at times wish they could be. If, as Ponge says, the confusion of genres is present at every instant in every one of his texts,[3] then each of the texts of *Le parti pris des choses* may be said to develop on a miniature scale (*"in petto"*) a project of central importance to Schlegel and the prose poem as well.

The project of a hybridization or con-fusion of genres which Ponge's texts share with Bloch's *Spuren*, the paradigmatic texts of the modern prose poem tradition we have previously examined, and Schlegel's notion of a *Universalpoesie* suggests two directions running counter to each other: on the one hand, a utopian aspiration toward unity, identity, the melting down of all oppositions into a harmonious oneness; on the other, a perhaps equally utopian drive toward the greatest possible difference and diversity, a breakdown of rigid categorical distinctions. A total homogenization of the "universal" threatens the one; a total fragmentation threatens the other. Ponge's texts are themselves, as he himself has acknowledged, "very diverse, contradictory, varied as to form . . . in *Le parti pris des choses* there is a little of everything; there are closed texts, there are open texts; each one proposes as well an *ars poetica*" (*CC*, 411–12). Although Ponge displays at times a nostalgia for the Book, he has himself said that for the most part he is concerned with *texts* (*CC*, 426). In other words, although Ponge sometimes entertains thoughts of a singular coherence of separate texts in some formal or other unity, more often he focuses his attention on particular phenomena, on the individual rather than the collective. What the prose poem leads Ponge to is less Schlegel's goal of a universal poetry than the nominalist fragmentation suggested by Schlegel's polemical contention that "every poem is a genre in itself" (*Jedes Gedicht eine Gattung für sich*).[4] Like Schlegel's fragments, however,

2. Claudine Giordan, "Ponge et la nomination," *Poétique* 28 (1976), p. 499. Lacoue-Labarthe and Nancy define the Bible, in their discussion of Schlegel's fragments, as a "plural book . . . and as such One," *L'absolu littéraire*, p. 65; hereafter cited as *AL*.
3. *Ponge, Inventeur et classique: Colloque de Cérisy*, ed. Philippe Bonnefis (Paris: Union Générale d'Editions, 1977), pp. 178 and 65; hereafter cited as *CC*.
4. Schlegel, *Literarische Notizen 1797–1801*, ed. Hans Eichner p. 120, frag. 1090; hereafter cited as *LN* followed by page and fragment number.

which are the specific articulation of an attempt to determine the properties of each genre, as we recall, in order finally to fuse them into one another, Ponge's texts suggest that existing literary and extraliterary forms must first be explored in all their particularity and isolation precisely in order to make it possible for a new universal to come into being. In order to construct a new unity allowing for the greatest possible diversity and difference, the poverty of received forms and the speciousness of any notion of an already given, preexistent unity must first be exposed. The possibility of a universal poetry must pass, in other words, *through* the fragmented world of prose, not around it. As the possibility of the universal coming into view is posited in Schlegel's work only through fragmentary articulations—what Lacoue-Labarthe and Nancy have referred to as "the totality of poetry as fragment" or "'form without form'" (*AL*, 63 and 184)[5]—so in Ponge's texts, according to that fundamental emphasis on the concrete which his texts share with other major examples of the prose poem as genre before and since, through what Ponge calls "a rhetoric by objects" (*une rhétorique par objects*) (*GRM*, 36).

The Pebble and the Prose Poem

Suzanne Bernard has remarked that it may be "troubling that one should be able to cite *Le Parti pris des choses* so easily by detached fragments, and also have the impression, quite often, that such a 'poem' could be indefinitely continued."[6] For the reader looking, as Bernard tends to do, for some kind of "organic" unity, Ponge's work will indeed be a source of frustration. With their aesthetic of discontinuity, their way of proceeding "by isolated fragments, by facets," their lack of transitions between various parts, Ponge's texts tend more toward the fragmentation and contingency of everyday life described by Hegel as characteristic of the world of prose than toward the appearance of

5. Of the "decomposition of *Gattung*, the decomposition of genre and of the mixture" represented by Schlegel's *Universalpoesie*, Lacoue-Labarthe and Nancy remark: "in that automanifestation, it is not only from literature to philosophy and from philosophy to literature that the identity cannot take place, but as well from literature to itself and philosophy to itself. The same, here, does not arrive at its sameness . . . it would be necessary to think that automanifestation of literature as a *neutral* manifestation, or as a *step* of manifestation" (*un pas de manifestation*). Historically, it is the prose poem that has carried forward, more self-consciously perhaps than any other genre, the fragment's revolutionary function as "the form, precisely, that ceaselessly dissolves the problematic of genre" (*AL*, 422), or of literary classifications.
6. Bernard, *Le poème en prose de Baudelaire jusqu'à nos jours*, p. 750.

necessity, well-roundedness, and organic wholeness commonly associated with poetry. In this Ponge's work carries forward the polemical
project of a sociohistorical reinscription or recontextualization of the
verse lyric exemplified by Baudelaire's *Le spleen de Paris*. *Le parti pris des
choses* does not represent a mere extension of this fundamental
Baudelairean project, however; rather than attempting to focus attention directly, as Baudelaire tends to do in his prose poems, on the
sociohistorical situatedness of lyrical/human subjects, Ponge radicalizes
Baudelaire's articulation of the ongoing poverty of social relations by
approaching these relations indirectly, through an almost exclusive
focus on *things*, objects of the material world, and an intense examination of the materiality of language. Every object, Ponge says, "should
impose a particular rhetoric on the poem. No more sonnets, odes,
epigrams; the form of the poem would itself be in some sense determined by its subject" (*GRM*, 36). Ponge's "rhetoric by object" points to a
prose utopia where objects—including reified human subjects—would
at last dictate their own language. In this respect, a collection of prose
poems such as *Le parti pris des choses* figures a utopian project for society
at large. No longer subjected to the domination of previously established hierarchies and levels of style, or received linguistic, literary, and
social conventions that limit the individual's freedom, the *objects* of
Ponge's utopia would be for the first time truly the determining *subjects*
of their own modes of discourse, their own ways of being in the world.[7]

Typically, for Ponge, the forms the world assumes imply a high
degree of tension between autonomy and interdependence, "organic"

7. The playful anthropomorphism of such a typically Pongeian proposition is obviously not to be taken too literally but, rather, as indicating an awareness that the
attitudes men and women take toward each other and the attitudes they take toward the
natural world (whether exploitative or respectful) may be more directly connected than
has been habitually acknowledged. As Ponge writes elsewhere: "*our* nature. We are
dealing with a tautology" (*GRM*, 144). To speak of "nature," whether human or non-
human is of course always, for Ponge, to speak of language as well. Like Stein and Bloch,
Ponge reveals through his focus on objects something of what Bakhtin (*The Dialogic
Imagination*, 276–78) refers to as the "socially heteroglot multiplicity of [their] names,
definitions and value judgments . . . the internal contradictions inside the object itself . . .
the unfolding of social heteroglossia surrounding the object." Yet although all three
writers novelistically confront the "multitude of routes, roads and paths that have been
laid down in the object by social consciousness," they also provide indications of the
desire for the "virginal fullness and inexhaustibility" of the object that Bakhtin associates
with poetic discourse. Robert Bly and Helga Novak, the two contemporaries I shall
examine in the final chapters, display a similar double orientation in the prose-poetic
focus on physical objects they share especially with Ponge, Bloch, Stein, Rimbaud, and
Novalis, and to a lesser extent with Jacob and Baudelaire as well.

wholeness and fragmentation. In "Fragments de masque," Ponge writes: "everything seems to me fragment, mask, fragment of habit, fragment of the common" (*TP*, 169). The artist's function, Ponge says, is to open a studio and begin to repair the world by fragments, as it comes to him (or her). Accompanying the artist's sense of an obligation not to misrepresent the world as a false organic unity is the "violent need to remain integrated there" (*GRM*, 193), or in the absence of such integration, to help construct one. In this drive toward integration, we can easily recognize an impulse toward the Book, a collection of texts that would be more than a mere collection, a unity of diversity rather than mere "pieces." Countering this impulse in Ponge is an equally strong drive toward disruption and fragmentation: "It's not a question of arranging things. . . . Things have to disturb you. It's a question of them obliging you to get out of the rut; that alone is interesting because only that could make the mind progress" (*GRM*, 257). Thus, for Ponge, poetry takes leave to a large extent of its more traditional organic, religious function of stitching together the appearance of a seamless unity, and takes on a more subversive, fragmenting orientation, even if finally, as with Schlegel's *Universalpoesie*, the "progressive" telos of a fragmented articulation is the organic unity of the Book.

"All poetic fragments," we recall from Schlegel, "must be parts of some whole." "Le galet" (The Pebble), from *Le parti pris des choses*, and the later "Introduction au galet" (Introduction to the Pebble), from *Proêmes*, provide two excellent early examples of the simultaneous presence in Ponge's work of a novelesque nostalgia for wholeness—the desire for a peaceful integration or harmonic coexistence of individual and collective phenomena Camus refers to in Ponge's work as a "nostalgia for the absolute"—on the one hand, and, on the other hand, an impulse toward fragmentation, the more lyrical sense of an inescapable isolation. Already in the first of the nine sections of "Le galet," that phenomenon manifests itself which Philippe Lacoue-Labarthe and Jean-Luc Nancy have called, with reference to Schlegel's fragments, "the copresence of the fragmentary and the systematic" (*AL*, 60). Ponge's text begins with an acknowledgment of the difficulties of (self)-definition: "The pebble is not an easy thing to define well" (*TP*, 104). The pebble, one might think, should not in itself be so difficult to define. As Ponge goes on to suggest, however, the problem is that even the simplest form can not be defined *in itself* but only by means of its relations to other forms. In writing of the difficulties of defining a pebble, Ponge is simultaneously addressing the difficulties of defining his own chosen literary form, both literary and nonliterary forms alike, the text on the page and the text of the world. Finding and losing itself in its own self-description, the text proves just how elusive and shifting such a definition may be. Beginning with dimension as its first category, "a form or a state of rock between the boulder and the small stone," the text's effort systematically to place the pebble as a natural form suggests, at the level of literary form, a genre such as the prose poem, which is situated between the largest and the smallest units of writing, the novel (*le rocher*) and the epigram (*le caillou*), a genre far closer to the latter than the former. The association stone/text is as old as the Ten Commandments, both historical and mythological; it is therefore necessary to go back a long way, to include practically everything in order to define even so "simple" a thing or text as the pebble/prose poem: "You will not reproach me in this matter for going back further than the Flood."

The second section of "Le galet" begins with the notion of an original unity and its fragmentation: "All rocks are born from fission of a single enormous ancestor." This evocation is immediately followed by the designation "this *fabulous* body" (*ce corps* fabuleux; my emphasis), which links the speaker's anthropomorphization of the sun to the realm of myth, narrative, and the imagination ("fabulous," from "fable," according to Ponge's beloved *Littré*, "imaginary. . . . That which relates to mythology. Fabulous antiquity. . . . The fabulous circumstances of a story"). Having no firsthand experience or memory of the formation of earth and the solar system, human beings are forced to invent or extrapolate its history from existing forms. Reason alone, the next paragraph indicates, is not able to comprehend "a hero of the world's grandeur" but discovers instead only "the ghastly trough of a death bed." Over the course of the following paragraphs, Ponge uses the word "hero" to evoke not only the earth but the other planets as well born of the "enormous forebear," the sun: "The heroes engendered by it [or him, *lui*], who gravitated in its [his, *son*] entourage have let themselves be eclipsed" (*TP*, 105). "Hero," according to *Littré*, is first of all a term of antiquity, a name given by Homer to men of courage and superior merit; it is also, by extension, a literary term designating the principal character of a poem, a novel, or a play. Thus, like the adjective "fabulous," "hero" suggests that although Ponge's manifest text is that of a history of natural forms, this natural history is itself intertwined with a history of literary forms and mythical, anthropomorphic, imaginative projections. Paragraphs four and five further reinforce these connections by using the language of theater to describe the planets ("an audience . . . of spectators") and the violent geological transitions of the earth ("dramatic upheavals"), and by attributing to the earth a hero's consciousness: "our hero, subdued/checkmated [*maté*] (by his consciousness)."

Following the violent, epic/heroic era evoked in section 2, section 3 begins by suggesting the advent of a more prosaic era in the world's (and in literature's) history which is still ours today and in which the "fabulous body" of myth has lost much of its affecting and unifying power:

> De ce corps une fois pour toutes ayant perdu avec la faculté de s'émouvoir celle de se refondre en une personne entière, l'histoire depuis sa lente catastrophe du refroidissement ne sera plus que celle d'une perpétuelle désagrégation. Mais c'est à ce moment qu' advient d'autres choses: la grandeur morte, la vie fait voir aussitôt qu'elle n'a rien de commun avec elle.

> [This body having lost once and for all its capacity to be moved and to recast itself into a whole person, history since the slow catastrophe of cooling will no longer be anything but a perpetual disintegration. But at this very moment other things happen: grandeur dead, life immediately makes clear that it has nothing in common with it.] (*TP*, 106)

In language strongly reminiscent of Baudelaire,[8] Ponge goes on to describe the ensuing period as one of fragmentation and individual isolation:

> Telle est aujourd'hui l'apparence du globe. Le cadavre en tronçons de l'être de la grandeur du monde ne fait plus que servir de décor à la vie de millions d'êtres infiniment plus petits et plus éphémères que lui. Leur foule est par endroits si dense qu'elle dissimule entièrement l'ossature sacrée qui leur servit naguère d'unique support. Et ce n'est qu'une infinité de leurs cadavres qui, réussissant depuis lors à imiter la consistance de la pierre, par ce qu'on appelle la terre végétale, leur permet depuis quelques jours de se reproduire sans rien devoir au roc.

> [Such is today the appearance of the globe. The mutilated cadaver of the being that was once the world's grandeur no longer does anything but serve as decor for the life of millions of beings infinitely

---

8. Cf. the passage from the preface to the *Petits poèmes en prose* quoted earlier: "Take away one vertebra and the two pieces of this tortuous fantasy come together again without pain. Chop it into numerous fragments and you will see that each one can get along alone" (*OC*, 1:275; *PS*, ix); see also the motif of the crowd ("Les foules," etc.).

smaller and more ephemeral [than itself, or himself, *lui*]. Their crowding is in places so dense that they completely conceal the sacred skeleton
which serves as their sole support. And it's only the infinity of their
cadavers which, succeeding since that time in imitating the consistency
of stone by what is called organic soil, has permitted them these few
days now to reproduce themselves without owing anything to rock.]
(*TP*, 106)

The fragmented, prosaic land mass that emerges with myth's demise
("The mutilated cadaver of the being that was once the world's grandeur") is actually one of the principal realms issuing from the *unified*
"fabulous body" (fabled, mythical) of the age "of the ancient hero who
was not long ago truly in the world" (*TP*, 107). The other realm, by
contrast to the sober, dry, prosaic element at issue in the above passage,[9] is the "liquid element," the sea, the poetic milieu par excellence,
"whose origin is perhaps equally ancient" (*TP*, 106). In aesthetic terms,
then, and more specifically in terms of the generic problematic within
which Ponge situates himself, these two realms suggest the "fission" of
myth, the "enormous ancestor" of all literature, into prose and poetry.
Having described the explosive birth of the solar system and of the
earth in section 2 and subequently, in section 3, the fission of the earth
into land and sea that brings with it a diminishing grandeur and increasing fragmentation, Ponge moves systematically down the scale of
natural forms to the "largest fragments, slabs almost invisible beneath
the interlacing plants. . . . " Metapoetically, Ponge's subsequent description of these fragments as repositories of the imagination and as
"mysterious blocks" suggest prose fiction, which is printed in "blocks"
of type. The large size of the blocks in question and the speaker's
evocation of the "ancient hero who was not long ago truly in the world"
further suggest that the genre of prose fiction at issue is the epic's
"prosaic" descendant, the novel: "Engaged in the imagining of great
things among the shadow and perfume of forests which sometimes
cover over these mysterious blocks, man by his mind alone supposes
continuity beneath them" (*TP*, 107). Of all the forms of imaginative
literature in the nineteenth century, Hegel's "age of prose," it is the
novel we most think of as engaged in "the imagining of great things"
and the presentation of a sense of continuity. Although the word

9. Cf. Ian Higgins, ed., *Le parti pris des choses* (London: Athlone Press, 1979), p. 35:
"All the poems in *Le Parti pris des choses* . . . have the vocabulary of encyclopedic sobriety."
Although this sobriety is certainly a striking feature of Ponge's work, more "poetic"
qualities are certainly not absent from the texts, which are, after all, *poems* in prose.

"blocks" figures the printed medium of prose, "the shadow and perfume of forests" and the adjective "mysterious" suggest oceanic, poetic
qualities overlaying the novel's prosaic form.

The sense of continuity man's mind alone may divine clearly depends as much on such poetic effects as the imagining of a mythical
past inaccessible to lived experience and hence, as section 2 suggests, to
reason alone. Without imagination, that element issuing from myth
which emphasizes connections and posits the existence of an underlying unity, the prosaic everyday world will continue to appear as a
"death-bed" (un lit de mort) (TP, 104) or "mutilated cadaver." Continuity is thus, as Ponge images it, an affair of the imagination which
finds only so much support in history and in nature as we are able or
inclined to conceive. And if the novel as a form has tended to offer a
sense of (narrative, historical) continuity, other forms, "numerous
smaller blocks . . . irregular stonecrumbs"—first hints of the metapoetical treatment of the pebble as prose poem in section 6—direct
attention, like the prose-poetic fragments of Ponge's "Le galet" itself, to
a fracturing of continuity and the speciousness of any putatively preex-
isting totality.[10] To a writer "en mal de notions" (at once bereft and sick
of notions), as Ponge has consistently defined himself, novelesque con-

10. In "On the Prose Poem's Formal Features," an essay in The Prose Poem in France
discussing Ponge's "Un rocher," from Proêmes (Paris: Gallimard, 1948), Michael
Riffaterre points out that for Ponge "every word that belongs to stone language, or stone
code, stands for poetic creativity." Riffaterre makes the case that "'Un Rocher' treats of
the writer's labors and of the agonies of creation" by first associating "rock" with "writer's
block," then by noticing that "right in the middle of the poem there is another stone, not
a rock but a pebble. And this pebble . . . brings together forest and boulder, inspiration
and what blocks inspiration, as two inseparable facets of the same creativity metaphor.
But only by means of the intertext is the pebble . . . able to accomplish this" (121–22).
The intertext Riffaterre has in mind is Mallarmé's poem on Poe, which allows him to
extrapolate bloc-notes (writing-pad) from a connection between Ponge's use of rocher, bloc,
and caillou and Mallarmé's use of bloc to indicate Poe's graven tombstone. Somewhat
surprisingly, Riffaterre never mentions "Le galet." Given its prior position within
Ponge's own oeuvre, the latter clearly functions as an intertext for the Pongean equation
of "stone language" with "poetic creativity" at least as well as the Mallarmé text Riffaterre
draws upon. In any case, all three texts read well as intertexts of and for one another.
Another parallel between "Un rocher" and "Le galet" lies in the proportion of imagery devoted to natural phenomena other than those indicated by the titles in both poems.
In "Un Rocher," as Riffaterre points out, "the boulder at the end (and) the rock of the
title . . . occupy very little space by comparison with the 'stifling forest' imagery, its varied
repetitions, and the author's insistence upon the intricate confusions of the under-
growth. . . . Rock and boulder remain marginal as image" (119). Much the same could be
said of "Le galet," where the object named in the title only becomes the actual focus of
attention quite late in the sequence. As the pebble (caillou) in "Un rocher" brings together
the dominant forest and boulder imagery Riffaterre identifies with "inspiration and what

tinuity and wholeness may appear mechanical, "too simple—like a watch" (*TP*, 109). If a "totality" is even to be grasped or imaged at all, Ponge writes, "even theoretically . . . we can only imagine a part of the phase of its very slow disintegration."

The same is true, of course, of "Le galet" itself, the fragments and sections of which do not quite add up to anything sufficiently whole to be held in our minds as easily and reassuringly as a pebble can be held in the hollow of a hand. All we can do is to retrace the lines that interest us in a *faulty* text ("reflect," as Ponge says in the final section, "on the faults [*défauts*] of a style that relies [or leans, *qui appuie*] too much on words") (*TP*, 115), a text that seems to allude metatextually now to a history of natural forms, now to a history of literary forms, without necessarily and systematically following through on all of the "crumbs" of thought it turns up. These faults in our reading/writing are not to be brushed away but are, indeed, precisely the point. As Derrida points out in a round table discussion of Ponge's work at the Cérisy Colloquium," . . . the thing is that which does not allow itself to be appropriated . . . somewhere the metatext fails to become the metatext" (*CC*, 148).[11] There is no accounting for everything. Nothing entirely disappears. "I will note, finally, as a very important principle," Ponge writes, "that all forms of stone, each of which represents some stage of evolution, exist simultaneously in the world. No generations here, no vanished races. . . . No conception: everything exists. Or rather, as in paradise, all conception exists" (*TP*, 111). This "paradise" may also be, as Rimbaud's work indicates, a kind of hell, making poetry seem, in Ponge's words, "a newspaper stand in ruins in its garden," the literature of our era "at the very best the nocturnal celebration that an enemy society gives to itself" (*GRM*, 183). Echoing the deliberate confusion of the synchronic and the diachronic, system and chaos, simultaneity and narrative history we find in Rimbaud's *Une saison en enfer* (including the latter's review of metrical verse and prose in "Alchimie du verbe"), Ponge continues: "We know that we reinvent one after the

blocks inspiration," in "Le galet" the pebble brings together the dominant ocean and land imagery I have identified as metapoetical figures of poetry and prose. The boulder is to the pebble, Riffaterre says, "what hyperbole is to understatement" (121). Transposing this analogy to the level of the imaginative/literary prose forms figured in "Le galet," we may say that the boulder is to the pebble what the novel is to the prose poem.

11. Other participants in the discussion, which took place following Derrida's delivery of the text of *Signéponge* (trans. Richard Rand [New York: Columbia University Press, 1984]), included Philippe Bonnefis, Jenny Batlay, Karlheinz Stierle, Raymond Jean, Irène Tschinka, Marce Spada, and Jean-Luc Steinmetz.

other the WORST errors of the stylistic schools of all eras. Well then, so much the better! . . . We want to be DISTURBED in our thoughts (Have I said it enough? I repeat it)" (*GRM,* 199).

In the sixth section of "Le galet," which focuses at long last on the pebble itself, nuances linking the pebble to the prose poem become quite clear. Speaking of the pebble's "perfection of . . . form," Ponge writes: "the fact that I can take hold of it and turn it over in my hand makes me choose the pebble" (*TP,* 111). Ponge's privileging of the pebble here, and of small, tangible natural forms and material objects generally, is not to be separated from his selection of the prose poem as a literary genre; the conceptual adequation of the literary to the natural form and vice versa is in fact fundamentally generative for Ponge's imagination. Like the prose poem, the limits of which they expand and break by "extension," the "definition-descriptions" Ponge speaks of as his chosen genre in "My Creative Method" are a genre *en mal de notions,* seeking out, as the prose poem has done historically, a maximum concreteness, what Serge Gavronsky has called a "denial of the lyrico-subjective" (*PL,* 9). This tendency manifests itself on a most "literal," one might also say "materialist," level in Ponge's virtually obsessive focus on elemental physical objects and the materiality of words: "TAKING THE SIDE OF THINGS *equals* TAKING ACCOUNT [also the "content"] OF WORDS" ("PARTI PRIS DES CHOSES *égale* COMPTE TENU [contenu] DES MOTS") (*GRM,* 19). "Nothing," Gavronsky has pointed out, "so materially violates the sacrosanct lyrical world as the appearance, and that *en masse* (in its double meaning), of the simplest objects, animate and inanimate" (*PL,* 17). Arranging for this material violation of the lyrical world through his focus on everyday objects impoverished by conventional discursive practices, Ponge places himself at the forefront of a tradition established by the prose poem which would emphasize not metaphysical absolutes but the world at hand.

If the "universal" is conceivable, Ponge suggests, it is only through its fragmentation that we may grasp it, as a large rock is grasped by means of its pebbles: "The pebble won the victory (the victory of existence, individual, concrete, the victory of falling under the eyes and being born into the word) because it is more interesting than the sky" (*GRM,* 26–27). Like the pebble, which is small enough to be held and turned over in the hand, the prose poem is a form "of a human measure" (*à la mesure humaine*) (*GRM,* 160). As the pebble is "the stone in

12. Serge Gavronsky, ed. and trans., *Francis Ponge: The Power of Language* (Berkeley: University of California Press, 1979), p. 230; hereafter cited as *PL.*

the era where the age of the person, the individual . . . the age of speech begins" (*TP*, 111), the prose poem is for Ponge the genre that most lends itself, by virtue of its characteristic brevity and its appearance on the page in the block-print of prose, to a treament of small, prosaic, individual phenomena such as the pebble itself. Born of the schism of poetry and prose, the prose poem moves away from the verse lyric's focus on individual *human* subjects to a corresponding focus on individual objects, whether animate or inanimate, of the material world. Compared to the novel's massive blocks of prose ("the rocky bank from which it directly descends"), it is a form, like the pebble, "already fragmented and polished into many nearly similar individuals." Cultivated by Baudelaire, Rimbaud, Mallarmé, Lautréamont, Jacob, and others in an age of art-for-art's sake and referred to by Jacob as a semiprecious stone or jewel, the prose poem has not been a genre easily assimilable to a "practical use" (*TP*, 111). As a subversively dialogizing form directed against other, better established genres such as the novel and the verse lyric, it was in its origins (though it may be becoming less so) the "stone still wild, or at least not domesticated," illegitimate heir of poetry as well as prose, "without meaning in any practical order of the world. . . ."

Having at last reached the pebble itself in section 6, and with it, metapoetically, the prose poem as Ponge's chosen form (what he calls his *forme d'élection*), in sections 7 and 8 Ponge expands his treatment of the form in order to situate it more exhaustively. Each pebble lies, Ponge says, "on the pile of its past and future forms" (*TP*, 112). Exemplary, like the prose poem, of a breakdown of existing forms, the pebble clears the way for new ones. Born of that "formless monster" the sea, on the one hand, and of the land, that "equally formless monster of stone," on the other (*TP*, 113), the pebble, like the prose poem, is a marginal form. As the pebble in Ponge's poem is located on a beach, the transitional space between land and sea, the prose poem is situated on the shifting terrain between prose and poetry.

Cependant sa forme à la perfection supporte les deux milieux. Elle reste imperturbable dans le désordre des mers. Il en sort seulement plus petit, mais entier, et, si l'on veut aussi grand, puisque ses proportions ne dépendent aucunement de son volume.

[Nonetheless in its perfection the form tolerates both environments. It remains imperturbable in the disorder of the seas, emerging a bit smaller, but intact and, as it were, just as grand, because its proportions do not at all depend on its volume.] (*TP*, 114)

Like the pebble according to Ponge's description of it, the prose poem is a form that must have greatness or grandeur, if it is to have these at all, in defiance of proportion. In the final section of "Le galet," the text breaks off abruptly with additional metapoetic indicators that are difficult to pin down but imply nonetheless some linkage between the forms of nature and those of writing (as, for example, "this idea of a disappearance of signs") (*TP*, 115). This linkage, and more specifically the analogy we have been tracing between the pebble and the prose poem, receives one last confirmation in Ponge's assertion in the text's concluding sentence that he is "Only too happy to have known to choose for these beginnings *the pebble*" (*Trop heureux seulement d'avoir pour ces débuts su choisir* le galet). As the final poem of *Le parti pris des choses*, the volume that marks Ponge's literary debut and places him among the major practitioners of the prose poem, "Le galet" is one of Ponge's most telling early reflections on the problem of form. Though it is probably too much to say that "Le galet" actually shows what Elisabeth Walther has called a "transition from the many into complex unity,"[13] its nine sections certainly display the problematic—foregrounded in the history of the prose poem in the relation of the individual text to the collection—of relating wholeness or totality to "a 'disjunctive diversity'" and (in)organic process.

Despite Ponge's insistent focus on physical objects and the concrete existence of things rather than on "ideas," increasingly since *Le parti pris des choses* his work has involved a great degree of "abstract" philosophical speculation. The second of the two early texts on the pebble, "Introduction au galet," is a case in point. The importance of "Le galet" to Ponge's work is underscored by Walther, who sees it as programmatic not only of Ponge's first collection but of almost all of his later texts as well. Of the relation between "Le galet" and "Introduction au galet," Walther has said that whereas the former presents a descriptive literary object language, the latter has as its subject the methodological preconditions and metalanguage of this object language.[14] In contrast to "Le galet," with its ordered "fable on the origin of the universe where the entity gives way to fragmentation,"[15] "Introduction au galet" presents a sequence of rambling quasi-philosophical specula-

13. Elisabeth Walther, *Francis Ponge* (Cologne: Kiepenheuer and Witsch, 1965), p. 158.
14. Ibid., p. 11.
15. This is the description given by W. D. Redfern in "Giono, Ponge et la Pierre," *La revue des lettres modernes* 4 (1976), p. 122.

tions on existence and discourse, the limits of language, man, and the physical world. More fragmented even than "Le galet," more devoid of transitions between sections, Ponge's "Introduction" arrives, paradoxically, *after* the fact of the actual text dealing with the pebble it is supposed to introduce. In this case, then, going back to the beginning, or even before the beginning, takes us closer to an absolute realm of mind than to a relativized, "concrete" world of objects. In the "Introduction," objects are not described in detail, as in "Le galet," but serve only as examples or notational illustrations. Indeed, the severely fragmented metalinguistic discourse of "Introduction au galet" resembles a work such as Schlegel's *Athenäums-Fragmente* much more than it does Baudelaire's *Petits poèmes en prose*. As Schlegel's collection offers a universalizing project in fragmentary form, Ponge's "Introduction" articulates a project aimed at concreteness (definition-descriptions) via abstract language. But where Schlegel attempts to offer, in quasi-epigrammatic fashion, a quintessence of thought in each verbal fragment, Ponge wants to show how "the simplest *things*" (*des* choses *les plus simples*) can be used to create "infinite discourses" (*TP*, 196; my emphasis).

Taken together, the two represent such extremely opposing directions we may suspect them of projecting a similar telos. Both Ponge and the prose poem choose to concentrate "on the first object at hand . . . the most elementary things . . . to say." Observation and description serve not merely as ends in themselves but to change the "intellectual atmosphere, to leave the dusty salons where everything there is that is alive in the mind is bored to death, to progress—finally!" (*TP*, 197). Like Schlegel's *Universalpoesie*, Ponge's project involves becoming conscious of undiscovered potential, "a million unspoken qualities [*qualités inédites*]" (*TP*, 198), but by means of the prose poem's emphasis on "the wealth of propositions contained in the least object . . . : a stone, a blade of grass, fire, a piece of wood, a piece of meat. . . ." In contrast to the temporal movement typical of Schlegel's thought, Ponge proposes "a voyage into the thickness of things, an invasion of qualities, a revolution or a subversion" that would turn up the "infinite resources of the thickness of things rendered by the infinite resources of the semantic thickness of words!" (*TP*, 200). Through a quasi-scientific "precise contemplation of the object," Ponge hopes to create a "De natura rerum," not mere poems—fragments of a missing whole—but a unity, "a single cosmogony" that would break through the poverty of objects and of language in contemporary society (the "slight thickness of things in the mind of men") (*TP*, 201) and offer a new, liberated usefulness ("you will serve me and you will serve men henceforth to many other expressions") (*TP*, 201–2). Throughout the history of the prose poem, the genre has exhibited great interest in clichés and proverbs, the reified verbal objects of "ordinary" or everyday language. If "subversion" can be successful in this most elemental level of discourse, the prose poem suggests, we may well be on our way to a permanent revolution that would extend beyond literature as such. Thus, at the conclusion of "Introduction au galet," Ponge writes: to create "some new proverbs or commonplaces: that is all my ambition."

Toward a "Post-Revolutionary Literature"

In 1974, in an introduction to the issue of *Books Abroad* celebrating Ponge's reception that year of the Neustadt International Prize for Literature, Ivar Iask wrote: "Ponge's bouts with ideologies and their perpetual promises of future salvation are a matter of the past."[16] In the atmosphere of the early to mid-1970s in America (the award was presented at the University of Oklahoma), with the student demonstrations of the late 1960s a fading memory, Watergate in the air and American involvement in the Vietnam War hastening to its inglorious end, one can imagine a certain amount of relief on the part of many that an author of Ponge's reputation should have ceased struggling with some of the more unsettling political implications of his own writing. Only a few years earlier, in 1970, Robert Greene had commented that the "heavy ideological content" of Ponge's writing made it difficult to conceive of much of his work as poetry or even prose poetry.[17] As Ponge has grown older, however, and as his work has become more widely read, both Ponge's commentators and Ponge himself have tended increasingly to deemphasize or belittle the political implications of his work.[18]

16. Ivar Iask, "Notes toward a Francis Ponge in Norman," *Books Abroad* 48, no. 4 (1974), pp. 650–51.
17. Robert Greene, "Francis Ponge, Metapoet," *MLN* 85 (1970), p. 572.
18. For a concise and useful overview of Ponge criticism through the mid-1970s, see Gerhard Butters's *Francis Ponge: Theorie und Praxis einer neuen Poesie* (Erlangen: Schäuble Verlag, 1976), pp. 8–25. A paradigmatic example of the tendency to belittle the political dimension of Ponge's work may be found in Ian Higgins's "Language, Politics and Things: The Weakness of Ponge's Satire," *Neophilologus* 63 (1979), pp. 347–62, which argues the inferiority of Ponge's early satires and more explicitly political poems such as "R. C. Seine no." and "Le restaurant Lemeunier rue de la Chaussée d'Antin" in comparison with the poems that deal with objects of the physical world. Though I would not entirely disagree with Higgins's conclusions, his arguments tend to support a narrowly

Even in Sartre's seminal essay on Ponge, "L'homme et les choses" (Man and Things), the political import of Ponge's work is largely misunderstood. With reference to "Le galet," Sartre writes accusingly: "Far from there being here a humanization of the pebble, there is a dehumanization, up to and including human feelings." The fact that Ponge "takes men deliberately for things" leads Sartre to condemn him as a "behaviorist" taking a *parti pris* "to treat men as mannequins,"[19] as if Ponge himself were somehow responsible for the massive reification his texts reproduce and expose. No less *engagé* in his way than Sartre, Ponge would nevertheless quite likely ascribe to Adorno's view that the contradictions and antagonisms of society are best presented in art indirectly ("Only through . . . mediation, not through direct parti pris").[20] Thus, Ponge takes *objects* as his immediate subject matter, although "it is man who is the goal" (*TP*, 215). Of the text on the pebble Ponge writes: "Here, one shrugs one's shoulders and denies all interest in these exercises because, I am told, there is nothing in them of man. And what should there be then? But it is of man unknown up to the present of man. . . . That is why it is of the highest interest. It's a question of the man of the future" (*GRM*, 25–26).

Taking the side of *things* is for Ponge a way of suggesting a possible world that reverses or overturns the existing world, with its stultifying exploitation of human beings and things alike. In "Réponse à une enquête" (Reply to a Questionnaire), Ponge writes:

> Ce qui me porte ou me pousse, m'oblige à écrire, c'est l'émotion que procure le *mutisme* des choses qui nous entourent . . . les hommes eux-

---

aesthetic appreciation of Ponge's texts and dismiss the political dimension without which his work might well suffer from preciosity. Ponge's "parti pris" is at its very core, as Jean Thibeaudeau has pointed out (*Francis Ponge* [Paris: Gallimard, 1967], p. 66; cited in Butters, *Theorie und Praxis*, 14), "a political matter." Butters rightly emphasizes (p. 39) that it was only through Ponge's political engagement that he was able to bring the problem of language sharply into focus.

19. Jean-Paul Sartre, "L'homme et les choses," *Situations 1* (Paris: Gallimard, 1947), pp. 269 and 289. Prior to Higgins, Sartre had already labeled the two poems "the only bad—but really bad writings of Ponge" (290); Albert Camus, on the other hand, was of a quite different opinion. Exhibiting a greater understanding of Ponge's project, Camus wrote: "I understand very well that you have not turned away from men. The texts on Hachette and on the restaurant are successes, perhaps relative, but surely astonishing" ("Lettre au sujet du *Parti pris des choses*," *La Nouvelle revue française*, no. 45 [September 1956], p. 388). For an early critical response that addresses Sartre's misunderstanding of the political implications of Ponge's texts, see Blossom Margaret Douthat, "Le Parti pris des *choses*?", *French Studies* 13, no. 1 (1959), pp. 39–51, especially pp. 46 and 49–50.

20. Adorno, *Ästhetische Theorie*, p. 479; *Aesthetic Theory*, p. 446.

mêmes pour la plupart nous semblent privés de parole, sont aussi muets que les carpes ou les cailloux. (*GRM*, 224)

[What carries me or pushes me, obliges me to write, is the feeling produced by the *mutism* of the things that surround us . . . men themselves for the most part seem to us deprived of speech, as mute as the carps or the pebbles.]

The problem of the "incommunicability of persons, of monads" (*GRM*, 224), which Baudelaire treats directly as a consequence of class and sexual differences in a poem such as "Les yeux des pauvres," is dealt with in Ponge's work, as we have seen, by a more indirect focus on "objects that have accompanied us . . . that are here with us, and that are forced to be silent—perhaps against their will—and of which we are never aware . . . " (*GRM*, 244). Ponge never lets us forget that, as Lukács reminds us, "human interrelations are not direct relations," but are " 'bound to objects' and . . . 'appear as objects,' " and that, as Lukács also points out, the objects of the empirical world must be understood, "as aspects of a . . . total social situation caught up in the process of historical change."[21] Like the objects of the physical world, human "subjects" cannot escape being caught up in this process, although the monadic character of life in capitalist society causes individuals to lose sight of the very social determinations that inhibit communication. As a consequence, human beings function in their own world as isolated objects. Suffering in isolation, and deprived of the possibility of speaking with a *collective* voice, they become as silent as things. In this context, as Ponge points out, " . . . between a perfect description and a cry, an appeal, there is not so much distance" (*GRM*, 278).

In "Le galet," "Introduction au galet," and other texts, Ponge reminds us that natural history and human history cannot be separated from each other. Where it is a question of relating the historical process to a human situation involving class struggle, Ponge's work allies itself with what Lukács calls "the standpoint of the proletariat." Thus, in *Le savon* (Soap) Ponge writes:

. . . je veux pouvoir être lu par des personnes d'une classe misérable, dont j'estime que le devoir et de s'élever . . . à une situation matérielle meilleure. Et je pense aussi que ces personnes et ces classes ayant eu la chance de trouver récemment une doctrine qui les exalte et un parti qui les conduit dans les chemins de la victoire, auraient bien tort de s'en

21. Lukács, *History and Class Consciousness*, pp. 176 and 162; hereafter cited as *HCC*.

détourner au profit de je ne sais quelles anciennes théories de résigna-
tion et de stoicisme, dont je crois bien qu'ils favorisent leurs exploiteurs.

[. . . I want to be able to be read by members of an unhappy, unfortu-
nate class, whose first duty I figure it to be to rise . . . to a materially
better situation. And I think also that such persons and such classes,
having had the luck to find recently a doctrine which exalts them and a
party which puts them on the path to victory, would be very wrong to
turn away from these to who knows what ancient theories of resignation
and stoicism, which I am aware of as favouring their exploiters.] (*LS*,
62; *LD*, 47–48)

As is easily imaginable, this political dimension of Ponge's work has not
taken very well in the English-speaking world. Thus, the translator of
Le savon writes apologetically in his brief notes about the author that
Ponge's "membership of the Communist Party from 1936 to 1946 was
a modest one" (*LD*, 99). Concerned to avoid "solemnities" and limit our
appreciation of Ponge's poems to their "first lightness and freshness,"
another commentator sees no remnant of Ponge's communism "except
a kind of materialism"; Ponge's texts were meant, he tells us, "only to
give pleasure to the mind."[22] In the American context especially, it is
important that such statements not be allowed to divert attention once
and for all from the profoundly Marxian basis of Ponge's work. Working at Hachette (the subject of the poem, "R. C. Seine no.") in the
1930s, Ponge had an intimate awareness of the objectification and commodification of self which is constitutive of the worker's position in
society; his choice of the prose poem as genre is bound up with this
experience:

Du fait de ma condition sociale, parce que je suis occupé à gagner ma
vie pendant pratiquement douze heures par jour, je ne pourrais écrire
bien autre chose: je dispose *d'environ vingt minutes,* le soir, avant d'être
envahi par le sommeil. . . . Ce qui m'importe, c'est de saisir presque
chaque soir un nouvel objet, d'en tirer à la fois une jouissance et une
leçon. . . .

[From the fact of my social condition, because I am busy earning my
living practically twelve hours every day, I could not very easily write
anything else: I have available *about twenty minutes* each evening before

22. Donald Sutherland, "Wonderful Things," *Parnassus* 1, no. 2 (1973), p. 60. See
also David G. Plank's *"Le grand recueil:* Francis Ponge's Optimistic Materialism," *Modern
Language Quarterly* 26, no. 2 (1965), pp. 302–17, in which Plank discusses Ponge's materialist aesthetic in such a way as to detach it for all practical purposes from any serious
political implications.

being invaded by sleep. . . . What matters to me is to seize nearly every evening a new object, to draw from it both pleasure and a lesson. . . .] (*TP,* 126)

Even if, like Sartre, we suspect this explanation of being perhaps too materialist, such material factors are certainly not without importance. Ponge's choice of the prose poem, that consummate "poem-object," and his *Parti pris des choses* suggest solidarity with people-as-things and a resistance to those forms of reification the working class experiences most intensely. If the proletariat is to become "the identical subject-object of the social and historical process" (*HCC,* 149), it is only, as Lukács has pointed out, by perceiving its own object status within that process, that is, by perceiving the mediation of all human subjects by objects both "natural" and man-made existing in the world. A similar insight lies behind Ponge's work, but although Ponge's "parti pris *des choses*" implies a critique of reification strongly related to that put forward by Lukács, it also suggests in a way Lukács did not the impasse of all narrowly defined "humanisms" that are based on an insufficient respect for the things of this world *other* than the human and that fail to take into account the determinate role of language ("*COMPTE RENDU DES MOTS*") in shaping both "nature" and "man."

Near the conclusion of "Notes premières de 'l'homme' " (First Notes of/on 'man'), Ponge writes: "*Le Parti pris des choses, Les Sapates* belong to a type of "post-revolutionary literature" (de *la littérature-type de l'après-révolution*) (*TP,* 248), and in "A chat-perché": "I will never rebound except in the pose of the revolutionary or the poet" (*TP,* 180). Today this constellation is still vitally important to Ponge's work, even if as the young revolutionary has gained increasing acceptance in the literary establishment his work has been subject to the aestheticist assimilation referred to earlier. In the 1970s, as Iask's remark suggests, Ponge himself withdrew increasingly from the politically engaged position of *Le parti pris des choses.* At the Cérisy colloquium held in his honor in 1977, Ponge remarked: "Revolution, as far as I am concerned, is to be taken in what you might call the physical sense; it is the revolution of the spheres; it is nothing else. It is revolution in the sense it is taken in astronomy, a kind of equilibrium without rest. . . . The word revolution must not at all be taken in the arch-banal sense of social subversion" (*CC,* 62). Certainly, a young Ponge would have thought, and spoken, differently, preserving along with the "physical" meaning, the historical materialist sense of the word which the older, more celebrated and widely accepted Ponge rejects as *arch-banal*. In the section of *Signéponge* that was first delivered at the Cérisy colloquium, Derrida justly calls attention to the feeling on reading Ponge of someone who is both engaged and disengaged at once (CC, 131). Although Ponge sometimes seems to refuse all prescriptive, didactic, or political strategies, his texts often engage in those very kinds of activity. Even as late as 1974, when Iask was putting Ponge's ideological struggles away in the closet, Ponge himself was continuing: "There is a morality that can be accorded to things [and quite possibly, he might say, to literary genres as well, such as the prose poem]. Above all, one shouldn't remain silent. In my opinion, this is very important, even on political grounds. . . . I do not believe it is sufficient to become ecstatic or revolt, all the while keeping silent. One must talk."[23]

One of the fundamental strengths of Ponge's writing is without doubt that, as Serge Gavronsky has pointed out, he does not fail "to account for the exigencies of class and economic factors, as these influence and even determine man's condition" (*PL*, 230). In "Les écuries d'Augias" (The Augean Stables), a text that bears striking affinities to Rimbaud's "Solde," Ponge writes of the "shameful order of things" which "crushes the eyes" and "staves in the ears" in Paris and speaks as well of "those streets where the honey of production flows in waves, where it will never again be a question of anything else for our high school friends who jumped with both feet tied from philosophy once and for all into the oils and the camembert" (*TP*, 175). It is this kind of situation which stands behind the quite *political* notion of a "parti pris des choses": "These governments of businessmen and merchants . . . if all that didn't speak so loudly, if that weren't the only thing to speak" (*TP*, 175–76). Given this state of affairs, Ponge writes, "the art of resisting in words [and of offering resistance *to* words, *résister aux paroles*] becomes useful . . . the art of founding one's own rhetoric is a work of public salvation" (*TP*, 177). Although Ponge's work certainly demonstrates a concern to preserve the distinction, in Gavronsky's words, "between poetry and polemic" (*PL*, 37), Ponge has nonetheless contributed on the whole to a *rapprochement* between poetry and political commitment. In "Pages bis" (Brown Pages), Ponge speaks of being "tormented by a feeling of 'civil responsibility'" (*TP*, 211) and of himself as an "'activist'. . . . (That is to say: communist, forbidden word in

23. Interview with Serge Gavronsky, *Books Abroad* 48, no. 4 (1974), p. 687.

1943.)" "I cannot conceive of myself," Ponge writes, "other than taking a stand [*prenant parti*], and I believe that not to take a stand is also to take one (the bad one). I choose therefore the one which—on the plane of political experience—seems to me the least bad. That is all. A sort of radicalism: yes, that is it indeed" (*TP,* 214).

Ian Higgins has quite correctly located Ponge's politics—albeit deprived of their social context—in what he calls the "explosive quality of the language" of Ponge's texts.[24] This explosive quality, characteristic of the prose poem at its best throughout its history, has been emphasized by Ponge himself on more than one occasion. At the colloquium in Cérisy, he referred to *Le parti pris des choses* as "a collection of bombs" (*CC,* 178), and in *Le savon* he asks if cakes of soap aren't themselves like hand grenades for which "it is a question of defeats, of course, much more than of victories" (*LS,* 119; *LD,* 87). If we read this passage in the metapoetic fashion for which it asks, Ponge's "cakes of soap" (*savonnettes*) suggest the prose poem (a sort of stone or pebble, as Ponge describes it, easy to grasp), that genre whose history since Baudelaire and Rimbaud does indeed concern defeats much more than victories. The true revolution, Ponge has said, lies in literature, in the subversive and revolutionary work on language which literary texts perform and which Ponge believes may have a greater power to help us change things than explicitly political discourse.[25] Although the prose poem is for Ponge without question the most modern, subversive, and revolutionary genre to emerge in the last half of the nineteenth century and first half of the twentieth, it is nevertheless the very space the prose poem occupies within literature, the small enclosure it defines, which Ponge's own "definition-descriptions" set out to explode:

> Dans *Le Parti pris des choses* même, qui est considéré et qui a été indiqué à un moment donné comme un recueil de textes clos, eh bien! ce n'est pas

24. Higgins, *Le parti pris des choses,* p. 36.
25. See Ian Higgins, *Francis Ponge* (London: Athlone Press, 1979), p. 132, and Ponge's remarks in *Cahiers critiques de la littérature,* no. 2 (December 1976), and *Entretiens de Francis Ponge avec Philippe Sollers* (Paris: Gallimard, 1970), p. 68, where Ponge speaks explicitly of having chosen the prose poem because its form is "the form of the bomb." The notion of the "exploding" text is further explored by Higgins (*Francis Ponge,* 9) in his explication of Ponge's "Le Magnolia": "First, there is the notion of a slow motion explosion. Second there is the tension between two sets of meanings for 'éclatement': . . . the destructive side, explosion or the bursting of a bubble, and . . . the creative side . . . the flower's opening into full maturity." This dual signification of "explosion" carries with it important implications for the idea of a post-revolutionary literature.

vrai, parce que c'est toujours l'histoire d'une rhétorique par objet. La rhétorique de l'eau, par exemple, m'oblige à faire un texte qui n'est pas clos. La "Faune et flore" est également un texte qui ne se clôt pas. . . . Déjà ce n'est pas seulement un recueil de bombes, au sens de choses parfaitement circonscrites. (*CC*, 178)

[In *Le parti des choses* itself, which is considered and was designated at a given moment a collection of closed texts, well! it's not true, because it's still the same story of a rhetoric by object. The rhetoric of water, for example, obliges me to make a text which is not closed. "Fauna and Flora" ["Le galet' as well, one might add] is also a text that doesn't close. . . . It is already at that point not simply a collection of bombs, in the sense of things perfectly circumscribed.]

The preoccupation with physical objects which has been so characteristic of the prose poem from Baudelaire to the present leads Ponge, in other words, to explode the very brevity and compactness that had given the prose poem its precarious identity among literary forms, and to move by so doing toward what he envisions as an even more concrete and objective imaging of texts/objects as an ongoing process: "I like to return to the reality of concrete things . . . since that time I have considered my sketches as definitive texts" (*CC*, 178–79).

Every poem, Ponge has said, should be able to be given the title, "Raisons de vivre heureux" (Reasons for Living Happily) (*TP*, 188). The possibility of living happily, for Ponge, can only come about in tandem with and as a result of the ongoing, ever renewed and self-renewing liberation of man and so of language. To write a post-revolutionary literature means to overcome the poverty of objects that inheres in the one-dimensionally utilitarian uses of language typical of capitalist society.[26] Such literature would explode this constricted usage, aiming at the forms of social organization that produce and are produced by it. It would be a destructive force, to be sure, but a force directed, finally, toward what Marx called an "all-sided production of the whole earth":

26. Evaluating Ponge's work from a communist perspective in 1949 in "L'anti-Pascal, ou La Poésie et les Vacances: Francis Ponge," *Critique*, no. 37 (June 1949), p. 497, Georges Mounin concludes that *Le parti pris des choses* is not simply (or does not have to be) "a poetry for the ten thousand privileged followers of art for art's sake." Mounin points out that it would be a "facile irony" to respond to Ponge's claim by saying "that it would be better to lay by each thing for its own time, to reserve the creation of a post-revolutionary literature for the times that will come after the revolution."

> The element of thought itself . . . *language*—is of a sensuous nature.
> The *social* reality of nature, and *human* natural science, or the *natural science of man*, are identical terms.
> It will be seen how in place of the *wealth* and *poverty* of political economy come the *rich human being* and rich *human* need. . . . Not only *wealth*, but likewise the *poverty* of man—under the assumption of socialism—receives in equal measure a *human* and therefore social significance. . . .
>   . . . since for the socialist man the *entire so-called history of the world* is nothing but the . . . emergence of nature for man, . . . he has the visible, irrefutable proof of his *birth* through himself, of his *genesis*.[27]

Creating a post-revolutionary literature means providing a foretaste of how "things" will be; it means for the artist "first of all doing nothing, sinking oneself into one's fecund leisure" (*GRM*, 194).[28] Intensely aware, like Schlegel and the major practitioners of the prose poem we have considered thus far, of a growing gap between the poet and society, as between poetry and life, Ponge addresses the need to make poetry living and social while making life and society poetic. Rejecting, on the one hand, any kind of "forced labor" on behalf of ideological dogma that would contradict the very principle of "free, conscious activity" Marx associates with artistic creation and life under socialism (*ME*, 76), Ponge comments: "They make me laugh with their talk of a *message* or *mission*" (*GRM*, 299). Expressing a somewhat astonishing confidence, on the other hand, in the power of literature to effect change, Ponge totally rejects the resignation of art-for-art's-sake: "Must we be reminded again that serene works of art have more power to change man than the boots of conquerors?" (*GRM*, 187–88). The aim of Ponge's "new claim" (*nouvelle prétention*) is the familiar utopian telos that would bring about a "reconciliation of man with the world" (*GRM*, 192) and show that "poets are people like anyone else . . . poetry is accessible to everybody" (*GRM*, 285).

Toward the realization of this utopian project, Ponge encourages us to turn our attention to things commensurate with man's stature in the world. Thus, first of all, for Ponge, nature must be accorded a respect

27. Marx, *Economic and Philosophic Manuscripts of 1844*, in *Collected Works*, 3:304–5.
28. In a discussion with Ponge and Breton published at the end of *Méthodes*, Pierre Reverdy remarks: "doubtless the poet is not by definition one of the most perfect social beings, but . . . his work . . . is a detour for inserting himself . . . taking back definitively a place in that society" (*GRM*, 300). The poet's function in bringing about social change is for Ponge, as Gavronsky has pointed out (*PL*, 14), that of a "laboratory technician" or a common laborer, a *worker* with language.

that man has not given it in the past. As Richard Vernier has pointed out, Ponge expressed such concerns in his poetry long before ecological concerns became as widespread as they are today.[29] Among the major poets of this century, there is none who displays more of what Lukács called "an aspiration towards the totality" (*HCC*, 175) than Ponge, none for whom man's "social redemption" and "the redemption of things in his mind" (*TP*, 248) are more expressly interwoven. Ponge's *parti-prisme* on the part of things gives a concrete dimension to the idealist utopian project of a *Universalpoesie* that is as "Romantic" in its fragmented articulation as it is "classical" in its projected telos: "Our tendency is toward a simple man [*C'est à un homme simple que nous tendrons*] . . . sober and simple" (*TP*, 246–47); "I choose order with calmness, but the new order, the *future order*, currently persecuted" (*TP*, 228). To arrive at the future order Ponge speaks of, a *new* classical work "according to the genres," it is first necessary to break down the barriers between existing genres. To begin, Ponge says in *Le savon*, "it is always necessary to break something" (*LS*, 64; *LD*, 49); hence both his initial choice of the prose poem, which has had the historical function, like that of Schlegel's *Universalpoesie*, of challenging generic hierarchies, and his subsequent "explosion" of that form into more amorphous "definitions-descriptions."

The "classical work" Ponge envisions, the true *livre* or book mentioned in the preface to *Le grand recueil*, is finally inseparable from the idea of living, as Ponge puts it, completely, fully ("*tout entier*"), in the "perfect society" that is to come into being "after the revolution" (*TP*, 217). In contemporary society, which Ponge describes as a "game of reciprocal abuse," such a work, such a society may only be articulated in fragments, by negation, indirectly ("that is why one should *speak indirectly*") (*TP*, 216); hence Ponge's choice of the prose poem as a point of departure and the focus on physical objects instead of human subjects:

> Quelqu'un a dit—je ne vois pas pourquoi je ne dirais pas qui—c'est Marx . . . —il a dit que *l'homme subjectif* ne pouvait se saisir directement lui-même, sinon par rapport à la résistance que le monde lui offre, sinon par rapport à cette résistance qu'il rencontre. . . .
> Il s'agit là d'un Grand Oeuvre, où les artistes sont dans une technique et les politiques dans une autre; il s'agit au fond de la même chose.

29. Richard Vernier, "De la poésie objective à la vénération de la *matière:* Francis Ponge," *Stanford French Review* 2 (1978), p. 23.

> . . . on pourrait aussi bien dire qu'il n'y a qu'un seul parti magique, et que c'est le parti communiste. . . .
> . . . Sortons, faisons-nous tirer . . . par nos objets. . . . l'homme n'est pas mon propos direct . . . mais . . . l'homme que nous ne sommes pas encore. . . .
> Allons! Cherchez-moi quelque chose de plus révolutionnaire qu'un objet, une meilleure bombe que ce mégot, que ce cendrier. . . . (*GRM*, 258–60)

> [Someone has said—I don't see why I shouldn't say who—it's Marx . . .—he said that *subjective man* could not seize hold of himself directly, but rather by means of the resistance the world offers him, that resistance he encounters. . . .
> Here it is a question of a Great Work, where artists pursue one technique and politicians another; when all is said and done it's the same question.
> . . . one could just as well say that there is only one magical party, and that it is the communist party. . . .
> . . . Let us go out, let us be drawn . . . by our objects. . . . mankind is not my direct concern . . . but . . . that mankind we have not yet become. . . .
> Go ahead! Find me something more revolutionary than an object, a better bomb than this cigarette butt, than this ash-tray. . . .]

These lines were written in 1947, around the time Ponge withdrew from active membership in the French Communist party. But if the party itself came to seem less and less "magical" to Ponge,[30] the impulse toward a new society, a new man, and a post-revolutionary literature accessible only by focusing on the reciprocal mediations of man and his objects does not diminish. The idea of the "Great Work"—in the inextricably political as well as aesthetic sense of Ponge's use of the term—remains crucially important to an understanding of Ponge's own project. Focusing on "the commonest, most indispensable objects of human making . . . those which one ordinarily utilizes without any thought for them, as Monsieur Jourdain used to do with prose" (*LS*, 125; *LD*, 93), Ponge's is indeed, as numerous critics have commented, a "materialist" aesthetic. As such, it is not to be separated without some violence from Ponge's Marxian commitment to a de-reification and liberation of the silent and oppressed "things" of the world, whether

---

30. For discussions of Ponge's disenchantment with the increasing Stalinization of the French Communist party, see Butters, *Theorie und Praxis*, pp. 120–23, and Sarah Lawall, "Ponge and the Poetry of Self-Knowledge," *Contemporary Literature*, 2, no. 2 (1970), p. 195. See also Ponge's *Pour un malherbe* (Paris: Gallimard, 1965), pp. 147–48.

we are speaking of subordinated classes of human beings, of physical objects per se, or of a "marginal" literary genre such as the prose poem.

Ponge's increasing distance from Marxist revolutionary political activity as he has grown older and more widely accepted should not now be allowed to obscure the political and historical context of his work and of his original *parti pris* in particular. Ponge's very choice of the prose poem as genre is bound up with what Christian Prigent describes as a "call to a future reconciliation," a "dream of a future without struggles (without divisions)" that is perhaps inevitably accompanied as well by a threat of "imaginary homogenization."[31] A highly concentrated form of the project of a fusion or reconciliation of genres such as that Schlegel envisioned on a more macrocosmic scale, the prose poem in Pronge's work gestures toward a concrete unity of the diverse by means of a deliberate focus on the physical world itself, the everyday poverty of objects, of language and of man Ponge would have liberated and realized as a new wealth. The problematics of homogenization and heterogeneity, of identification, difference, and opposition, and of genre (as also of gender and class) are, as we have seen, crucially important to the prose poem's development from its very beginning. Like Schlegel's *Universalpoesie*, the prose poem characteristically gestures both toward unity and sameness and toward fragmentation and difference. If it aspires, on the one hand, to a hybridization or "fusion" of generic difference in order to resolve false contradictions and oppositions (as of poetry and prose, literary and ordinary language), it aspires also to a breakdown of generic, textual, and class barriers which would allow for the greatest possible heterogeneity and diversity.

In keeping with the prose poem tradition from which they are derived, Ponge's "definition-descriptions" aspire toward nothing less than a full flowering of generic potential.[32] In this, perhaps, more than

31. See Christian Prigent, "La 'Besogne' des mots chez Francis Ponge," *Littérature* 22 (1978), pp. 97, 96. This desire for reconciliation carries with it, as Prigent also points out, the vision of "an imaginary recomposition of the unity of the person, whose ideological base is very much the myth of the unity of the social body in its entirety" (94). The prose poem's history is intimately involved with this myth, the desire for what Giordan, "Ponge et la nomination," p. 495, has called a "(polysemic) re-union . . . a 'certain adequation,' giving the impression of a homogenization of two different orders, seized as contrary in that writing and fought as such to resolve."

32. See also "Tentative orale" (*GRM*, 253): "No . . . I am not a mystic! May humour, or if you like, quite simply, the sense of the ridiculous save me from that! It is not unity I seek but variety." Certainly, there is evidence of both in Ponge, but of the former perhaps more indirectly and less decisively than the latter.

anything else, they display traces of a postrevolutionary literature and a classless society where positive differences would flourish. One crucial difference between Ponge's use of the prose poem and Schlegel's use of the fragment is that whereas Schlegel aims more or less directly at the absolute he calls *Universalpoesie,* Ponge directs his attention more to the concrete physical/linguistic material at hand. Where Schlegel emphasizes a fusion of oppositional terms, Ponge is more intent, finally, on what he calls "the differential quality" of things (*GRM*, 42). Although absolutes are by definition inaccessible, it is still possible, as Ponge has said, to arrive at "positive results" in the political organization of human life and in human society generally, as well as in the "mastery of human history and of the antinomy individual-society" (*TP*, 209). The problematic of the antinomy "individual-society," so important to the prose poem since Baudelaire, has continued to be at issue in organizational strategies for dealing with the relation between the individual prose poem and the collection. From Baudelaire to Ponge, collections of prose poems have characteristically refused to offer the reader a reassuringly novelesque sense of wholeness or totality. Playing off the possibility that its block-print format seems to indicate the need for a teleological reading emphasizing the chapter-to-chapter development and coherence conventionally expected of novels but not of collections of verse, collections of prose poems typically reject such development and coherence, thereby allowing for a greater autonomy of the individual texts themselves as well as for a greater variety of possible relations between and among them.

In such poems as "Le galet" and "Introduction au galet," Ponge undermines what Jean-François Chevrier has called a "fetishism of the closed object" (*CC*, 405). Although Ponge has himself doubtless participated in this fetishism along with other writers of the prose poem, in "Le galet" and "Introduction au galet," among other early texts, this fetishism gives way to a severe fragmentation that would deny for all practical purposes the existence of any pregiven or already existing totality or unity. Like "Pages bis" and "Notes premières de l'homme," in which Ponge articulates his vision of a new man, these two texts suggest what Walther has referred to as "not the concentrating but the disruptive character" of Ponge's intention. That Ponge never finished his "Notes premières de l'homme" is itself, as Walther has pointed out, "an important indication of Ponge's concept of man."[33] As intended

33. Walther, *Francis Ponge,* pp. 148, 34.

contributions toward the ongoing project of a postrevolutionary literature, Ponge's "Le galet" and "Introduction au galet" suggest that a reconciliation of man with the world and of man with himself is to be imaged, if at all, by negation, fragmentation. We are still, Lacoue-Labarthe and Nancy have remarked, in the era of the Romantics, the age "of the chaos of works, or of chaotic works" (*AL*, 72). Like Schlegel's fragments—"unformed forms in the chaos of the epoch"— such texts of Ponge as "Le galet" and "Introduction au galet" may well teach us "that the future itself is fragmentary—and that there is *no place* there to project a work" (*AL*, 423; my emphasis). They also suggest that the utopian project of finding such a place and of constructing such a work can and must not stop.

PART V

Beyond French Borders:
Two Contemporaries

CHAPTER 9

Politics and Solitude:
The Prose Poetry of Robert Bly

Politics, Form, and the Prose Poem

"Once a poet takes a political stand," Robert Bly wrote in the introduction to his selected translations of Pablo Neruda, "the wise assure us that he will cease writing good poetry. Neruda became a Communist in the middle of his life and has remained one: at least half of his greatest work, one must admit, was written after that time. He has written great poetry at all times of his life."[1] Appearing near the beginning of Bly's

---

1. Robert Bly, ed., *Neruda and Vallejo: Selected Poems* (Boston: Beacon Press, 1971), p. 15. Further references to Bly's work will be indicated in the text by the following abbreviations followed by page number: *This Body Is Made of Camphor and Gopherwood* (New York: Harper and Row, 1977), *CG*; *The Light around the Body* (New York: Harper and Row, 1975), *LB*; *The Man in the Black Coat Turns* (New York: Penguin Books, 1983), *MBC*; *The Morning Glory* (New York: Harper and Row, 1975), *MG*; "The Network and the Community," *American Poetry Review* (January/February 1974), *NC*; "Poetry in an Age of Expansion," *The Nation*, April 22, 1961, *PE*; "On Political Poetry," *The Nation* (April 24, 1967), *PP*: *Talking All Morning* (Ann Arbor: University of Michigan Press, 1980), *TM*; *This Tree Will Be Here for a Thousand Years* (Haprer and Row, 1979), *TT*; "The Two Stages of an Artist's Life," *Georgia Review* 34, no. 1 (Spring 1980), *TS*; "A Wrong Turning in American Poetry," *Choice*, no. 3 (1963), WT. "Written Forty Miles North of a Spreading City" and a portion of "August Rain" from *The Morning Glory: Prose Poems by Robert Bly*, copyright © 1972 by Robert Bly and copyright © 1973 by Robert Bly, and "A Dream of What Is Missing" and "The Left Hand" from *This Body Is Made of Camphor and Gopherwood: Prose Poems by Robert Bly*, Copyright © 1977 by Robert Bly, are reprinted by permission of Harper & Row, Publishers, Inc. "Eleven O'Clock at Night" from *The Man in the Black Coat Turns*, copyright © 1981 by Robert Bly, is reprinted by permission of Double-day & Company, Inc.

career in 1962, the year of publication of his first relatively apolitical collection, *Silence in the Snowy Fields,* these remarks indicate a long-standing interest on Bly's part in the relationship between poetry and politics. Five years later, in an essay published in *The Nation,* Bly would go on to say that the result of the American tendency to discourage artists and writers from writing political poetry has been the absence in American letters of a man like Boris Pasternak "who wrote great poetry, who took a clear stand, and whose work itself has a serious political meaning" (PP, 522). With Bly's politically charged second book, *The Light around the Body,* on its way to winning the National Book Award the following year, in 1968, Bly himself was emerging as one of America's most respected poets and a formidable social critic. Applying the criteria Bly himself used to appraise Neruda, we might say that although Bly may not have written great poetry all his life, the period of this second collection encompasses much of Bly's strongest work as well as his greatest influence on American society and literature; it is also the period of his most intense involvement politically.[2] In the early 1970s, as evidenced by the appearance in Bly's third major collection, *Sleepers Joining Hands* (1973), of such poems as "Condition of the Working Classes: 1970" and above all the long poem, "The Teeth-Mother Naked at Last" (1971), Bly continued to write in an explicitly polemical and political vain. Since that time, however, Bly's work has demonstrated relatively little resistance to the increasingly conservative trend of American politics and consequent privatization of American poetry. No writer's fate over the last twenty years suggests more emphatically than Bly's that, as Bly himself has said, "everything that happens to the country happens to the literature" (*TM,* 59). Following the end of American involvement in the Vietnam War, Bly's poetry has turned, as has America generally, more "inward." As a consequence, traces of sociopolitical awareness have largely faded by comparison with his earlier work.

2. Extended discussions of Bly's poetry may be found in Charles Altieri's *Enlarging the Temple* (Lewisburg: Bucknell University Press, 1979), hereafter referred to as *ET;* Charles Molesworth's "Domesticating the Sublime: Bly's Latest Poems," *Ohio Review* 19, no. 3 (Fall 1978), pp. 56–66, hereafter referred to as DS, and his *The Fierce Embrace* (Columbia: University of Missouri Press, 1979), hereafter referred to as *FE;* and in Howard Nelson's "Welcoming Shadows: Robert Bly's Recent Poetry," *The Hollins Critic,* no. 2 (April 1975), hereafter referred to as WS, and his full-length study, *Robert Bly: An Introduction to the Poetry* (New York: Columbia University Press, 1984), hereafter referred to as *RB.*

For our purposes here, what is crucial to note about Bly's turn away from sociopolitical content is that it largely coincided with the shift in his poetics toward the prose poem. In 1969, Bly commented in an interview: "I think that the poem is a tiny model of the society in which it's born. The Elizabethan sonnet is a tiny model of the closed society and the class structure of the Elizabethans" (*TM*, 149). Through the work not only of Bly but also of other well-established verse poets such as W. S. Merwin, David Ignatow, and James Wright, the prose poem enjoyed an unprecedented surge of interest in America in the 1960s and 1970s.[3] Although Bly's initial experimentation with the "new" genre drew sharp criticism, his publication by 1977 of two full collections of prose poems, *The Morning Glory* and *This Body Is Made of Camphor and Gopherwood*, demonstrated Bly's commitment to the genre and greatly contributed to its currency on the American scene. By the late 1970s, in stark opposition to Paul Lacey's early appraisal in his book, *The Inner War*,[4] Charles Molesworth, one of Bly's most devoted critics, was saying that Bly had "slowly, unobtrusively, and patiently *mastered* the prose poem" (my emphasis). At the same time, Molesworth also remarks that Bly's prose poems are "completely without political content"; in this, they are without question closer to what Molesworth calls "the idiom of pastoral ecstasy" (*FE*, 119) in *Silence in the Snowy Fields* (which itself contained two prose poems) and the more recent verse collection, *This Tree Will Be Here for a Thousand Years*, than to the sharply political poems of *The Light around the Body* and *Sleepers Joining Hands*.

In an early essay entitled "Poetry in an Age of Expansion," Bly demonstrates his awareness of the political ramifications of the French prose poem tradition when he says that for Rimbaud: "No division existed necessarily between politics and literature. A rebel against the upper class or against class forms in general might also rebel against certain forms in poetry." Although Bly goes on to use Whitman as the prime example of an American poet "who broke the old idea of the poem, and also announced the end of class in society" (*PE*, 350), Rimbaud clearly occupies a similarly exemplary status among French poets.

3. For discussions of Bly's verse and prose poetry in the context of developments in American poetry in the 1950s and 1960s, see Nelson, *Robert Bly*, pp. 1–7 and 129–31. For a concise overview of the prose poem's status in the United States, see especially the introduction to Stephen Fredman's *Poet's Prose: The Crisis in American Verse* (New York: Cambridge University Press, 1983), pp. 1–11.

4. Paul Lacey, *The Inner War* (Philadelphia: Fortress Press, 1972), p. 48.

Acknowledging, on the one hand, that "the reimposition of form is a failure" (the more traditional, rhymed, metrical forms of verse, for example), Bly also insists that a revolution of forms is itself a thing of the past: "The breaking of forms, in the poem and in society, has already taken place." For Bly, the urgent problems of literature and society no longer concern form, but content: "The poet said, See, I have broken the forms in my poem, and the essence remains. Do the same, and the essence of society will remain" (PE, 352). No more "out-ward"-directed revolutions, Bly insists; what we need is a quiet, "in-ward" revolution. In the nineteenth century, Bly says, "the poem be-came longer and looser" in response to increasing social "constriction"; in the twentieth century, in response to increasing "expansion," "the poem will grow shorter and more intense . . . it is not the form of the poem that will be changed, but the poet's life. . . . The presence of forms, or the breaking of forms—is not central" (PE, 353). The twen-tieth century is, Bly says, a "totally new situation" by comparison with the nineteenth, yet clearly more continuity exists than Bly admits. Though Bly refers to our own century as one of "expansion" and to the nineteenth as one of "constriction," one must surely acknowledge that, for example, industrial, capitalist expansion was as unprecedented in its way in the nineteenth century as it has been in the twentieth. This recognition is important because Bly's approach to *literary* form corre-sponds, as we have seen, to his perceptions of forms in society at large. Bly writes that free verse, with which he was primarily working when "Poetry in an Age of Expansion" was written, is not today "a reaction against fixed forms, as it actually was in 1915," but "a movement into something new . . . impelled by a vision of something ahead" (PE, 353–54). What this something is, Bly does not indicate in great detail; it is "something that does not yet exist . . . concerned also with privacy and solitude." Having called attention to American poetry's docile recep-tion of "old forms," Bly himself nevertheless steps back from Rimbal-dian gestures of provocation. "It is not a matter of iconoclasm," Bly says, "poetry is beginning again" (PE, 354).

To writers of the prose poem such as Baudelaire and Rimbaud, for whom questions of form and content were inextricably interwoven, one can easily imagine that Bly's project would sound a bit odd. On the one hand, poetry is to move "into something new." On the other hand, the continuing crisis of forms is simply to be ignored; it is all a matter of changing the content, the "essence," to use Bly's revealing term. In any case, although Bly is certainly right to hold up Whitman's "longer and looser" free-verse poetry as the exemplary model for the liberation of poetic form in American poetry, the situation of poetry in America and the situation of poetry in France in the nineteenth century stand in need of further differentiation than Bly's essay provides. What the essay does not make clear, and what has tended to be overlooked by American poets and critics for over a century, is that in the French tradition it is the prose poem much more than free verse which provides the most significant liberation of both form and content in the last half of the century. Baudelaire, the founder of modern poetry in France, did not write *vers libre,* and although Rimbaud was familiar with Whitman's work, it is the prose poem, not free verse, that dominates the final stages of his experimentation with poetry. Like free verse, the prose poem does of course represent a break with traditional metrical forms; it also represents, however, a reaction against the effusive expansiveness of Romantics such as Lamartine and Hugo. Far from being a longer and looser form, the prose poem in the hands of Baudelaire and Rimbaud displays an explosive compactness, the very brevity and intensity Bly predicted for American poetry in the 1960s.

In this respect, Moleworth's assessment of Bly's prose poetry, the most extensive available prior to the recent appearance of Howard Nelson's book-length study of Bly's work, includes a potentially misleading characterization of the French prose poem tradition. The prose poem may indeed be thought of, as Molesworth says, as exemplified by a Rimbaldian "series of aggressively scintillating but fragmented insights," but to speak of the genre as "a rather bourgeois invention" (*FE,* 120) is to risk seriously misrepresenting its historical function. Emerging in the mid-nineteenth century in the France of Napoleon III, the prose poem was certainly deeply embedded in bourgeois culture. In the work of its major practitioners from Baudelaire and Rimbaud to the present, however, as we have seen, the prose poem has itself figured in various ways a revolt against the bourgeoisie and the exclusions of genre, gender, and class by means of which it has managed to maintain its hegemonic position in society. If we ask ourselves why a prose poem tradition developed in France from Baudelaire to the present but did not take root in America until quite recently, the constellation 1848–1871–1917 is highly suggestive. The revolutionary political activity that occurs at each of these crucial moments in European history corresponds roughly in the history of the prose poem, as we have also seen, to the periods of (1) Baudelaire, (2) Rimbaud, Lautréamont, and Mallarmé, and (3) Max Jacob and Gertrude Stein. In all these periods, the failure of bourgeois society radically to alter its own forms of organization yields to experimentation with a genre that has as its project the undermining of received literary and extraliterary discursive practices. The prose poem's dialogizing gesture toward a genreless genre (neither prose nor poetry alone, both prose and poetry) symbolically enacts at each of these crucial historical junctures the dismantling of restrictive, hierarchically ordered forms and institutions still in place in society at large.[5]

Clearly, one of the prose poem's dominant historical functions has been to call attention to a crisis of forms in society as well as in literature. It is thus not surprising that not until the late 1960s, when revolutionary impulses reached their peak in student movements and antiwar and civil rights demonstrations in the United States, does the prose poem began to attract widespread attention among poets in America. In this context, it is significant that Bly, who at the height of this activity was awarded the National Book Award for a highly political book of verse, should soon become perhaps the most vocal protagonist of what presented itself to American poets over one hundred years after its appearance in France as a revolutionary new genre. As Rimbaud had turned to the prose poem around the time of the failed revolution of 1871, so Bly in the period surrounding the intense activism of 1968. In both cases, a poet critical of directions taken in society as well as in literature turned to the prose poem as to a new *form* of liberation. Like Rimbaud and Whitman, Bly displays in his work what Molesworth has called an "essentially Utopian vision" (*DS*, 61). Yet although Bly's own transition at the end of the 1960s and in the early to mid-1970s from a primary focus on free verse to an intense preoccupation with the prose poem is itself a sufficient indication that form is more important to Bly than he sometimes suggests, Bly's choice of the prose poem is, as the "Poetry in an Age of Expansion" essay demonstrates, as bound up with the idea of ignoring form as a constitutive element of utopian vision as Rimbaud's work in the genre is with stressing its importance. In France in the nineteenth century the prose poem emerged in response to the exhaustion of more traditional metrical forms; similarly, its emergence in America in the 1960s was a

---

5. Cf. Fredman (*Poet's Prose*, 2–3), who describes Baudelaire's prose poetry as an "abdication of previous generic (and therefore social) underpinnings" and characterizes the prose poem as "a leading agent in the nineteenth-century breakdown and amalgamation of genres that foreshadows the massive hybrids of the twentieth century . . . a kind of 'last genre.'"

response to the ascendancy and rapidly increasingly exhaustion of free verse. Taken up by respected verse poets such as Bly, Merwin, Wright, and Ignatow, the prose poem in the 1970s had the effect of shifting the poetry establishment's attention away from an exclusive preoccupation with free verse. Yet although the prose poem's appearance in America in the late 1960s and early 1970s carried with it something of the revolutionary aura the genre held in the nineteenth century, it would be a mistake to attribute to it the same force and function. The sudden surge of interest in the prose poem and its newfound acceptance in America raise the possibility that the genre may in fact be losing its polemical force by becoming, not a genreless genre symbolically gesturing toward a breakdown of received generic hierarchizations as it was for Baudelaire and Rimbaud, but just another genre or literary niche in which younger writers may obediently ensconce themselves.[6]

That Bly understands what is at stake politically as well as aesthetically in the prose poem's hybridization of various modes of discourse and its consequent undermining of distinctions based on genre, gender, and class is clear; what he himself does with the genre is, however, another matter. With Bly as one of its principal proponents, the genre that once gestured toward and contributed to the breakdown of existing class and generic barriers inside and outside literature has come to be used for quite different purposes. Whereas Rimbaud's involvement with the prose poem represents for him an all-or-nothing, last chance moment within literature, Bly seems to be attracted to the genre for the potential he sees in it to relate rather cozily to an already acquired audience. Thus, in an interview conducted in 1972, Bly likens the prose poem not to the radical French tradition of the nineteenth and twentieth centuries but to Chinese poetry, "low key all the way through."[7] His aim in working with the genre is not to break down any class or generic barriers but "to calm the language down," not to smash forms

6. Cf. Nelson (*RB*, 129), who writes that by the 1970s "prose poems were being written by scores of poets of all levels of renown," and Fredman (*Poet's Prose*, 3). Pointing out the prose poem's paradoxical status as the genre that marks a "codification of a moment of generic dissolution," Fredman writes: "The expanding history of the prose poem gives testimony that the urge to stand inside the socially and literarily sanctioned sphere of a genre survives even within a form of writing dedicated to the destruction of genre."

7. Similarly, in his brief introduction to *The Morning Glory*, Bly makes explicit reference not to Baudelaire, Rimbaud, and the French tradition of the *poème en prose* but to Taoism and the Basho haiku from which Bly draws the title of his collection. What the Basho poem teaches us is, Bly says, "the idea that our disasters come from letting nothing live for itself," from our inability, in other words, to leave things alone.

but to "bring in all sorts of details" (*TM*, 103), not to democratize poetry in revolt against the elitism and exclusiveness of traditional metrical forms but, as we read in the notes on the author at the conclusion of *This Body Is Made of Camphor and Gopherwood,* to talk "in a low voice to someone he is sure is listening" (*CG*, 61). Although Bly rejects the subversive historical function of the prose poem, opting for a more comfortable and, in the jargon of the 1970s, "laid-back" approach, his use of the prose poem does carry forward two characteristic aspects of the French prose poetry tradition. The first, which we will return to later in more detail in looking at two poems from *This Body Is Made of Camphor and Gopherwood,* is a very definite utopian tendency, articulated within a framework more mystical and religious than sociopolitical. Second, Bly's prose poems consistently exhibit the prose poem's tendency to focus attention on the concrete, the everyday, inconspicuous physical objects and events, a tendency already evident in the work of Baudelaire, Rimbaud, and Jacob but manifest to an even greater extent, as we have seen, in such later texts as *Tender Buttons, Spuren,* and above all *Le parti pris des choses.*

In considering the latter tendency, it is revealing to compare two of Bly's essays published almost twenty years apart which appear to flatly contradict each other. In "A Wrong Turning in American Poetry," which appeared in 1963 at a time when he was working principally with free verse, Bly attacks T. S. Eliot for constantly looking over the public world "for reliable sets of objects." Criticizing all poets who, like Eliot and William Carlos Williams, "want to concern themselves with objects," Bly praises Rilke for believing "the poet actually experiences the soul" (WT, 33–36). Following his critique of the poem of objects, Bly turns his attention once again to the apolitical orthodoxy of American letters. The poetry we have had in America, he says, is "without a trace of revolutionary feeling—in either language or politics." He is startled that "in the last twenty years there have been no poems touching on political subjects, although such concerns have been present daily" (WT, 38). Coupled with Bly's insistence on the need to move from a poetry of objects to a poetry of inwardness and "revolutionary feeling" is an antipathy to "descriptive prose" and a poetry "defined as something more prosy than prose" (WT, 44). "A man cannot turn his face," Bly says, "at the same moment toward the inner world and the outer world" (WT, 36). What we have had is "picturism," "a poetry without the image," abstraction, which is one form of the "flight from inwardness," and objectivism, the "flight into the outward world, which is another" (WT, 39–40). By contrast, Bly wants a poem that does not involve the "extinction of the personality" but one "in which the image is released from imprisonment among objects" and human effort is not "dissipated among objects" as in our age of "technical obsession" and "business mentality" (WT, 46–47). In the context of the early 1960s, following the revolt against "academic" verse in the 1950s and the ascendancy of "objectivist" verse with the poets of the Black Mountain school, the purpose of Bly's essay is to resituate American poetry from an internationalist perspective and redirect attention away from what Bly considers the typical preoccupation in American poetry with matters of poetic "technique." With regard to the prose poem, however, what is perhaps most significant about Bly's polemic is that, although Baudelaire and Rimbaud each conceived of the genre in their different ways as an objectivizing (re)inscription of the subjective, lyrical self into the social context, with revolutionary implications both aesthetically and socially, Bly sees an "objective" poetry or "poetry of objects" as antithetical to true revolutionary feeling.

In light of Bly's 1963 condemnation of a poetry of objects and "descriptive prose," let us now turn to an essay written a number of years *after* Bly's turn to the prose poem which is about Rilke and Ponge, "The Two Stages of an Artist's Life" (1980). As in the earlier essay, Bly stays with the opposition he so favors between the "inner" and the "outer." Now, however, we may be surprised to read the following: "In the last sixty years, a wonderful new poem has appeared. It is the object poem, or thing poem" (TS, 105). What Bly considers "new" is not, of course, quite so new as all that; the object or thing poem certainly has a much longer history than he suggests. In the modern era, in particular, its history is deeply involved with that of the prose poem, the poem-object Jacob referred to as a "jewel." It is thus not a coincidence that Bly, following his own commitment to the prose poem and the revelations of Ponge, should suddenly find "wonderful" what seventeen years earlier he had polemicized against. Clearly, it is not the "same" object poem; nor does Bly's advocacy of this particular kind of poem in 1980 in fact contradict his condemnation of it in 1963 as utterly as it might first seem. Objects, as Stein's *Tender Buttons* insistently reminds us, are subject to many uses. What Bly continues to find limiting in the use of objects in the work of such American poets as Eliot and Williams is what he perceives as a manipulative, instrumentalist, technique-ori-

ented approach to the world,[8] a way of relating to the world exemplified in the decade preceding Bly's "Two Stages" essay by the narcissistic
"me generation" America of the 1970s. In the object poems of Rilke
and Ponge, by contrast, Bly finds two examples of a kind of writing that
seems to synthesize subject and object. Despite his continued allegiance
to Rilke (the writer of *Dinggedichte* as well as of prose poems), what Bly
evidently finds so wonderful and new at this point in his development
is certainly the work of Ponge, whom Bly has not written on before,
where the object poem emerges *qua prose poem*.[9] Although Bly says
Ponge "*adopted* primarily the prose poem for his thing poem" (*TS*, 107;
my emphasis), it would be more correct to say that, as the example of
"Le galet" demonstrates, Ponge's choice of the prose poem as form and
his focus on material objects went hand in hand.

Bly forces Ponge into a mold of "inwardness" toward which Ponge
himself would doubtless have been skeptical. The prose poem, or object poem, Bly says, "implies that we have the longing to give honor to
objects again, and that we don't feel them so distant" (*TS*, 106). Perhaps
because great detail is possible when the object is described in the prose
poem, Bly says, something surprising happens: "It is as if the object
itself, a stump or an orange, has links with the human psyche. . . ." In
terms Ponge would probably not assent to without qualification, Bly
goes on to speak of a "*union* of the object with the psyche" (TS, 107).[10]
Justly remarking the Pongean (and Baudelairean) strategy of emphasizing both sobriety *and* spontaneity, as well as the 1960s' lack of under-

8. Cf. Fredman's discussion (*Poet's Prose*, 54) of Bly's prose poem, "The Dead Seal
near McClure's Beach."

9. Cf. Nancy Willard, "A Poetry of Things: Williams, Rilke, Ponge," *Comparative
Literature* 17 (1965), pp. 311–24 and Willard's chapter on Ponge in her *Testimony of the
Invisible Man* (Columbia: University of Missouri Press, 1970). Nelson's chronology of
Bly's life and work (*RB*, xxvii–xxxvii) notes that Bly translated Ponge's "object poem"
"L'huître" (The Oyster) in 1963, the same year the essay "A Wrong Turning in American
Poetry" was published in *Choice*. It is not until 1980, however, that Ponge is mentioned as
figuring among Bly's important reading. Nelson describes Ponge (*RB*, 137) as the writer
to whose work *The Morning Glory* bears the strongest kinship precisely because his prose
poems on objects elude subjective/objective categories. Although Bly shares Ponge's
interest in physical objects, his approach is obviously not, like Ponge's, self-consciously
metalinguistic. Cf. Molesworth (*DS*, 63), who writes that for Bly "the opacity of language . . . is simply to be willed away," and Altieri ("From Experience to Discourse:
American Poetry and Poetics in the Seventies" [*Contemporary Literature* 21 (Spring 1980)],
200 and 202), who remarks that since Bly wants his rhetoric to count "as immediate
concrete perception," he "must shrink from acknowledging his own rhetorical acts."

10. It is Ponge, after all, who has spoken of seizing "the differential quality" as "the
goal, progress." See his *Méthodes*, in *Le grand recueil*, 2:43.

standing of the former (TS, 105), Bly points out that the politics of
Ponge's *parti pris* imply a refusal "to exploit things, either as symbols or
as beings of a lower class." Ponge's title certainly suggests such a refusal, but politically it implies, as we have seen, much more: a solidarity
with people-as-things, and a recognition that in our world it is misleading to act as if "things," including people, did not continue to be exploited. With Bly, on the other hand, the political importance of
Ponge's "parti pris des choses" tends to be largely displaced by an
emphasis on individual transcendence and quasi-mystical reconciliation.

A good example of the emphasis placed by the prose poem in
general and by Bly in particular on the concrete objects of everyday
experience may be found in the last paragraph of "August Rain," from
The Morning Glory:

> The older we get the more we fail, but the more we fail the more we
> feel a part of the dead straw of the universe, the corners of barns with
> cowdung twenty years old, the chairs fallen back on their heads in
> deserted houses, the belts left hanging over the chairback after the
> bachelor has died in the ambulance on the way to the city. These objects
> also belong to us, they ride us as the child holding on to the dog's fur,
> these appear to us in our dreams, they are more and more near us,
> coming in slowly from the wainscoting, they make our trunks heavy,
> accumulating between trips, they lie against the ship's side, and will
> nudge the hole open that lets the water in at last. (*MG*, 70)

Writing on this poem, Nelson remarks Bly's relative accessibility for
people "who are not specialists in poetry" (WS, 14). This accessibility,
like the emphasis on physical objects, is an important part of the prose
poem's relative democratization of the verse lyric. In the poem's final
paragraph, quoted above, Bly draws together with impressive skill concrete images of feelings familiar to everyone. The focus becomes increasingly precise, moving from the relatively abstract awareness of the
inevitability both of growing old and of knowing failure to the cosmic
concrete/abstract image of the "dead straw of the universe" to the final
three images that are at once closer to home ("more and more near us")
and more and more definite: "the corners of barns . . . the chairs fallen
back on their heads . . . the belts . . . over the chairback. . . ." This first
sentence testifies to the capacity Bly sees in the prose poem for incorporating detail. Bly's typical strategy of proliferating image clusters like
those above suggests the expansion of feeling "into" or toward the

objects of the physical world rather than a reduction of feeling to any single object among them. Syntactically, here as elsewhere, Bly's use of commas allows for a quite mobile sentence structure suggestive of a liberation of objects from their usual contexts into new, if vaguely defined, relations, a liberational contiguity in which practically any-thing—a child, a dog, wainscoting, trunks, a ship's side—might appear next to anything else by virtue of a synthetic leap of the imagination. Where that leap leads in "August Rain," as so often in Bly's work, is to an affirmation of oneness in death, but what is most interesting about the poem is perhaps less this affirmation itself than the concrete sense it gives of our relations to *things*, things that "belong to us," but also "*ride* us" (my emphasis), in other words own us and rule our lives as much if not more than we do them. There is playfulness in these objects but also a tenaciousness, as in "the child holding on to the dog's fur," that may be harmful. Appearing in our dreams, growing nearer to us, weighing us down, accumulating and bearing pressure on our lives as on the hull of a ship, these objects (including also "deserted houses," the dead bachelor's "belts left hanging" with its hint of suicidal loneliness) are emblematic of the impoverished relations among human beings, among people-as-things, which threaten to bring on the final catastrophe.

"Written Forty Miles South of a Spreading City"

Bly's prose poetry may well involve what Molesworth has referred to as a desire to "domesticate the sublime." To the extent this is true, howev-er, it is important to remember that such a domestication is at odds with the radically antigeneric, dialogizing tradition of the prose poem we have been considering. Emerging as it does with Baudelaire as a reac-tion *against* the "sublime" isolation of the lyric self, the prose poem is a provocation not a whisper. Its most representative texts provide evi-dence of a verbal detonation in the manner of Baudelaire's "It was the explosion of the new year" ("Un plaisant" [A Joke]) or Rimbaud's "A tap of your finger releases all sounds and begins the new harmony" ("A une raison" [To a Reason]).[11] Consisting mainly of what Molesworth calls "heightened descriptions" (DS, 123), Bly's prose poems resemble the condensed, anecdotal narratives of Baudelaire's *Petits poèmes en*

---

11. Baudelaire, *Petits poèmes en prose (Le spleen de Paris)*, in *Oeuvres complètes*, p. 279; Rimbaud, *Illuminations*, in *Oeuvres de Rimbaud*, p. 168.

prose more closely than they resemble the texts of Rimbaud's *Illumina-tions* or *Une saison en enfer,* works that self-consciously display, as we have seen, what Rimbaud calls in *Une saison en enfer* "an absence of descriptive or discursive faculties." The brusque directness and ex-plosive quality manifest in many of Bly's own more powerful texts— "The Hockey Poem" from *The Morning Glory,* "Galloping Horses" from *This Body Is Made of Camphor and Gopherwood*—are themselves charac-teristic, however, of the prose poetry of both Baudelaire and Rimbaud.

One of the more successful poems of *The Morning Glory,* placed close to the end of the collection, is entitled "Written Forty Miles South of a Spreading City":

It is early dawn. The city forty miles away draws airplanes, as if it were a Sabbath. They appear and disappear. They are like flakes of powdered milk that appear in the water an instant, and then disappear. There are still paths that the cows have woven through the weeds, fences that mark the limits of the 75 × 40 barn the farmer pushed before him all his life. The barn is now only used for hay, the stanchions cold, it is like some African trading post, abandoned when the secrets the Europeans kept caught up with them, and no one could give a "simple and sincere account of his own life"!

The Germans and Norwegians who opened this land tore it away from the mother-love of the Sioux. They have sunk back now into their family Bibles; the great hinges have closed on them, and they sleep, a coarse sleep—not forgiven—they know they have done wrong, and they go over and over the harness-hours, trying to see how they threw on the harness, how they happened to buckle things in the wrong order. And the souls of their women float crippled through the hayloft, the floating souls are missing an arm, or a leg, the missing parts have been sent back by kidnappers in Persia. The feminine dries up early, and is easily torn away by the wind; pieces of it flying into the gully, or the tree split open, bare wood showing. The masculine like the windmill from Chicago, replaced after the Second World War by a pump set between the three legs.

In early dawn, sunlight gleaming on the tops of the cars in the yard, the farm is neither living nor dying. The dolphins go on speaking their high-pitched and playful thoughts, the whale sees himself less in the wide oceans, the high school girl in the suburbs makes love, and feels a bit detached, she is surprised to see what the ass of a man looks like; she is drawn to the hair on her arms. I too swim on, like those tortoises nearing a beach, or a coral reef, their great leather wings rising and falling in the friendly ocean, waking after long sleep, I feel secrets being discovered everywhere, thoughts that can save, rising, the sea at dawn littered with schools of live jellyfish, half soul and half body. (*MG*, 65–66)

Given the fact that Bly spends most of the year on his farm in Minnesota at some distance from urban life, the title of this poem nicely situates his own relation to the times. The airplanes of the second sentence are emblematic of the modern fascination with "things" of only passing importance, machines that "appear and disappear." By contrast, "There are still paths that the cows have woven through the weeds," "fences" and a farm, a barn "now only used for hay. . . ." In accordance with a long-standing pastoral convention, Bly's juxtaposition of nature with the city attributes to the former something of the "eternal": airplanes come and go; the cow paths remain. Similarly, the barn recalls an "African trading post," a primitive, precapitalist or early capitalist economy in which exchange-value had not yet gained hegemony over use-value, and displays nostalgia for the days when a man could give " 'a *simple* and sincere account of his own life' " (my emphasis). In the second paragraph, the past rises up in a less idyllic light, bringing with it the guilt connected with the treatment of the Indians by European whites, "Germans and Norwegians" being Bly's own ancestors and the chief settlers of his native Minnesota. Having "done wrong," buckled things "in the wrong order," America's white males inherit a world of fragmentation for which they themselves are responsible, "souls of their women . . . crippled," "pieces" of the feminine "flying into the gully, or the tree split open. . . ." While the tree split open suggests the death of the organic, a way of life supplanted by airplanes and the mechanical pump set that replaces the windmill after the Second World War, the feminine implies virtues of simplicity and sincerity at one with the "mother-love" of the Indians and in stark contrast to the exploitiveness of their European conquerors.

The opposition "male-female," which goes back a long way in Bly's work and remains central to his thinking, is used in this particular case to evoke the same sorts of contrasts between the public and the private, the materialistic and the spiritual, the bad "outer" and the good "inner" life, fragmentation and wholeness, the mechanical and the organic that one finds in such earlier verse poems as "A Man Writes to a Part of Himself" (*Silence in the Snowy Fields*), "The Executive's Death," "The Busy Man Speaks," "Romans Angry about the Inner World," and "After the Industrial Revolution, All Things Happen at Once" (*The Light around the Body*). Although males of European descent bear primary responsibility for the fragmented, impoverished relations that have continued from an unjust, often cruel past into a precarious present, women's souls and the world of "things" as well, both human and nonhuman, are "crippled" by these relations. The result, as the last paragraph indicates, is a state of suspension in which "the farm is neither living nor dying," whales are disappearing from the oceans and a narcissistic culture thrives in which the high school girl making love feels detached, vainly drawn "to the hair on her arms."

In its synoptic figuration of the estranged conditions, uncertainty, and disconnectedness of contemporary American life and its suggestion that current problems are an inevitable and perhaps irredeemable consequence of past individual and cultural failures, "Written Forty Miles South of a Spreading City" retains, in contrast to the majority of poems in *The Morning Glory*, something of the sociopolitical content of *The Light around the Body*. Significantly, however, this content is metaphorically "drowned" by the notion of a "friendly ocean" with which the poem concludes. The speaker, whom Bly would not hesitate to identify as himself, claims he feels "secrets being discovered everywhere, thoughts that can save," yet what he offers us is merely the familiar dichotomy, "half soul and half body," intimations of a transcendence in stark contrast to the images of fragmentation that precede them, a closural strategy dangerously close to what Charles Altieri has called, after Hegel, the "'bad infinite,' a form of mystery depending more on vagueness and surprise than on any sense that the mind has located structures that genuinely exceed its own powers of comprehension" (ED, 206).[12] Like Novalis, to whom he bears important affinities, Bly often seems to be looking everywhere for the absolute and everywhere finding only things. In his detailed attention to the concrete objects of everyday experience and the continuing impoverishment of daily life, Bly develops in his prose poetry the characteristic object orientation and critical-utopian function that have been so crucial to the genre since Baudelaire. Bly's concreteness typically breaks down, however, precisely when he attempts to offer us a sense of community, for it is a community still more imagined than real, a community that has yet to arrive and that neither Bly nor anyone else can single-handedly deliver.

12. Charles Altieri, "From Experience to Discourse," p. 206; hereafter referred to as *ED*. "The aim," as Altieri says, "may be to bring despair to a point of religious transcendence, but the result is a capitulation to society's view of poetry as mere emotive cries seeking desperately to escape realities and ironies that only a lucid and demystifying consciousness can face."

"A Dream of What Is Missing"

More than most American poets, Bly has made an effort to reach out beyond what he has referred to as "a network of like-minded people" (NC, 21) to establish some kind of meaningful connection with the "community" at large and bring about the kind of reciprocal, revivifying relationship between poetry and society which Schlegel projected as a fusion of genres. Bly's desire for community is nowhere more evident than in his second prose poem collection, *This Body Is Made of Camphor and Gopherwood*. Here, in its entirety, is one of the texts containing the phrase from which the collection takes its name:

The Left Hand

My friend, this body is made of camphor and gopherwood. Where it goes, we follow, even into the Ark. As the light comes in sideways from the west over damp spring buds and winter trash, the body comes out hesitatingly, and we are shaken, we weep, how is it that we feel no one has ever loved us? This protective lamplit left hand hovering over its own shadow on the page seems more loved than we are. . . . And when we step into a room where we expect to find someone, we do not believe our eyes, we walk all the way over the floor and feel the bed. . . . (*CG*, 15)

From the very first words of this brief text—the direct address, "My friend," that recurs frequently in the collection as a whole—to its telling conclusion in an empty room, the longing for an authentic form of community currently lacking in society is clear. Although the demonstrative "this" of "this body" suggests the assumption of a common humanity, Bly's subsequent assertion—"Where it goes, we follow, even into the Ark"—implies an apocalyptic, religious frame of reference for the idea of community. In the remaining sentences, the pronoun "we" occurs another eight times in just seven lines: "we are shaken, we weep . . . we feel no one has loved us . . . the page seems more loved than we are . . . we step into the room . . . we expect to find someone, we do not believe our eyes, we walk all the way over the floor and feel the bed. . . ." Clearly, large demands and claims are being made: "we" are all "friends" (presumably anyone reading Bly's text); we are all "one body," "this body." Though Bly does not tell us *which* body exactly he has in mind, one plausible reading given Bly's protestantism and the text's own internal evidence is that it is the body of Christ,[13] the spir-

13. Cf. Molesworth (*FE*, 34; quoted also in Nelson, *RB*, 182), who describes the friend

itual, transcendent body sent because "God so loved the world," the crucified God incarnate whose followers were shaken and wept in early spring over his crucifixion, the resurrected body that "comes out hesitatingly" and is supposed to sit, on the day of judgment, at God's right hand. As the right hand recalls Christ, so the "protective lamplit left hand hovering over its own shadow" brings to mind the dove or holy spirit that sits at God's other side. Given "this" body, Bly's speaker suggests, whatever differences exist do not really exist but are superficial; they are as transitory as was the world of prose in the eyes of Novalis. Though the right hand does not know what the left hand is doing, the left hand that seems more loved than "we" are is, after all, part of "this" body, the unified body of the Trinity.

And yet, although the image of the Ark and the allusions to the body of Christ and the Holy Spirit suggest unity and salvation, they also carry with them the old antinomian dualism: those who believe will be saved; those who do not will be lost. "We" go by twos. Set as it is at evening ("As the light comes in sideways from the west . . ."), the time of day when the sun goes down, and in springtime, the time of year that marks the death of the Son and his exile from earth, if also the possibility of his return, Bly's text images both the waning of old opportunities and the onset of new ones. Occupying as it does the uncertain, transitional space between the prosaic, lingering despair of "winter trash" and the poetic hopefulness of "damp spring buds," it figures the distance between the shadowy reality that is and the luminous reality that might be. Although the discovery of an empty bed at the text's conclusion recalls Christ's empty tomb and Easter ascension, its hint of salvation is at best ambiguously utopian. When Bly writes that "we do not believe our eyes," he may be implying that the doubting Thomases of the world should learn to accept on faith what they cannot see; on the other hand, the two Marys who expected to find Christ did indeed find an *empty* tomb, a sign that the kingdom of heaven was yet to be realized on earth.

The "Hand" of Bly's title, the one that governs the text, is thus not the right hand that does the writing, the hand of the Son that would be itself the Word incarnate, but the *left* hand, the hand of a missing, alternative politics and of the absent presence of the Holy Spirit. The

---

in *Gopherwood* as "the savior, or us, or the savior-in-us, less a social force than a private, inner healer." For another prose poem in which Bly associates the body with Christ see the text from *The Morning Glory* entitled "Christmas Eve Service at St. Michael's."

hand that writes the text is not, apparently, the hand that can right the world, however much it longs to do so. What the image of the "protective lamplit left hand" draws our attention to is not, finally, an image of actual community but, rather, "its own shadow on the page," a sobering reminder of the lack of community in the world as it is, if also of the enduring utopian aspiration for the realization of such a community. In marked contrast to Baudelaire, who called attention in his preface to *Le spleen de Paris* to the distance separating the life of the collective from the life of the individual ("la vie moderne . . . *une* vie moderne"), Bly attempts to efface the ongoing separation between these by means of a single pronoun, the first-person plural, "we," a deictic, like "this," which points to a unity that can only be, at our own historical juncture no less than in the mid-nineteenth century of Baudelaire, either a mystification of the present or a project for the future. As the conclusion of Bly's prose poem suggests, if we really "expect to find someone," if we expect to find a transcendent, Christ-like salvation and true community in the prosaic reality of the here and now, we are likely to be disappointed. When "we walk all the way over and feel the bed . . . ," there are only Bly's ellipses to greet us, a concrete indication of the absence of an authentic collective "we" from which to speak.

One of the more revealing texts from *This Body Is Made of Camphor and Gopherwood* to develop the prose poem's utopian tendency is entitled "A Dream of What Is Missing":

> Last night such glad powerful dreams, each tile laid down of luminous clay. . . . The dream said that The One Who Sees the Whole does not have the senses, but the longing for the senses. That longing is terrible, and terrifying—the herd of gazelles running over the savannah—and intense and divine, and I saw it lying over the dark floor . . . in layers there. The one who thinks does not have feeling, but the longing for feeling—that longing makes the lines of force at the bottom of Joseph's well. In the dream I saw the lumps of dirt that heal the humpbacked, what rolls slowly upward from the water, and prowls around the rocky edges of the desert, keeping the hermit inside his own chest. . . .
> (CG,27)

Throughout the history of the prose poem's fundamentally utopian project, a strong sense has developed among the genre's major practitioners of the appropriateness of the form to dream content.[14] It thus comes as no surprise that Bly's own utopian vision should express itself

14. Cf. Molesworth, "Domesticating the Sublime," p. 612.

so intensely in a prose poem that has its inspiration in dreams. Although "A Dream of What Is Missing" begins by describing the dreams that gave rise to the poem in wholly positive terms as "glad," "powerful," and "luminous," the sober distinction Bly goes on to make between the longing for the senses and for feeling and the actual possession of these measures the distance between the utopian dream of what might be and the prosaic reality of what is. One of the inspiring things about Bly has always been the evidence his work provides of a desire for community and a resistance to the idea that the society of the monadic, isolated individual is inevitable. As so often in Bly's work, however, so here in the image of "The One Who Sees the Whole" and the allusion to Joseph, the possibility of realizing the utopian dream of an authentic community is itself figured through the mediation of a single, charismatic individual.[15]

Although Bly's emphasis on charismatic individuals is unsurprising in light of his protestantism, from a collectivist point of view it has to be considered one of the most problematic aspects of his work. Such an emphasis is characteristic of that "affirmative culture" that Herbert Marcuse describes as asserting the existence of a "universally obligatory, eternally better and more valuable world . . . essentially different from the factual world of the daily struggle for existence, yet realizable by every individual for himself 'from within,' without any transformation of the state of fact."[16] It is symptomatic of the difficulties Bly encounters in attempting to conceive a transformation of the state of fact that "A Dream of What Is Missing" offers as its imaginary solution to the real problem of an absence of community a miracle, "the lumps of dirt that heal the humpbacked." What is perhaps most revealing about the text's conclusion, however, is that the ecstatic moment of healing yields to the threatening image of something that "prowls around the rocky edges of the desert, keeping the hermit inside his own chest. . . . " Reading this last line in the context of Bly's earlier work, we cannot help but recall the short poem called "The Hermit" in *The Light around the Body*. Even in Bly's most politically engaged book, the hermit is there as a positive symbol, albeit of "joyful death." He makes us "calm," and yet, his identity is less than reassuring: "There is

15. "Fall Poem," a verse poem from Bly's *Old Man Rubbing His Eyes*, is highly suggestive in this context: "Something is about to happen!/ Christ will return!/But each fall it goes by without happening" (Greensboro, N.C.: Unicorn Press, 1975), p. 17.

16. Herbert Marcuse, *Negations*, trans. Jeremy J. Shapiro (Boston: Beacon, 1968), p. 95; hereafter cited as *N*.

a man whose body is perfectly whole," Bly writes, " . . . He is no one." Isolated much of the year as he is on his farm, Bly himself is doubtless his own prototype for the hermit in his poems, the very type of the poet Altieri speaks of who sets himself up as "prophet or exemplary figure whose rhythms of perception we must imitate" (*ED*, 206). Although Bly knows well that he cannot claim to be "The One Who Sees the Whole," the suggestion is often there, and Bly's poems lose credibility the stronger that suggestion comes through.[17]

In poetry, Marcuse has said, "men can transcend all social isolation and distance and . . . overcome the factual loneliness in the glow of great and beautiful words." The ecstatic unity Bly attempts to portray in *This Body Is Made of Camphor and Gopherwood* is, however, only "the counterimage of what occurs in social reality" (*N*, 102). Though such counterimages may have the utopian function of projecting a world in which things would be different, they may also serve to mystify the world as it is. "A Dream of What Is Missing" provides a paradigmatic example of the interconnectedness in Bly's work of two forms of ideology, what might be called in Theodor Adorno's terms an ideology of inwardness, on the one hand,[18] and, on the other hand, the American ideology par excellence, the belief in the power of the lone charismatic individual to effect dramatic change and control his or her own destiny. That the hermit is trapped "inside his own chest" at the text's conclusion suggests the limited capacities of both these ideologies to raise *collective* awareness. As Adorno has pointed out, "Even in works of art the concrete can scarcely be named other than by negation" (*AT*, 203). In the European, and especially the French tradition, the prose poem as genre has exhibited a strong tendency toward the concrete in

17. Cf. Nelson (*RB*, 173), who writes that the body in *Gopherwood* is "not just a temple, but also a kind of priest, or shaman, or wise uncle." The "strident voice of the preacher" Jonathan Chaves identifies in his article "Chinese Influence or Cultural Colonialism: Some Recent Poets," *Ironwood* 19 (Spring 1982), pp. 115–23 (quoted also in Nelson, *RB*, 164) has drawn negative reactions from a number of commentators, including Nelson (*RB*, 165). The most biting, from Philip Dacey, is in the form of a review entitled "This Body Is Made of Turkey Soup and Star Music," *Parnassus* 7 (Fall/Winter 1978), pp. 34–45. As Nelson points out (*RB*, 167), *Gopherwood* is not only more baldly didactic than *The Morning Glory*, it is also more abstract, a depature from the object-poem orientation of the earlier collection.

18. Adorno, *Ästhetische Theorie*, p. 177; *Aesthetic Theory*, p. 169—hereafter cited as *AT*: "As the helplessness of the individual subject grew more pronounced, inwardness became a blatant ideology, a mock image of an inner realm in which the silent majority tries to get compensation (*sich schadlos halten*) for what it misses out on in society. All this tends to make interiority increasingly shadowlike and insubstantial."

large part, as we have seen, by polemically negating established literary classifications and generic distinctions. In Bly's hands, however, attention to this important formal/functional dimension of the genre gives way to a preoccupation with "pure" content and, in *This Body Is Made of Camphor and Gopherwood,* in particular to what might be called in Bakhtinian terms a monological, single-styled affirmation of ecstatic moments that bear only a surface resemblance to those of a dialogical, hybrid, politically charged collection like Rimbaud's *Illuminations.*[19] Whereas in Rimbaud's prose poetry the utopian is self-consciously inscribed as a project not yet realized rather than as a *fait accompli,* in *This Body Is Made of Camphor and Gopherwood,* by contrast, Bly's attempt to present as already healed the very fragmentation a writer such as Rimbaud exposes often results—as such an attempt inevitably must given the state of society—in a sense of unreality. If such poetic/prophetic phrases in Bly's second prose poem collection as "this body" and "The One Who Sees the Whole" have the unintended function of compounding our sense of isolation and lack of community, however, what is most genuinely utopian about a prose poem like "A Dream of What Is Missing" is that despite a certain pomposity it succeeds in maintaining the distinction between the *longing* for something—"the senses," "feeling"—and its realization. This is where Bly is at his most concrete, insisting that what is missing is still missing, and that a real community has yet to be created.

"Eleven O'Clock at Night"

In an essay written in 1975, Bly explicitly contrasts political poetry, in which, he says, "you have to use generalizations often," with the prose poem, which he sees as an exercise in "moving against 'plural consciousness.'" "In the prose poem," Bly writes, "we see the world is

---

19. See Bakhtin, *The Dialogic Imagination,* especially pp. 266–68 and 285–88. Despite the prose-poetic form of its texts, the monological character of *This Body is Made of Camphor and Gopherwood* makes the collection decidedly more poetic than prosaic in the following Bakhtinian sense. "The world of poetry," Bakhtin says, "no matter how many contradictions and insoluble conflicts the poet develops within it, is always illumined by one unitary and indisputable discourse. Contradictions, conflicts and doubts remain in the object, in thoughts, in living experiences—in short, in the subject matter—but they do not enter into the language itself. In poetry, even discourse about doubts must be cast in a discourse that cannot be doubted. . . . The poet is not able to oppose his own poetic consciousness, his own intentions to the language that he uses, for he is completely within it and therefore cannot turn it into an object to be perceived, reflected upon or related to" (286).

actually made up of one leaf at a time" (*TM*, 116). Bly's opposition notwithstanding, the prose poem, as I have argued, has been historically very much a political mode of writing, a norm-breaking genre gesturing by virtue of its antigeneric dialogizations toward new, liberated forms of collective reorganization in literature and in society at large. Although the prose poem's identity is bound up with a mixing or fusion of genres and a breakdown of hierarchizations of genre, gender, and class, its norm-breaking function has depended to a large extent on its capacity to resist being assimilated as just one genre among others.[20] Given the fact that the principal aesthetic target of the prose poem's polemic at its emergence with Baudelaire was the verse lyric, it is doubtful that the *Petits poèmes en prose* would have had the polemical force it did had its integrity as a collection been violated by the inclusion of poems in rhymed, metrical verse. Similarly, in the late 1960s and early 1970s, by which time free verse had gained ascendancy over rhymed, metrical verse as the dominant lyrical mode, the prose poem's unprecedented rise to prominence in America was given its momentum by writers such as Bly, Russell Edson, and Merwin who preserved the prose poem's autonomy and polemical force, like Baudelaire, by not mixing prose poems and verse poems in the same collection. Since the mid-1970s, however, the proliferation of collections that offer a loose mixture of prose and verse poems suggests that the prose poem may now be on the verge of forfeiting much of its autonomy and polemical force even as it enjoys a newfound respectability.

Bly's recent turn from the prose poem to a brief verse form of his own invention, the *ramage*,[21] and his mixing of verse and prose poems in his latest collection, *The Man in the Black Coat Turns*, provide additional evidence of the extent to which the prose poem now risks becoming, not the dialogizing, genreless genre or genre to end all genres gestured toward in the work of such writers as Baudelaire, Rimbaud,

---

20. Fredman (*Poet's Prose*, 3) draws attention indirectly to the importance of such resistance when he points out that the integrity of the French prose poem's antigeneric project has been compromised over the last century as it has increasingly become "another genre within the purview of the lyric poem." Exemplifying what Fredman refers to as "a moment in which poetry, philosophy, and criticism begin to coalesce" (10), the work of Francis Ponge demonstrates perhaps the most concentrated and forceful resistance to such a reduction of the prose poem's potential among French writers who have situated themselves with reference to the prose poem tradition.

21. See *Poetry* 138, no. 5 (August 1981), pp. 283 and 306, and The *Ohio Review* 19, no. 3 (Fall 1978), pp. 52–55.

and Ponge but merely one genre among many. In contrast to other recent mixed collections by such poets as Ignatow and Wright, *The Man in the Black Coat Turns* does preserve something of the prose poem's autonomy by grouping all of the collection's prose poems together in the second of its three sections. Like Bly's first two collections of prose poems, however, these most recent examples contribute to a de-politicization of the genre which is at odds with its initial norm-breaking function. Although the verse poems of the book's first and third sections include such politically oriented texts as "The Convict and His Radio" and "Kennedy's Inauguration," the vast majority are relatively apolitical by comparison with Bly's earlier verse collections. Bearing titles like "The Dried Sturgeon" and "A Bouquet of Ten Roses," the six prose poems of the second section demonstrate an even more peripheral interest in issues of an explicitly public, political nature.

To further situate Bly's work in the prose poem with reference to Baudelaire's social reinscription of the lyric in the *Petits poèmes en prose,* it is instructive to compare Bly's "Eleven O'Clock at Night," the text that opens the prose poem section of *The Man in the Black Coat Turns,* with the paradigmatic text from Baudelaire's collection considered earlier entitled "A une heure du matin." In addition to the close resemblance of their titles, a number of striking parallels between the two prose poems suggest that Bly is consciously following Baudelaire's example. Like "A une heure du matin," "Eleven O'Clock at Night" begins by focusing on the speaker's sense of relief at being alone at the end of a harried day. Like Baudelaire's text as well, Bly's goes on to recount in anecdotal fashion a litany of the day's events which has confessional overtones:

> I lie alone in my bed; cooking and stories are over at last, and some peace comes. And what did I do today? I wrote down some thoughts on sacrifice that other people had, but couldn't relate them to my own life. I brought my daughter to the bus—on the way to Minneapolis for a haircut—and I waited twenty minutes with her in the somnolent hotel lobby. I wanted the mail to bring some praise for my ego to eat, and was disappointed. I added up my bank balance, and found only $65, when I need over a thousand to pay the bills for this month alone. So this is how my life is passing before the grave? (*MBC,* 17)

As this passage indicates, the close of the day causes Bly's autobiographical speaker to reflect, like the speaker in "A une heure du matin," on his unwilling indebtedness to and dependence on others, the web of relations which daily entraps him. In the second and third paragraphs, additional close parallels emerge in Bly's speaker's avowed dissatisfaction with himself compared to others ("I am aware of the consciousness I have, and I mourn the consciousness I do not have") (*MBC*, 17) and in the desire he expresses to escape this dissatisfaction through poetry ("Many times in poems I have escaped—from myself. I sit for hours and at last see a pinhole in the top of the pumpkin, and I slip out that pinhole, gone!") (*MBC*, 18). Although these parallels between "A une heure du matin" and "Eleven O'Clock at Night" reveal real continuities between Bly's approach to the prose poem and Baudelaire's approach, the two texts also provide evidence of important differences in the aesthetic and historical situations of the two writers. Where Baudelaire's speaker must find whatever solitude he can within the confines of an urban environment, Bly's finds what peace he can at his home in rural Minnesota. Where the entanglements of Baudelaire's speaker have specific reference to the horrors of city life and professional and class struggle, those of Bly's speaker have to do with such private, domestic, family concerns as cooking and reading to the kids and getting a daughter on the bus. Although both "Eleven O'Clock at Night" and "A une heure du matin" articulate a sense of entrapment, Bly's version of the motif suggests that the possibility of liberation figured in and by Baudelaire's prose poetry has if anything diminished over time. Despite his relentless imaging of reified social relations, Baudelaire is still able to conclude "A une heure du matin" on the relatively hopeful note of the speaker's request to produce "some beautiful verses." By contrast, Bly writes of the "genie" of poetry he raises up roughly halfway through "Eleven O'Clock at Night" that "no one can get him back in the bottle again" (*MBC*, 18). Dispersed virtually beyond recall by the prosaic wreckage of modern life, he is "hovering over a car cemetery somewhere." The possibility of creating beautiful poetry that remains open at the conclusion of "A une heure du matin" gives way in "Eleven O'Clock at Night" to total intransigence; the alternative, poetic world that had been figured by the "dreaming" furniture of Baudelaire's "La chambre double" yields to an unwavering insistence in Bly's text on the poverty of objects of everyday experience and the impossibility of change:

> Stubborn things lie and stand around me—the walls, a bookcase with its few books, the footboard of the bed, my shoes that lay against the blanket tentatively, as if they were animals sitting at table. . . . There is no way to escape from these. . . .

Now more and more I long for what I cannot escape from. . . . My shoes, my thumbs, my stomach, remain inside the room, and for that there is no solution. Consciousness comes so slowly, half our life passes, we eat and talk asleep—and for that there is no solution. Since Pythagoras died the world has gone down a certain path, and I cannot change that. . . . Air itself is willing without pay to lift the 707's wing, and for that there is no solution. Pistons and rings have appeared in the world; valves usher gas vapor in and out of the theater box ten times a second; and for that there is no solution. Something besides my will loves the woman I love. I love my children, though I did not know them before they came. I change every day. For the winter dark of late December there is no solution. (*MBC,* 18)

As earlier in "A Dream of What Is Missing," so here in the expression of the desire for the presence of the eternal in the here and now, Bly maintains the indispensable critical-utopian distinction between what is longed for and what the actual state of things really is. In marked contrast to the prose poems of *This Body Is Made of Camphor and Gopherwood,* however, in the world of "Eleven O'Clock at Night" and the other prose poems of *The Man in the Black Coat Turns* there is no reassuringly "affirmative" image of "The One Who Sees the Whole." The at times narcissistic, ecstatic mode of Bly's second prose poem collection has given way in his most recent book to a tone that is, as Nelson has pointed out, more somber, sober, and reflective than any of Bly's collections since *The Light around the Body* (*RB,* 193). Though Bly indicates the possibility of transcendence through poetry in the image of the self slipping out the pinhole in the top of the pumpkin, the car cemetery the genie of poetry hovers over serves as a reminder of the continuing intractability of the world of prose. Similarly, although Bly speaks of himself in "Eleven O'Clock at Night" as changing every day, the prose poem concludes by acknowledging the limits of his ability to effect change. In its sober refusal to gloss over the negative aspects of modern life, its realistic assessment of the relative powerlessness of the individual, and its insistence on the difficulty, if not the impossibility, of finding solutions to deep-seated problems, "Eleven O'Clock at Night" is fundamentally Baudelairean. On the other hand, despite allusions to technological innovations and such twentieth-century phenomena as the 707, Bly's assertion that since the death of Pythagoras the world has gone down a path Bly cannot change suggests a fatalism that stems from an essentially ahistorical, idealist view of the world.[22] In contrast to Baudelaire, who tends to focus on *social* relations, Bly tends to be

22. Cf. Nelson, *Robert Bly,* pp. 193, 196, 214, 219–20, 224–25, and 230–32.

concerned with *human* relations. Where "A une heure du matin" figures the *spleen* of its speaker with specific reference to the sociohistorical situation of mid-nineteenth-century urban life, the speaker's concerns in "Eleven O'Clock at Night" remain, as we have seen,
essentially domestic, private, family-centered, transhistorical. Having
begun with references to bed, cooking, and stories, "Eleven O'Clock at
Night" circles back on these concerns by concluding with the speaker's
thoughts of his love for his wife and children and the "winter dark of
late December" that is emblematic of things beyond human control.

The prose poem has historically been a form selected by poets who
have felt intensely the split between the individual and the collective,
yet who have fought against resigning themselves to the inevitability of
individual isolation. It is thus significant that Bly, who has had one of
the largest readerships of any American poet in the last twenty years,
should have also contributed so prominently to the first major surge of
interest in that genre in the United States. "It's possible," Bly has said
recently, "that originality comes when the man or woman disobeys the
collective. The cause of tameness is fear . . . that we will lose the love of
the collective. I have felt it intensely. What the collective offers is not
even love, that is what is so horrible, but a kind of absence of loneliness"
(*TM*, 308). Questions of "originality" aside, *The Morning Glory* and *This
Body Is Made of Camphor and Gopherwood* attest to Bly's steadily less
provocative relation to collective life in America during the period of
his most concentrated work in the prose poem. The utopian impulse
that has manifested itself in the prose poem from the very beginning in
its drive toward a fusion of genres can still be strongly felt in Bly's own
work in the genre: in the focus of *The Morning Glory* on the everyday
physical objects that wait, along with us, upon a kind of liberation;[23] in
the healing gestures and the deliberate, subtle narrative and thematic
connections of individual texts to the collection as a (wished-for) whole
apparent in the sequential arrangement of the prose poems of *This
Body Is Made of Camphor and Gopherwood;* and in the attention given to
fragmented human relations and male grief in *The Man in The Black
Coat Turns.* Despite this manifestly utopian dimension, however, Bly's
work in the prose poem has not contributed greatly toward a dialogization of the relationship between poetry and society at large but has
instead tended to reinstitute the split between the lyrical self and social

23. Cf. Altieri, who has written of Bly's work in connection with the desire to be
"'released from imprisonment among' the objects of the *prose* world" (*ET*, 90; my emphasis).

reality which had been contested both by Bly's own verse poetry in the late 1960s and early 1970s and by the prose poetry of Baudelaire and Rimbaud. Despite its history as a genre of revolt, the prose poem in Bly's case draws him away from political poetry rather than deeper into it. His tendency has been rather to depoliticize what has been historically a highly charged, polemical, form-smashing genre for the sake of ecstatic religious content and a focus on domestic concerns and the inner life.

Commenting on the "Lack of Thinking on the Left" in the mid-1970s, Bly has said that the students "never did realize how much the antiwar protests really moved the bourgeoisie; they didn't pass a confidence in that down to the kids in high school now." Ironically, the same might be said of Bly in relation to a younger generation of poets. What William Heyen has called a "sense of fatality" in Bly's work, accompanied by a "move toward affirmation" (*TM*, 81) reveals itself in Bly's prose poems in the inability to move beyond notions of individual "transcendence" to a more concrete notion of community. In *This Body Is Made of Camphor and Gopherwood* in particular, the concrete, collective "We" of a movement Todd Gitlin said in 1971 was "in the process of gathering" has been displaced by the pseudo-community of the cosmic "We" of such prose poems as "The Left Hand."[24] "The cliché of the last ten years," Bly said in 1978, is: " 'I want to say something positive. If I can't say something positive I don't want to say anything at all' " (*TM*, 293). In lines such as the following from the conclusion of another text in Bly's second prose poem collection, Bly gives evidence of having succumbed himself at times to this cliché, the dubious consolations of a mystical, private, all-too personal "affirmative culture" whose sense of community scarcely extends beyond one or two. In "Snowed In," "A man and woman . . . sit quietly near each other" while the rest of the world continues on its unsettling course: "In the snowstorm millions of years come close behind us, nothing is lost, nothing rejected, our bodies are equal to the snow in energy. The body is ready to sing all night, and be entered by whatever wishes to enter the human body singing" (*CG*, 56). Bly's generous-minded acceptance of whatever comes, what Altieri has called his "sense of cosmic unity" (*ET*, 91), certainly has its appeal. What has been missing in Bly's prose poetry, however—perhaps unavoidably, symptomatic of what is missing in the fragmented, unreconstructed totality we call society—is not utopian longing but a firm collectivist

---

24. Todd Gitlin, "The Return of Political Poetry," *Commonweal*, July 23, 1971, p. 378.

grounding for that longing coupled with a clearly articulated critical stance toward society which would give us more a sense of where "we" really are, and hence a more concrete sense of where real community might be.

Writing on American poetry in the 1970s, Altieri has pointed out that in general younger poets turned away from the efforts of poets in the 1960s to transform values and articulate fresh epistemological stances to an emphasis on "the importance of recognizing limits and appreciating the value of quiet reflection" (*ED*, 209). On the strength of the poetry he has written in both verse and prose, Bly has by now been assimilated into the mainstream of American letters. Far from offering strong resistance to the shift in American poetics from public, political concerns to private, domestic ones, however, Bly's prose poems have tended in that very direction. The only artist the middle class has difficulty assimilating, Bly has said, is the one who lives "relatively apart" and tries to preserve "a certain solitude" (*TM*, 61). Since "the issues aren't clearly drawn" in America, Bly adds, "the U.S. poet has to feel his way, like a blind man along the wall" (*TM*, 63). These statements, and Bly's oft-repeated claim that the only true political poetry comes from intense inwardness, have come to seem more and more a potential rationalization for poets and other writers who would prefer to concern themselves not with the direction society is taking but only with the state of their art. Having held on throughout his career to what Gitlin has called "the myth of the lone hero,"[25] Bly has recently indicated his own readiness to give up this myth: "Heroes were needed in the sixties. I offered to be one which was very generous of me. But you can't do that for very long, it's not quite human. The hero always tries to solve things. . . . "[26] In light of the problematic emphasis on charismatic individualism evident especially in Bly's second prose poem collection, the desire expressed in the above quotation to jettison the hero complex points to an important reassessment of the poet's role in society. As the verse poems of *The Light around the Body* and *Sleepers Joining Hands* testify to Bly's heroic engagement with the social and political problems of the 1960s and early 1970s, however, the prose poems of *The Morning Glory* and *This Body Is Made of Camphor and*

25. Ibid., p. 376. "The shallowness of the American poetic consciousness," Gitlin goes on to say, "is revealed in the fact that the poet thinks the public sphere is only for visiting. Like it or not, he has to live there."

26. Cited in *Of Solitude and Silence: Writings on Robert Bly,* ed. Richard Jones and Kate Daniels (Boston: Beacon Press, 1981), p. 68.

Gopherwood attest to Bly's increasing detachment from such problems and his turn toward a more personal, private sphere dominated by the intersection of poetry, family, and religion much more than of poetry and politics.

With its mix of verse and prose poems and its attempt to come to terms with limitations in both the public and private spheres, *The Man in the Black Coat Turns* offers a compromise between these two general orientations which focuses on the family as the principal mediating instance between the self and others. In contrast both to the object orientation of *The Morning Glory* and the self-directed focus on the inner life in *This Body Is Made of Camphor and Gopherwood,* Bly's latest collection is concerned primarily, as its third-person title suggests, with an objectified self, the self in its relations to others. In this, Bly's latest collection reaches back behind the prose poem's twentieth-century pre-occupation with objects to a more direct Baudelairean approach to societal relations. Where the Baudelairean tradition of the prose poem serves, however, to draw poetry back into the realm of the social, *The Man in the Black Coat Turns* remains a relatively asocial, apolitical, private collection, a collection situated, in the words of the verse text entitled "Fifty Males Sitting Together," "far . . . / from working men!" (*MBC,* 57). Significantly, it is the prose poems even more than the verse poems that reveal what the book's jacket hails as an "intensely introspective sensibility." Having reconfirmed, in an interview conducted with Deborah Baker in 1981, "that community in the U.S. is very hard to come by," Bly goes on to say that he has learned to take comfort in "the community of poets."[27] Although any sense of authentic community is doubtless better than none, Bly's newfound willingness to take refuge among fellow writers certainly represents a retrenchment from his earlier call to reach out beyond a "network of like-minded people." As "Eleven O'Clock at Night" suggests, the world of prose which caused Baudelaire to turn to the prose poem in the nineteenth century is still very much with us in the twentieth. In such a world, from the perspective of the Schlegelian project of making society poetic and poetry social, it would surely be crucial to continue looking for solutions, as Bly's career teaches us, without necessarily looking for heroes.

27. Ibid., p. 70.

CHAPTER 10

Time Doesn't Pass: Helga Novak and the Possibilities of the Prose Poem

Born in Berlin-Köpenick in 1935 and a citizen of East Germany after the war, Helga Novak is the author of several collections of verse and of short prose, including most recently a selection from previous volumes entitled *Palisaden* (1980), and two autogiographical novels, *Die Eisheiligen* (The Ice Saints, 1979) and *Vogel, Federlos* (A Bird, Featherless, 1982).[1] Although a 1968 recipient of the Bremen Prize for Literature, Novak has only recently begun to receive a small measure of critical attention in West Germany,[2] where she has taken up residence since giving up her East German citizenship in 1966. Not surprisingly, Novak is considerably less well known in the United States, although translations of her work have appeared in *Field* as well as Michael Benedikt's

---

1. *Die Eisheiligen* is the partial subject of a recent study by Helga W. Kraft and Barbara Kosta, "Mother-Daughter Relationships: Problems of Self-Determination in Novak, Heinrich and Wohmann," *The German Quarterly* 56, no. 1 (January 1983), pp. 74–88.

2. See Otto Knörrich, *Die deutsche Lyrik seit 1945* (Stuttgart: Alfred Kröner Verlag, 1978), pp. ix and 393; Helene Scher, "Helga Novak: Ballade von der reisenden Anna," in *Geschichte im Gedicht: Texte und Interpretationen,* ed. Walter Hinck (Frankfurt: Suhrkamp, 1979), pp. 265–70; and Sigrid Weigel, "'Woman Begins Relating to Herself': Contemporary German Women's Literature (Part One)," trans. Luke Springman, *New German Critique*, no. 31 (Winter 1984), pp. 72–73, and "Overcoming Absence: Contemporary German Women's Literature (Part Two)," trans. Amy Kepple, *New German Critique*, no. 32 (Spring–Summer 1984), pp. 3–22. See also Christel Göbelsmann's anthology *Mörikes Lüfte sind vergiftet. Lyrik aus der Frauenbewegung 1970–1980* (Bremen: Schreiben, 1981).

international prose poem anthology.[3] The selections of *Palisaden* stem mainly from four collections. Of these, *Wohnhaft im Westend* (1970) and *Aufenthalt in einem irren Haus* (1971) both contain texts of short-story length and need not concern us here. The more compact texts of the remaining two collections, however, those of *Geselliges Beisammensein* (1968) and *Die Landnahme von Torre Bela* (1976), may clearly be situated both formally and functionally within the modern prose poem tradition as it has developed since Baudelaire and Rimbaud.[4]

Geselliges Beisammensein

When *Geselliges Beisammensein* first appeared it consisted of four sections, "Reisen" (Travels), "Das Gefrierhaus" (The Freeze-House), "Die Teppichweberei" (The Carpet Mill), and the title section, demonstrating an impressive range of formal, narrative, and thematic possibilities

3. *Field*, no. 9 (Fall 1973), pp. 22–24, and no. 10 (Spring 1974), pp. 94–95; Benedikt, *The Prose Poem: An International Anthology*, pp. 235–43.

4. Helga M. Novak, *Geselliges Beisammensein* (Neuwied: Luchterhand, 1968), and *Die Landnahme von Torre Bela* (Berlin: Rotbuch Verlag, 1976). References for both these works will be to the texts as they are reprinted in *Palisaden* (Neuwied: Luchterhand, 1980; © 1980 by Hermann Luchterhand Verlag, Darmstadt and Neuweid, and quoted with their permission), and will be indicated by *P*. Translations drawn from Benedikt's *International Anthology* will be cited as *IA*. Since my intention here is especially to emphasize the international character of what is at stake in the prose poem by calling attention to formal and functional continuities between Novak's texts and those discussed in the preceding chapters, my principal concern is not with the question of influence. As Ulrich Fülleborn has noted in *Das deutsche Prosagedicht* (31; hereafter cited as *DP*), the contemporary renaissance in the prose poem does not guarantee that all writers working in the genre are equally familiar with its history or even that they are aware they are working within its formal parameters. The prose poetry of Baudelaire and Rimbaud has nonetheless achieved so classical a status in the twentieth century and been so readily available in translation that as a rule one may assume familiarity with it among established writers of brief, highly condensed prose texts in Western countries and many non-Western countries as well. In my discussions of Schlegel and Novalis in the first two chapters, I indicated the extent to which the prose poem's fundamental project was anticipated in Germany well before Baudelaire. In the twentieth century, nevertheless, in Germany and elsewhere, it is above all the French prose poem tradition that gives the genre its currency. As Fülleborn points out, although as early as 1730 Gottsched maintained that true poetry need not be written in verse, the German term *Prosagedicht* makes its appearance only in the late 1800s and is itself derived from the French term *poème en prose*. For further discussion of the impact of the French prose poem on major German writers in the late nineteenth and early twentieth centuries, including especially Nietzsche, Kafka, Rilke, Georg Trakl, and Georg Heym, see Fülleborn, *DP*, pp. 7–8, 25–26, 52, 55–59, and Bernard, pp. 538–39, 724–27; see also Fülleborn's useful survey of twentieth-century German prose poetry and its relations to the French tradition in the introduction to his collection of texts, *Deutsche Prosagedichte des 20. Jahrhunderts* (Munich: Wilhelm Fink Verlag, 1976), pp. 15–43; hereafter cited as *DPJ*.

among as well as within individual texts. That *Geselliges Beisammensein,* unlike Novak's remaining collections, is reprinted in *Palisaden* almost in its entirety suggests its importance and weight relative to her other work. The texts of *Geselliges Beisammensein* are a *worker's* texts, a record above all of the four years Novak spent in factories in Iceland between 1961 and 1965, the years before her final immigration to the West. It is thus logical and fitting that, among other changes, Novak should choose to begin *Palisaden* with the section called "Das Gefrierhaus," and that she should begin this section with the brief text entitled "Arbeitnehmer—Arbeitgeber" (Employer-Employee). Placed eighth in *Geselliges Beisammensein,* in *Palisaden,* by contrast, this text is appropriately resituated to suggest what is perhaps *the* fundamental and determinant opposition of the earlier collection. It is appropriate, too, as the opening text of a collection of prose poetry, the genre that has shown itself since Baudelaire to be intensely conscious of oppositions and antagonisms within society and within literature, a concrete, utopian, antigeneric genre articulating conflicts of gender and class:[5]

> Dem das Gefrierhaus gehört, der nimmt meine Arbeit. Er nimmt sie mir ab. Ich, da mir nichts gehört, gebe ihm meine Arbeit. ER ist der Arbeitnehmer. Der ArbeitGEBER bin ich.
> Arbeitnehmer und Arbeitgeber—an seinem lodengrünen Tisch begegnen wir uns mit vertauschten Namen und taxieren einander. (*P, 7*)
>
> [The man who owns the freeze-house takes my work. He takes it away from me. I, because I own nothing, give him my work. HE is the one who takes work. I am the one who GIVES it.
> The one who takes work and the one who gives—on his green coarse woolen cloth table we meet with exchanged names, and tax each other.]

The attention to social motifs which Benjamin considered a conquest of the lyric in Sainte-Beuve's works and which is so intensely evident in such prose poems of Baudelaire as "Le joujou du pauvre," "Les yeux des pauvres" and "Assommons les pauvres!" manifests itself in Novak's

---

5. Fülleborn also calls attention to the prose poem's critical, utopian function (*DP,* 43, 56, and 58, *DPJ,* 16–17, 28, and 39–43). As we have seen, the prose poem in France and the United States has tended to flourish around periods of revolutionary activity and/or great social as well as aesthetic upheaval. Fülleborn points out a similar constellation in Germany, describing the genre as a consequence (*Auswirkung*) of the "radicalization of the bourgeoisie's drive for emancipation" (*DP,* 43), the extreme result (*Ergebnis*) of a "revolutionary literary movement," a "revolutionary, anticlassical impulse" (*DPJ,* 16–17).

text as the most basic of economic relations. With a sobriety of expression surpassing Baudelaire's which is typical of her work, Novak suggests the rituallike way in which capitalist relations repeat themselves. The meeting of the two parties involved is presented as a litany and response in which the patriarchal, Jehovah-like employer has the power to give and the power to take away. The capitalized "HE" and the quasi-religious tone of the entire text recall the biblical invocation to render unto both secular and religious authority what belongs to each. Here, by implication, these two kinds of authority have merged in the figure of the factory owner. That the employer and employee meet "with exchanged names" suggests the extent to which, in capitalist society, a reversal has taken place so that the one who *gives* labor is looked upon as the one who *takes* it, and vice versa. Thus, the speaker/employee's polemical corrective, with its evocation of class struggle through the euphemistic language of postwar notions of social partnership:[6] "I am the one who GIVES work" (*Der ArbeitGEBER bin ich*).[7] Although the employer/employee relationship is asymmetrical—the balance of power lying more in the hands of the one who owns than the one who owns nothing—the phrase "tax each other [*taxieren einander*]" suggests that each side exhausts the other. The reciprocal acts of assessment take place on all levels, physical, emotional, mental and economic, as both employer and employee are subject to the same laws of exchange.

In its new position at the beginning of *Palisaden*, "Arbeitnehmer-Arbeitgeber" functions in much the same way as Baudelaire's "L'étranger" does at the beginning of the *Petits poèmes en prose*. Like Baudelaire's equally brief text, Novak's offers an account of a dialogue that is characterized especially by the alienation of one speaker from the other. Compared to Baudelaire's text, however, where questions and answers are presented directly and the alienated "I" still has recourse to

6. My thanks for this insight to Irving Wohlfarth.
7. Noting that the modern prose poem in German begins to take root with the rise of expressionism, Fülleborn contrasts the more lyrical tradition of the prose poem developed in Germany by Trakl under the influence of Rimbaud's *Illuminations* with the "prosaic, sober" Baudelairean tradition of the prose poem developed by Heym which focuses on "the 'Prose' of social reality" (*DPJ*, 25–28). In their sober anecdotal strategies and their decidedly prosaic content, Novak's texts clearly belong more to the Heym-Baudelaire tradition than to that of Trakl and Rimbaud. As we shall see, however, the attack on narrative in a text such as "Gepäck" suggests that Novak also has affinities to the latter. On the Trakl-Rimbaud connection, see Reinhold Grimm's "Georg Trakls Verhältnis zu Rimbaud," *Germanisch-Romanische Monatsschrift* 40 (1959), pp. 288–315.

the poetic consolation of "the marvelous clouds," Novak's emphasizes the obstacles to authentic communication by presenting the exchange indirectly, through narration, and by concluding with employer and employee alike locked in a reified encounter that offers no poetic recourse for either party. Their world is not that of the soft, cottony clouds envisioned by Baudelaire's stranger but rather, that of the prosaic "coarse woolen cloth table" on the opposite sides of which the two must face each other. Despite the enormous changes in capitalist production since the mid-nineteenth century, when Baudelaire was writing, the fundamental employer-employee relation remains, Novak's text suggests, as much a struggle for survival, power and dominance as it was in the early days of capitalism. In the perpetuation of these kinds of relations, the frozen, reified relations of which the "freeze-house" is itself emblematic, contemporary forms of capitalism merely reproduce one of the underlying causes of social antagonism and conflict. From the perspective of the utterly prosaic situation within which both parties are inscribed, any dialogization of prose and poetry such as that Baudelaire undertook cannot help being crushed by the utter impossibility of conceiving the kind of poetic alternative that even Baudelaire's stranger could still envision. In its imaging of the intractability of the worker's situation, "Arbeitnehmer-Arbeitgeber" is a programmatic text for *Geselliges Beisammensein* as a whole. The most prosaic content and a parodically poetic, quasi-religious repetition, patriarchy, capitalism and ritual—all these are brought together by Novak in a compact, latently explosive text.

In Baudelaire's prose poems on the poor, the lyrical subject is reinserted into the social context, as we have seen, chiefly through a direct focus on human subjects-as-objects. By contrast, in a way that calls to mind the attention to physical objects we have been considering in the work especially of Stein, Bloch, Ponge, and Bly, Novak's approach to reified human relations is to treat these *indirectly*, through a focus on *things*. In Novak's case, however, this focus involves a milieu not previously explored by any of these other writers, that of the physical objects of factory labor. Rather than attempting to give a glimpse of what Bloch calls "the other side of things" or show everyday objects, as Ponge typically does, as objects of liberation set free from the everyday world of work, Novak insists in *Geselliges Beisammensein* on the unliberated, prosaic character of the objects of alienated labor. The collection's acidly ironic title prepares the way for us to share one woman's experience of one of the most extreme forms of dehumanization. Appropriately since, as Lukács says, in bourgeois society "a relation between people takes on the character of a thing,"[8] Novak approaches reification not only through a direct focus on its human "subjects" (as in such poems of the second section as "Jonina—die Gütekontrollerin" [Jonina—the Quality Controller] and "Herr Jons—der Chef" ["Mr. Jons—the Boss"]; we will return to the latter in detail) but also through a direct focus on the objects of factory labor and the means of production which rob the laborer of her individuality.

Two paradigmatic texts exemplifying Novak's focus on objects are "Der Filetiertisch" (The Fileting Table) (*P*, 7–8), arranged sequentially into five brief sections, one for each day of the week, and its companion piece, "Das Fischfilet" (The Fish Filet). In the first of these—evidence of the extent to which Novak's utopian aspiration is articulated in *Geselliges Beisammensein* negatively, by a series of concrete descriptions of how things actually are—twenty-four of forty-five sentences are constructed with forms of the verb *sein* (to be). Eleven sentences begin with such component parts as "Glass Cases," "Iron Stand," "Neon Tubes," and "Lid." As the table and its parts go through their Monday–Friday cycle, sterile cleanliness yields to increasing griminess, with the original cleanliness restored only at the end of the week and human involvement present only as an implication of the stages through which the machine passes. With her short, hard-hitting, monotonous sentences and ruthless, concrete observations, Novak offers a mimesis of the rhythms of factory labor which both suggests a fierce resistance to those rhythms and refuses to turn away from even the most prosaic content merely for the sake of creating a "poem."

As "Der Filetiertisch" focuses on the means of production, "Das Fischfilet" (*P*, 10–12; *IA*, 237–38) focuses on its object, the process of transforming a once living being into a packaged product. As in "Der Filetiertisch," the sequential arrangement of "Das Fischfilet" exemplifies what Lukács has called after Marx "the translation of economic objects from things back into processes" (*HCC*, 183). Novak images these objects and processes and the human relations behind them with stubborn indirectness, deliberately excluding up to a point any sign of human involvement. Accordingly, in the first section, she describes the fish filet as an object that arrives (implictly, at her work station) "with other things in a steel tub on the conveyor belt." The lack

8. Lukács, *History and Class Consciousness*, p. 83. Hereafter referred to in the text by *HCC* followed by page number.

of individuality, the utter anonymity of any given fish is of course paralleled by the anonymity of the unmentioned laborer. The fish swimming quite literally "in its juice" (*im eigenen Saft*) and the frustrated worker metaphorically "stewing in her own juice" are one in that very concrete sense Lukács describes when speaking of the proletariat as that class "able to discover within itself on the basis of its life-experience the identical subject-object" (*HCC*, 149). What happens physically to the fish, the splitting in two of its living body into two filets, the rubbing off of its scales and casually violent deboning "against the grain" (*gegen den Strich*) also happens on the psychic level to the human "subject." In fact, as is indicated by the line "The fileting machine halved the fish," the principal subject of action is the machine, which comes to have a life of its own, not the human being who operates it. Only after the second section's evocation of the size, shape, and texture of the new object in negative images recalling those of "Der Filetiertisch" ("It flakes into layers. . . . Thick chunks fall off"), and the one-sentence third section's connections among fact, memory, and the sense of smell ("Its smell reminds you of salt baths in drugstore windows, with minerals [*Heilerde*] in them") do we get the first direct mention of an acting "I": "I cut out the blood clots and the worms, straighten it where the meat is torn." The (re)inscription of the subjective self as a mere object in an economic process is here carried out to its most extreme, where the individual human worker, the mundane violence of the act of production (reduction), the tool of production, and its object are, for all practical purposes, indistinguishable: "The cut of my knife is three fingers long. . . . With one stroke I cut globs of fat from the edge."

From minute to minute at her place on the production line, the anonymous worker has to witness and contribute to routine violence to once living organisms. In section 5, the transformation of the object of production from the animate to the inanimate is complete: "It's no fish." As the pun in the German on the words "ist" and "isst" ("*Es ist kein Fisch*") suggests, since the filet has ceased to *be* a fish, it no longer *eats* other fish but has itself become a mere object of consumption. Having contributed to the production of a consumable commodity and having been transformed by that very process into a commodity herself, the worker is clearly repulsed by the idea of consuming the product she has been partly responsible for creating; hence the line, "It's supposed to be eaten." As society's prosaic commodity structure routinely shows a violent disregard for personal feelings, the "inner" life of the individual which has become one of poetry's conventional domains,

Novak's prose poem may be considered a poem largely by negation: like the fish/filet on which it focuses attention, it is "free of innards" (*frei von Innereien*), objectified, stripped of any ennobling subjectivity.[9] In the internal organization of a factory, which may be seen as figuring, in Lukács's words, "the whole structure of capitalist society" (*HCC*, 90), there is no room for the Schlegelian project of making poetry living and social, and life and society poetic. On the contrary, all human complexity is reduced by factory labor to a simple commodity function, the very opposite of a truly "Geselliges Beisammensein." "Households," Novak writes in "Das Fischfilet," "sometimes have pudding molds that look like fish. The filet doesn't look like a fish at all" (*P*, 11). Resisting the discrepancy between the worker's view of the commodity and the domestic, decorative view of the same represented by "pudding molds," Novak exposes the commodity for what it really is, a violent dissociation of life and death, of the individual and society. Brushing against the grain of the social imperative not to question the source of things as well as against all efforts to conceal thoughtless consumption beneath a veil of prettiness and the lies of packaging and advertising, Novak takes as her subject matter the hidden violence of the commodity structure, the reified relations of human beings as a process among things.

"It is true," Lukács points out, "for the capitalist also there is the same doubling of personality" as for the worker (as in the halving of a fish), "the same splitting up of a man into an element of the movement. But for his consciousness it necessarily appears as an activity (albeit this activity is objectively an illusion) in which effects emanate from himself" (*HCC*, 166). Since employer and employee are both continually subjected to the process of reification, the principal difference between them is not that the employee lives a reified daily existence from which the employer is entirely liberated. The difference lies rather in how reification is perceived. Where the worker feels destroyed by it, the employer feels confirmed precisely because he has the illusion of being "in control." In the text, "Herr Jons—der Chef" (*P*, 28–30; *IA*, 239–40), Novak records something of this illusion. The text opens with a description of the boss standing under the picture of his founding father, an image of the same kind of interdependence of patriarchal and

---

9. In their precise descriptions and insistent negations of the "poetic," Novak's texts participate in the process of "delyricization" Fülleborn has identified as characteristic of the type of prose poem manifest in Kafka's parables (*DPJ*, 35).

capitalist forms we have seen in "Arbeitnehmer-Arbeitgeber." Significantly, the boss stands "on the same level as the face of the large wall clock," on the glass door of which is written: "punctuality is a matter of trust [*Vertrauenssache*]." As these dry notations suggest, although reification may be no less real for employer than for employee, the worker appears to herself through her own laboring time not as a controlling subject of the work process but, rather, as one of its interchangeable objects; by contrast, the employer perceives such time as a self-affirmation. In the phrase, "Punctuality is a matter of trust," a relation of dominance and exploitation is rationalized and presented under the guise of a pact among equals. Ironically, the clock that bears a slogan of mutual trust also clocks in and out the employees the employer does not trust to put in an honest day's labor. Similarly, what might at first appear to be a matter of personal concern—"He hires new workers personally"—is in fact a matter of watching out for business interests; what may appear to be selfless dedication ("Mr. Jons gets up every morning at seven") is in fact something to hold over the heads of employees who are certainly well aware that equal dedication reaps drastically unequal rewards.

Requiring a binding contract of no less than one year, the employer, Mr. Jons, prefers to hire foreigners and people without families; perhaps because they are more dependent, unprotected by unions, easily fired at any time, in the first case, and in both cases have less involved personal lives. Despite his material advantages—he does not hesitate to show off his fine clothes to the workers—the employer is subject to the same dehumanization as the employee. For him, no less than for those under him, all human demands and needs, including sleep and health, are subservient to the demands of the market. Urging his employees to work more quickly, not to dose off, not to feign sickness (". . . come on, you're not sick"), Mr. Jons is not himself in the best of shape; "*magenkrank*" (with stomach problems), he suffers from an illness suggestive of the psychosomatic repression not infrequently produced by the capitalist work ethic. Obsessed with his father, who taught him to be obedient, "strict and efficient," Mr. Jons gets on poorly with his lamed older brother ("Mr. Jons doesn't notice him. Mr. Jons is not noticed by him") and perpetuates the quasi-feudal capitalist and patriarchal social conflicts that have been handed down to him. So utterly is Mr. Jons not in control of his life that he buys a German knitting machine unusable for Icelandic wool merely to rationalize a trip he wants to take to Germany to attend a handball tournament. In Novak's conclusion, patriarchy, the myth of the benevolent factory owner, the small consolations of capitalism and the big lie of brotherhood and community are soberly imaged in terms of that festival par excellence of "Geselliges Beisammensein," the coming and going of Christmas:

> Zu Weihnachten schenkt Herr Jons jedem eine Schachtel Konfekt. Er sagt, Kinder, Kinder. Ihr erlaubt es mir selten, gut zu sein. Weihnachten ist vorbei.
> Der Bruder zieht die Uhr auf. Er wischt das Glas mit dem Armel sauber.

> [At Christmastime, Mr. Jons gives everyone a box of sweets. He says, children, children. You don't often let me be good. Christmas is over. The brother winds the clock. He cleans the glass with his sleeve.]

We have seen how Novak's texts share with the prose poem tradition established by Baudelaire a social reinscription of the subjective, lyrical self, and how she approaches this project, like Baudelaire in his prose poems on the poor, through a direct focus on human beings as decidedly *social* beings ("Herr Jons—Der Chef"), as well as through an indirect focus on things ("Der Filetiertisch")—the physical objects that mediate and are mediated by human relationships—which recalls the various object-oriented approaches of Stein, Bloch, Ponge, and Bly which we have considered in previous chapters. We have also seen how Novak tends to present the world, in a manner quite appropriate and familiar to the form of the prose poem, through oppositions and antagonisms based on gender and class ("Arbeitnehmer—Arbeitgeber") as well as through an emphasis on process ("Das Fischfilet"). Another possibility of the prose poem, the earliest example of which is Rimbaud's *Une saison en enfer,* is as a compact space within which to dismantle narrative logic and sequentiality. Although Jacob made perhaps the most extensive and explicit use of this possibility in such poems as "Roman populaire" and "Encore le roman feuilleton," *Geselliges Beisammensein* has itself some fine examples.

One of the more effective of these, the second text of the section entitled "Travels" (retitled "Up in the Air" ["In der Luft hängen"] in *Palisaden*) is called "Gepäck" (Luggage) (*P*, 35–36; *IA*, 242–43):

> Wir haben kein Geld. Wir haben viel Gepäck. Alles, was wir besitzen, tragen wir in Koffern und Säcken verschnürt bei uns. Es sind fünf Gepäckstücke.
> Wir kommen in einem Dorf an. Die Bürgermeisterei, die Kirche, ein

Gasthaus mit Saal liegen eng beieinander.
Wir fragen nach Arbeit. Der Wirt sagt, wir haben selber Arbeitslose.
Noch dazu Männer.
Wir übernachten in dem Gasthaus. Das Zimmer ist billig. Es hat kalte
Fliesen. Die Fliesen sind marineblau und torfrot gemustert. Das Zim-
mer hat einen Balkon. Der Balkon hängt über dem Markt.
Auf dem Markt wird angepriesen, gefeilscht, geschimpft, gelobt, alles
angefasst und berochen. Auf den Obstständen türmen sich rote, gelbe,
grüne Pyramiden aus Früchten. Es riecht nach Kaffee.
Die Pfanne in der Kaffeerösterei dreht sich. An langen Stangen werden
enthäutete Lämmer vorübergetragen. Gerda und ich packen. Wir tragen
das Gepäck in den Hof. Während ich hinaufgehe, um einen schweren
Koffer zu holen, bewacht Gerda das Gepäck.
Ich komme mit dem schweren Koffer hinunter. Gerda ist weg. Ich rufe.
Ich suche. Ich gerate in die Menschenmenge auf dem Markt. Ich werde
aufgehalten. Ich schreie. Ich drehe mich im Kreis. Ich kehre zurück. Es
sind nur noch zwei Gepäckstücke da. Ich rufe. Ich weine. Ich heule.
Gerda kommt. Sie lacht.
Ich sage, wo warst du?
Sie sagt, in der Küche, Bohnen brechen.
Ich sage, derweil haben sie uns das Letzte gestohlen.
Sie sagt, leider nicht.
Ich sage, aber die grössten Stücke.
Sie sagt, wir hatten sowieso zu viel.
Ich sage, jetzt haben wir gar nichts mehr.
Sie sagt, wir haben allerhand gewonnen.
Ich sage, ich habe an dem Zeug gehangen.
Sie sagt, entweder irgendwohin gehören oder gar kein Gepäck haben.
Jetzt sind Gerda und der Wirt schon lange verheiratet.
Sie haben mich adoptiert. Ich bewohne das Zimmer mit den ma-
rineblauen und torfroten Fliesen und dem Balkon, der über den Markt
hängt.

[We have no money. We've got lots of luggage. Everything we own we
carry in suitcases and laced-up sacks. There are five pieces of luggage.
We arrive in a village. The town hall, the church, an inn with a dining
room are all close together.
We ask for work. The innkeeper says, we have our own unemployed.
Men, even.
We spend the night at the inn. The room is cheap. It has a cold tile
floor. The tiles are marine-blue and decorated with peat-red. The room
has a balcony. The balcony overlooks the market-place.
Down there in the street, continual hawking, haggling, nagging, com-
mending; everything grabbed up and sniffed over. At the fruitstands
red, yellow, and green pyramids tower up. You can smell coffee.
The pan of coffee beans at the roasting stand goes around and around.
Skinned lambs are carried by on long spits. Gerda and I pack. We carry

our luggage down into the courtyard. While I go up to get a heavy
suitcase Gerda guards the bags.
I come down with the heavy one. Gerda's gone.
I call, Gerda, Gerda. I go upstairs again. I come back down. Two pieces
of luggage have disappeared. I call. I look all over the place. I get
dragged into the crowd of people in the marketplace. I'm stuck. I
scream. I wander around in circles. I go back. Now there are only two
pieces of luggage there. I call. I cry. I howl. Gerda comes. She laughs.
I say, Where were you?
She says, in the kitchen, shelling beans.
I say, meanwhile they've stolen our last stitch.
She says, unfortunately not.
I say, the biggest pieces anyway.
She says, we had too much anyhow.
I say, now we have hardly anything.
She says, we've come out ahead all around.
I say, I was counting on that stuff.
She says, either you belong somewhere or why have bags at all.
Gerda and the innkeeper have been married a long time now.
They've adopted me. I live in the room with marine-blue and peat-red
tiles, and the balcony, over the marketplace.]

In Novak's text, money, private property, and identity are not to be
dissociated. From the very beginning, the "we" of the poem is identifiable by the *absence* of money. Although they are said to have "lots of
luggage," and although they (whoever "they" are here; anonymous,
lacking a proper introduction) feel what property they have a burden,
we soon learn how much at a disadvantage they are in relation to the
permanent residents of the town they are passing through. The town's
council building, church, and inn are side by side, suggestive of the
close interdependence of government, religion, and business. Evidently, the existing social structure is not working for everybody.
There are unemployed, and for the jobs that exist women are treated
as second-class citizens; class conflict and conflicts based on gender are
one. At the center of everything is the marketplace, full of colorful fruits
and good-smelling coffee, a wealth of commodities available only to
those who have money, unlike the narrator and her partner. The latter is
introduced only after their situation in the marketplace has allowed for
further definition and then only by name: "Gerda and I." In typically
dry, straightforward style, Novak presents the two as a kind of composite "everyman" or "everywoman." Unable to get a job and missing
her partner as well as some pieces of luggage whose disappearance
remains unexplained, the narrator falls into a panic that goes un-

heeded by those around her. The neglect of her urgent cries for help suggests the small degree to which individual problems are of consequence in a market society. There is no sense of community for her, and since she has no money, there is not even a pretense of such. Had she been calling out to buy or sell something she would certainly have been heard; according to the laws of the marketplace, however, there is no "logic" that pleads her case.

What flat narrative continuity is established in the text is violently disrupted at the conclusion in the shock of the last paragraph, where the background setting of a market economy and the narrative of Novak's text suddenly yield a conventional "comic" resolution (marriage, happy ending) which is no resolution at all. Unable to get any other job, and without any apparent psychological motivation that would give the text a semblance of narrative coherence other than the purely economic, Gerda marries into a position of subservience, "adopting" the narrator and leaving everyone, as the title of the section in *Palisaden* suggests, "up in the air." No real narrative transformation is accomplished, merely a repetition of traditional forms of patriarchal and economic domination. With the marketplace and the balcony that hangs over it at the text's center, Gerda ends by prostituting herself out of a desperate situation rather than risking some untried alternative. The narration stalls in resignation under the sign of traditional class and gender relations, and private ownership ("we've come out ahead all around") emerges as the poor man's (or woman's) consolation for flat, impoverished relations that seem to go on, like the narrator's "I live in the room . . . ," in an eternal present without the possibility of a noticeably different past or future.

The deliberate flatness that characterizes not only "Gepäck" but all of the texts we have considered here and that is manifest on virtually every page of Novak's collection, figures the monotonous, prosaic world the worker experiences daily. Sacrificing psychological "depth" for a complexity of "surface" observation, Novak's texts offer a critique of poetry and prose alike, problematizing both the conventional lyrical focus on the inner life of the individual ("Der Filetiertisch," "Das Fischfilet") and the narrative emphasis on well-roundedness of plot and character ("Gepäck"). Reproducing the ennui of a world where people are reduced to mere functions of the machines they serve, a world characterized, in short, by a poverty of objects that is itself a poverty of human relations, the texts of *Geselliges Beisammensein* suggest that the ideologically reassuring function of such categories as "well-roundedness" and "inner life" is itself in need of demystification. In the relations it sets up between discrete individual texts and the collection as a whole, the attention it devotes to concrete social relations and the prosaic daily existence and monadic isolation of the individual in bourgeois society, and its critical-utopian emphasis on conflicts of genre, gender, and class, Novak's first collection of prose poems manifests its engagement with concerns that have been crucial to the prose poem's development as a genre since the appearance of Baudelaire's *Petits poèmes en prose*.[10]

The situation of the writer was imaged by Baudelaire, as we recall, as a prostitution of one's innermost being, thoughts, and feelings. Something of that sense of an absolute prostitution of the self we get in a poem such as "A une heure du matin," the sense of the extent to which the individual subject remains a mere object for the ends of others, makes itself felt in the newly included prose poem of *Palisaden* called "Hauptpost" (Main Post Office) (*P*, 55–56). Like "Gepäck," and unlike Baudelaire's more traditional approach to narrative, "Hauptpost" offers little in the way of reassuring transitions or helpful introductions to better situate its characters. Again, as in "Gepäck," the time is the eternal, seemingly unalterable present: "It is morning. The main post office is very busy [*In der Hauptpost herrscht viel Betrieb*]" (*P*, 55). As the latter sentence suggests, the house of communication, the quasi-allegorical main post office, is also the house of business. Economic exchange and linguistic (including literary) exchange are not to be separated from each other.

Seating herself at one of the typewriters located along one wall, the narrator begins composing sentences she is aware are implicated in the exchange process ("I snatch up sentences: we don't exchange prostheses . . .") (*P*, 55). One of the first things she realizes as a writer (the phrase, "I write" [*Ich schreibe*] being repeated no less than nine times) is that "The public is in a hurry." For someone working in a brief form such as the prose poem, this fact is obviously not without consequence. In the work of such writers as Baudelaire, Jacob, Ponge, and Bly, the

10. The prose poem's inclusion since Baudelaire of "the language of economic and social reality" (*DPJ*, 41) is, as Fülleborn points out, a crucial dimension of the genre's important epistemological function. As Fülleborn also points out, the prose poem's future continues to depend in large measure on the kind of openness to extra-aesthetic impulses already evident in the genre's beginnings (*DPJ*, 43).

prose poem is conceived of, as we have seen, as a preeminently *convenient* form, a form that demands little time of its readers and allows them to come and go as they please, an alternative short ("lyrical") form especially well suited for a prosaic, busy world. In this case, the dialogization or hybridization of genres the prose poem shares with Schlegel's project of a *Universalpoesie* is developed through a rapprochement between the prose poem and the epistolary mode: "I sit down on a stool in front of the typewriter and write a letter" (*P*, 55). While the narrator is writing, two women stand by stereotypically gossiping about a "tramp" (*Schlampe*), finally referred to outright as an "unabashed whore" (*unverfrorene Dirne*) (*P*, 56). There can be little doubt that the woman referred to is the narrator/writer herself, who is writing to an unidentified person addressed in the second-person familiar (*Du, Dich*) of her desire to eat, drink, go out, make love, and spend the night together. The writer's unabashed expression of her desires ("I write, my dearest You, I kiss You all over") is received by a prudish, bourgeois public as an affront ("The one lady says, and all that in public too") which is, nevertheless, apparently of great vicarious interest.

It is a highly ambiguous text. On the one hand, for example, the brevity of the prose poem/letter suggests itself as a way of reaching a public with no time for longer "serious" literature such as the novel, a public otherwise virtually impossible to reach ("One can never reach You" [*Dich erreicht man ja nie*]) (*P*, 55). On the other hand, with its banishment of difficult and quasi-aristocratic metrical devices, the prose poem may be considered, for all its potential readability, as a sellout of the verse lyric. On the one hand, as with Baudelaire, the prose poem may seem to offer itself as a form more accessible than the verse lyric to a large bourgeois public. On the other hand, it may resist—as it does, for example, in the work of Mallarmé, Lautréamont, Rimbaud, Jacob, and Stein—the prostitution of everyday speech into easy communicability and linguistic/literary exchange (as contaminated by economic): "I write, I would like to go looking for mushrooms with you or amber or feed zoo animals with silver paper or smash in display windows full of prostheses because they are excluded from exchange" (*P*, 56). Although the speaker's particular motivation for wanting to feed zoo animals and break in display windows full of artificial limbs is far from clear, the very arbitrariness of such actions is itself doubtless part of the point, her willfully gratuitous actions intended as a defiance of the laws of exchange (*Umtausch*) which would assimilate everything.

Feeding zoo animals silver paper might suggest offering a domesticated public texts it cannot easily digest; the act of smashing a display
window full of mannequins implies violent resistance to the dehuman-
izing commodity structure of society. On the one hand, the text suggests that literature may be used to express real, and even and especially prohibited (rebellious, violent) desires; on the other hand, even
these desires seem prostituted by the existing hegemony of exchange-
over use-value. On the one hand there is the writer's fear of being
without an audience, on the other, the suspicion that any communication or exchange with an audience brings with it unwished-for compro-
mises and complicities with the status quo.

In Baudelaire's "Perte d'auréole," the speaker is so conscious of the
risks involved in playing the role of poet that he abandons the writer's
unholy "halo" with a gesture of aristocratic superiority, leaving it to be
picked up by someone else. At the end of Novak's text, the writ-
er/speaker undergoes a humiliation similar to that the speaker experiences in Baudelaire's poem when his halo falls into the mud. Thrown
out of the main post office, which for the writer suggests being put out of
circulation, out of print, barred from communication, the speaker
emerges with "a lot of pieces of paper" (*lauter Papierstücke*) clinging to
her hat and coat. The final image—"Outside I brush myself off" (*P*,
56)—is more ambiguous than the end of Baudelaire's poem and suggests two possible consequences. The speaker/writer may have decided,
like the speaker of "Perte d'auréole," to let someone else take the risks of
being a writer. On the other hand, the fact that she brushes herself off
also suggests the possibility that she will start all over again: not resignation but its opposite, the will to continue; not writing as an actual
prostitution but writing as a potential liberation; not the phoniness of
"Geselliges Beisammensein" but the determined resistance indicated by
"Entkommen," the title of the section in which "Geselliges Beisammensein" is reprinted in *Palisaden*.

Anticipatory Forms, Collective Practices

The prose poem's utopian project of fusing genres manifests itself in
Geselliges Beisammensein, as we have seen, by negation, the presentation
of a reified, utterly prosaic world where the poetic possibility that
things might be different is inscribed only as a conspicuous absence. In
Novak's second volume of prose poems, by contrast, *Die Landnahme von
Torre Bela* (The Expropriation of Torre Bela), a more directly positive
utopian but no less concrete vision is offered which contrasts strongly

with the concrete negations of the earlier collection.[11] "The liberation of the individual was effected," as Herbert Marcuse has pointed out, "in a society based not on solidarity but on the conflict of interests among individuals. The individual has the character of an independent, self-sufficient monad."[12] This situation, already indicated by Baudelaire in his preface to the *Petits poèmes en prose,* is still ours today, and it is evident on every page of *Geselliges Beisammensein.* Evident too is Novak's awareness that as long as this situation continues there can be no true escape (*Entkommen*), no individual transcendence that does not wait upon the social. The project of overcoming the monadic isolation of the individual entails the establishment of what Marcuse has called "real solidarity . . . the replacement of individualistic society by a higher form of social existence" (*N,* 111). Noteworthy not least of all for the rare articulation it seeks to provide of such a higher form of social existence, *Die Landnahme von Torre Bela* is an experimental collection both aesthetically and politically. By alternating compact, original texts with excerpts from newspaper articles, it brings about a rapprochement of prose poetry and journalism which further develops the prose poem's dialogization of "literary" and "nonliterary" discourse. In so doing, it contributes to the prose poem's undermining of hierarchizations of genre, gender, and class and the critical, utopian project of making society poetic and poetry social. Beyond this, it is experimental in bringing together political and aesthetic concerns by means of an organizing strategy that follows chronologically a precise social experiment in collective reorganization. In its effort to present the whole movement of a single peasant uprising by means of a series of texts chronicling its progress from the outbreak of a rebellion to the text's own present, *Die Landnahme von Torre Bela* demonstrates something of that kind of praxis Lukács has described as directed toward a transformation of the social totality (*HCC,* 174–75).

The text entitled "Losungen, die in Rauch aufgehen" (Slogans That Go up in Smoke) (*P,* 165) exemplifies Novak's dialogization of the aesthetic and the political in *Die Landnahme von Torre Bela* and her use of the prose poem as a form for gesturing towards as yet unrealized social as well as literary forms that would be truly collective:

11. Taken together, Novak's two collections offer examples of all of the major tendencies—lyrical, narrative, objective, and politically engaged—Fülleborn identifies (*DPJ,* 33–34) as characteristic of German prose poetry both before and after 1945. The fundamental heterogeneity that characterizes Novak's collections was already characteristic, as we have seen, of the prose poem collections of both Baudelaire and Rimbaud.

12. Marcuse, *Negations,* p. 111; hereafter cited as *N.*

Wir schleifen tote Aste zum Feuer. Die Zeit vergeht langsam, sie bleibt stehen. "Pele" beglückt uns jeden Morgen mit einer Losung. Es ist stets dieselbe Losung, die er auf Deutsch und auswendig gelernt hat.
Por-tu-gal darf nicht das Chi-le Eu-ro-pas werden!
Eines Tages hat sein Eifer uns angesteckt, und wir bringen ihm stündlich neue Losungen bei. Nachdem wir sie haarklein auf französisch, spanisch, portugiesisch usw. erklärt haben wiederholt er auf deutsch—holpernd, stockend und gurgelnd—die kompliziertesten Vorschläge.
Lissabon soll nicht das Washington der Südostflanke werden!
Portugal soll nicht das China Westeuropas werden!
Lissabon soll nicht das Moskau Südeuropas werden!
Portugal soll nicht das Vietnam der Iberischen Halbinsel werden!
Hinter jedem Reisighaufen schwirren neue Losungen hervor, und die Zeit verfliegt wie der Rauch.
Cuñhal soll nicht der Stalin der Vereinigten Iberischen Republik werden!
Soares soll nicht der Nixon Portugals werden!
Spinola soll nicht der Franco des Lusitanischen Volkes werden!
Wir bilden mehrere kleine Sprechchöre und rufen uns quer übers Brachland Losungen zu.
Portugal soll nicht das Taiwan des Ostatlantischen Ozeans werden!
Vollkommen heiser kehren wir zurück und überlassen alle unsere vergänglichen Losungen dem Rauch.

[We drag dead branches to the fire. The time goes by slowly, stands still. "Pele" blesses us each morning with a slogan. It is always the same slogan, which he has learned by heart in German.
Por-tu-gal must not become the Chi-le of Eu-rope!
One day his enthusiasm has caught on with us, and we teach him new slogans by the hour. After we have minutely explained them in French, Spanish, Portuguese and so forth, he repeats in German—tripping up, faltering, gurgling—the most complicated suggestions.
Lisbon must not become the Washington of the southeast flank!
Portugal must not become the China of western Europe!
Lisbon must not become the Moscow of southwestern Europe!
Portugal must not become the Vietnam of the Iberian Peninsula!
Behind every pile of brushwood new slogans swirl up, and time dissipates like smoke.
Cuñhal must not become the Stalin of the United Iberian Republic!
Soares must not become the Nixon of Portugal! Spinola must not become the Franco of the Lucitanian People!
We form several small choruses and call slogans to each other across the fallow land.
Portugal must not become the Taiwan of the east Atlantic Ocean!
Completely hoarse we turn back and leave all our passing slogans to the smoke.]

With its suggestion that a work of art may be the expression of an explicit political intention that defies the traditional aesthetic separa-

tion of poetry and politics and the deeply seated notion that real art
should be somehow "eternal," the very title of Novak's text is itself
particularly striking. As Breton had declared surrealism to be "in the
service of the revolution,"[13] so here Novak makes use of a prose-poetic
compact space for an unabashedly political purpose. Revolution is imaged not in Romantic terms but, as is typical for Novak, soberly and
concretely, as the hard labor of clearing ground and dragging dead
wood to the fire. As with the stultifying work of "Hering Packen"
(Packing Herring) (*P*, 9–10; *IA*, 237) where "Time doesn't pass" (*Die
Zeit vergeht nicht*), the dangers of resignation and stagnation are great:
"Time passes slowly, stands still." Here, however, there is a difference.
Whereas the art of Novak's earlier poem is to render the monadic
individual's quasi-eternal damnation under factory labor in all its mo-
notony and boredom, the function of the slogans of "Losungen die in
Rauch aufgehen" is to provide encouragement for a collective solution
that will get "things" moving again.

The effort to use language for political purposes is at the outset
slow and ineffectual ("It's always the same slogan, which he (Pele) has
learned in German"), and the interaction between the foreign speaker
and Pele, the Portuguese national, is not developed with any psychological depth. Pele typifies the committed, perhaps somewhat unim-
aginative but zealous revolutionary. One day, however, the text suggests, the radical split between imaginatively "aesthetic" and doggedly
"political" uses of language may be overcome, giving way to a fruitful
interpenetration of politics and art: "One day his enthusiasm has
caught on with us, and we teach him new slogans by the hour." Once
this revolution has come about, once work presents itself not as slow
drudgery but as an occasion for collective enjoyment and communication, once language has been set moving again, "time dissipates like
smoke." The slogans of Novak's text exhibit both a ritualistically poetic
repetition and a restlessly prosaic negation and criticism directed toward all sides, Washington, China, and Moscow. Through this interpenetration of the poetic and the prosaic, Novak's text offers a sense of
real community ("We form several small choruses and call out slogans
to each other across the fallow land") that contrasts starkly with the
pseudocommunity indicated by the phrase "Geselliges Beisammensein." The negations and criticisms the text offers are clearly not conceived as ends in themselves but as the necessary prelude for the realization of a Blochian "Noch nicht" (Not yet) or "Novum," an "open

13. Breton, *Manifestes du surréalisme*, p. 156.

system." Compared to this goal, fixations on the permanence of art and the fetishism of art objects seem of little consequence. Thus, the text suggests that the collective might gladly leave behind "all our passing slogans to the smoke," like so much dead wood for the fire. Although the title is itself potentially ambiguous, the context of *Die Landnahme von Torre Bela* as a whole makes it clear enough that though the word "slogans" (*Losungen*) is often loaded with negative connotations, it is here subject to a positive semantic reversal. Although the term could suggest the transience of political enthusiasms, it seems more likely that Novak's use of it is meant to imply the possibility of creating and using certain phrases for political purposes without regard for traditional notions of aesthetic permanence or timelessness. The political function of art, as Novak presents it here, is not to set up monuments to the future but, rather, to serve present needs, not to be set off in a corner, untouchable and eternal, but to clear the way in the present for what is yet to come. It is a function at once critical and utopian.

"Collective small-group modes of production," Adorno has said:

> are already conceivable today—indeed, they are required by some media—and yet even here the locus of experience in all existing societies is the monad. Individuation along with the suffering it involves is a fundamental fact of society. By implication society can be experienced only by the individual, not by groups. To try and undergird experience with an immediate collective subject is to engage in subterfuge, condemning the work of art to being untrue. It would deny to art the only chance it has today of experiencing reality.[14]

The active coproduction of the text by the reader encouraged by writers of the prose poem from Baudelaire to Ponge suggests the extent to which the genre has presented itself, as it presents itself also in *Die Landnahme von Torre Bela*, as a gesture toward collective form. Like Baudelaire, Novak feels intensely the constrictions of monadic individualism. But if she is wary of a pseudo-collective subject and conscious of the individual's role as the locus of experience in all existing communities, she is also able to give a glimpse in a way Baudelaire could not, through her experience with the Torre Bela collective, of what it might mean to experience real community, to live in a world in which things would be truly different.

In the text called "Oliven Pflücken" (Picking Olives) (*P*, 166), Novak provides a vision of such a world:

---

14. Adorno, *Ästhetische Theorie*, p. 385; *Aesthetic Theory*, p. 367.

Der Ölbaum ist wahrlich kein prunkvoller Baum, so mit Schorf be-
deckt, so verkrüppelt.
Die Früchte sind matt, tiefdunkelblau. Sie sind nicht viel grösser als ihr
Kern und in rohem Zustand fast ungeniessbar. Einige sind noch grün,
gefleckt, unreif. Andere sind verschrümpelt und trocken wie Rosinen.
Seit vorgestern brechen die Olivenbäume unter den Pflückern zusam-
men. Fünf, sechs Leute hocken in einer Krone, deren Durchmesser
nicht mehr als dreieinhalb Meter beträgt.
Die Erde unter dem Baum ist dicht mit Sackleinwand, Planen und
Netzen bedeckt.
Ich sitze auf einem Ast und kämme die Blätter mit den Fingern durch.
Ich streife junge Rüten ab. Ich schüttle, schlage, breche kleine Büschel
ab und lasse mit schlechtem Gewissen auch Beeren dran.
Andere Arbeiter stehen unterhalb des Baumes und schlagen mit lan-
gen Stangen die Oliven von den äusseren Asten ab. Sie wedeln mit den
Stangenspitzen. Sie hauen, stossen, rütteln und füchteln in der Krone
herum. Es ist schwer, die vibrierende Stange längere Zeit steil in die
Höhe zu halten.
Die vom einsetzenden Regen berieselten Früchte blinken wie Pferdeau-
gen.
Nie habe ich so gründlich einen Olivenbaum betrachtet wie in Torrebela. Dabei sieht man ihm tatsächlich nichts als das biblische Alter
an—so anspruchslos, so eigenwillig verwachsen.

[The oil tree is truly not a gorgeous tree, so covered with scabs, so
stunted.
The fruits are dull-colored, deep dark blue. They are not much bigger
than their seed and almost inedible raw. Some are still green, flecked,
unripe. Others are shriveled up and dry as raisins.
Since the day before yesterday the olive trees have been collapsing
beneath the pickers. Five, six people crouch in the crown, whose diame-
ter amounts to not more than three and a half meters.
The earth under the tree is thick with sackcloth, covered with awnings
and nets.
I sit on a branch and comb through the leaves with my fingers. I strip
off young switches. I shake, hit, break off small bunches and, with a bad
conscience, leave some berries on.
Other workers stand beneath the tree and knock off the olives from the
outer branches with long poles. They wag with the pole-ends. They
hack, push, shake and wave their hands about in the crown. It is difficult to hold the vibrating poles stiff for a long time in the air.
The fruits speckled with rain just setting in blink like horse-eyes.
Never have I looked so closely at an olive tree, as in Torrebela. When
you do, all you see is its biblical age—so unassuming, so willfully
deformed.]

Significantly, the text's initial characterization of the olive tree refers to
the tree's utility for man (its oil) and its lack of it ("The fruits. . . . almost

inedible raw") rather than to any of its conventionally beautiful, "aesthetic" qualities. Much of the first sentence's effectiveness stems in fact from its sober, prosaic rendering of its subject matter and its manifest refusal to poeticize ("no gorgeous tree . . . so stunted . . ."). This sobriety is an important dimension of the text's overall effect in part because it instills in the reader a certain trust in the speaker's observation. A second factor contributing to this trust is the fact that the speaker approaches the subject not from the contemplative stance of a poetic speaker but from the standpoint of a worker. Her experience of the tree is not from a distance, from outside it, but from inside, and not as a lone individual but as a member of a group engaged in similar activity. The speaker is all the more believable because she claims no particular charismatic or oracular status; she is, rather, one among many ("Other workers"): "Since the day before yesterday the olive trees have been collapsing beneath the pickers. . . . I sit on a branch and comb through the leaves with my fingers. I strip off young switches."

The "vision" of the speaker is at once illuminating and concrete. Hers is not the isolated lyric "I" but the "I" of a person who is able to work with others while preserving a sense of individual choice: "I shake, hit, break off small bunches and, with a bad conscience, leave some berries on." The speaker's bad conscience doubtless stems from her awareness that the collective might not approve of her not picking all the olives. Whether she does not do so out of laziness or out of a conscious revolt against the collective's unecological, exploitative use of nature (the trees collapsing beneath the weight of the pickers), her actions suggest the ongoing need, all the more present in a collectivist society, both for resistance to excessive encroachments on individual freedom and for that respect for "things" which Ponge, for example, would consider as essential to well-being as respect for human beings. It is in large part this need for a simultaneously resisting and respectful orientation to the world of human beings and things alike which makes believable the shift to a more aesthetically appreciative, less utilitarian perspective evident in the joyously poetic image that follows: "The fruits speckled with rain just setting in blink like horese-eyes." In the *Economic and Philosophic Manuscripts of 1844*, Marx remarked that "the *senses* of the social man *differ* from those of the non-social man."[15] Offering her readers a glimpse, in "Picking Olives," of what the senses might be like in an authentically socialist society, Novak suggests that

---

15. Marx, *Economic and Philosophic Manuscripts of 1844*, in *Collected Works*, 3: 301.

what the isolated, monadic individual perceives as a poverty of objects may be overcome only to the extent that we are able to see these objects in the light of our collective potential, the potential of the collective to reorganize itself and transform nature into what Marx called "*humanized* nature."[16] Having begun by focusing on the question of utility, however, Novak's text moves toward a conclusion which intimates that such a humanized nature may well reside as much in a certain willingness to let people and things alone as in the determination to turn them to good use: "Never have I looked so closely at an olive tree, as in Torrebela. When you do, all you see is its biblical age—so unassuming, so willfully deformed."

In such passages, as also especially in the text entitled "Reminiszenzen" (Reminiscences) (*P,* 169), the prose poem's critical, utopian, and concrete axes converge in an affirmative moment that carries forward into the latter part of the twentieth century the interanimation of poetry and prose and of the aesthetic and the political already manifest in the nineteenth century in the prose poetry of Baudelaire and Rimbaud.[17] Significantly, this moment occurs in the context of what Novak calls an "enclave of the revolution" ("Bourgeoise Sorte" [Bourgeois Brand]). As Novak herself is well aware, even in this context, such a moment would not be credible were it to be articulated by a repression of the deep-rooted struggles and unresolved tensions suggested by the olive tree's "biblical age" and the actions of the individual worker, who may be as "unassuming" as the tree she sits in but is nevertheless, like the tree in this respect as well, "willfully deformed" from the collective's point of view in her resistance to yield to its organized demands. In addition to "Picking Olives," *Die Landnahme von Torre Bela* contains a number of other texts—most notably "Bourgeoise Sorte," "Bombe!", "Nach der Demonstration" (After the Demonstration), and "Streit bei der Arbeit" (Fight on the Job)—that emphasize even more pointedly the unresolved, ongoing conflicts of genre, gender, and class which have been fundamental concerns of the prose poem from its very beginnings; in fact, the collection ends on a less than positive note, with the future of the hard-won collective cast into doubt by the intervention of the military. *Die Landnahme von Torre Bela* is fundamentally a book that affirms utopian possibilities, however, rather than one that

16. Ibid., p. 89.
17. Noting the prose poem's functional resistance to a "dogmatic antithesis of l'art pour l'art and engagement," Fülleborn emphasizes the genre's contribution to a "living form-content dialectic" (*DPJ,* 38).

emphasizes, as *Geselliges Beisammensein* does and needs to do, the severe limitations of a seemingly endless, intensely prosaic existence and socioeconomic structure. It thus seems fitting to conclude with the text "Reminiszenzen" (Reminiscences), which itself affirms these possibilities, as it attests also to the possibilities, and limits, of the prose poem.

> Ich reiße die stabilen Fensterläden auf, die jeden Abend sorgfältig verriegelt werden. Sechs Uhr und dunkel. Die Sachen sind klamm von der nächtlichen Feuchtigkeit. Ich tappe in die Küche, um Kaffeewasser aufzustellen. Wohltuende Leere. Die Absätze meiner Holzschuhe klappern auf den Fliesen.
> Ich habe viele solcher Häuser gekannt, denn ich bin in einem Land aufgewachsen, wo wir Villen, Gutshöfe und Schlösser schon vor dreissig Jahren enteignet haben.
> Die Fenster unseres Badezimmers gehen nach Osten. Bewaldeter Horizont, wellige Ebene, gelbe Gräser, die das erste Licht einfangen. Das Ohr vernimmt ein leises Bimmeln—Ziegenglocken. Keinen Steinwurf entfernt sitzt ein Paar krächzender Raubvögel.
> Ich habe viele solcher Häuser gekannt. Oberschulinternat, politische Lehrgänge, Parteischulen, Studentenwohnheim—sie alle waren in Villen, Gutshöfen, Schlössern untergebracht.
> Um halb neun kommen in der Küche zwei Papiersäcke voll heißer Brötchen an. Große Brötchen, in denen die Butter schmilzt und der tiefgefrorene Schinken auftaut, den Céléstina stöhnend mit der Brotmaschine in Scheiben schneidet.
> Ich habe viele solcher Häuser gekannt, doch in keinem habe ich wie hier ohne Normen, ohne Dressur, ohne Zeremonien, ohne eingefleischte Hierarchie arbeiten dürfen.
> Ich schreibe in der Frühe, bevor es losgeht. Um Horst nicht zu wecken, schreibe ich mit der Hand. Die Morgensonne wirft ein leichtes Rot auf die gekalkten Mauern.
> Ich habe viele solcher Häuser gekannt, doch in keinem habe ich wie hier, wenn auch kurzfristig, innegehalten und meinen Frieden gemacht.
> [I throw open the solid window shutters that are carefully barred every evening. Six o'clock and dark. Our things are clammy from the nightly dampness. I grope around in the kitchen to put on coffee water. Welcome emptiness. The soles of my shoes clatter on the tiles.
> I've known many such houses, for I grew up in a country where we took over villas, estates and castles some thirty years ago.
> The windows of our bathroom look east. Wooded horizon, wavy plain, yellow grasses that take in the first light. A light tinkling comes to the ear—goat bells. Less than a stone's throw away, a couple of birds of prey sit cawing.
> I've known many such houses. Private school, political instruction,

schools of the party, student housing—they were all housed in villas, estates, castles.

At half past eight two paper sacks full of hot rolls arrive in the kitchen. Large rolls the butter melts into and the deep-frozen ham thaws out in and which Celestina cuts groaning into slices with the bread machine. I've known many such houses, yet in no other have I been able to work as here without norms, without regimentation, without ceremonies, without fleshed-out hierarchies.

I write in the early morning before everything gets underway. So as not to wake Horst I write by hand. The morning sun throws a light red on the whitewashed walls.

I've known many such houses, yet in no other have I paused, as here, however briefly, and made my peace.]

CHAPTER 11

Conclusion: Uses
of the Prose Poem

Form follows function no less than function follows form. We give meaning to things above all in the various uses we make of them, even if our decision is, finally, to leave things alone. The prose poem has demonstrated its power as a mode of discourse by addressing and symbolically enacting dominant social conflicts at critical historical junctures and by calling attention, in more narrowly aesthetic terms, to the limitations of various literary genres, the lyric and the novel in particular. Within prose poem collections generally, the individual prose poem occupies a position that is neither quite as autonomous as what we might normally expect for a verse lyric, nor as bound to what precedes and follows it as what we might expect from a chapter in a novel. Its objects are the unresolved conflicts of daily life, the world of prose, the prosaic reality that drags on with no end in sight from day to day in contrastive tension to the brief, interruptive, poetic space where the prose poem takes place.

Like all genres a specific "form for conceptualizing the world,"[1] the prose poem owes much of its particularity to its conceptualization of social and aesthetic discourse as a system of interpenetrating oppositions—a system, in other words, of inescapable power relations, not mere differences—such as those that give it its name. A good portion of the significance of the term "prose poem," and one of the better

---

1. Bakhtin, *The Dialogic Imagination*, p. 292; hereafter cited as *DI*.

CONCLUSION

reasons to choose to write in the genre and designate a text accordingly, might well lie in the opportunity it provides to give formal, thematic,
and critical expression to the ongoing struggles of society. These
struggles manifest themselves in part in the sociolinguistic stratification
accomplished by and figured in the conflictual relationship between
literary and nonliterary discursive practices and in part in the competition among such specifically literary genres and modes as the novel, the
lyric, the short story, the parable, the journalistic or philosophical essay, the fairy tale, the aphorism, and even the well-told personal
anecdote.

The poetry/prose conflict is of particular interest in the history of
intra- and extraliterary discursive struggle because of its conceptual
double valence. In the prose poem, two fundamental struggles overlap:
that *between* literary languages—"Literature" with a capital L, Literature as a putative unitary language—and extraliterary or "ordinary"
languages; and that *within* literature between dominant/ascendant genres like the novel and other genres, like the verse lyric, of apparently
declining socio-aesthetic importance. In the context of these struggles,
the abstruseness and privatization of language in much twentieth-century poetry may serve as a paradoxical index of the accelerating difficulty of reserving for oneself a world and a language that might seem
unimpinged upon by society's dominant cultural, linguistic, and economic forces. Through her cubist fracturing of the sentence as an
elemental narrative/poetic/linguistic unit, Gertrude Stein suggests, for
example, that the notion of a "natural" cohesiveness and logic of language is no less ideological than that of the "natural" hegemony of men
over women assumed by Victorian society. Situated midway between
the poet's efforts to strip words of their prior socioideological embeddedness and the prose writer's exploitation of this embeddedness to
serve her own intentions, Stein's struggle to wrest language away from
patriarchal control becomes the reader's struggle to make sense of a
mutilated speech. Similarly, Max Jacob's comic fragmentations of plot
expose the conventional novelist's pretense of an unmediated apprehension of the social totality as being as problematic as the notion
that society itself is a harmonious, organic whole.

The dialogical role of the prose poem *as form* may no longer be said
to be as subversive or polemically provocative as it once was.[2] Nonethe-

---

2. On the continuity of counter-discursive struggle between the nineteenth century
and the present, see Terdiman, *Discourse/Counter-Discourse*, p. 340; hereafter cited as

less, the genre can continue to keep faith to varying degrees, as do the contemporaries who conclude my study, with its original revolt against the hegemonic uniformity and monoglossia of established single-styled "poetic" genres and the aesthetic exclusions that contribute to reproducing a society still grounded in hierarchical relations of gender and class. Literary language is, as Mikhail Bakhtin has observed, both "the oral and written language of a dominant social group" (*DI,* 291) and the subject of its own internal stratification. Given these facts, the twofold decision to write texts occupying the formal and functional space of the prose poem and to designate such texts as prose poems might be more than a mere "aesthetic" choice in the narrow sense or a choice arrived at purely on the basis of individual temperament and personal affinity. Thus, the critical decision I have made here to include texts of Schlegel, Novalis, and Bloch because of the close family resemblance they bear to the prose poem both formally and functionally and despite the fact that their authors have not designated their work as such might serve as a reminder of the long-standing international character of the kinds of struggles designated now for over a hundred years in France, if only more recently elsewhere, by the name "prose poem." Such a decision is also a way of affirming the solidarity of these texts with a genre whose very identity and historical significance have been bound up with the recuperation of the marginal, a recuperation that emerged in response to a principle of exclusion operating at a particular moment in the history of genres when that principle had become subject to question. In the still functional opposition between poetry and prose, as elsewhere, this principle remains today conventionally accepted and deeply entrenched in the logic of noncontradiction that is one of the governing principles of a social order based on a variety of exclusions, including especially those of gender and class.

The problem of the prose poem is a problem of limits. Although Mary Ann Caws generously remarks in her preface to *The Prose Poem in France* that the collection "in no way represents an attempt to set limits upon a genre as complex and controversial" as the prose poem,[3] the setting of limits—however provisional or heuristic—is clearly in one

---

DCD. Though counterdiscursive forms of the last 150 years have mutated, says Terdiman, they "could hardly be said to have advanced." On the "proto-dialectical" nature of counterdiscourses such as the prose poem and the diminution of their effect over time, see pp. 115 and 199.

3. Caws, "Preface," *The Prose Poem in France,* p. vii.

sense an indispensable step toward discussing any subject, the very choice of which is already a limitation. In Hermine Riffaterre's introduction to the same volume, the impulse to set limits not only for the sake of intelligibility but also to achieve agreement as to the nature of a given phenomenon manifests itself clearly: "Despite the diversity of approaches evident in this volume, or perhaps because of that very diversity, a clear consensus emerges as to what traits will define a genre too often thought undefinable: brevity, closure, inner 'deconventionalized' motivation of forms."[4] Such has been, and still is, the prose poem. But the limits of the prose poem have reference, as we have seen, not only to form but to history and politics as well. Although recently there has been substantial agreement among critical theorists—Julia Kristeva, Barbara Johnson, and Richard Terdiman in particular—concerning the subversive character of the prose poem as it emerged in the nineteenth century, its position in contemporary society is more complex. Having undermined generic distinctions in order to claim a space for its utopian project of a fusion of genres, has the prose poem finally lost its critical dimension in an atmosphere in which aesthetically—though certainly not politically in a country, for example, such as the United States—anything goes? Once a form of "radical change,"[5] the prose poem today is at a crossroads of its history, arrived at by what we may call a "crisis of respectability." With respect to form alone, abstracted from the social, historical, and political contexts that have played such a crucial role in the genre's emergence and its subsequent development, the liberation figured by the prose poem might be regarded as a fait accompli:

> And now that the liberation has been achieved it would seem that none of them—not the genre, not its texts, not the authors—need any longer seek their definition in this rupture with tradition; it is no longer this rupture that justifies their creation of poetic experience or their winning of a readership. The attitude is obsolete. If the prose poem is a valid genre for us, it should be able to dispense with such purely historical traits of perhaps only temporary significance.[6]

Although most critics of the prose poem, Suzanne Bernard included, would agree with Hermine Riffaterre that the prose poem was

4. Hermine Riffaterre, "Introduction," *The Prose Poem in France*, p. xi.
5. Hermine Riffaterre, "Reading Constants: The Practice of the Prose Poem," in *The Prose Poem in France*, p. 98.
6. Ibid., p. 99.

once a kind of "revolutionary" genre,[7] even if it cannot still be so today, others may question if it ever has been: "Despite its origins as an expression of the striving for poetic freedom in form and language of the post-romantic era, it remains largely faithful to typographical linearity, to accepted syntax, and above all, to clearly marked boundaries . . . the great tradition of the *poème en prose* is, in its formal expression of the ceremonial of closure, anything but avant-garde."[8]

Albert Sonnenfeld's point here about the purely typographical limitations of what has come to be defined as the prose poem is well taken. His remarks about the genre symptomatically reveal two dangers, however, which critics of the prose poem as well as of other genres would do well to keep in mind. The first is that of isolating aesthetic experimentation and judging past achievements by present standards—or, to put it another way, past answers by present questions—to such an extent that the historical specificity of a particular act is lost. Resituated within a larger context, the prose poem draws much of its significance from the fact that the form's "ceremonial of closure" and its spatial, syntactical, and typographical limitations may themselves be read as symptomatic of the ideological impasses and political aporias that overdetermine even the most advanced aesthetic productions of any historical period.[9] By today's standards, the prose poem *as form* may appear relatively tame. Its recent reception in America and elsewhere suggests that what was once revolutionary may not be so any longer. On the other hand, it is difficult to overestimate the genre's impact among French poets working to break with reified forms of both verse and

7. See, for example, the subtitle of Barbara Johnson's book: *Défigurations du langage poétique: La seconde révolution baudelairienne.*

8. Albert Sonnenfeld, "L'adieu suprême and Ultimate Composure: The Boundaries of the Prose Poem," in *The Prose Poem in France,* p. 210.

9. Cf. Terdiman, *DCD,* p. 278: "The defining trait of the dissident intelligentsia, of the avant-garde particularly, was its situation *at the absolute limit* of consciousness of a class ideology, of a dominant discourse, while never transgressing it. The impulse to distinction from the dominant ideology which framed their very existence proved by nature contradictory." Against its every impulse, as Terdiman points out (272), the prose poem figures "a limit of practice and of ideology" which it does not itself go beyond. Despite its "intensely critical . . . powerfully negative and reformist" posture toward dominant literary and social formations, it has not managed to issue into "the authentically revolutionary stance (save in its projection of an *esthetic* revolution) which would have fulfilled essential dynamics within its project." As Terdiman also observes, however, although the struggles of counterdiscourses such as the prose poem to "forge and consolidate a counterhegemonic consciousness" have thus far come up "*short* of the revolutionary," each counterdiscourse may be said to retain its significance as a "differential language" (72 and 160).

prose in the mid to late nineteenth century. What is not revolutionary today may yet have gestured *toward* the revolutionary in an earlier historical context.

Although some contemporaries, Robert Bly for example, see to it that the designation "Prose Poems" appears on the covers and title pages of their collections, others, like Helga Novak, do not acknowledge their adherence to the genre quite so explicitly. Perhaps it is the slim market for poetry and the increasingly unpoetic times in which we live which induce an author such as Novak (or her publishers) to present texts bearing such a striking, even obvious formal and functional resemblance to the prose poem merely as "Prose." In any case, the problem of naming a text, the problem of its generic identification, was for Baudelaire inextricable from the problem of writing a text at all. Given the prose poem's ongoing polemic against "single-styled" genres, it might be ironically appropriate for writers of prose poems at our own historical juncture to refuse to name their texts as such and thereby fit themselves neatly into a once subversive form that risks becoming increasingly traditional and canonized. In this sense especially the prose poem today is a genre that must perhaps risk giving up its own traditional self-designation and dismantling its conventionally accepted formal identity, as the later work of Francis Ponge suggests, in order paradoxically to retain the aesthetic and political force of its polemic against generic exclusions. The refusal to identify one's work with the prose poem would then be in keeping with the utopian project of a genreless genre, a genre that is not a genre, a form fixed once and for all to be handed down reassuringly from age to age like the fixed verse forms against which the prose poem was itself a revolt.

A second danger Sonnenfeld's remarks suggest, and one that I myself have doubtless not entirely avoided, is that of homogenizing writers as different in so many ways as those I have selected into what Sonnenfeld calls a "great tradition of the *poème en prose*."[10] As a partial corrective to this tendency, which nevertheless may have some strategic value, it is perhaps useful to remember that traditions, like genres, are at best heuristic constructions, not eternal givens, and that such categories may themselves be cheerfully abandoned, as Fredric Jameson has put it, "like so much scaffolding when the analysis has done its work."[11] The problem of tradition and that of genre are intimately connected; both

---

10. Sonnenfeld, "L'adieu suprême," p. 210.
11. Jameson, *The Political Unconscious*, p. 145; hereafter cited as *PU*.

are bound up with questions of identity and difference, the singular and the plural, the individual and the collective. In keeping with its oxymoronic designation, the prose poem has proven to be an unusually self-thematizing genre foregrounding a variety of conflicts and oppositions, a genre whose counterdiscursive resistance has served as a persistent reminder of the importance of reconceiving the aesthetic "as a mode of struggle."[12] Many of its authors have also demonstrated a preoccupation with material objects which suggests the appropriateness of the prose poem as form to a focus on the tangible, prosaic realities of everyday life. Returning to the issue I posed in the introduction, it seems clear that the prose poem's predominant aesthetic function in both the nineteenth and twentieth centuries has been primarily that of a norm-breaking genre, rather than of a norm-sustaining one. After years of tradition and norm-building within the "genre itself," however, that is to say, among those texts that have been called prose poems either by their authors or by critics or both, many recent manifestations of the genre seem less resistant to dominant culture than their more illustrious predecessors in France. Perhaps inevitably given the process of historical assimilation the genre has undergone, the prose poem's current function risks becoming, by contrast to its initial historical tendencies, perhaps more norm-sustaining than norm-breaking. Nevertheless, the prose poem has been historically, at least until recently, a subversive utopian genre critically oriented toward received aesthetic and political conventions.

My principal points concerning the prose poem may now be summarized as follows: (1) as the genre with the distinction of having "an oxymoron for a name,"[13] the prose poem has shown itself historically to be an exceptionally self-reflexive genre foregrounding a variety of generic tensions, conflicts, oppositions, and attempted resolutions; (2) the increasing preoccupation of prose poetry with material objects, particularly in the twentieth century, suggests the extent to which influential writers in the genre have considered it one of the most appropriate and suggestive forms available for emphasizing the tangible, prosaic realities of everyday life; (3) the prose poem has typically displayed a marked interpenetration of the critical and the utopian in response to existing aesthetic and political conventions; (4) this interpenetration of

12. Ibid., p. 202.
13. Michael Riffaterre, "On the Prose Poem's Formal Features," in *The Prose Poem in France*, p. 117.

the critical and the utopian has been largely responsible for the prose poem's predominant historical function as a norm-breaking rather than a norm-sustaining genre; (5) as the prose poem has gradually come to be assimilated within literature, thereby undergoing the risk of becoming merely one genre among many, its function as a norm-breaking, utopian genre has become increasingly threatened. Accordingly, since its present function among contemporary writers risks being at least as much that of a norm-sustaining genre as of a norm-breaking one, the current resurgence of interest in the prose poem also betokens a crisis with regard to its predominant historical role as a genre *against* genres, a dialogical, novelistic genre whose function it has been to resist exclusions, recuperate lost voices, and undermine forms of generic hierarchization.

Such texts of Baudelaire as "A une heure du matin" and "Assommons les pauvres!" demonstrate well how prominently unresolved and perhaps irresolvable social and aesthetic struggles for power and dominance figured in the emergence of the prose poem as a genre. As we have seen, the genre that appeared at its beginnings to gesture toward the democratic comes itself to enjoy, over the long run, some of the dubious privileges of being one genre among many (although its privileges are still those of a relatively "minor" genre), a form in danger of undergoing the same canonic reification against which it had offered, and at its best still offers, determined resistance. What may have looked like a democratization of the lyric in Baudelaire, a liberation of poetry from its verse constraints, a journalistic, anecdotal prose at least relatively more accessible to the public than the alexandrine, had already become in Jacob the most esoteric of genres, inaccessible to all but a small, initiated, aesthetic elite. In its inability over the last century successfully to resist recuperation and assimilation, the prose poem has continually displayed a double impulse toward the poetic—in the sense of what is aristocratic, divorced from life, secure in discrete, formal isolation, resistant to change—as well as the prosaic, with the accompanying risk of presenting the trivial, the uninteresting, the unadorned expression of an all-too personal ennui. In this sense, the prose poem has had and continues to have, perhaps more than ever, a clearly ideological function. The genre's characteristic double gesturing is also the source, however, of its actual and potential strengths. For just as the impulse toward the poetic is also the desire for a world in which things would be different and better than they are, so too the impulse toward the prosaic affirms a continual revaluation of the marginal, a leveling of harmful privilege, and a renewed attention to everyday struggles of gender, genre, and class. Though often prematurely excluded by aesthetic, critical, theoretical, and sociopolitical perspectives alike as "banal," such struggles might well be seen from a more penetrating angle of vision such as that which the prose poem often provides as being of the highest interest for the fate not merely of literature, which seems to be able to take care of its own interests quite well, but of society as a whole.

To the extent that the prose poem has itself become, since its heroic age with Baudelaire and Rimbaud, one of those cultural treasures Benjamin says the victors of history carry over the prostrate bodies of their victims,[14] its victory can never be compensated for entirely. It may be partially compensated, however, by commentators and practitioners of the genre who continue to emphasize the importance of including the excluded and of listening to those whose voices have been submerged amid the general clamor of *things* and of people-as-things, our poverty of objects. Accordingly, I have attempted to make my own analyses *anticipatory* in the Jamesonian sense (*PU*, 296) as well as functionally descriptive. It has been my intention to identify, where it has seemed possible and plausible to do so, traces of the prose poem's utopian gesture toward becoming a genreless genre and thus a displacement, projection, and symbolic enactment at the level of literary generic struggle of the Marxian project of a classless society. To the extent that such a society remains for us, in Jameson's words, the "as yet untheorized object" (*PU*, 294) that would continually transform the poverty of everyday experience into a communally shared wealth, the prose poem as well may be said to wait upon a theory of itself which it will draw not from the past but from the future.

Currently, the antigeneric impulses manifest throughout the prose poem's history may well seem to have been dispersed. Although no longer as potent as it once was in nineteenth-century France, the prose poem has nevertheless reemerged over one hundred years after Baudelaire as a significant force in the drive toward what Paul Ricoeur has called a "decategorization of our entire discourse." Contributing to this project, the prose poem also redirects critical energies toward the text of the world, providing a focus on the concrete, prosaic realities and unresolved conflicts of everyday life which might receive somewhat less attention in discussions of ordinary language/poetic language

14. Benjamin, "Theses on the Philosophy of History," *Illuminations*, p. 256.

and literature/theory. Significantly, recent preoccupations with such terms have not preempted the international prose poem renaissance that has taken place over the last twenty years but have instead grown up alongside it. Whatever the prose poem's future might be, its continued vitality may lie largely in keeping faith with its past, not only with its critical orientation toward aesthetic and extra-aesthetic modes of discourse and the concrete realities they articulate but also with its utopian aspirations for a resolution of the conflicts of genre, gender, and class which we have traced from the prose poem's beginnings to the present. It is to this interpenetration of the critical and the utopian that the genre owes much of its norm-breaking force within literature.

Frequently Cited References

ADORNO, THEODOR. *Ästhetische Theorie*. Frankfurt: Suhrkamp, 1970.
——. *Aesthetic Theory*. Trans. C. Lenhardt. London: Routledge and Kegan Paul, 1984.
——. "Blochs *Spuren*." *Noten zur Literatur*. In *Gesammelte Schriften*, vol. 2. Frankfurt: Suhrkamp, 1974.
——. "Rede über Lyrik und Gesellschaft," *Noten zur Literatur*. In *Gesammelte Schriften*, vol. 2.
——. "Lyric Poetry and Society." Trans. Bruce Mayo. *Telos* 20 (Summer 1974), pp. 56–71.
BAKHTIN, MIKHAIL M. *The Dialogic Imagination: Four Essays*. Trans. Caryl Emerson and Michael Holquist. Ed. Michael Holquist. Austin: University of Texas Press, 1981.
BAUDELAIRE, CHARLES. *Oeuvres complètes*. Ed. Claude Pichois. 2 vols. Paris: Gallimard, Editions Pléiade, 1975.
——. *Paris Spleen*. Trans. Louise Varèse. 1947 reprint, New York: New Directions, 1970.
BENEDIKT, MICHAEL. *The Prose Poem: An International Anthology*. New York: Dell, 1976.
BENJAMIN, WALTER. *Illuminations*. Trans. Harry Zohn. New York: Schocken Books, 1976.
BERNARD, SUZANNE. *Le poème en prose de Baudelaire jusqu à nos jours*. Paris: Nizet, 1959.
BRETON, ANDRÉ. *Manifestes du surréalisme*. Paris: Gallimard, 1948.
CAWS, MARY ANN, AND HERMINE RIFFATERRE, EDS. *The Prose Poem in France: Theory and Practice*. New York: Columbia University Press, 1983.
DERRIDA, JACQUES. "La loi du genre." In *Glyph* 7 (1980), pp. 176–201. Baltimore: Johns Hopkins University Press, 1980.

————. "The Law of Genre." Trans. Avital Ronell. In *Glyph* 7, pp. 202–29 and *Critical Inquiry* 7, no. 1 (Autumn 1980), pp. 55–81.

————. *White Mythology.* In *Margins of Philosophy.* Trans. Alan Bass. Chicago: University of Chicago Press, 1982.

EAGLETON, TERRY. *Walter Benjamin, or Towards a Revolutionary Criticism.* London: Verso Edition, 1981.

FOUCAULT, MICHEL. *L'ordre du discours: L'archéologie du savoir.* Paris: Gallimard, 1971.

————. *The Order of Things: An Archaeology of the Human Sciences.* New York: Random House, 1970.

FÜLLEBORN, ULRICH. *Das Deutsche Prosagedicht.* Munich: Wilhelm Fink, 1970.

HEGEL, G.W.F. *Vorlesungen über die Ästhetik* 3. In *Werke,* vol. 15. Frankfurt: Suhrkamp, 1980.

ISER, WOLFGANG. *Der Akt des Lesens.* Munich: Wilhelm Fink, 1976.

————. *The Act of Reading.* London: Routledge and Kegan Paul, 1978.

JAMESON, FREDRIC. *Marxism and Form: Twentieth-Century Dialectic, Theories of Literature.* Princeton: Princeton University Press, 1971.

————. *The Political Unconscious: Narrative as a Socially Symbolic Act.* Ithaca: Cornell University Press, 1981.

JAUSS, HANS ROBERT. *Aesthetische Erfahrung und literarische Hermeneutik.* Munich. Wilhelm Fink, 1977.

————. *Aesthetic Experience and Literary Hermeneutics.* Trans. Michael Shaw, Minneapolis: University of Minnesota Press, 1982.

————. "La douceur du foyer—Lyrik des Jahres 1857 als Muster der Vermittlung Sozialer Normen." *Rezeptionsästhetik.* Ed. Rainer Warning. Munich: Wilhelm Fink, 1975.

————. "Racines und Goethes Iphigenie." *Rezeptionsästhetik.*

JOHNSON, BARBARA. *Défigurations du langage poétique: La seconde révolution baudelairienne.* Paris: Flammarion, 1979.

LACOUE-LABARTHE, PHILIPPE, AND JEAN-LUC NANCY. *L'absolu littéraire.* Paris: Seuil, 1978.

LOTMAN, JURIJ M. *Die Struktur literarischer Texte.* Trans. Rolf-Dietrich Keil. Munich: Wilhelm Fink, 1972.

LUKÁCS, GEORG. *History and Class Consciousness.* Trans. Rodney Livingston. Cambridge: MIT Press, 1971.

MACHEREY, PIERRE. *A Theory of Literary Production.* Trans. Geoffrey Wall. London: Routledge and Kegan Paul, 1978.

MARCUSE, HERBERT. *Negations.* Trans. Jeremy J. Shapiro. Boston: Beacon, 1968.

MARX, KARL. *Economic and Philosophic Manuscripts of 1844.* In *Collected Works,* vol. 3. New York: International Publishers, 1975.

————. *The Eighteenth Brumaire of Louis Bonaparte.* In *Collected Works,* vol. 11. New York: International Publishers: 1979.

————. *The German Ideology.* In *Collected Works,* vol. 5. New York: International Publishers, 1976.

————. *Manifesto of the Communist Party.* In *Collected Works,* vol. 6. New York: International Publishers, 1976.

_____. *The Marx-Engels Reader.* Ed. Robert C. Tucker. New York: Norton, 1978.

_____. "Theses on Feuerbach." In *Collected Works,* Vol. 5. New York: International Publishers, 1976.

NOVALIS (FRIEDRICH VON HARDENBERG). *Schriften.* Ed. Paul Kluckhohn and Richard Samuel. Vols. 1–3. Stuttgart: W. Kohlhammer, 1960.

PONGE, FRANCIS. *Méthodes.* In *Le grand recueil,* vol. 2. Paris: Gallimard, 1961.

RICOEUR, PAUL. *The Rule of Metaphor.* Trans. Robert Czerny. Toronto: University of Toronto Press, 1977.

RIMBAUD, ARTHUR. *Oeuvres de Rimbaud.* Ed. Suzanne Bernard, Paris: Garnier, 1966.

_____. *Rimbaud: Complete Works, Selected Letters.* Trans. Wallace Fowlie. Chicago: University of Chicago Press, 1966.

SARTRE, JEAN-PAUL. *Qu'est-ce que la littérature?* Paris: Gallimard, 1948.

SCHLEGEL, FRIEDRICH. *Kritische Friedrich-Schlegel-Ausgabe.* Ed. Ernst Behler. Vol. 2, ed. Hans Eichner. Paderborn: Ferdinand Schöningh, 1967.

_____. *Literarische Notizen 1797–1801.* Ed. Hans Eichner. Frankfurt/M.: Ullstein, 1980.

TERDIMAN, RICHARD. *Discourse/Counter-Discourse: Theory and Practice of Symbolic Resistance in Nineteenth-Century France.* Ithaca: Cornell University Press, 1985.

Index

Library of Congress Cataloging-in-Publication Data

Monroe, Jonathan   1954–
    A poverty of objects.

    Bibliography: p.
    Includes index.
    1. Prose poems—History and criticism.   I. Title.
PN1059.P76M66   1987   809.1   86-24026
ISBN 0-8014-1967-0 (alk. paper)